Blowhard

Windbaggery and the Wretched Ethics of Clarence Darrow

Mike Farris

Other books by Mike Farris

Fifty Shades of Black and White: Anatomy of the Lawsuit behind a Publishing Phenomenon
The Bequest
Isle of Broken Dreams
Manifest Intent
Rules of Privilege
Kanaka Blues
Wrongful Termination
Every Pig got a Saturday
A Death in the Islands: The Unwritten Law and the Last Trial of Clarence Darrow
Call Me Lucky: A Texan in Hollywood (with Robert Hinkle)
Poor Innocent Lad: The Tragic Death of Gill Jamieson and the Execution of Myles Fukunaga
The Catch
Something Unfortunate
Miles Apart
Forty Hours

© 2024 Mike Farris
All Rights Reserved
Print ISBN 978-1-960405-09-8
ebook ISBN 978-1-960405-10-4

This book is sold subject to the condition that it shall not, by way of trade or otherwise, be lent, resold, hired out or otherwise circulated without the publisher's prior consent in any form of binding or cover other than that in which it is published and without a similar condition including this condition being imposed on the subsequent purchaser.

STAIRWAY PRESS—APACHE JUNCTION

Cover Design by Guy D. Corp, www.GrafixCorp.com

STAIRWAY≡PRESS

www.StairwayPress.com
1000 West Apache Trail Suite 126
Apache Junction, AZ 88120 USA

The great enemy of truth is very often not the lie—deliberate, contrived and dishonest—but the myth—persistent, persuasive and unrealistic. Too often we hold fast to the cliches of our forebears. We subject all facts to a prefabricated set of interpretations. We enjoy the comfort of opinion without the discomfort of thought.
—John F. Kennedy

Dedication

To Susan—words fail me.

Mike Farris is a retired attorney whose practice in Dallas included commercial litigation and entertainment law. A multi-time published author of both fiction and non-fiction, he is an adjunct professor in the Political Science Department at the University of Texas at Arlington, where he teaches Entertainment Law and Lawyers in Popular Culture.

Acknowledgments

WHEN WRITING HISTORY, an author can't help but be indebted to those who came before in writing about the particular subject. In addition to primary sources, such as trial transcripts, I relied heavily upon the work of those I have identified in the Bibliography. For them, and their work, my deepest appreciation.

I also owe a debt of gratitude to the team at Stairway Press, particularly Ken Coffman and Stacey Benson. This is my fourth book with Stairway and, as before, they do yeoman's work in ensuring the quality of their books. Thank you.

I couldn't continue to write without the love and support of my wife Susan. I rely upon her keen eye as an editor and razor-sharp mind as an attorney as the best quality control any writer could hope for. She has my enduring love and gratitude.

Introduction

Legend: A lie that has attained the dignity of age.
—H.L. Mencken

LIKE A LOT of lawyers, I have always held Clarence Darrow in the highest esteem. To me, he was (note the past tense) a hero and icon for the profession.

It almost seemed as if it were a job requirement for lawyers to revere Darrow.

Oh, sure, there was always *To Kill a Mockingbird*'s Atticus Finch, though his stature is dimmed by the sequel *Go Set a Watchman*, which revealed his character arc to bend from idealist to racist.

But, hey, that was a fictional character, right?

Atticus could be whatever author and creator Harper Lee wanted him to be.

Clarence Darrow, though, was the real deal. A genuine flesh-and-blood lawyer fighting for justice. Attorney for the damned, as dubbed by muckraking journalist Lincoln Steffens. An idealist who honored principle above expediency. Who honored justice over money. Now there was a role model!

Or so I thought.

When I started researching for my book *A Death in the Islands*, about Hawaii's infamous Massie Case, I learned some things about Darrow that troubled me.

I was astonished to find that, not only was he not the hero for justice that I had always believed him to be, he often subverted the justice system. In fact, he really didn't believe in the concept of justice at all.

Of course, the Massie Case came at the end of his illustrious career. Some might even say it came *after* his career, since he literally had to be lured out of retirement—I say "had to be," but it only took money to do so, which flies in the face of the Darrow legend—to take on one last case.

Maybe worse, he suborned perjury in that trial by putting his client on the stand to lie because it suited his defense. And that begged the question: Was his unethical, even criminal, conduct in the Massie Case an aberration, or was it simply the continuation of a pattern of conduct?

Perhaps there was more to Clarence Darrow than I had previously known.

I decided I needed to dig a little bit deeper, go back farther, and see whether, in fact, my role model and idol was as flawed as his swan song[1] case revealed him to be.

Could it be that his feet had always been made of clay[2] and I simply didn't know it?

I read everything I could find about what others had to say about him.

He had, of course, his apologists and his detractors, as do all historical figures, and their works were my starting point. But I decided that, to fully know and understand Darrow, I needed to go to the source.

To the man himself.

I needed to know what he said and what he thought, not

---

[1] *Merriam-Webster* defines "swan song" as "a farewell appearance or final act or pronouncement."

[2] The popular notion of the term "feet made of clay" refers to weaknesses or character flaws in prominent or powerful people. The term is Biblical in origin. In *Daniel* 2, the prophet Daniel interpreted King Nebuchadnezzar's dream about an image, or statue, made of gold, silver, brass, and iron, but with feet partly made of clay. When those feet of clay were struck, they broke and were unable to sustain the weight of the image, causing it to crumble.

merely what others said and thought about him.

Only then could I draw any valid conclusions about Clarence Darrow based upon...Clarence Darrow.

I began digging into Darrow's own words.

What better place to begin this part of my discovery journey than Darrow's autobiography, titled *The Story of My Life*?[i]

But that was just as biased, if not more so, than works by his apologists, and was sometimes flat-out dishonest.

I learned that I had to take his words with a grain of salt.

I read many of his other writings, as well, which could fill a library, but I also consumed his spoken words, both inside and outside of the courtroom.

That meant, among other things, excavating court records and transcripts. Those kinds of things might bore the average person into a coma, but I found them to be fascinating.

And while they gave me an appreciation for the man's keen wit and quick mind, as well as for his oratorical skills, I found that plenty of less complimentary words and phrases—of all parts of speech, including nouns, verbs, and adjectives—begin to spring to mind. Words like blowhard, windbag, bloviate, sophistry, con man, misdirection, deflection, sleight of hand, and—dare I say it?—criminal.

What I discovered was that Darrow was a very flawed individual, as we all are, but also that he was a very flawed lawyer.

I realized that my blindly placing him on a pedestal was because I, like so many other lawyers, had been awed by popular culture's presentation of Clarence Darrow.

But legend and reality are quite often, if not almost always, mutually inconsistent. Popular culture did not portray the real Clarence Darrow, but instead it portrayed the legendary Clarence Darrow.

Several things I learned about him, and which exploded the legend I had clung to for so long, included:

Darrow didn't really believe in law and justice.

In fact, Darrow did not even equate law with justice.

In his closing argument in the Massie Case, he said:

> *I fairly well know what law is, but I don't often know what justice is—it is a pattern according to our own personal conceptions.*

In other words, justice was personal to each individual, and he believed he had the right to decide what it was in any particular case—law be damned!

Darrow believed that the end justified the means.

That allowed him to rationalize unethical, even criminal, behavior. So long as his actions achieved the end he desired—one that comported with his own personal sense of justice—then he was justified in taking those actions. In his closing argument in the Leopold and Loeb case, he said:

> A great many people in this world believe the end justifies the means. I don't know but that I do myself. And that is the reason I never want to take the side of the prosecution, because I might harm an individual. I am sure the State will live anyhow.

Do you understand what he's saying? Because the end justifies the means, the prosecution might hurt an individual by acting accordingly and he couldn't bring himself to do that. But if he acted accordingly on the defense side, well, no big deal if it harmed the prosecution because the prosecution would still survive to bring the next case.

And the next.

And the next.

So, he was perfectly willing to take actions in his cases that may have violated the law, but if it accommodated his own personal perception of justice and his desired end, then it was okay.

He spelled this out in one of his trials in Los Angeles when he was charged with bribing jurors in the McNamara case. That case, which we'll discuss in more detail later, involved the bombing of the *Los Angeles Times* building in 1910, during a time of intense labor unrest, resulting in more than twenty deaths.

In Darrow's closing argument, he persisted in asserting the righteousness of the cause of labor, which he had championed for years. He even impliedly suggested that the bombing was justified since the bombers "had no thought of harming human life" and, thus, "[n]one of the perpetrators of this deed was ever morally guilty of murder."

And what about the bribes he was accused of orchestrating?

While complaining bitterly that the prosecution had advantages not available to the defense, and had acted unethically and even illegally,[3] he said, "Of course I did not pass $500 in the elevator, but if I had, I had just as much right to give that $500 for that purpose as I would have to buy $500 worth of hogs, just exactly. I was doing exactly what they were doing...."

Just fighting fire with fire. Just buying hogs. The end justified the means. *If* he did it, that is.[4]

Darrow didn't believe in free will.

He had this remarkable belief that we are all the victims of our circumstances and heredity and, thus, we have no control over our acts. Accordingly, we should not be held accountable for them.

We see that in his argument in Leopold and Loeb:

> Why did they kill little Bobby Franks? Not for money, not for spite, not for hate. They killed him as they might kill a spider or a fly, for the experience. They killed him because they were made that way. Because somewhere in the infinite processes that go to the making up of the boy or the man, something slipped, and those unfortunate lads sit here hated, despised, outcasts, with the community shouting for their blood. Are they to blame for it?... It is one of those

---

[3] One wonders if he ever appreciated the irony of that complaint. If the end justified the means, wasn't the prosecution entitled to do the same if it comported with their sense of justice?

[4] You can almost hear the Monty Pythonian "Nudge nudge. Snap snap. Grin grin, wink wink, say no more."

things that happened; that happened, and it calls not for hate but for kindness, for charity, for consideration.

He also stated that belief in an address to the prisoners at the Cook County (Illinois) Jail in 1902, in which he said:

> I do not believe that people are in jail because they deserve to be. They are in jail simply because they cannot avoid it on account of circumstances which are entirely beyond their control and for which they are in no way responsible.

Darrow seemed to have no real adherence to, or belief in, the concept of right and wrong—just inevitability.

If you have no control, no free will, over what you do and, thus, bear no responsibility for your acts, how can there be right or wrong? According to Darrow, we do only that which we are programmed in our genes to do. Our actions are inevitable, almost a Calvinistic form of predestination, and we are not responsible for those actions.

In Leopold and Loeb: "I do not know what remote ancestors may have sent down the seed that corrupted him, and I do not know through how many ancestors it may have passed until it reached Dickie Loeb."

And again, "Now, I have said that, as to Loeb, if there is anybody to blame, it is back of him. Your Honor, lots of things happen in this world that nobody is to blame for."

Darrow didn't believe that punishment should be meted out to those who had committed crimes.

This was a logical outcropping of the inevitability concept.

After all, if we have no control over our actions, and we simply do that which we are programmed by our genes to do, imprisonment would, itself, be a crime.

As he told the prisoners at the Cook County Jail, "There ought to be no jails; and if it were not for the fact that the people on the outside are so grasping and heartless in their dealings with the people on the inside, there would be no such institution as jails."

***

Our basic belief in a system of laws, a nation of laws, crumbles if we accept the notion that the end justifies the means, and the appropriate end is subjective, depending upon personal conception.

Darrow seemed to advocate that a partisan lawyer's concept of the proper result of a particular case should prevail and, thus, justify whatever the lawyer did to achieve it. That leads to a whole slew of other problems on a slippery slope.[5]

If a lawyer gets to decide the outcome of his or her case based upon their personal sense of justice, what about the opposing lawyer? Doesn't the same concept apply to them? Or does the victory simply belong to the lawyer who can better articulate their position, can be a better advocate for their personal sense of justice? Or can cheat the best?

And if that's the case, then there is no need for a trial, is there? Just allow the lawyers to debate.

But who gets to decide?

And if there is no right or wrong, just inevitability, why don't we do away with the criminal justice system entirely? Just click our tongues and say to people who do things of which we don't approve—can't really call them crimes under this theory—"there, there, we know you didn't mean it," and let them go.

Darrow seemed to believe that he should be the arbiter of what is or is not the preferred outcome, thereby justifying anything he had to do in order to achieve it.

It's a surprise, I suppose, that he didn't change his name to Solomon. It is arrogance that is hard to comprehend. It is this same notion that allows some people, even today, to believe that they are above the law because, after all, they know better than the rest of us.

This book is not intended as a biography or a history of Clarence Darrow, full of details and dates, but rather as an analysis of, and commentary upon, Darrow's overwrought

---

[5] *Merriam-Webster* defines "slippery slope" as "a course of action that seems to lead inevitably from one action or result to another with unintended consequences."

oratory and abysmal ethics as a lawyer.

I didn't choose to write this book for the purpose of denigrating Darrow, although it may appear that way, and that certainly is the result. Rather, it is to point out the flaws in the application of his belief system as applied to the justice system and the way he practiced law.

At its heart, this is intended as a morality tale.

Hopefully, it will provide lessons all lawyers need to learn. For that matter, I believe they are lessons that all *people* need to learn: that we are a nation of laws, that there are rights and wrongs, that justice is real and is bigger than one individual's opinion or interest, and that one person doesn't get to decide for all of us.

As Spike Lee said: "Do the right thing."

---

[i] Clarence Darrow, *The Story of My Life*, Charles Scribner's Sons, 1932.

Table of Contents

PART ONE: 5
Popular Culture and the Legend of Clarence Darrow 5
Chapter One: Dazzlement or Bafflement 6
Chapter Two: The Legend of Clarence Darrow 12
    The Legend of Clarence Darrow 16
PART TWO: 20
Bombs and Bribes—The Bribery Trials of Clarence Darrow 20
Chapter Three: Bombs 21
    A Bomb in Idaho 21
    A Bomb in Los Angeles 28
    Déjà vu: Darrow and Dollars 32
    "For it is Mary, Mary, plain as any name can be." 37
Chapter Four: Necessity Knows No Law 40
    Ortie McManigal: the Harry Orchard of the McNamara case ... 42
    Kidnapping Witnesses 48
    Bribing Robert Bain 49
    Bribing George Lockwood 52
    Changing Pleas: Backlash 57
Chapter Five: The Trials and Tribulations of Clarence Darrow 62
    Indicted 62
    Darrow Hires a Lawyer 64
    The Lockwood Trial 67
    Darrow Testifies 70
    Darrow the Thespian 74
    "That'd I'd been crying..." 77
Chapter Six: That's Not My Dog 79
    The Prosecution is Being Mean to Me 82
    Big Business is Being Mean to Me 89
    Serial Non-Denials 92
    Guilt Trips 95
    Does it Make Sense? 98
    Fighting Fire with Fire 100
    Jury Nullification: So What if I Did It? 101
    The Golden Rule 102
    Don't Hold What the McNamara Brothers did Against Him .. 103
    They Didn't Mean to Hurt Anyone 105
    They were Justified because Their Cause was Just 107
    Invoking God 110
    Special Defense for the Second Trial 113
    Waxing Poetic 114

Chapter Seven: Did He, or Didn't He? 119
    Popular Belief that Darrow was Guilty 120
    Bribing the Bribery Jurors?.. 131
    John Brown's Body.. 136
    "I'm going to kill myself."... 139
PART THREE: 141
The Smartest Guys in the Room—Leopold and Loeb 141
Chapter Eight: A Fair Fee 142
    Money, Money, Money, Money 143
    I Can't Think without my Glasses 145
    You Have the Right to Remain Silent 151
Chapter Nine: My Kingdom for a Lawyer 160
    You Must Save our Two Boys! 162
    Affluenza 163
    Darrow's Bully Pulpit.. 167
Chapter Ten: A Plea in Mitigation... 170
    Crazy 171
    Not Crazy, Exactly; Just Mentally Diseased 174
    Windbaggery on Display 179
    Arguments in Mitigation 180
    Leopold and Loeb were the Real Victims 180
    What Would Jesus Do?... 182
    Bobby Franks Might Never Have Amounted to Much............. 185
    Leopold's and Loeb's Youth 187
    The Murder was Not Particularly Cruel or Cold-Blooded 188
    Bobby's Parents are to be Envied 192
    Pity the Mothers. Again. Except Flora Franks. 193
    Dickie and Babe... 194
    The Senselessness of the Crime Proved the Disease of the Minds 196
    They Couldn't Help Themselves... 198
    Do it for All Children Everywhere 202
Chapter Eleven: Someone Else's Fault 205
    Pointing Fingers—The Wealth of his Clients' Families 206
    Leopold's and Loeb's Parents 209
    Richard Loeb's Governess 211
    Detective Stories.. 212
    Lack of Proper Training 213
    Youth 214
    Puberty and Sexuality... 217
    Society.. 220
    Friedrich Nietzsche... 220
    Books [Part Two] 222
    World War I 223

Happenstance 224
Spared from the Gallows 225
Chapter Twelve: Bye Dickie; Hello New and Improved Babe 229
    The Violent Demise of Dickie Loeb 230
    Repairing Fine China 232
    Compulsion 234
    Babe's Final Chapter 241
    Meanwhile, Back at the…Darrow 242
PART FOUR: 244
A Barrel of Monkeys—The Scopes Trial 244
Chapter Thirteen: An Act Prohibiting 245
    Divine Creation v. A Lower Order 247
    He that Troubleth his own House… 249
    Something is Afoot at the Drugstore 252
Chapter Fourteen: Under the Big Top 259
    The Great Commoner and the Attorney for the Damned 262
    View from the Fourth Estate 265
Chapter Fifteen: Send in the Clowns 269
    Trial and Error 270
    Motions and Speeches and Prayers—Oh My! 277
    Give Me that Old-Time Religion 286
    "Your Honor has the right to hope." 291
Chapter Sixteen: The Sun Stood Still 298
    "A Lot of Fellows who are Profusely Ugly…" 300
    Find the Defendant Guilty 306
    And on the Eighth Day, the Court Rested 308
Chapter Seventeen: Folding the Tent 311
    The Sleep of the Just 313
    The Judgment Must Accordingly be Reversed 316
    Whatever Happened to John T. Scopes? 318
    Whatever Happened to the Butler Act? 319
PART FIVE: 325
Aloha Oe—Massie 325
Chapter Eighteen: "I Better Go to Hawaii" 326
    "I Needed the Fee" 327
    High-Minded, Honest, Kindly, and Sympathetic Clients 330
Chapter Nineteen: The Ala Moana Case 333
    Assault on a Woman 335
    License Plate 58-805—Close Enough 343
Chapter Twenty: Hung Jury 347
    Thalia Takes the Stand 350
    Shady Tactics 354
    Six to Six 357

- **Chapter Twenty-One: The Murder of Joe Kahahawai 359**
  - A Bundle in the Back Seat 361
  - Convening the Grand Jury 363
  - A High-Powered Attorney Who Needed the Fee 367
- **Chapter Twenty-Two: Darrow's Final Trial 371**
  - Picking a Jury 373
  - The Trial Begins 376
  - Crazy—Leopold and Loeb Redux 378
  - Thalia Returns to the Stand 386
- **Chapter Twenty-Three: Darrow's Final Courtroom Bloviation . 389**
  - The Unwritten Law 390
  - More Windbaggery 392
  - The Golden Rule 393
  - Darrow's Clients were the Real Victims 396
  - Mothers 397
  - There was No Intent (Just Gross Indifference) 400
  - Ends Justify the Means 401
  - Loyalty 402
  - It Doesn't Matter who Fired the Shot 402
  - Victims, Again 404
  - Crazy, Again 404
  - Darrow Assumed the Ala Moana Boys were Guilty of Rape 405
- **Chapter Twenty-Four: Paradise Lost 409**
  - Leniency Recommended 410
  - A Miscarriage of Justice 412
  - No Retrial for the Ala Moana Boys 417
  - You're Goddamn Right I Shot Him 419
- **PART SIX 421**
- **Stop the Presses 421**
- **Chapter Twenty-Five: The Hard Death of a Legend 422**
- **Blowhard Bibliography 424**
  - Published Materials 424
  - Court Cases 429
  - Court Records 430
  - Newspapers, Magazines, and Periodicals 430
  - Internet and Video 431
  - Endnotes 433

PART ONE:
Popular Culture and the Legend of Clarence Darrow

Sometimes legends make reality, and become more useful than facts.
—Salmon Rushdie

Mike Farris

Chapter One: Dazzlement or Bafflement

History has its truth, and so has legend. Legendary truth is of another nature than historical truth. Legendary truth is invention whose result is reality.

—Victor Hugo

W. C. FIELDS FAMOUSLY said, "If you can't dazzle them with brilliance, baffle them with bullshit." He could have been talking about Clarence Darrow, though he wasn't.

At least not specifically.

On the other hand, Adela Rogers St. Johns *was* talking about Darrow when she expanded on the notion. St. Johns, the daughter of attorney Earl Rogers—who represented Darrow in his criminal prosecution for bribery—wrote in her biography of her father:

> [Darrow] *had the debater's trick of sliding off a question—ask him about the ten-thousand-dollar check to* [labor leader Olaf] *Tvietmoe or the thousand dollar check to Bain, and he would be found discussing The Rich and Social Conflict.*[i]

Darrow, she believed, was a "phony" who would, she was

"pitifully sure...betray us anywhere along the road without a qualm for any reason that seemed good to him."[i]

Or, as Rogers biographers Alfred Cohn and Joe Chisholm wrote:

> Rogers, more than once, when the drinks were coming thick and fast, confided to intimates that he had little respect for Darrow's ability as a lawyer, attributing his success mainly to wide publicity and his wonderful gift in delivering emotional appeals to juries.[iii]

Emotion seemed to be a major weapon in Darrow's arsenal of rhetoric. Reports from Darrow's closings in multiple cases are full of comments on the flow of tears in courtrooms. Tears from judges. Tears from jurors. Tears from audience members. And plenty of tears from the Attorney for the Damned, himself.

In addition to tears, Darrow also flooded courtrooms with rhetoric. From his four-hour-and-twenty-minute closing argument in Hawaii's Massie case, which was short by Darrow standards, to his three-day argument in Leopold and Loeb, his almost nonstop torrent of words may well have baffled far more than they dazzled.

Reading those speeches today—and they truly are speeches appealing to emotion rather than reasoned legal arguments appealing to logic—engenders a tremendous amount of sympathy for the original hearers, juries and judges tasked with sorting through a mountain of often irrelevant verbiage to apply law to Darrow-obscured facts.

Darrow's favored tactic was to confuse and distract those hearers, particularly juries, although not all judges were immune to his verbosity.

Darrow's rambling arguments conjure up the term bloviation, once defined by President Warren G. Harding as "the art of speaking for as long as the occasion warrants and saying nothing."

William Gibbs McAdoo, progressive leader and son-in-law

of President Woodrow Wilson, defined it as "an army of pompous phrases moving over the landscape in search of an idea."

Paint Darrow as the poster boy for that expression.

Perhaps even worse, his bombast provided cover for a tortured sense of ethics that is hard to fathom, particularly in the modern world. In *The People v. Clarence Darrow*,[iv] historian Geoffrey Cowan wrote that Darrow appeared to justify his ethical breaches by a fervent belief in the righteousness of his legal positions and causes that often led him to discard inconvenient facts as collateral damage.

As it turns out, that may or may not be true—sometimes it appeared as if simply the desire to win was justification enough for him. But even if true, as Alan Dershowitz pointed out in his introduction to a reprint of Darrow's autobiography, *The Story of My Life*, "[t]here is simply no justification for corrupting the legal system, even if it is done to level the playing field."

Long considered an icon and role model for lawyers everywhere, Darrow's legend, largely crafted by his own words, doesn't bear up to scrutiny. He seems to admit as much in *The Story of My Life*. "If I tell anything it will be but a plain unvarnished account of how things really have happened," he wrote, then added the qualifier, "as nearly as I can possibly hold to the truth."[v] That hearkens to former president Donald J. Trump's qualifier to ABC News's Jonathan Karl in an interview in which he said, "When I can, I tell the truth."

In a flash of self-realization, Darrow added that "[a]utobiography is never entirely true. No one can get the right perspective on himself."

What Darrow was telling the reader is that everything he says about himself and his career must be taken with a grain of salt. Grains of salt. Mounds of salt. Telling the truth is nearly always possible but, for Darrow, whether to tell the truth in any given instance was a choice dictated by self-interest.

If the truth helped his cause or his image, then he would champion it. If it didn't, or if it harmed it, then truth was expendable, to be left in a heap in his wake.

Ironically, he had slipped and told the unvarnished truth about himself and his philosophies, in a sort of forerunner to the quoted statements above from his memoir, in a fictionalized account of his youth in rural Ohio called *Farmington*, published in 1904.

In it he wrote that the book told "an expurgated story of a life." Elaborating, he said, "But so far as I can really tell my story, I shall make a brave endeavor to tell it truthfully, at least as near the truth can be told by one who does not tell the whole truth—which, after all, is not so very near."

> *I have always had the highest regard for integrity and have ever by precept urged it upon people; therefore in these pages I shall try, as I have said, to tell the truth; still I am afraid that I shall not succeed, for, after all, I can tell about things only as they seem to me.... So, to be perfectly honest with the reader—which I am bound to be as long as I can and as far as I can—I will say that this story is only a story of impressions after all. But this is doubtless the right point of view, for life consists only of impressions, and when the impressions are done the life is done.*

In other words, Darrow would tell the truth as he saw it—something he expressly said in his autobiography: "I can tell of my life only as I see it...." [vi]—and as it fit with his preferred narrative.

Almost any list of America's greatest lawyers will include Darrow somewhere, often at or near the top. We tend to idealize historical figures and, admittedly, it is often unfair to judge any historical figure's conduct in the past by the standards of today. But certain basic principles of legal ethics transcend time—principles like honesty in the courtroom and sanctity of the judicial process.

Whether viewed by the standards of the late 19th and 20th

Centuries or those of the 21st Century, Darrow's conduct in multiple cases, including those for which he is best known and highly lauded, falls short. This was not just the occasional aberration but instead represented a pattern of conduct.

For example, it was commonly believed at the time that, in his defense of union officials charged with killing the former governor of Idaho in 1905, Darrow tampered with the jury and even kidnapped or paid off witnesses. In the case of the McNamara brothers accused of dynamiting the *Los Angeles Times* building in 1910, he sought to align his close friend, Charles Erskine Scott Wood, as co-counsel. Wood declined because he feared Darrow would resort to his customary nefarious tactics to win, including bribery and perjury.

Past is often prelude and made a prophet of Wood.

During his defense of the McNamara brothers, Darrow resorted to witness intimidation—one account has a Darrow agent telling a witness that if he persisted in testifying for the prosecution, "he will not die a natural death."

Darrow was ultimately indicted and tried for attempting to bribe two jurors in that case. Although he was acquitted of one charge and obtained a hung jury in the other, journalists who covered the trials, as well as his own closest friends and the attorney who defended him at trial, believed he was guilty.

In the Leopold and Loeb case, he sought to avoid a jury trial by pleading his clients guilty and then proceeding on a defense of mental illness to mitigate their culpability and escape the death penalty. It was critical that he walk a fine line between mental illness and insanity because proceeding on the latter would automatically trigger the requirement for a jury trial, which he was desperate to avoid. But while walking that line, he suppressed his own experts' reports that concluded that Leopold and Loeb were insane—then he leaked those reports to the press in an effort to paint a more favorable view of his clients in public opinion.

And in Hawaii's Massie case, he relied upon the unwritten law (that a man is justified in avenging the dishonor of his wife) and the theory of jury nullification to defend his clients on a murder charge.

To advance his defense, though, he suborned perjury by knowingly putting a witness on the stand to lie.

The only logical conclusion is that Clarence Darrow was a highly unethical attorney.

As you read the pages that follow, you can judge for yourself.

Mike Farris

Chapter Two: The Legend of Clarence Darrow

When the legend becomes fact, print the legend.
—Maxwell Scott in *The Man Who Shot Liberty Valance*

IF ALL LAWYERS behaved the way they are portrayed in popular culture, Lord help us! Would we really want to operate in a system full of Saul Goodmans, the eponymous sociopathic character from television's *Better Call Saul*?

Notwithstanding a final *kumbaya* moment in a New Mexico federal courthouse at the end of Season 6 that provides Saul, nee Jimmy McGill, a modicum of redemption, to call him a bad role model for lawyers would be the understatement of all understatements. But for those who are fortunate enough to avoid courtrooms and law offices in their day-to-day lives, pop culture, with its Saul Goodmans, often offers the only window into that mysterious world. And the windowpanes provide a decidedly distorted view, resulting in a variety of myths that urgently need to be dispelled, but likely never will be.

The term "popular culture" refers to the influence of cultural products on a society's views on a particular topic.

Those products include[1] music, art, literature, film, television, radio, mass media, and social media. In other words, it is how society is led by those products to perceive a particular subject or aspect of that society, as opposed to reality. For the profession of law, that perception has been shaped—or maybe more accurately, misshaped—over the centuries, and none too favorably, at that.

Plato espoused the rule of law in his aptly titled *Laws*,[2] noting that the "lawgiver…will appoint guardians to preside over these things…." Presumably, "lawgiver" is a reference to what we, today, call lawyers. Socrates seemed to advocate that those guardians should be seen but not heard, writing, "The law presumably says that it is finest to keep as quiet as possible in misfortunes and not be irritated, since the good and bad in such things aren't plain…."

This clearly doesn't represent the modern lawyer in any manner.

And then, in *Henry VI*, Part 2, Shakespeare's Dick the Butcher said: "First thing we do, let's kill all the lawyers." Sounds grim, but when considered in context, what the villainous Dick the Butcher is actually suggesting is that, in order to succeed in a rebellion against King Henry, they must first eliminate the defenders of justice in society.

Supreme Court Justice John Paul Stevens analyzed the line in a dissenting opinion, in which he was joined by Justices Brennan and Marshall: "As a careful reading of that text will reveal, Shakespeare insightfully realized that disposing of lawyers is a step in the direction of a totalitarian form of government."[3]

---

[1] Perhaps the lawyer in me says I should add the qualifier "but are not limited to…" I suppose I've done one document request too many in my career.

[2] Not only aptly entitled, but also maybe a little on the nose—a phrase that, according to the Urban Dictionary, means "unsubtle or overly and clumsily direct."

[3] *Walters v. Radiation Survivors*, 473 U.S. 305, 371, fn. 3/24 (1985) Stevens, dissenting.

Overall, not so bad a portrayal of our profession.

Lawyers didn't fare as well in *The Bible*. The prophet Isaiah bemoaned that "none calleth for justice, nor any pleadeth for truth: they trust in vanity and speak lies; they conceive mischief and bring forth iniquity." *Isaiah* 59:4 (KJV).[4] While that verse isn't specifically addressed to lawyers, it could sure be interpreted to apply to them. But to remove any Biblical ambiguity, St. Luke wrote in the *New Testament*: "Woe unto you also, ye lawyers! For you lade men with burdens grievous to be borne, and ye yourselves touch not one of the burdens with one of your fingers." *Luke* 11:45 (KJV). Just a few verses later, he doubled down: "Woe unto you, lawyers! For ye have taken away the key of knowledge; ye entered not in yourselves, and them that were entering in ye hindered." *Luke* 11:52 (KJV).

The good news is that the term "lawyers" as used in the *New Testament* actually refers to religious leaders of the time, who were supposedly experts in Mosaic Law, and not lawyers operating within a justice system as we know them today. So, Luke's indictments don't really apply.

Or do they?

More modern assessments still go back a lot of years, although maybe not to Biblical days. Charles Dickens's *Bleak House* was first published as a 20-episode serial in 1852 and 1853, and, on this side of the "pond," *The Leavenworth Case* was published in 1878 by Anna Katharine Green. The former involves a long-running case involving conflicting wills in England's Chancery Court,[5] while the latter is really more of a detective novel, albeit utilizing a lawyer named Everett Raymond to get to the truth, along with investigator Ebenezer Gryce.

---

[4] King James Version.

[5] Oh, boy, a will dispute! The topic makes one absolutely giddy at the thought of potential thrills it might conjure up. And then one remembers the steamy *Body Heat* and its plot point centered on the Rule Against Perpetuities. Maybe I diss will contests unfairly.

Blowhard

We are likely more familiar with 20th Century literary works about lawyers, like those of lawyer-turned-novelist Erle Stanley Gardner, who introduced the Perry Mason series in 1933 with *The Case of the Velvet Claws*. The novel version of Mason ended with *The Case of the Postponed Murder*, number 82 in the series, published in 1973 as the second of two posthumous final editions to the series.

Other lawyer-authors picked up the mantle after Gardner left it beneath an urn of his ashes, which were scattered over the Baja California peninsula. The next generation of champions for the profession includes the likes of Scott Turow, John Grisham, James Grippando, and Robert Dugoni.

A number of literary efforts, including some from non-lawyer authors, ended up gracing the big screen, such as *The Firm*, *Presumed Innocent*, *The Verdict*, and Harper Lee's *To Kill a Mockingbird*.[6] Since lawyers and the law offer such fertile ground for storytelling, there have, of course, also been big-screen originals, like the comic *My Cousin Vinny* and *From the Hip*, and adaptations from other mediums, including stage plays such as the overly dramatic *A Few Good Men*.

Perry Mason climbed out of the pages of Gardner's novels and entered our homes via the television screen, along with a host of others. Typically hour-long dramas, and some that were combined with police procedurals, the list includes *The Defenders*, *Matlock*, *LA Law*, *Judd for the Defense*, *The Practice*, *Suits*, and *Law & Order*s ad nauseam. There were even a few half-hour sitcoms that introduced clownish lawyers into our perceptions,

---

[6] *To Kill a Mockingbird* was first published in 1960 and made into a movie in 1962. The timing places it in the waning years of Gardner's Perry Mason run, but my reference to picking up his mantle refers to lawyer-authors, which Harper Lee was not—though she missed it by only a hair. Lee's father was a lawyer and member of the Alabama legislature. Lee, herself, studied law at the University of Alabama though, to her father's chagrin, she left school a semester shy of acquiring her law degree. Some might say it was the best semester she never had.

such as *Night Court*'s public defender Daniel R. Fielding and the silver-tongued Jackie Chiles on *Seinfeld*. Each of these contributed in part, some more than others, to the popular culture view of lawyers.

For better or worse.

But it's not just the generally considered forms of cultural products, like movies, television, and books, that are at play. We all know the world of lawyer jokes, negative contributors to pop culture, and we also see lawyers depicted in the comics, such as Steve Dallas in *Bloom County* and Snoopy as the "World Famous Attorney" in *Peanuts*.

Regardless of the source of the depiction, a chicken or the egg riddle has been created. Does popular culture reflect the conduct of lawyers, or is the conduct of lawyers more and more a reflection of how they are perceived by popular culture? Either way, a mythology has been created about lawyers that longs for a reality check because, while there are myths about lawyers, there are also truths. The trick is distinguishing them.

While much of popular culture creates its impressions based on fictional lawyers, sometimes popular culture reshapes, or rewrites, history. In *The Man Who Shot Liberty Valance*, newspaper editor Maxwell Scott (played by Carleton Young) says to attorney-turned-senator Ransom Stoddard (played by James Stewart), "When the legend becomes fact, print the legend." And so, legends have often stood the tests of time because of popular culture's disdain for facts.

One of those is Clarence Darrow.

The Legend of Clarence Darrow

Clarence Darrow and the Scopes Monkey Trial[7] is no exception to the "print the legend" admonition. That legend, largely shaped by *Inherit the Wind*, a play later made into a movie

---

[7] We'll discuss Scopes in more detail later, but it provides a good illustration of how pop culture hijacked reality when it came to Darrow.

starring Spencer Tracy and Fredric March, holds that, in 1925, a poor, beleaguered biology teacher in small-town Tennessee defied a criminal law forbidding the teaching of evolution in schools. His freedom and livelihood were imperiled, but then none other than Clarence Darrow rode into town on his white horse to challenge William Jennings Bryan, spokesman for organized religion and the anti-evolution forces, and to defend academic freedom and the beleaguered educator. Makes for good copy. Made for a darn good play and movie. But it doesn't comport with the facts.

A particular part of the Darrow pop culture legend deserving to be debunked is the notion that he was the "attorney for the damned," as he was dubbed by his friend, Lincoln Steffens. The Darrow legend at the time, and even today, is that he was a lawyer who always stood up for the underdogs, even at his own financial expense. We know that was Darrow's reputation because...well, because Darrow told us so.

He wrote in his autobiography, "My sympathies always went out to the weak, the suffering, and the poor." He went on to say, "I have always stood with the minority against all popular causes and mass hysteria...." and it is "impossible to deny help to those in trouble and pain...." In pursuing those cases, "I never cared much for [money] nor tried to get much of it or ever had a great deal...." [vii]

It's nice, though, when the "weak, the suffering, and the poor" have money. In the Haywood case, his fee was reputed to be anywhere from $35,000 to $50,000 in 1907 money, approaching a million and a half in today's dollars. In the McNamara case, he demanded that the American Federation of Labor guarantee him a minimum fund of $200,000 to finance the defense—and apparently a bribe or two—and allow him to retain at least $50,000 of that as his fee, roughly $1.57 million dollars in today's money. The families of Leopold and Loeb paid him $70,000 in the mid-1920s while the friends and family of the Massie parties paid $50,000 in 1932, both more than a million dollars in today's money. Lincoln Steffens made no mention of these payments. Apparently, he only raked muck from those who were not already his friends.

Some say that the legend was really created following his near-disastrous trials for bribery of jurors in the McNamara case in Los Angeles in 1910, that Darrow learned his lesson and "rebuilt his practice and his reputation by taking cases that other lawyers would not touch." [viii]

Gerald Uelmen wrote that reflecting on Darrow's role in the bribery of jurors led him to conclude "the man who inspired my own ambition to become a lawyer, turns out to have been not just unethical, but a lousy lawyer to boot." But, he added the hopeful note that Darrow lived for another twenty-six years and "pursued a very different direction in his legal career...He truly redeemed himself and gained his place as an inspirational model for future generations of lawyers." [ix]

The three cases that most prominently figured in the Darrow legend, as we know it today, were Leopold and Loeb, Scopes, and Massie. Adela Rogers St. Johns,[8] daughter of Darrow's Los Angeles attorney Earl Rogers, wrote that had it not been for that acquittal, "Darrow would not have had a chance to win the moral victories of the Leopold-Loeb, Scopes, Scottsboro, and Massey trials. All of which, of course, he lost in court." [x]

She was correct that Darrow lost Leopold-Loeb, Scopes, and Massie (which she misspelled as Massey) but, although the NAACP offered the services of Darrow to the Scottsboro defendants in their appeals, the defendants declined the offer in favor of lawyers retained on their behalf by the International Labor Defense. The United States Supreme Court ultimately reversed the trial court convictions of what became known as the "Scottsboro Boys" on ineffective assistance of counsel grounds, in the landmark case of *Powell v. Alabama*, 287 U.S. 45 (1932). By then, Darrow had already retired, unretired when his finances took a hit to take on one final case, earned a hefty

---

[8] I'll refer to her throughout this book as either Adela or St. Johns.

fee losing the Massie case in Hawaii, and then retired again, all while doing nothing on the Scottsboro case.

W.W. Robinson was a student at USC when the *Los Angeles Times* building was bombed in 1910, and he attended the bribery trials of Clarence Darrow. In a chapter from his book *Lawyers of Los Angeles*, Robinson agreed with St. Johns that Darrow's "greatest days as a defender were ahead of him—with spectacular victories to be won in the Loeb-Leopold, Massie-Fortescue, and Scopes cases." [xi] Reporter Hugh Baillie, too, noted that Darrow's greatest fame would follow the Los Angeles bribery trial, naming the same three cases—Leopold-Loeb, Massey [sic]-Fortescue, and Scopes—and also misstating the results of those cases, referring to them as "his most spectacular triumphs." He wrote, "Today he is part of the history in the history books, largely because of the cases he tried after his escape from Los Angeles." [xii]

The phrases "spectacular victories" or "spectacular triumphs" very much overstate the matter—Darrow lost all three of those cases. Still, unquestionably, the foundation of the Darrow legend today largely had its genesis with those cases. It's important that Darrow and his legacy stand on their own rather than be propped up by unrealistic views of his legend.

St. Johns, who was highly critical of Darrow during the time her father represented him in his bribery trial, probably said it best:

> *Legends grow.*
>
> *Facts are forgotten. Darrow went down in history almost entirely for cases he tried after his escape from the jury bribery charges in Los Angeles and, to pin it down, few of them had much to do with the poor the weak and the helpless.*
>
> *If the Darrow legend is really founded upon a rock, this eyewitness account I've given cannot harm it.*
>
> *If it was built on sand, it should fall like all else that is phony in the history books.*[xiii]

PART TWO:
Bombs and Bribes—The Bribery Trials of Clarence Darrow

When people ask me what sort of man Darrow is, I ask them the apparently irrelevant question: When? And my answer is that at three o'clock he is a hero for courage, nerve, and calm judgment, but at 3:15 he may be a coward for fear, collapse, and panicky mentality.
—Lincoln Steffens

Chapter Three: Bombs

My dynamite will sooner lead to peace than a thousand world conventions. As soon as men will find that in one instant, whole armies can be utterly destroyed, they surely will abide by golden peace.
—Alfred Nobel

ON OCTOBER 1, 1910, the *Los Angeles Times* building was destroyed by a bomb blast. It was not the first bombing tied to labor unrest in the United States, nor would it be the last. And it was not the first bombing that drew Clarence Darrow into a courtroom to defend members of organized labor accused of being behind the bombings, but it very nearly marked his last appearance in a courtroom, at least as a lawyer.

To fully understand and appreciate Darrow's role in defending the McNamara brothers—Jim and J.J.—on charges of bombing the *Los Angeles Times* building, and his utilization of tactics that led to his indictment, one only has to go back a few years to a bomb blast that killed a former Idaho governor.

A Bomb in Idaho

With labor union support, Frank Steunenberg served two terms as governor of the State of Idaho but, instead of seeking re-election in 1900, he moved from the governor's mansion in

Boise to the town of Caldwell, about thirty miles west, to go into private business. On the evening of Saturday, December 30, 1905, Steunenberg returned home, on foot, from the Caldwell Banking and Trust Company, the bank that he and his brother had erected. As he opened the gate to his yard, a bomb exploded, killing him. Suspicion focused on leaders of Idaho's labor movement who had come to view the once pro-labor Steunenberg as a traitor.

As governor, he had tamped down labor violence in the mining industry by, among other things, declaring martial law and asking President McKinley to send in federal troops to Coeur d'Alene in 1899. Perhaps even more egregious, particularly in the eyes of the white, mostly European immigrant members of the Western Federation of Miners, Steunenberg had acquiesced to the use of black troops from the Twenty-fourth Infantry Regiment to restore order.

In a subsequent federal investigation, Steunenberg accepted full responsibility for that military intervention. To the labor movement, accepting responsibility was tantamount to a confession of disloyalty. Revenge was in order. And, as the expression goes, it was a dish best served cold. Though five years had passed since Steunenberg exited the governor's office, organized labor had the memory of an elephant, long and unforgiving. Hence, the murderous explosion in Caldwell on the cusp of a new year.

Hired by the State of Idaho, detective James McParland of the Pinkerton Detective Agency tracked the origin of the explosive device to a man named Harry Orchard, who had a history of labor-related bombing. McParland arranged to have Orchard spirited away, by dubious means, to the Idaho state penitentiary in Boise where, under days of relentless questioning, he confessed to the Steunenberg bombing.

He also confessed to multiple other violent murders of non-union men, including politicians and judges in Colorado. He claimed that he committed all the crimes at the direction of leaders of the Western Federation of Mining: William "Big Bill"

Blowhard

Haywood, Charles Moyer, and George Pettibone. The three men were arrested and brought to trial in Boise, with Orchard as the prosecution's star witness.

The International Workers of the World hired Clarence Darrow to undertake the defense of Big Bill, *et al*. Darrow told labor organizer Mary Harris Jones, sometimes known as Mother Jones, that it would likely be a long trial and that it "will need a great deal of finance to carry it on."

It's not entirely clear what he meant by "great deal of finance," but it turned out to be a considerable sum. Darrow's law partner, Edgar Lee Masters, said it was $50,000, though Darrow claimed he received only $35,000. Either way, in today's money, that was *beau coup* dollars: either $1.2 million or $1.7 million, depending upon whose figure you accept.

Darrow argued before the United States Supreme Court for a writ of habeas corpus on behalf of George Pettibone arising out of the circumstances under which the three men had been arrested in Colorado and extradited to Idaho for trial—illegally, Darrow claimed; in fact he argued they had been "kidnapped," a term he would revisit a few years later in the McNamara case. The high Court ruled against him, essentially (and perhaps irrationally) saying that, since Pettibone was already within the jurisdiction of the Idaho court, it didn't matter how he got there.

> [T]*he vital fact remains that Pettibone is held by Idaho in actual custody for trial under an indictment charging him with crimes against its laws...it is not necessary to go behind the indictment and inquire as to how it happened that he came within reach of the process of the Idaho court in which the indictment is pending.*[9]

The three men (Haywood, Pettibone, and Moyer) were tried separately, with Hayward first up. The key witness against him

---

[9] *Pettibone v. Nichols*, 203 U.S. 192 (1906).

was Harry Orchard, the confessed bomber.

A basic principle of criminal law is that a jury may not convict on the uncorroborated testimony of a co-conspirator, and corroboration for Orchard existed in the form of a confession by an accomplice, Steve Adams. But a problem developed regarding that confession, thanks to Darrow.

Pulitzer Prize-winning author J. Anthony Lukas described it this way:

> *Though Darrow's closing deserves substantial credit, nothing he did in the courtroom can compare to his master stroke of persuading Steve Adams—whether by bribe, threat, or otherwise—to renege on his confession, thus depriving the state of that corroboration.* [xiv]

Pinkerton detective McParland believed that Darrow utilized James Lillard, uncle of Adams's wife Annie, to assist in turning Adams. McParland said that "Darrow had paid Lillard $75,000, of which $25,000 had specifically been promised to Adams if he'd repudiate his confession." [xv]

To further exert pressure on Adams, Darrow used the carrot-and-stick approach, coupling the offer of bribe money with a threat to implicate Adams in another murder case if he didn't recant. This, again, was a tactic Darrow would revisit in the McNamara case.

Referring primarily to Darrow, McParland said that he had never before seen "men who called themselves reputable attorneys" obtain a repudiation of prior statements by acting under the "pretext of being his best friend," and then to "place him in a position where he would be convicted of a capital offense...." [xvi]

It worked.

With Adams recanting, that left only the uncorroborated testimony of Orchard to be used against Haywood, which paved the way for an acquittal.

But even with that successful tactic, Darrow wasn't about

Blowhard

to leave anything to chance. There was widespread belief, in yet further foreshadowing of the McNamara case, that Darrow engaged in various other nefarious tactics.

Darrow's friend Charles Erskine Scott Wood reported that he heard stories about Darrow creating and destroying evidence. Attorney John McLane said that another lawyer, a friend of Haywood's named John Nugent, referred to Darrow as "Old Necessity," because Darrow followed the creed that "necessity knows no law." [xvii]

Edgar Lee Masters, Darrow's law partner, later wrote, "The newspaper grape vine [sic] is that Darrow bribed the Steunenberg jury," a sentiment echoed by Oscar King Davis of *The New York Times*, who said that there were rumors that "the jury had been bought."

While the truth of the rumors has never been conclusively established, they were widely accepted as true at the time, and they fit a pattern of conduct chargeable to Darrow; hence, they were imminently believable.

In keeping with his pattern of windbaggery and performance art, Darrow's closing statement in the Haywood trial lasted more than eleven hours. Part lawyer and part snake oil salesman, his argument was less about the facts of the case than it was about emotion and misdirection—a hallmark of Darrow arguments.

After Darrow completed his argument, prosecutor William E. Borah told the jury:

> [The defense lawyers] *are men of wonderful powers. They have been brought here because of their power to sway the minds of men…*[to] *draw you away from the consideration of the real facts in this case, to beguile you from the consideration of your real and only duty.*

Author David Grover succinctly nailed Darrow's rhetoric: "The speaking of Clarence Darrow defies analysis." [xviii] Dissecting Darrow's closing argument in the Haywood case, Grover detected "no clear pattern of organization." [xix] That is consistent with many of Darrow's arguments in other cases, which often seemed to follow a stream of consciousness, albeit with certain repetitive themes, no matter the facts of any particular case. In a word: bloviation, designed to bludgeon the listener into submission.

A major Haywood theme, that later recurred in McNamara, was justification of violence as a tactic of labor. For example, Darrow argued to the Idaho jury:

> *I don't care how many wrongs they have committed—I don't care how many crimes—these weak, rough, rugged, unlettered men, who often know no other power but the brute force of their strong right arm, who find themselves bound and confined and impaired whichever way they turn, and who look and worship the God of might as the only God that they know; I don't care how often they fail—how many brutalities they are guilty of. I know their cause is just. I know that trouble and strife and contention have been involved, yet through brutality and bloodshed and crime has come the progress of the human race.*

Prosecutor Borah was not moved by this appeal, telling the jury about Darrow's "startling doctrines":

> *...you must have said to yourselves at once, this man justifies murder, coldblooded, deliberate murder, openly in the courts of our country. If Haywood felt as his counsel feels, who speaks for him, if this is the creed of the W.F. of M.* [Western Federation of Miners], *why should they not kill and murder? ...Shame, oh shame....*

The media was even more vicious in attacking Darrow's Haywood closing. "[A] vicious appeal to class prejudice" said the *New York Sun*, while the *New York Tribune* termed it "untenable and ridiculous." Even Darrow's hometown *Chicago Tribune* piled on, calling it the "most unseemly, abusive, inflammatory speech ever delivered in an American courtroom" and went on to tag Darrow as "a master of invective, vituperation, denunciative humor, pathos and all the other acts of the orator except argument." [10]

The *New York Times* said:

> Darrow was not making an argument upon the facts that have been presented to the jury. He was expressing with passionate eloquence his views on certain phases of life.

The *Times* reported that, before he finished, the jurors "were tired of Darrow's talk" and that "they certainly took no pains to conceal the fact that they were bored almost to the limits of endurance." It said that one juror, Samuel F. Russell, whom the paper dubbed "Grandfather Russell," had discovered a squeak in the spring of his revolving chair and "put in the greater part of the afternoon giving it encouragement."

But regardless of their wandering minds during the second day of Darrow's argument, the jury managed to acquit his client. There were perhaps at least two major factors behind the acquittal.

The first, as mentioned above, was Darrow's ability to persuade Steve Adams to recant his confession, depriving Orchard's testimony of corroboration.

The other was the possibility, suspected but never proved, that Darrow bribed jurors. With the acquittal of Haywood, an acquittal followed for Pettibone, prompting the prosecution to dismiss the charges against Moyer.

---

[10] *Merriam-Webster* defines argument as "a coherent series of reasons, statements, or facts intended to support or establish a point of view." Maybe the *Tribune* was on to something.

Mike Farris

A Bomb in Los Angeles

At 1:07 A.M. on October 1, 1910, sixteen sticks of dynamite exploded at the *Los Angeles Times* building located at First Street and Broadway. It blew a hole in the first floor of the building and cratered a portion of the street.

As the building burned, a secondary explosion occurred when fire from the first ignited barrels of ink behind the building in what was called Ink Alley. In a chain reaction, a large printing press, dubbed the Old Guard by the newspaper's owner Harrison Otis, fell through the floor into the basement, demolishing a gas main, which led to yet another explosion. Before the blaze could be contained, the building had been virtually destroyed, twenty lives had been lost, and dozens more hospitalized.

Suspicion focused almost immediately on the forces of organized labor. This was a time of incredible labor unrest, not just in Los Angeles, and bombings were one of their favored tactics when strikes failed. The *Times*, under the leadership of owner and publisher Harrison Otis, spearheaded the battle against unions in California. Otis—a veteran of the Civil War, in which he had been twice wounded, as well as the Spanish-American War and the 1899 insurrection in the Philippines—had cut his anti-union teeth fighting the typographers union. At one point he had even brought in strikebreakers from Kansas City to get the paper out during a strike.

He was also a strong admirer of German philosopher Friedrich Nietzsche and his theories of the *Übermensch*, or superman, that there were some people who simply were not bound by rules that applied to lesser mortals. Nietzsche later found another admirer in the form of Nathan Leopold, who was six-years-old at the time of the Los Angeles bombing.

Otis was instrumental in creating the Merchants and Manufacturers Association (M&M), a staunchly anti-union organization that controlled Los Angeles and represented as much as 85 to 90 percent of Los Angeles businesses.

Under the leadership of Otis and M&M, Los Angeles had become known as "Otistown of the Open Shop." As author Howard Blum wrote, "From its inception, the M&M was uncompromising. Either employers ran an open shop or they would suffer consequences...."

Consequences included financial institutions cutting off credit, and sometimes, "customers would be 'persuaded' to go elsewhere." [xx] Make what you will of the word "persuaded." Naturally, this made the *Times* a target of organized labor.

By contrast, San Francisco was a labor paradise with a significant majority of jobs unionized. San Francisco's labor leaders yearned to export their unionizing to their neighbor in the southern part of the state. Olaf Tvietmoe, secretary-treasurer of the California Building Trades Association, sent organizers to Los Angeles, with financing from labor organizations in San Francisco as well as the national American Federation of Labor (AFL). "Strike fever" ensued and unrest intensified. The AFL even attempted to mobilize a national boycott of companies that advertised in the *Los Angeles Times*.

Because of the fierce resistance labor forces faced from Otis and the M&M, leadership determined that something had to be done.

That was when Eugene Clancy, a San Francisco leader in the west coast Bridge and Structural Iron Workers Union, made a key, and fateful, strategic move: he sent a letter to the union's chief operating officer in Indianapolis, John J. "J.J." McNamara, asking for help.

Attorney/author Nelson Johnson wrote: "[Clancy] wanted *help of a different kind*. McNamara agreed on the need for such help, but he had a decision to make. Whom should he send to the City of Angels?" [xxi] [emphasis in original]

Picketing had already been tried in Los Angeles and had failed. Something more dramatic was needed. Using dynamite to send messages was a common labor tactic, as witnessed in the bombing death a few years earlier of Frank Steunenberg. In fact, over the course of a few years, overlapping with the *Times* bombing, agents of the Iron Workers union were reputed to have planted bombs at approximately seventy-five sites or more across the country, although with "only" one fatality.

For the "whom," J.J. settled on his younger brother, Jim, and a man named Ortie McManigal, both trained and experienced bombers, to be the instruments of destruction.

They planted bombs at the *Times*, as well as at the homes of newspaper owner Otis and Felix Zeehandelaar (known as "Zee"), executive secretary of M&M.

After the *Times* explosion, police arrived at Otis's house and found the bomb in a suitcase beneath a window. They escaped just in time to avoid the blast when it went off. Otis was not at home at the time, but was traveling in Mexico. The bomb at Zee's house failed to go off; apparently the triggering alarm clock had been wound too tight, and it was discovered the next day by workmen.

Initially, there was some speculation that the *Times* had been destroyed by a gas explosion—an accident—while conspiracy theorists suggested that Otis had bombed his own building in an effort to focus suspicion on the labor unrest. The most logical theory, though, was that the bomb had been planted by labor interests as part of the bitter conflict racking Los Angeles and the *Time*'s unrelenting assault on labor unions.

Beginning on October 25, 1910 and extending to October 13 of the following year, a Los Angeles County grand jury conducted an investigation and issued a final report on the cause of the explosion.

It concluded, after providing "full consideration" to the "possibility of gas being the destroying agent, the explosive force," that "there was placed in the Times Building, in that part thereof commonly known as Ink Alley, a high-power explosive in the nature of dynamite or nitroglycerine, and that the origin of the catastrophe may be found in the destruction wrought by this agency." The evidence, it said, "makes the theory of exploding illuminating gas not only untenable, but puerile." [11]

It also concluded "that the perpetrators and instigators of this terrible catastrophe have been members of labor unions and officials and organizers therein, and, moreover, intimately associated and connected with certain leaders and high officials of labor unions."

It did not, however, reach any opinion as to who, specifically, was responsible. That would be up to other investigations. There would be two of them.

The City of Los Angeles hired detective William J. "Billy" Burns of the Burns Detective Agency, reputedly the most famous detective in America, to investigate the bombing. But, as Nelson Johnson tells us, "Equally important as his fame, the Burns Detective Agency provided guns, spies, and agents provocateurs for hire in the war between capital and labor." [xxii] This would be a significant part of Darrow's later justification for his clients', and his own, actions in the ultimate prosecution of J.J. and Jim McNamara.

The second investigation was commissioned by M&M, which hired as its investigator noted Los Angeles attorney Earl Rogers, who had authored the city's anti-picketing ordinance.

Rogers then assembled his own investigative team, working with detective Sam Browne of the Los Angeles County sheriff's office. The Rogers team ultimately obtained information that led to murder indictments against Matthew Schmidt and David Kaplan (or Caplan), as well as against J.B. Bryce.

For his part, Billy Burns was able to trace the bombing back to J.J. McNamara and his brother, having uncovered the real identity of J.B. Bryce as Jim McNamara. He also implicated Ortie McManigal, who would later turn state's evidence.

Through a sequence of secrecy and trickery, the McNamaras were extradited to Los Angeles to stand trial. The union and Clarence Darrow would later contend that the

---

[11] *Merriam Webster* defines puerile as "juvenile, childish, silly." That word will come up again later.

brothers had been "kidnapped" by Burns because all the legal niceties for extradition had supposedly not been complied with.

In fact, some of those involved in the "kidnapping" were later arrested and charged with that crime. Only a couple of those were actually indicted—the grand jury refused to indict the others—and charges were ultimately dismissed against the ones who were indicted.

The McNamara case seemed to have all the hallmarks of the Haywood case—as Yogi Berra was reputed to have said, "It's déjà vu all over again"—with bombs, arrests (or kidnappings) of union leaders, allegations of frame-ups by capitalist leaders, and confessions of accomplices—Harry Orchard in the Haywood case and Ortie McManigal here.

The *International Socialist Review* published an article by "Big Bill" Haywood that itemized the similarities, and journalist/socialist Frank Wolfe published a pamphlet called *Capitalism's Conspiracy in California: Parallel of the Kidnapping of Labor Leaders in Colorado and California*.

The Idaho case had seen acquittals or dismissals of all those charged, and labor forces, convinced of the McNamaras' innocence, envisioned the same thing happening in Los Angeles.

To do that, though, they would require the services of the man many of them believed to be the best lawyer in the country, the man who had won Haywood for them: Clarence Darrow.

Déjà vu: Darrow and Dollars

At this point in his career, more than thirty years since first being admitted to the Ohio bar, Clarence Darrow had abandoned, for all practical purposes, getting involved in "causes."

Following the Haywood case, he had been desperately ill for months with an ear affliction ultimately diagnosed as mastoiditis, which was surgically repaired. When the *Times* was bombed, he was focusing his practice on more mundane matters, primarily for the Chicago Title and Trust Company and other corporate clients. He needed steady work, steady fee payments, and less stress.

The constant flood of union litigation he had previously been involved in had nearly bankrupted those unions, forcing him to "take much less than my contract entitled me to..." [xxiii] The corporate clients, though, helped pay the bills.

And he really needed it just then.

A financial crisis had swept the country, wiping out investments and closing banks. The Darrows had invested in a gold mine, Black Mountain, in Mexico, though Clarence had not told his wife, Ruby, of the investment. As the value of the investment plummeted, Darrow's business partner in the venture sent repeated messages to him, seeking his signature to authorize liquidation of the interest.

But Darrow was in the midst of his mastoiditis infection and Ruby, concerned about her husband's health and fearful that, in his weakened state, he wouldn't be able to handle the stress, kept it from him—until it was too late and the entire investment had been wiped out. Biographer Irving Stone describes the scene when Darrow was finally told.

> *After several weeks, when he had regained his strength and was judged able to leave the hospital, Ruby and the doctors told him as gently as they could that his investment was gone, that the Black Mountain gold mine was no more. Darrow jumped out of bed, broke away from the grasp of the doctors who were trying to keep him quiet and charged like a bull across the room.*
>
> *"Do you realize what you've done to me?" he cried at his wife. "You've thrown away my life savings, my dream of retiring. Now I'll have to begin all over again—be a slave to that irksome law work—we'll never be able to travel the world, write all those books! I'll never forgive you for this—never, never!"*
>
> *But he did, husband-like, when he learned that she had probably saved his life by letting his money go.* [xxiv]

So now he needed a big payday, as he would again later when he accepted employment in the Massie case in Hawaii following reversals in the stock market from the crash of 1929.

Though he was content to steadily represent paying clients, he still had his labor roots. He had championed labor from his involvement in the Pullman Strike and representing Eugene V. Debs to the Oshkosh Woodworkers and Anthracite Coal strikes and the Haywood case.

Organized labor, aware of those deep roots, made a hard rush at him. It even called out its biggest gun, Samuel Gompers, who had founded the AFL, to add pressure.

At least for a while, Darrow resisted. He was tired of fighting battles like this.

He wrote in his autobiography:

> *"I realized that the men should be defended, but I felt that I had done my share of fighting. It was not easy to combat the powerful forces of society in the courts, as I had been doing for many years, and I was now weary of battling against public opinion."* [xxv]

But he was agreeable to at least meet with union leaders in Indianapolis while he pondered the request. While there, he demonstrated his own particular brand of windbaggery and bloviation.

> *Darrow gave the union leaders a lesson in the nexus between propaganda and law. To make it a crusade, he told them, the focus would have to shift. The public would have to stop thinking about the twenty men who had died. As long as those men were on the public's mind, there would be a cry for revenge and McNamara would be sucked down by the demand for blood. McNamara's friends would have to make J.J. the victim and make the forces of capital the villains.* [xxvi]

Blowhard

It was a page straight out of the Darrow playbook, one he would follow almost to the letter, himself, in Leopold and Loeb in 1924.

He also talked to Gompers by telephone. Gompers, who had known Darrow for two decades, sincerely believed it was vital to obtain Darrow's representation for the McNamaras, and he knew how to push Darrow's buttons.

> [Gompers] *knew that Darrow could be reached by flattery, impressed by money, and touched by sentiment. If all else failed, he could also be moved by fear.*

Gompers checked that last box by telling Darrow:

> *You will go down in history as a traitor to the great cause of labor if now, in our greatest hour of need, you refuse to take charge of the McNamara case.* [xxvii]

Darrow admitted to being worn down.

> *But the representatives of the Federation of Labor were so urgent that at last I could not refuse. How many times thereafter I wished that I had insisted upon some one younger and stronger and more anxious for the task. But I could not turn back.* [xxviii]

So, Darrow reluctantly agreed, and he and his wife Ruby temporarily relocated to Los Angeles for the trial.

He failed to mention in his autobiography that the AFL also beat him over the head with a checkbook. His conditions, which the AFL agreed to, were for it "to let him control the case and choose his own co-counsel; turn the case into a national crusade; and guarantee him a fund of at least $200,000, of which $50,000—after expenses—would be his fee." [xxix]

That $50,000 in today's money is north of $1.6 million dollars. That'll pep a fellow up pretty good.

Darrow continued to stay on top of the money issue throughout.

On July 8, 1911, he wrote Gompers:

> *I received your telegram today that a second 15,000 on the way. I hate to urge you about money but none of the lawyers have had any thing [sic]—except I was given $5,000 by the Structural Iron Workers at first & took 5,000 of the 15,000—but I must do something for them. Then we have a first class man for the detective work, who will need help. He is from Chicago & trusty [sic]. We have the ablest evidence gatherer I ever saw from Chicago—he needs help.*[12] *Then the McManagel [sic] matter, has cost & is costing money.*[xxx]

He wrote Gompers again a week later, on July 15.

> *It is necessary that the money matters must be clearly understood at least so far as possible—There is no way to try this case with a chance of winning without a great deal of money.... This will need all together [sic] $350,000 to $400,000 between now and Jan 1st—& should have $100,000 now & the balance at about 35,000 or 40,000 a month until that time. After this I should say it would need $20,000 a month until it is done.*

Then, probably understanding how all that money talk must have sounded, he threw in, "In this I am not thinking much of myself."[xxxi]

But Gompers was no dummy. Geoffrey Cowan wrote:

> *Like Erskine Wood, Gompers had undoubtedly heard*

---

[12] This appears to be a reference to John Harrington, who will be discussed again later.

> *rumors about the improper use of money in some of Darrow's previous cases. He insisted on scrupulous record keeping. He would not even allow anyone else to give money to Darrow and his team. When Olaf Tvietmoe offered to send money to Darrow from San Francisco, Gompers turned him down cold. All money had to be sent to Darrow through the AFL, with checks signed by Frank Morrison, the union's longtime secretary.*[xxxii]

Morrison sent $65,000 by August 3 and two $10,000 checks later that month, August 18 and 21.

Thereafter, the money flow slowed to a bare trickle, and by the first of September, the defense was nearly bankrupt.

Darrow did not cash or deposit the second $10,000 check but, through a series of transactions, it ended up in the hands of Tvietmoe, a leading labor figure in San Francisco, who converted it into cash.

Some of it would find its way into the hands of jurors.

"For it is Mary, Mary, plain as any name can be." [13]

Mary Field graduated from the University of Michigan in 1902, where she was exposed to the pragmatist philosophies of William James and John Dewey. Her ideals led her into social work and landed her in Chicago. Maybe it was fate, but there she worked with Jane Addams at Hull House, a settlement house, which on occasion featured Clarence Darrow as a speaker. It was probably inevitable, then, that the two would meet. Perhaps less inevitable, Mary soon became his protégé and, next thing you know, his lover.

Mary, whom Darrow sometimes referred to as Molly, wanted to be a writer. So, Darrow introduced her to his friend Theodore Dreiser in New York, editor of the women's

---

[13] "Mary's a Grand Old Name," songwriter George M. Cohan, written for 1906 Broadway musical *Forty-Five Minutes from Broadway*.

magazine *The Delineator*, who hired her as a reporter, and Darrow financed her way to New York to pursue a career. Not entirely unselfish in his motives, it was also to help cover up their romance so Ruby wouldn't find out. Author Howard Blum explained it this way:

> [G]*uilt ate at Darrow. He was betraying Ruby, and, he came around to conceding to himself, he was also betraying Mary. He could not leave Ruby; she was the anchor that weighed him down, yet at the same time she kept him moored. And if he wasn't going to marry his Molly, what would become of her? ... Their parting was a sadness. It would not do for her to remain in Chicago; proximity would bring memories and new temptations.*[xxxiii]

Which was not to say that Darrow didn't miss her. He wrote her on March 15, 1910, and said:

> *I miss you all the time. No one else is so bright & clever & sympathetic to say nothing of sweet and dear & I wonder how you are & what you are doing in the big city.*

He closed that letter with "But I really am going to NY to live...."

Whether he intended such a move or not, it's what he told Mary. But it took the bombing of the *Los Angeles Times* to reunite the two lovers, though on the west coast, not the east.

Now established as a writer, Mary had been asked by several pro-organized labor publications to cover the McNamara trial, which she agreed to do over Darrow's objections. He had already paid once to separate his spouse and his lover by half a continent, and he surely didn't want his girlfriend taking up residence again, even if only temporarily, in the same city in which he and Ruby were, themselves, going to be temporarily residing. It certainly throws into question the seriousness of his promise to Mary to move to New York.

But Mary had a mind of her own, and she and her sister, Sara, moved into an apartment together in Los Angeles. Even though Darrow had initially objected, he was a pragmatist. A lustful pragmatist, one might say. After all, they were both now once again in the same city, so it only made sense for him to pay her regular visits.

Geoffrey Cowan described Mary's apartment as "a hideaway for Darrow, a second home where he could retreat from the office and from his life with Ruby." [xxxiv] It was also a place where he could, apparently, make sexual advances on Sara in addition to Mary, although the sister rebuffed his repeated advances.[xxxv] And Darrow would pay a particularly significant visit to that apartment later.

Somehow, Ruby learned of the relationship, "a wound that remained raw for the rest of her life." [xxxvi]

Nelson Johnson wrote that, after Darrow had passed away and Ruby was corresponding with Irving Stone as he researched his biography on Darrow, *Clarence Darrow for the Defense*:

> Ruby bitterly denounced the very thought of allowing Mary to 'embroider her life' into Stone's book.
> She chided him: Why don't you ignore her, forget her? Why let her try to fasten herself onto a dead man as a bloodsucker that he once shook off, but is powerless to do?

Although Stone did not include Mary in his book, Ruby never forgot Mary.[xxxvii]

Chapter Four: Necessity Knows No Law

I will talk the matter over with Clarence Darrow and he will fix it.
—Bert Franklin

ONCE DARROW CAME on board to head up the McNamara defense team, he figured out quickly that his clients were guilty. He was a virulent opponent of capital punishment, so that meant his defense strategy would revolve around saving them from the death penalty, the same philosophy he later would apply in Leopold and Loeb.

But he figured he still had one shot at an acquittal, long though it might be.

The McNamara case presented many of the same issues and same difficulties on matters of proof as the Haywood case had, but he had been successful there.

So why would anyone expect him to use any different tactics now?

Darrow's friend Charles Erskine Scott Wood was perhaps the most vocal, or at least the most literary, in expressing his concerns about Darrow. A prolific correspondent in an age where letter-writing was as commonplace as emailing and texting is today, Wood liberally expressed his concerns that Darrow would do anything to win. That included bribery and perjury, not to mention hiding or whisking away unfavorable witnesses, tactics Wood considered legally, morally, and ethically wrong. When Darrow asked him to be his co-counsel, Wood refused for the very reasons he expressed in his letters.

Writing to Sara Field Ehrgott, sister to Darrow protégé and girlfriend Mary Field, Wood said that, while it might be "fun" to work with Darrow on the McNamara case, "I knew it would be these tactics because I know what was done at the Moyer-Pettibone-Haywood trial at Boise," a case in which "the defense was manufactured." [xxxviii]

He also predicted that Darrow would:

> ...use bribery where safe, perjury where safe. He will manipulate and marshal labor all over the United States at psychological moments to appear in masses and utter threats, arousing a bitterness, a recklessness meant to intimidate a jury in Los Angeles, but thereby arousing a sentiment of clan against persons and individuals more dangerous than dynamite.... [xxxix]

Detective William Burns had his own take on Darrow's handling of the case. Biased, to be sure, but it offers an additional viewpoint to consider when evaluating Darrow's conduct. He reduced it to writing in his own book under the self-aggrandizing, and more than on-the-nose, title of *The Masked War: The Story of a Peril that Threatened the United States by the Man Who Uncovered the Dynamite Conspirators and Sent Them to Jail.*

According to Burns, the defense, Darrow in particular, pulled out all the stops to thwart justice.

> Every possible effort to beat us out was made by the agents for the defense. Threats of murder were openly made to witnesses, evidence was manufactured or destroyed, plans were laid to kill me, as I have told before, my offices were broken into and searched, bribes were offered my men and the veniremen drawn for the jury. One man, employed by

> counsel for the defense, was caught red-handed bribing a juror the day before the McNamaras pleaded guilty. Detective Biddinger, traveling from Chicago to Los Angeles with important documentary evidence, was offered a large sum of money if he would permit himself to be hit over the head and the evidence taken from him.[xl]

Ortie McManigal: the Harry Orchard of the McNamara case

Burns and his detectives had been able to track down and arrest Jim McNamara for the *Times* bombing and Ortie McManigal for bombing the Llewellyn Iron Works, also in Los Angeles. When arrested, the two men were carrying a suitcase full of explosives.

To save his own hide, McManigal agreed to cooperate with prosecutors and to testify against both McNamara brothers. Darrow knew he had to undercut McManigal's testimony, just as he'd had to defuse Harry Orchard's in the Haywood case by eliminating any corroboration. The question in McNamara was a little different. It was how to get Ortie McManigal to recant. Darrow tried two approaches, both using family members of McManigal—his uncle, George Behm and his wife, Emma.

Burns wrote, "The defense was eminently successful with Mrs. McManigal...and she sold out after trimming us and trimming her husband." [xli]

"Trimming us" refers to the fact that Emma McManigal, who lived in the Midwest, had initially offered to help the prosecution. She convinced the Burns Agency to pay for her travel to Los Angeles, but once she arrived, she:

> ...calmly turned us down and worked so hard to influence her husband in prison to go back on his confession that at times we were fearful she would succeed.... As we were soon to learn, Mrs. McManigal's task was to whip her husband around for the defense and she kept at it to the very end. [xlii]

There had been reports that J.J. McNamara had promised Emma fifty dollars if she could convince her husband to keep quiet, which certainly would explain her change of heart.

Prosecutor John Fredericks served her with a subpoena, but she promptly sought out Darrow for advice. He told her to refuse to answer any questions in court when she responded to the subpoena. He also prepared a note for her to take to her husband to sign, recanting his testimony, and in exchange, Darrow promised to represent him. To add pressure, when Emma presented the note to Ortie, she told him that if he didn't sign it, he would never see her again.

He signed.

After learning this, Burns met with Ortie and convinced him to sign a second note, recanting his recanting. Ortie also promised to never see Darrow.

Score one for the prosecution.

On July 4, Darrow wrote to his son, Paul, and reported on these efforts. "Have not yet got McManagel [sic] but have hopes." [xliii] He had other cards to play.

Darrow's next step was to solicit the assistance of Ortie's uncle, George Behm. Ortie had always been very close to his uncle, but Darrow and the defense team had a particularly dastardly psychological scheme in mind utilizing Uncle George.

Before Behm arrived in Los Angeles from his home in Wisconsin, he and Emma had met with Darrow in Darrow's office in Chicago. In his testimony at Darrow's bribery trial, Behm said that Darrow started by asking him if he was a "union man" and whether "I was in sympathy with the labor movement, about the McNamara and McManigal cases." Darrow then "…asked me if I would be willing to go out there and see what I could do with my nephew in regard to changing his testimony…."

When Behm responded that he had to put his crop in before he could go anywhere, Darrow acceded to that short delay, then gave Behm $100 to make the trip. Behm testified, "He [Darrow] says, 'that will help you out there,' he says, 'to pay your railroad fare and your sleeping car and your meals; when you get out there,' he says, 'I will take care of you.'"

As to what he should say to Ortie when meeting with him in jail, Behm said Darrow told him, "George, do all you can with Ortie out there and get him to come across..." and "...that if he [Ortie] came across that he would get to be a free man; that he could come back here to Chicago and he [Darrow] would see that he had a good job back here; that he wouldn't be climbing around on buildings to make a living."

But when Behm got to Los Angeles, he was unable to convince Ortie to recant his recanting of the recanting.

In fact, Behm said, "He told me that he was guilty of the deeds that were charged against him" and that he was better off behind bars because, if he was out on the street, "Somebody was going to blow my head off." Ortie insisted to Uncle George that "I am going to tell the truth and nothing but the truth in this case, no matter where I end at."

After reporting this to Darrow, the attorney for the damned told Behm to meet with Ortie again. "He [Darrow] says, 'You tell him if he ever gets out of here on this case they will indict him back in Chicago on a murder trial.... Spring that on him and see if he will come across then.'"

This was similar to the threat used with Steve Adams in Haywood to implicate him in another murder if he didn't recant. It worked with Adams, but didn't work on McManigal. "Ortie says, 'No, Uncle George, you tell Darrow to go to it, I am not afraid of him.'"

Next step? Deeper psychological warfare.

On the way to the post office one day with Ortie's five-year-old son, Behm walked past the jail cell where Ortie would see them. Ortie called out for Uncle George to bring the boy closer so he could talk to his son, but Behm refused. After leaving the post office, Behm returned to Darrow's rented Los Angeles office, where he recounted what had happened. "He [Darrow] says, 'That is right, God damn it,' he says, 'tease him,' he says, 'and then he will come across.'"

Burns claimed that they did exactly that, parading Ortie's son back and forth. "This third degree work from the sidewalk was kept up for some time, the trips of the uncle being timed carefully so that McManigal would be at the window." [xliv]

According to Behm, Darrow also "told me that she [Emma] should make out an application and he would get her a divorce from him [Ortie] because he would never be any account for her any more [sic] and he was going to make arrangements so that she could get about $3,000 and she could buy a place in Chicago or somewhere east out near where her folks lived and get a little home where she could bring up her children."

Burns wrote: "The tactics the attorneys for the defense are using, look to me as if they were trying to unbalance Mac's [McManigal's] mind. First, they have turned his wife against him; second they have refused to bring his children to see him; third, they have paraded his uncle past the jail where they knew Mac would see him..." [xlv]

Burns believed this was part of a deliberate effort to undermine McManigal's testimony by asserting that he was "mentally defective." He said that the defense lawyers even went so far as to line up testimony of friends and relatives, going back to childhood, of Ortie's mental state.

But Darrow wasn't finished with Uncle George. When the grand jury sought testimony from him, Darrow and his co-counsel held a pow-wow and "they all decided that when I was called before the grand jury I should not answer any of the questions they asked me any more [sic] than my name and my residence."

At Darrow's first bribery trial (for the George Lockwood bribe), prosecutor Fredericks presented Behm with the transcript of his grand jury testimony and started his questioning with, "Which one of the attorneys, if you remember, instructed you that you should refuse to answer all the questions?"

Behm answered that it was Darrow.

"'Well, George,' he [Darrow] says, 'you go over to the grand jury and every word they ask you outside of your name and residence, just tell them that don't concern the case.' That was my answer for every question that was asked me in the grand jury during that time."

The result of complying with Darrow's instruction was that Behm was arrested and cited with contempt, along with an order to answer all questions he had previously refused to answer.

Upon Behm's return to court to purge the contempt and answer questions, he would be accompanied, not by Clarence Darrow, but by LeCompte Davis, Darrow's co-counsel.

Presumably, Darrow wanted to distance himself from any court backlash that might befall his client in court for having followed Darrow's instructions. But Darrow met with Behm again, along with Davis, one more time before the fateful day in court, to coach Behm on how to answer the questions.

Behm described it this way:

> *Well, Mr. Darrow told me, he says, "Well, now," first off, Mr. Darrow says, "Now, George, you ain't afraid to go to jail, are you?" I says, "No, not unless it is necessary." "Well," he says, "we are not going to let you go to jail if we can possibly help it, but," he says, "you may go to jail for this." I says, "I don't want to go to jail, it looks kind of bad for my folks back home to go to jail for what I came out here for." He says, "We will take care of you, we will get you out of here if we have to carry it up to the higher court." Now, the conversation was between the three of us. They undertook to drill me on those questions and how I should answer.*

Procedurally in that meeting, "Mr. Davis would ask me the question, and Mr. Darrow would tell me how to answer it."

Behm met one last time with Darrow prior to that return visit to the grand jury, this time without Davis. "He questioned me on these questions and he told me how I should answer them." But, Behm, said, Darrow told him not to answer any

Blowhard

questions about what Behm told McManigal that Darrow would do for him.

Instead, Darrow said "that I should deny those charges."

> Well, he says, "I can tell you," he says, "you answer those all with the exception of the questions they asked you concerning what you said to McManigal as what answers you got out of McManigal, and what you told McManigal, so in the fall term of court he could use me for a witness against McManigal's testimony," and then he told me that those questions they would ask me up there would be just the same as they had asked me, and I should fix it up in my own mind in a way I could answer him **so as to keep him out of trouble** and myself, and deny all questions asked of me about what I told McManigal that he would do for him if he changed testimony. [emphasis added]

The "him" in "keep him out of trouble" referred to Darrow. In other words, Darrow was telling Behm to lie to cover Darrow's butt. It's called perjury, and Darrow's conduct is called suborning perjury, apparently for the express purpose of, not protecting his clients, but *protecting Darrow*.

When questioned at the bribery trial about what he had told the grand jury about promises from Darrow, Behm was hardly able to answer due to frequent vociferous objections from Darrow, himself. Darrow apparently didn't want the answer to come out. It must have been a relief to Darrow when Behm acknowledged that he actually denied, to the grand jury, "the charge of interfering with a state witness."

But his testimony before the court in the Lockwood bribery trial proved that he had perjured himself at the grand jury.

Wiktionary defines scumbaggery as "the behavior of a scumbag."

Apt.

Kidnapping Witnesses

John Harrington was an attorney whom Darrow brought with him from Chicago and was one of Darrow's top investigators on the McNamara case. He appears to be the attorney referenced above in Darrow's July 8, 1912, letter to Samuel Gompers as "the ablest evidence gatherer I ever saw from Chicago."

But as trial of the McNamara brothers loomed, prosecutors sought Harrington's cooperation. They knew he had knowledge about certain nefarious activities of the defense team, including whisking witnesses away to prevent them from testifying. Ironically, that was exactly what Darrow wanted to do with Harrington: to whisk him away.

According to Erskine Wood, Darrow summoned him to San Francisco to discuss a project for which he wanted the help of Larry Sullivan, a detective that Darrow had hired following a recommendation from Wood.

As Wood later wrote to Sara Field Ehrgott, younger sister of Mary Field, Anton Johannsen requested a favor.

> He wanted a letter to Sullivan from me which would stimulate Larry into doing for Darrow a great service—no other or less than kidnapping Harrington, the lawyer who has turned state's evidence against D.[xlvi]

Detective William Burns suggested that Sullivan and Harrington had previously worked in concert to influence and intimidate witnesses to change their testimony. He wrote that, after one meeting with a witness, a man named William Flynn, packing foreman at the Giant Powder Works (where the explosives for the bomb came), Sullivan told Flynn, "Remember, everything said to-night [sic] dies here; if not, look out." Harrington told him, "They have no evidence against the McNamaras; they are just trying to job them."[xlvii]

Sullivan and Harrington questioned Flynn about George Phillips, also of the Giant Powder Works, who had actually sold the explosives to Jim McNamara.

As an implied threat to cooperate with the defense, the two men impressed upon Flynn that they had an "intimate knowledge" of him by "asking if he did not have a deaf and dumb child, a girl." [xlviii]

For his part, Phillips was told that if he changed his story about being able to identify McNamara, he would be well rewarded, but if not, he would meet a "horrible death," [xlix] or, as Cowan wrote, "he will not die a natural death." [l]

Obviously, then, Harrington's testimony could be very detrimental to Darrow if he wasn't either kept in line or kept out of reach. Hence, the "favor" requested by Johannsen to have Sullivan kidnap Harrington.

There is no specific evidence that it was done with Darrow's knowledge, but Wood wrote in that letter to Sara:

> I am sure Darrow knows of it. I am sure he set Johannsen on this, yet he talked with me so guardedly that he is perfectly safe in saying that "I never thought of such a thing."

Bribing Robert Bain

Although Darrow figured out pretty quickly that the case was likely unwinnable—at least not if he handled the matter ethically and legally—when you are able to convince yourself that your cause is just, and that the ends justify the means, your prospects brighten just a bit. And with the brightening, suddenly the path forward ventures into shadows and dark corners.

It had done so in Haywood, and it would do so in McNamara. With jury selection on the horizon, Darrow commenced one of the other tactics his friend Erskine Wood had anticipated. The one that got him indicted and tried.

He retained Bert Franklin, a private detective in Los Angeles, to develop background information on those in the McNamara jury pool. Franklin had opened his own private detective agency in Los Angeles after leaving his position as head of criminal investigations for the LA County sheriff's office, which had followed a stint as chief deputy U.S. marshal. With his background, he was the perfect choice for the investigative job.

If you believe Franklin's later testimony, his job, as directed by Darrow, was broader than just background investigation. It also included spreading around a bit of the AFL's money that ended up in Darrow's hands to fund the litigation. Recall that Darrow had demanded $200,000, with three-quarters of that for expenses and the remainder for his fee.

Specifically, Franklin was to ensure that favorable jurors made it onto the jury, if not to ensure acquittal then to at least hang the jury. If you don't believe Franklin's testimony, then it is still undisputed that he spread money around to buy jurors, just not at Darrow's instruction or with his knowledge or blessing.

The latter seems highly unlikely since Darrow had demanded of the AFL that he be allowed to control the case for the defense. By all accounts, he did exactly that.

The first potential juror Franklin approached was Robert Bain, an elderly Civil War veteran who lived with his wife Dora in their Los Angeles home, where he struggled financially while trying to earn income as a carpenter.

Bain was not home when Franklin first visited the house on October 6, 1911, so he spoke to Dora. She testified that, when she told him she was selling subscriptions to the *Los Angeles Examiner* to raise money for a blind friend, Franklin bought one. Nothing wrong with that.

But then Franklin asked how much she and her husband owed on their modest home. "I am not asking out of curiosity," she testified he said, "but I am asking as a friend."

He bemoaned with her how unfair it was that her husband had to work so hard and that "he is getting pretty old to do carpenter work." After a few more moments, Franklin got to the point of his visit.

Referring to the McNamara case, he said, "Mrs. Bain, I

want Bob to serve on that jury. I will make it worth his while."

As she told the story in court, Franklin told her:

"'If he will agree to serve on that jury,' he says, 'I will give him $500 tonight,' and he says, 'then if he stays through, qualifies, he stays through to the end of the trial,' he says, 'I will give him $3500 more at the end of the trial, providing he votes for acquittal or hangs the jury...'"

The prosecution, Franklin said, was "'buying witnesses and jurors, and' he says 'we have got to use the same tactics that they do to keep even.'"

To fully understand the enticement that was dangled in front of Dora Bain, the Bains owed $1,800 on their home and were paying fifteen dollars a month. The $4,000 bribe would more than erase that debt. By way of comparison, that amount equals about $130,000 in today's purchasing power. When her husband arrived home, Dora told him about the offer, and the Bains were hooked.

Franklin later met with Robert to make the "down payment," but he had only $400 with him. He promised he would make good on the other hundred—but not out of his own pocket.

Bain testified that Franklin told him: "'Of course, I am not good for that, you know me, you have known me a long time, I am not responsible for that, but', he says, 'Darrow furnished me $20,000 to use."

That equals about $650,000 in today's money. You can buy a lot of jurors with that.

Franklin told Bain that: "both sides was [sic] doing dirty work, buying witnesses and getting rid of witnesses." He also told him that "You are not the only man...there will be others in the boat." He then cautioned Bain to be careful with the money, lest anyone become aware that he seemed to have extra, unexplained cash on hand. Bain's only obligation in exchange? "I was to hold out for acquittal," Bain testified.

And so the deal was done, to Bain's apparent disgust, maybe the result of a guilty conscience. When he handed the cash to Dora, Bain said, "Here is the money, I do not want it, I never want to see it." As to what his wife ultimately did with the money, he testified that "She told me she paid most of it back to the District Attorney."

Bribing George Lockwood

Less than two months after passing a bribe to Robert Bain, Bert Franklin was ready to make his next payment to fulfill his promise to Bain that "there will be others in this boat."

This time his target was a former sheriff's deputy named George Lockwood. Franklin first made contact with Lockwood in early November at his home, but it was late in the evening so Lockwood rebuffed him until they could meet a few days later, on the morning of November 9, at Franklin's office.

According to Lockwood's testimony, "I think his first remark was, that he would like to have me as one of the jurors in the McNamara case." Franklin told him that he was "looking after the jury" for the defense and that "there was $2,000 in it for me, if I would act as a juror on that case." Franklin then bid against himself, saying that "possibly he could make it $2,500."

That number would continue to rise until it reached the same $4,000 promised to Robert Bain. That seems fair. After all, it was for the same job.

Franklin told Lockwood that "he had already one juror that was fixed," and specifically named him: Robert Bain. As he had with Bain, Franklin cautioned Lockwood that "your wife wants to be careful about how she spends money just now, don't want to flourish too much of it."

"Not a problem," Lockwood replied. He testified, "I told him that in case that the matter went through as outlined, that my wife would be the last person I would want to know anything about it."

It's unclear what Lockwood meant by that. In fact, Darrow counsel Horace Appel raised a laundry list of objections to it: "We move to strike that statement on the ground that it is incompetent, irrelevant, immaterial and hearsay...."

Blowhard

One can almost hear an echo of *Seinfeld*'s Jackie Chile objecting that, "I am shocked and chagrinned, mortified, stupefied," and that the question is "outrageous, egregious, preposterous."

The objection was overruled.

Ultimately, the Lockwood bribe was to be paid in two installments, as was the Bain bribe, $500 up front with the additional $3,500 to be paid later. The only uncertainty was ensuring the latter payment, since a bribe wasn't exactly the kind of promise that could be reduced to an enforceable writing.

Lockwood told Franklin that, "when the case would be over, there might be no one know anything about the balance of that money."

Well, Franklin told him, "I will talk the matter over with Clarence Darrow, and he will fix it."

The men agreed that a third party would hold those funds until after the trial, but then there was disagreement as to who that third party would be. Ultimately a deal was struck.

Unbeknownst to Franklin, before the date when the first payment was to be made, Lockwood reported the bribery effort to District Attorney John Fredericks, who also had been told about the bribe to Bain. A trap was laid. Lockwood was to meet with Franklin and the third party, Captain C.E. White, a mutual friend who had been the county jailer when Franklin and Lockwood both worked for the county sheriff, to receive the initial payment. White, as the stakeholder, would display the remaining funds to satisfy Lockwood that it existed. The meeting was to take place on Tuesday morning, November 28, at the corner of Third and Los Angeles Street.

At the appointed hour and place, Lockwood arrived to meet White, but Franklin wasn't there. Lockwood asked White, "What's new?" to which White replied, "Nothing except a mutual friend of ours intrusted [sic] me with some money to be paid to you on certain conditions." I'm to give you $500 and hold $3,000, White said.

This was not the deal that was made.

Lockwood testified, "I says, 'It don't go. There was to be $3,500 held, not $3,000." Then he asked, "Where's Franklin?"

"Franklin," White said, "just went away from here."

White walked away for a moment, as if to scout things out, then returned. Yep, you're right, he said, there was actually $3,500 in the roll he held in his hand, the correct amount, as if he had just counted it. When White handed Lockwood a $500 bill, Lockwood dropped it, then bent to pick it up—either a prearranged signal with the authorities or an attempt to buy time until Franklin returned.

When Franklin appeared, emerging from a saloon, Lockwood told him, "Bert, I'm afraid there is something wrong."

About that time, Franklin spotted police detectives he recognized. "Don't look around; don't look around," he said to Lockwood. Then, "The sons-of-bitches. Don't look around. Let's get out of here."

About that time, Lockwood spotted a man he didn't recognize coming across the intersection. That man was Clarence Darrow, who reportedly said to Franklin, "Bert, they are on to you." Before anything else could happen, detectives swooped in and arrested Franklin while Darrow made his escape. His presence at the site of a bribe payoff seemed damning, though.

Adela Rogers St. Johns wrote that Darrow testified that he received a call telling him:

> *If you want to save your man Franklin, you'd better hurry. They're onto him. If he passes that money at Third and Los Angeles, you're all for it.* [li]

That is inconsistent with the trial transcript and, one supposes, calls into question her other recollections of the trial—at least those that are not corroborated.

On the other hand, it's also possible Adela overheard Darrow tell that to her father, just not from the witness stand.

She writes that, in a private meeting with her father, Earl asked, "What were you doing there, Mr. Darrow?" Darrow responded, "I went there in response to an anonymous telephone call. I thought probably they were trying to frame Bert."

This is consistent with Franklin's testimony that Darrow said, as he crossed the street to where Lockwood stood with Franklin, "they are on to you."

That, after all, begs the question: On to Franklin about what?

Darrow, of course, had his own story for why he was there that morning. He and his attorneys claimed that he had received an anonymous call telling him he was wanted at the offices of the Socialist Party, the route to which would take him past Third and Main, near where the payoff was taking place.

So said reporter Frank E. Wolfe, a correspondent for a number of eastern newspapers and magazines, in response to questioning from Darrow.

Describing a meeting with Darrow on the fateful morning, this exchange between Darrow and Wolfe occurred at trial:

> **Q:** *First, what was done, what did you see me do?*
> **A:** *Saw you receive a telephone call.*
> **Q:** *And what was said?*
> **A:** *You stated you had to go away.*
> **Q:** *Was anything said as to where?*
> **A:** *Yes.*
> **Q:** *Whereabouts?*
> **A:** *You said you were going to headquarters.*
> **Q:** *What headquarters?*
> **A:** *Socialist headquarters.*
> **Q:** *And state whether I went away soon after or about that time?*
> **A:** *Yes, you went at that time.*

This testimony, of course, begs another question: Who placed that call? The defense team initially speculated that it was a cohort of either detective William Burns or perhaps *Los Angeles*

Times owner Harrison Otis, all part of a scheme to lure Darrow to the scene and set him up.

With George Lockwood on the stand, Earl Rogers asked him, "Don't you know that Darrow was telephoned for to come down to Third and Main Streets so that you could pull this play off?"

"No, sir, I don't know anything of the kind," Lockwood said.

But then Darrow undercut his own story by calling insurance broker Charles O. Hawley, a friend of Job Harriman, who was running for mayor of Los Angeles on the Socialist Party ticket. Hawley testified that, at about nine o'clock AM, he "telephoned him [Darrow] in the morning to meet me and Mr. Harriman at Socialist headquarters."

In other words, it wasn't some big plot or trap by the authorities, but was all just a huge coincidence.

Seems like a classic case of trying to confuse the jury by floating different theories. They couldn't both be right. And neither story explained what Darrow purportedly said to Franklin: "Bert, they are on to you."

The remark, if it was made—and in fairness, it should be pointed out that Darrow denied it—only makes sense if Darrow knew what they were "on to" him about. Of course, there is always the possibility that Franklin lied under oath. There is also the possibility that Darrow lied under oath.

But, detective Samuel Browne, who arrested both Franklin and Lockwood on the corner that morning, has an even more damning story to tell about Darrow. He testified that he later met Darrow on the street near the old post office, and Darrow made what seemed to be an admission.

Browne said he told Darrow that he [Darrow] should have known better than to hire Franklin "to do this work." Darrow replied that Franklin had come highly recommended, then said, "My God, I wouldn't have had this happen for the world; if I had known that this was going to happen *this way* I would never have allowed it to be done." [emphasis added]

He seemed to be acknowledging concern about the *method* of the payoff, not the *fact* of it. Browne also said that Darrow asked if there was anything he [Browne] could do to help.

"He [Darrow] says, 'This is terrible, you do the best you can for us,' he says, 'and I will take care of you.'"

Three days later, the McNamara brothers changed their pleas to guilty. Yet another remarkable coincidence.

Changing Pleas: Backlash

The Associated Press reported that, upon learning of the McNamaras' guilty pleas, Samuel Gompers said:

> *My credulity has been imposed upon. I am astonished at such news. Only a short time ago, I visited the McNamaras in the Los Angeles jail and they asked me to deliver to the Labor interests the message that they were innocent. I knew nothing at all of any plan for change of plea or any reason for a confession. I was not consulted about this step. I had raised $300,000 for their defense, believing them innocent.*

The president of the United Mine Workers of America was quoted by a UP reporter as saying:

> *I have believed confidently in the innocence of the McNamara brothers, I had always sincerely believed the Times blowing up was an accident, not a crime. Darrow was sent to defend them because we all believed their assurances of innocence.*

Obviously, then, the guilty pleas undermined all trust and confidence the labor leadership, as well as the rank-and-file, had held in the brothers' innocence. But it also provoked suspicion of Darrow, that he had engineered the change of pleas to save his own hide from a bribery charge.

Darrow insisted that a change of plea was already in the

works, and that the sole motivation behind the plea agreement was the obvious guilt of his clients and an unwinnable case against a potential death penalty.

In a conversation with his friend, journalist Lincoln Steffens, he mentioned his desire to reach a settlement, a suggestion that Steffens claimed to have picked up and run with on his own, with the goal being to get local business leaders to approve so as to pressure authorities to acquiesce. In his autobiography, Steffens described the inception of the idea this way:

> ...Darrow was at his cynical norm when, lighting up a cigarette, I said, "Darrow, you were talking yesterday about a settlement of the case. Do you mean that?"
> "Yes. I'd like to settle it, but it's impossible, of course."
> "I think not. I think I could work it out, if you'd let me."
> "What! And save the boys?"
> "Yes." And I outlined my plan: to get a group of employers or, anyhow, capitalists to do it.
> He reflected, tempted, no doubt, but he soon threw up his hands. "Do you think for one moment that the local employers would consent to let those prisoners go? And if they did, would the eastern employers who have suffered from dynamite let them? It's impossible. Impossible.[lii]

With Darrow's consent, Steffens claimed he proceeded to broker the deal. He pitched the idea to Meyer Lissner, a "sort of political box for the reformers, then in power in Los Angeles."

This was Steffens's pitch to Lissner:

> "Well," I said, "here it is, tearing your city to pieces—for a year, perhaps; arousing hate, intensifying the class war which you don't believe in. However it turns out, whether you hang those men or not, you won't settle anything or satisfy anybody. A law fight is a fight, perjury, suborning

> *of witnesses, jury bribery, and when one side wins there is no public conviction, only a running sore left. Why not try the other, the kinder, the finer way? Call together the leading men of your city and say to them, 'Here we've got labor down; we can hang two dynamiters who the workers think are innocent if we want to. But let's not. Let's let labor up and let their heroes go. And then we have a conference of leading employers with labor leaders and see if we can't handle our labor problem in such a fashion that we can afford to make Los Angeles the best instead of the worst town in the country for labor.'"* [liii]

A deal was reached, and the pleas were changed from "not guilty" to "guilty."

J.J. McNamara, the shot-caller, was to be sentenced to a term of less than ten years, while Jim, the actual bomber, would receive a life sentence.

Judge Walter Bordwell accepted the agreement as to Jim, but sentenced J.J. to fifteen years. There were even a few reports that Darrow wanted to include any potential bribery charges against himself in the deal, but Steffens disputed that.

> *Darrow drew me aside and said, 'Tell the prosecution to leave my case out of the settlement. They can have me—to try, if they'll let these prisoners off.'* [liv]

Many continued to believe that Darrow had convinced his clients to change their pleas because he feared he would be arrested for bribing jurors and that guilty pleas provided him a defense. Why would I bribe jurors, the argument would go, if I knew there would be no trial due to the guilty pleas?

While that might have carried some weight as to the Lockwood bribe, since it had occurred during a time when the settlement discussions were supposedly already in progress, it wouldn't wash as to the Bain bribe. That had occurred six weeks prior when there weren't even arguable settlement discussions in process.

But even as to the Lockwood bribe, many who knew Darrow didn't buy his defense.

C.P. Connolly of *Collier's* magazine said, "My own judgment is that Darrow turned the affair for his own salvation."

He also discounted the possibility that bribe money could be spread around without Darrow's knowledge.

> *No agent would dare attempt to account for the disappearance of four thousand dollars to a man of the world like Darrow by saying he had fed it to the pigeons.*

And O.N. Hilton, attorney for the Western Federation of Miners told the *Denver Post:*

> *Mark my words, you will see that Darrow has not acted in good faith. There isn't a man who has once been associated with him in the profession of law that will not tell you the same thing. Not one of them cares to associate with him again.* [lv]

Even Judge Walter Bordwell, who was presiding over the McNamara case, believed the change of pleas was related to the attempted bribery and not something that had already been in the works.

He issued a statement to correct some of what he considered misstatements and misconceptions in an article written by Steffens, and published in the *Los Angeles Express*, in which Steffens outlined the supposed timing and his role in brokering the deal.

Judge Bordwell's statement blew a hole in the defense.

> *The District Attorney acted entirely without regard to Mr. Steffens and upon lines he had decided to follow before the latter appeared on the scene. As to the McNamaras' defense, the public may rely on it that the developments of*

*last week as to **bribery and attempted bribery of jurors were the efficient causes of the change of pleas which so suddenly brought these cases to an end**...Those interested in the defense continued to urge the District Attorney's acceptance of propositions for ten days or more until **the bribery development revealed the desperation of the defense**...then it was that the change of the pleas of these men was forthcoming.* [emphasis added]

Chapter Five: The Trials and Tribulations of Clarence Darrow

I had no conversation with him whatever in reference to Mr. Bain, excepting, possibly, as I would any other juror on October 6th, and I gave him no check on October 6th.

—Clarence Darrow

Indicted[lvi]

DARROW COULD SMELL an indictment coming for bribing jurors, but the suspense seemed to be killing him. On December 29, 1911, he wrote to his son Paul and said, "I am no doubt in some danger here & don't know how things will turn…but my mind is at ease & any thing [sic] that comes is all right."

It's not exactly clear exactly how "at ease" his mind was, particularly in light of a visit he paid to Mary Field at roughly the same time. That will be discussed later.

On New Year's Day of 1912, he tried to reassure Paul:

> I think I was too pessimistic when I wrote you last—Of course there is danger here but I don't believe there is one chance in twenty that they could get me even if they try which they might. There is really nothing to it except

some suspicious circumstances...you know that every step I have taken has been out of devotion to the cause & I have done nothing wrong.

As the suspense built, he wrote again to Paul, on January 13, that "my mind and conscience are at ease," and on January 17, "I have very direct information that I will be indicted tomorrow. I believe I will win—but may not.... I know that all I did has been for the poor & the highest motives & I am content & want you not to worry."

On January 25, he wrote to Mary Field, who had left town, telling her:

Things are as they were when you left. It looks for sure for an indictment early next week. Of course there might be a slip but I don't think so. Will keep you posted. I believe I can win & of course shall give them a good fight.

On January 29, the indictment was handed down. Darrow was informed and permitted to voluntarily come to the courthouse, along with his lawyers, rather than having police dispatched to arrest him.

The next day, the *San Francisco Examiner* reported that Darrow was "white and plainly stirred to the depths of his being."

The Los Angeles Times reported:

"Well, boys, is everything fixed?" This is the remark attributed to Clarence Darrow as he stepped between Bert H. Franklin and George N. Lockwood at the intersection of Third and Los Angeles streets on the morning of November 28. It is alleged that evidence went before the grand jury during the past few weeks that showed Darrow was standing close by when Franklin is said to have paid $500 to Lockwood.

> *According to the theory of the prosecution, Darrow was on the spot to see that his confidential man, Franklin, paid over the agreed amount of money. There are at least ten or more detectives or attachés of the District Attorney who will swear that the scene took place and that Darrow placed his arms confidently on the shoulders of Franklin and Lockwood.*

After the indictment, Darrow sent a telegram to his older brother, Everett, in which he advised him of the indictment and said, "Can't make myself feel guilty. My conscience refuses to reproach me."

He also wrote his partner Edgar Lee Masters, saying:

> *As you know the ax has fallen—but I feel very confident that I shall win—though of course it is a hard blow— Well I chose my life & must stand the consequences.*

And to Paul:

> *I know the truth and am satisfied & feel sure that nothing better could happen to me or to you & that it would do more for me & the cause than any thing [sic] I could do....*

It's interesting that in these letters to his son, to Mary, and to his brother, Darrow didn't protest his innocence, but simply asserted that his conscience was clear for whatever he may have done.

They were more assertions of justification for his conduct than denials of the conduct. Interpret that as you see fit.

Darrow Hires a Lawyer

Earl Rogers, arguably, never should have undertaken to represent Darrow. For starters, there might have been a conflict of interest, since Rogers had been hired by the Merchants and

Manufacturers Association to investigate the bombing of the *Los Angeles Times* building and Darrow had represented the men who destroyed that building.

But Rogers was one of the premier defense attorneys in the city, so why not hire the best? Rogers's daughter, Adela Rogers St. Johns, objected, though. She thought that Darrow was a "phony," believed from the start that he was guilty, had a hunch that "he was going to do us dirt somehow," and was "pitifully sure" that he "would betray us anywhere along the road."[lvii]

Throw into the mix the fact that Rogers's wife hated, or at least severely disliked Darrow, while Ruby Darrow appeared to be equally as disdainful of Rogers and never wanted him from the start.

In what can only be termed irony, Ruby was reported to have told reporters: "'He [Rogers] was too theatrical for my taste.... He wasn't a lawyer, he was just an actor.'"[lviii]

Adela Rogers said that Ruby created unnecessary discord between the two lawyers.

> Without her needling, her jealousy, her insistence that Earl Rogers was nothing but a shyster, a ham actor, a drunk, Rogers and Darrow might have achieved what I **know** my father longed and strove for—a friendship.[lix] [emphasis in original]

In the scientific world, opposites might attract, but it's different in the ego-driven realm of lawyers. Geoffrey Cowan offers an interesting contrast between the two men, whom he describes as, not just opposites, but "polar" opposites.

The "public Darrow," Cowan wrote, "was a candidate for a certain kind of secular saint...." He had a reputation as "something of an idealist, a defender of righteous causes, the lawyer for the weak against the powerful, the poor against the rich. Even if not precisely accurate, that was how Darrow was best known."

That was the Darrow-created legend. He had his flaws, of

course:

> As a legal tactician, he...from time to time, felt obliged to find a way to get rid of unwelcome witnesses and to make sure that the jury contained some members who were committed to vote for his client.

But he carefully tended that legend he had sown:

> He played, at once, to the compassion of the jury and the passion of the public, building sympathy for his clients' cases and admiration for his own noble qualities. If an affair or two found their way into his personal life, the story never found its way into the press. [lx]

The "public Rogers," on the other hand, had created a legend of his own. He was:

> ...a candidate, indeed a deliberate candidate, for sinner.... It was a reputation he relished—and cultivated—despite the pleas of his father, the minister, who tried in vain to persuade his son to confine his cases to the defense of the innocent or, at worst, the **honest** defense of the guilty. He wasn't the attorney for the damned. He was the attorney for the guilty. [lxi] [emphasis in original]

Another difference was that Ruby Darrow, unlikeable though she may have been to Adela Rogers, was a "stand by your man" kinda wife, even though she knew of his ongoing affair with Mary Field.

Earl Rogers, on the other hand, had a very contentious relationship with his wife, apparently reaching its zenith in the Rogers household during the Darrow trial. Adela wrote that "things were at their worst at home" after a "period of relative peace." She and her brother Bogart had welcomed a new baby sibling named Thornwell, "born as an attempt at the tie that binds. But the terrible sickening quarrels had begun again." ˡˣⁱⁱ

A divorce followed a few years later.

Those outside his family also tried to talk Rogers out of representing Darrow, including an old family friend named Harry Carr.

Adela wrote that Carr told her father:

> This man Darrow is a discredited mountebank.[14] I don't believe in his cause or his fight—Rich against Poor—Capital against Labor—I think he's building up unnecessary class hatreds everywhere. But by God I thought he believed in it. Now even his own labor unions know he sold them down the river.

What could possibly go wrong?

The Lockwood Trial

The bribe to George Lockwood was the subject of Darrow's first trial, scheduled to start on May 24, 1912. Given their differences, it was no wonder that Darrow and Rogers clashed mightily throughout. Much of their conflict was the result of Rogers's apparent belief that, not only was his client guilty, but also that he *looked* guilty in front of the jury.

Following the cross-examination of Lockwood by Rogers, the two quarreled over the client's in-court manner. According to his daughter, Rogers told Darrow:

> I must ask you to stop looking so guilty. Only guilty men hang their heads and won't look the jury in the eye.... I work all day to prove you innocent. They look at you and see a Portrait of a Guilty Man. They remember this at night—they will remember it when they take the case into

---

[14] Defined by *Merriam-Webster* as "a person who sells quack medicines from a platform" or "a boastful unscrupulous pretender: charlatan."

the jury room. [lxiii]

Hugh Baillie echoed Adela's account of her father browbeating Darrow for looking guilty in the courtroom, writing that Rogers did so "often within the hearing of others in the courtroom." [lxiv]

Darrow, used to being in charge and with an ego the size of the *Times* building that had been destroyed, chafed at being chastised.

> *You want me to be cheerful when my heart is broken.... I am crucified daily, tortured by false accusations, burned at the stake in the flames of injustice.* [lxv]

If Adela's account of Darrow's dialogue is accurate, he couldn't refrain from windbaggery and bloviation even in private conversation with his lawyer.

At one point, Rogers disappeared for a couple of days, leaving courtroom duties to his co-counsel while he went on a bender. This, apparently, was not unusual, as Rogers was a notorious drinker.

His daughter wrote:

> *We had certain cover-ups ready by this time, a sheaf of doctor's certificates on hand, outposts in bars, honky-tonks, Turkish baths, hospitals, backstage, and on the police force, prepared to notify us.* [lxvi]

This time, though, Adela blamed it on Darrow:

> *Now I had a feeling that he* [Rogers] *had begun to look at Darrow from time to time like a pitcher watching a shortstop boot away four unearned runs behind him.*

When Darrow flat-out asked her if her father was drunk, the use of the term "drunk" floored her. "I could have smacked him.... Around our office nobody ever said that."

Blowhard

In a fit of anger, Adela replied, "If he is you're enough to drive anybody to it, I will say that for you, Mr. Darrow."[lxvii]

Ruby Darrow had to pitch in her own insult. "I knew it. He drinks secretly all the time, I smell it on him." To which Adela retorted, "I'm surprised he ever lets you get close enough to him." That wasn't good manners, she admitted, "but at least I didn't say anything further about *smelling* people. There were no deodorants in those days so you had to be very careful about *bathing* and talcum powder and clean clothes and all."[lxviii] [emphasis in original]

If that weren't enough conflict between the Rogerses and the Darrows, there was apparently the issue of money. Money, as in Darrow wasn't paying his lawyer. Even on this point, there was a difference in viewpoint, or at least in characterization, depending upon whether you were the unpaid attorney or the non-paying client.

According to Adela, when Darrow grew indignant at her father's absence, possibly because he was on a drunken bender, and demanded that he be in court the next morning, she called him on it:

> *Yes, and you had better be here, too, Mr. Darrow, with some cash of the realm.... If I was your chief counsel, I would not show up until you paid up* **some** *dough, so far we have put all of it up out of our own funds, but we are not John D. Rockefeller, nor Andrew Carnegie.*[lxix] [emphasis in original]

Adela's mother confirmed this, claiming that:

> *Earl never got any part of his fee from Darrow...except maybe running expenses. They were always pleading poverty, right on the verge of starvation. It got so I couldn't pay our bills at the stores.*[lxx]

Ruby's take was a bit different, although she appears to

acknowledge they were in arrears on the fees.
She said:

> *Earl Rogers came to us every morning and blackmailed us. If we didn't give him money he wouldn't go to court that day.*

And so:

> [E]*ach morning Clarence Darrow would dig into his pocket for a roll of bills.*[lxxi]

But when Rogers returned home after the disappearance, his response to inquiries from his wife as to his whereabouts was particularly interesting. "'Oh, that son of a bitch has been up to his old tricks again,' from which Mrs. Rogers deduced that Darrow had been trying to bribe members of his own jury."[lxxii]

With tensions at a breaking point, Darrow took over his defense from Rogers, including making his own final appeal to the jury in closing argument. When he was acquitted, Adela contended that Darrow was so convinced his own brilliance had won the day that he discharged Rogers and did not use him in the second trial.

However, she said, the verdict was sealed before Darrow ever spoke a word in closing. Hugh Baillie agreed, writing in his memoir that he already knew, a week ahead of that final speech, that the jury had already decided to acquit Darrow.

His source?

Juror Fred Golding.

More about Golding later.

Darrow Testifies

Darrow took the stand in his own defense on Monday, July 29, 1912, and finally stepped down at the end of the day on Monday, August 5, 1912. A significant portion of the time was consumed by lawyers arguing various objections, but Darrow was responsible for much of that because of his meandering answers to questions. Once a blowhard, always a blowhard, whether at counsel table, in the well before the jury, or on the witness stand.

On Darrow's first day on the stand, Earl Rogers objected to objections from prosecutor Joseph Ford on the basis that:

> *Mr. Ford is doing nothing but trying to break up Mr. Darrow's testimony with objection after objection, puerile and infinitesimal, done for no purpose in the world but to break up the continuity of the narrative and destroy the effect of the testimony of Mr. Darrow, which is proceeding in a very general way, it is true, but in a way which we have a right to ask the witness.*

Several times Rogers repeated his description of the prosecutor's objections as "puerile," the same term the Los Angeles grand jury used to describe claims that the explosion at the *Los Angeles Times* was caused by gas and not a bomb.

Prosecutor Fredericks responded that:

> *...we maintain that he should be bound by the same rules that other witnesses, [sic] and if he is going to stray afield and try to make a speech on the witness stand, and compel us to make these objections—we are making them against our will; we would rather not have to make them; we would rather he would go along without objections, but if he doesn't observe the rules or his counsel does not observe the rules, we have got to make them, that is all.*

After the court sustained the objection, prosecutor Ford next asked the court to:

> *...protect me from such words as puerile and rotten...I have a right to be protected from such language in this court, and I ask your Honor to take some steps to protect*

me from such language.

The judge responded, "You are quite right in that."
He admonished counsel that they...

> ...must curb their inclination to use terms of that kind. They have been used too much in this case, and if we are going to get along with this case and get through in any reasonable time, it must be eliminated. Counsel must restrain that impulse, no matter what he thinks. Counsel sometimes in an excited argument, when a lawyer might have a very unkind thought towards another, it passes off and he forgets it, but he ought not give expression to it.

He specifically directed Earl Rogers not to use the phrase "puerile objection."

Horace Appel, co-counsel with Rogers for Darrow, argued that the rules somehow did not apply to, nor constrain Darrow, who...

> ...is not a witness like the average witness, your Honor, that he is a witness who has his peculiar way of expressing his idea, his narrative way of expressing his ideas. He probably has a better command of language than the ordinary witness, and that there is no particular rule of law by which the witness must frame and clothe his ideas or convey them to the jury.... I have seen lots of lawyers who were absolutely so deficient in knowledge, both as to human experience and as to law and as to rhetoric that they couldn't spell their names right, and it would be a shame to put an intelligent witness on the stand and have him answer questions in the manner that would convey ideas to the ignorance of the one examining him....[15]

---

[15] So, like Yogi Bear, who is smarter than the average bear, Darrow was supposedly smarter than the average witness.

Blowhard

The prosecution's complaint, at its core, was that Darrow was speaking in a narrative fashion—making speeches or extended storytelling—rather than engaging with his counsel in a question-and-answer process as required by court rules.

In other words, bloviation and windbaggery. Based on a review of the transcript, the objection is well taken. Here is just one example of Darrow's speechifying in a portion of his response to a question as to why he believed there was no motive to bribe a juror on the late date of November 28.

Note that this is not even the entire answer.

> *As we went on in the preparation of this case it kept growing on all of us that there was no possible chance to win the case; we first commenced gathering all the evidence we could to ascertain all the facts we could and it grew on us from day to day and from week to week, the exact condition we were in and that our clients were in, which a lawyer never knows at once, the same as a doctor learns that his patient is going to die. We felt that owing to the number of lives lost, the bitter feeling there was in the community, that it was going to be difficult to avoid the death penalty; we wanted to save their lives, if possible, and believed that at some time there would be a better understanding, probably a commutation or pardon. It had seemed hopeless to me for sometime [sic] and I think to my associates. On the 19th day of November Mr. Steffens and I went down to San Diego and had a visit with Mr. Scripps,[16] who read to us an article which he had prepared, or somebody prepared and sent to him on belligerent rights in labor controversies on the theory of belligerent rights in warfare. I made a remark, coming from that statement, that I wished the people of Los Angeles could see it that way and believed that it was to*

---

[16] Edward Willis "E.W." Scripps was a newspaper publisher and founder of the media empire known as the E.W. Scripps Company.

the best interests of the community and also right and just to get rid of this case without shedding any human blood. That was all that was said at that time; the next day Mr. Steffens referred to that conversation and we came up that night from San Diego, and we got our breakfast at the Van Nuys Hotel...[prosecutor Ford corrects him as to the day in question]...I meant Sunday night. Sunday night we came up from San Diego, and got our breakfast at the Van Nuys; during the time we were taking breakfast, Mr. Steffens referred to the statement I had made, and he asked whether I really meant it. I told him I did, but I didn't believe it would be possible to bring any such thing about; that the feeling was too bitter on both sides, and the people were not in a reasoning state of mind and I did not think it could be done. He said he thought he could, and that if I didn't object, he would see some people and see what could be done. I told him I was perfectly willing that he should do it, but if he saw anybody he must make it very plain, it did not come from me or from our side, for if it should get to the community that we were making overtures, it would make it that much more difficult to defend these men and save their lives....

Darrow the Thespian

It was ironic that Ruby Darrow objected to Earl Rogers as not being a lawyer, but instead being an actor, especially since Darrow, himself, was a dramatic performer, right down to his calculated appearance.

Observers of the Haywood trial took note of his deliberate sloppiness in attire and some drew the same conclusions as had Adela Rogers as to what it was intended to convey: a pretentious lack of pretense. Martin Maloney called it an aspect of his "Lincolnesque personality" and his desire to look less like an attorney and more like an everyman member of a jury. Maloney wrote that Darrow, a "devil's advocate by profession," was a myth in his own time.[lxxiii]

Hugh Baillie, who, as a twenty-one year old just two years removed from art school, covered Darrow's bribery trials for the *Los Angeles Record*, an E.W. Scripps paper and client of the United Press, shared the opinion.

> [H]e dressed sloppily. His clothes hung on him in folds and drapes, and there were soup spots on his tie and his vest.[lxxiv]

Nathan Leopold would later echo this in describing his first meeting with Darrow.

> Mr. Darrow was wearing a light seersucker jacket. Nothing wrong with that, surely. Only this one looked as if he had slept in it. His shirt was wrinkled, too, and he must have had eggs for breakfast that morning. I could see the vestiges.[lxxv]

Beyond his attire, there was his subtle theatricality, which itself was likely a façade. Ethel Barrymore, the acclaimed actress, was in Boise during the Haywood trial for a one-night stand of her road company's performance of *Captain Jinks of the Horse Marines*.

She was invited, as a guest of publisher Calvin Cobb, to sit in on the trial for a day.

In her memoir, she expressed distrust of Darrow—whom she referred to as "A man named Clarence Darrow"—and his slickness.

> That was the first time I had heard of the flowery Mr. Darrow. He had all the props, an old mother in a wheelchair and a little girl with curls draped around Haywood. I don't know whether she was his daughter or just one of Mr. Darrow's props.[lxxvi]

If anyone should know an actor when she saw one, it was Ethel

Barrymore.

Hugh Baillie also recognized Darrow's theatricality during his coverage of McNamara and the subsequent bribery trials.

> *From the moment I met him, I knew I was in the presence of an actor who would never forget this public role, never removed his make-up. He was carrying the weight of the world on his shoulders and his gestures were calculated to express his reactions to his burden. He could shamble, or stride vigorously, as the occasion demanded, use his smile as a gesture of gratitude or as a formal grimace.*[lxxvii]

Baillie, like Ruby Darrow, noted that Earl Rogers was equally a thespian in the courtroom, though of a different ilk than Darrow. Rogers was "obvious and flamboyant," while Darrow was more subtle and "always *seemed* to have scored his point by pure logical argument, and you had to watch him carefully to see that he was acting."[lxxviii] [emphasis in original]

The two females Barrymore referred to (the old mother in a wheelchair and a little girl with curls) were, in fact, Haywood's mother and daughter, about whom Darrow would wax eloquent in his closing. He loved to talk about mothers in his addresses to juries—the Leopold and Loeb and Massie cases would be examples.

And in Haywood:

> *I have known Haywood—I have known him well and I believe in him. God knows it would be a sore day to me if he should go upon the scaffold. The sun would not shine or the birds would not sing on that day—for me. It would be a sad day, indeed, if any such calamity would come to him. I would think of him, I would think of his wife, of his mother. I would think of his children. I would think of the great cause that he represents. It would be a sore day for me, but, gentlemen he and his mother, and his wife and his children are not my chief concern in this case. If*

> you should decree that he must die, ten thousand men will work in the mines and send a portion of the proceeds of their labor to take care of that widow and these orphan children, and a million people throughout the length and breadth of the civilized world will send their messages and good cheer to comfort them in their bereavement and to heal their wounds.

"That'd I'd been crying…" [17]

At some point in his career, Darrow learned that tears were an effective weapon to influence a jury. It worked in the Haywood case, where he primed the jurors' pumps with his own tears.

As he tried to align himself with the struggles of the lower classes, historian David Grover wrote:

> Darrow unleashed his most emotional eloquence. His voice by now was harsh and pathetic, and his eyes were full of tears. Women were openly crying in the courtroom; Haywood's wife sobbed audibly and his mother shed silent tears.[lxxix]

Arthur Weinberg described the closing this way:

> Darrow spoke for eleven hours. As he talked there were tears in his eyes, Haywood's wife and mother were sobbing, and women in the courtroom wept.[lxxx]

It's an open question whether Darrow's tears were merely a tactic or if they were sincere, heartfelt tears. The betting odds seem to be on the former. Baillie noted in the Lockwood bribery trial, "He could weep at will—real tears." [lxxxi]

Either way, at least moving forward from the Haywood case, he nearly always resorted to them.

After being exposed to multiple episodes of Darrow tears,

---

[17] "Crying," lyrics by Roy Orbison

both in her home and in the courtroom, Adela Rogers dismissed them almost out of hand.

"Before long," she said, "I got so I had learned to plain pay no attention to Darrow crying. The young can be very hardhearted." [lxxxii] But apparently Darrow saved the granddaddy of all cries for his final appeal to the jury as he pled for his own future. A headline in the August 16, 1912, *Chicago Tribune* screamed: JURORS WEEP AS DARROW PLEADS.

Adela described it this way:

> *Darrow's mild tears and gentle sobs had taken on hurricane proportions. His great bony frame, from which so much weight had fallen in the long, long weeks, shook like a scarecrow on a pole in the midst of his convulsive sobs. He wept each handkerchief into a sodden ball, cast it from him, and Ruby Darrow supplied another, which soon suffered a like fate. At last he began to wipe the floods on his sleeves, they clung as though he'd plunged them into a rain barrel.* [lxxxiii]

Her father, fearing that Darrow's melodramatic outburst was going to cost him the favor of a jury everyone believed was already prepared to acquit him, walked out of the courtroom in disgust. Adela followed her father out, only to see "the maddest man I had ever seen...."

He told her, "He will get himself convicted yet.... If he doesn't stop this wailing-wall weeping-willow blubber and snivel—That's not a speech, it's a lament. They might change their minds and lock the melancholy Dane up somewhere." [lxxxiv]

Adela acknowledged that "perhaps" Darrow's closing was one of the greatest jury speeches, but that it "reads better than it heard." The reason? Its "excessive self-pity."

She explained, "I didn't know then that self-pity is the final mark of the true egotist and sweeps him far beyond his own control." [lxxxv]

Blowhard

Chapter Six: That's Not My Dog

Let me say this, gentlemen, there are other things in the world besides bribery, there are other crimes that are worse.
—Clarence Darrow

IN A FIT of ego—perhaps "fit" is not the right word because it suggests something sudden, while Darrow had already been securely in the clutches of ego for a sustained period of time—Darrow had his closing argument in the Lockwood bribery trial, in which he was acquitted, published for all the world to read.

The title under which it was published seems a bit on the nose: *Plea of Clarence Darrow in his Own Defense to the Jury that Exonerated Him of the Charge of Bribery at Los Angeles, August 1912.*

But that was just one of two juries he faced with bribery charges.

Interestingly, he didn't publish the second argument, in the Bain bribery trial, which would have to have been entitled: *Plea of Clarence Darrow in his Own Defense to the Hung Jury that was Deadlocked 8-4 in Favor of Convicting Him of the Charge of Bribery.*

The former argument was published by Golden Press of Los Angeles-San Franciso, and sold, along "with portrait" for twenty-five cents.

In his Foreword, Luke North (who "prepared [the

argument] for publication") wrote:

> *Clarence Darrow is like no other man. His position in the nation and at the bar is unique—his life, his ideals, his 'view of things' are his own. He is often silent; but when he speaks men listen.*

Of course, it's difficult to find a time when Darrow ever was silent.

In a further break from reality, North said:

> *Those who seek rhetorical flourishes and flights of mere oratory need not search the following, or any pages, of the man Darrow.*

He claimed that the argument was "delivered impromptu without even the assistance of notes," which, if true, probably explains the stream of consciousness rhetorical flourishes and flights of oratory that Darrow employed.

North's actual name was James Griffes, whom Darrow described as someone "who wrote beautiful things that did not pay but were a delight to read," and "whose devotion dated back to our youth in Chicago, and who found no day too long and no night too dreary to work in my behalf." [lxxxvi] Maybe we can forgive North a pair of rose-colored glasses through which to view his old friend.

Darrow, himself, misrepresented his manner of speaking in much the same way as North a/k/a Griffes had. In his autobiography, Darrow wrote that when he was younger:

> *I was rather oratorical. Like many other young men of that day, I did the best, or worst, I could to cover up such ideas as I had in a cloud of sounding metrical phrases. In later years nothing had disturbed my taste along that line more than being called an "orator," and I strive to use simpler words and shorter sentences, to make my*

> statements plain and direct and, for me, at least, I find
> this the better manner of expression.[lxxxvii]

It is unclear whether this is poor self-perception or self-delusion, or whether Darrow was again simply slinging nonsense to convince readers that up was down. You can judge for yourselves as you review his courtroom speeches.

There is an old joke on the progression of arguments that a defendant might make when on trial for owning a dog accused of biting someone. You start with "I don't have a dog," progress to "My dog doesn't bite," then fall back to "That's not my dog."

Darrow's defense of his conduct had a similar progression mixed with other deflections and non-denials. He started by attacking the prosecution, which merged with "everybody is out to get me," then progressed to "they're out to silence me," and devolved into "the prosecution is corrupt."

The *Chicago Inter-Ocean* headlined an April 15, 1912, article: "Chicago Lawyer on Trial for Alleged Jury Bribery Assails his Enemies as Liars and Conspirators Against His Freedom," with a sub-heading that declared, "No Prosecutor Immune from Denunciation in 3-Hour Talk." [18]

His response to the straightforward charge of bribery was classic misdirection.

He put off denying it for as long as he could, deflecting the accusation, sometimes impliedly conceding the allegations, and claiming that this wasn't actually a case about jury bribing but about his role as a champion for labor, martyred to the cause.

For the last one, he had to climb upon a metaphorical cross with his arms outstretched. He repeatedly asked the jury whether the claims against him made sense before offering a lukewarm denial, but then progressed to "it's better to bribe someone than to lie" and finally settled on "it would have been all right if I did it."

Taken as a whole, it puts into question whether he ever

---

[18] Three hours was just the first day.

seriously denied committing the criminal act of bribery. It sounds a lot like "I don't have a dog" blending into "my dog doesn't bite."

The Prosecution is Being Mean to Me

Darrow opened his argument by channeling Blanche DuBois's dependence on the "kindness of strangers" in Tennessee Williams's *A Streetcar Named Desire*.

> *I am a stranger in a strange land, 2,000 miles away from home and friends—although I am proud to say that here, so far away, there have gathered around me as good and loyal and faithful friends as any man could have upon the earth. Still I am unknown to you.*

He reiterated it in the Bain case, the second of his bribery trials.

> *Is it possible that here in California, a western state, liberal, broad, a jury is seriously asked to send a man to the penitentiary? A man who has lived a long life, has done his best, has had the respect of his fellow men. Upon evidence like that, because I am a stranger and they want me a stranger.*

He later added:

> *But here is a stranger within your gates and* [the prosecution] *want*[s] *you to send him to the penitentiary. Gentlemen, if a jury of California should do that...I would be the victim. But it would leave a blot upon your state greater than all the frosts that could come down from the north.*

It should be pointed out that the "stranger in a strange land" line was merely a variation of the rhetoric he had trotted out in Idaho defending the men accused of the bombing death of Frank

Blowhard

Steunenberg.

> *Gentlemen, we are here as aliens to you...before people, if not unfriendly, who at least we do not know....*

In Lockwood, he lamented that not everyone in Los Angeles had been good to him, this poor stranger in a strange land. There were some who treated him poorly, certainly not as nicely as he would have been treated back home in Chicago.

In particular, he pointed his finger at the prosecutors.

> *I think I can say that no one in my native town would have made to any jury any such statement as was made of me by the district attorney in opening this case. I will venture to say he could not afterward have found a companion except among detectives and crooks and sneaks in the city where I live if he had dared to open his mouth in the infamous way he did in this case.*

It's not entirely clear just how nicely he expected a prosecutor to characterize a criminal defendant at trial, accused of committing crimes, but apparently Darrow's feelings were hurt, and he wore them on his sleeve before the jury.

He seemed particularly incensed by the words of Joseph Ford, who, himself, was a budding windbag—although not in Darrow's league. Anticipating Darrow's plea of his own noble character, Ford started with a history of "men of noble character" who had, nevertheless, committed crimes and betrayed others. He cautioned jurors to "remember that previous good reputation is no guaranty against the commission of an offense."

Even the best of men, he argued, can stumble and fall.

He started with Judas Iscariot, who betrayed Christ.

> *Notwithstanding his great reputation for honesty, notwithstanding his great reputation for integrity, his*

> *apparent love of charity and disdain for the things of this world, he sold his God for thirty pieces of silver.*

It should be noted that a *Bible* scholar, Ford was not. While Ford characterized Judas as an honest man with great integrity, John, the disciple, disagrees. When Mary, the sister of Lazarus, anointed Jesus's feet with a precious ointment, Judas complained that it should have been sold and the proceeds given to the poor.

> *He did not say this because he cared about the poor but because he was a thief; as keeper of the money bag, he used to help himself to what was put into it.*
> —John 12:6 (New International Version)

Ford next moved to the treasonous Benedict Arnold, who, "notwithstanding the great reputation for truth, for honesty and integrity, for noble, patriotic and unselfish devotion to duty," became "synonymous over the whole civilized world with treachery and treason."

But even the ranks of treasonous traitors don't compare with Darrow's act, he said.

> [T]*he act of the jury briber is worse than all of these, for it strikes the very foundation of government. For without courts of justice to maintain the relations between the individuals of a commonwealth, there is no government, and we might as well...revert at once to a state of anarchy and let the strongest prevail.*

From there, Ford launched into a discussion of the necessary, and certainly honorable, role of defense attorneys. But Darrow, he believed, had corrupted that role.

> *The law provides that it is the attorney's privilege to see that his client, even though his client is guilty, is not*

> *convicted except upon legal evidence, and in accordance with the established rules of law. But, to the disgrace of our civilization, many criminal lawyers have enlarged this privilege. They have extended it into an excuse for committing all sorts of chicanery and fraud.*

At this point, Ford directed his remarks personally at Darrow. Although he didn't mention Darrow by name, it was clear from the context and his reference to published positions advanced by Darrow, about whom he spoke.

> *He has used it as an excuse for subornation of perjury on the part of witnesses,[19] for the bribery of judges and juries.[20] They have taught by their acts, by their conduct, by their preaching to the criminal classes of this country, that there is no such thing as crime, as the word is generally understood.[21] They have taught the criminal classes of these United States that there are no courts of justice; that courts of justice are merely instituted by society as an instrument for making reprisals upon them; that there is warfare between society and them; that the beligerent [sic] rights on both sides are equal; and that they have the right to do anything necessary to defeat and obstruct justice; that there is no difference between the people in jail and those out of jail, except this, that if you are in jail, it is better if you have a smart lawyer like Clarence Darrow.[22]*

---

[19] An unwitting foretelling, perhaps, of Darrow's conduct in the Massie Case in the Territory of Hawaii twenty years hence.
[20] Likely at least a partial reference to the Haywood case.
[21] This likely refers to Darrow's address to the prisoners in the Cook County Jail in 1902, which Darrow also made sure got published.
[22] Another reference to the address in the Cook County Jail, where Darrow said, "When your case gets into court it will make little difference whether you are guilty or innocent, but it's better if you have a smart lawyer. And you cannot have a smart lawyer unless you

Almost as if to echo the last point, Darrow later told the jury, "I have been, perhaps, interested in more cases for the weak and poor than any other lawyer in America...."

One supposes that Darrow didn't like being lumped with the traitors Judas and Arnold, but he might have been most incensed by Ford's implied argument that Darrow bore some responsibility, personally, for the bombing of the *LA Times* building.

> *The unfortunate Brice* [J.B. McNamara pseudonym], *the poor, deluded Brice, when he placed that bomb of dynamite that hurled twenty unsuspecting souls into eternity, knew that if he were caught, that he could get a smart lawyer, like Clarence Darrow, and he believed that Darrow could free him; and when he was arrested and carried from Detroit to Chicago, he said, "If you don't take this money Darrow will get it."*

Darrow decided to fight fire with fire, a theme for him in this case. Because he felt that the prosecution was being mean to him, he launched personal attacks on the prosecuting attorneys individually, as well as on everyone and everything else he could think of who might be behind the charge against him.

This approach seems telling.

In litigation, most lawyers typically start by attacking the substance of the charge. You would think, then, that Darrow would have started by debunking the validity of the bribery accusation.

But no, he went after the opposing lawyers first, and aimed most of his vitriol at Joseph Ford.

> *I don't object to a lawyer arguing the facts in his case and the evidence in his case, and drawing conclusions as he will; but every man with a sense of justice in his soul*

knows that the attack of Ford's was cowardly and malicious in the extreme.

He had other colorful terms to employ, as well, such as referring to the "villainy and infamy of this prosecution which reeks from beginning to end with crime and corruption, and with bloodlessness and heartlessness to the last degree."

He used these attacks and characterizations as groundwork for a jury nullification argument that since he, a stranger in a strange land, had been foully mistreated, the jury would be justified in acquitting him regardless of whether he had committed the crime of bribery.

On the morning of the second day of his argument, he seemed to admit that he had not yet addressed the main issue.

For the balance of my argument I shall confine my talk almost entirely to the main charge brought against me, and say no more about these outside issues, which mean nothing except an effort on the part of the State, cruel, unjust and unlawful, to prejudice you against me. The question which you are to decide here is this: Did I give Franklin four thousand dollars on the morning of the 28th of November to bribe Lockwood? That is all there is to it.

It was almost as if, after giving it some thought overnight, it occurred to him that it might be to his benefit to address the specific charge brought against him. At long last he had arrived at "that's not my dog."

The meanness of prosecutors was also a theme in his closing argument in the Bain case.

Apparently Darrow thought it had worked well enough in the first trial, an acquittal, that he saw fit to run it up the flagpole again.

Attacking the prosecutors as "this gang of brigands who soak my life's blood," he said:

> *This prosecution is not a prosecution but a persecution. It is not fair, it is not honest, and it is not decent. Had I been a midnight robber or a burglar or a bank robber, had been tried once and acquitted, nobody would ever have dared, in a free community of intelligent men, to place me on trial again.*

Just as he lambasted prosecutor Joseph Ford in the Lockwood case, he went after special prosecutor Wheaton Gray in the Bain case.

> *I don't like to talk ill of any of my fellow man, but if I didn't in this case I couldn't talk about Gray; and he brought it on himself.... He said I was a coward, among other things. Now Gray is brave, isn't he? Here I am in Los Angeles under indictment, and he stands here, a prosecutor, abusing and vilifying me, when he is not my equal, morally, intellectually—he may be my superior physically—he weighs more, and he is brought in here; and the hard part of it is, it is my sad duty to make Gray immortal.*

So, Darrow believed he was thrusting immortality on Gray by making him the man who persecuted the great Clarence Darrow, but he said, it will backfire on him. "You may break, you may shatter the vase if you will, but the stench of the polecat will hang round it still."

Interestingly, after both bribery trials had ended and the "stranger in a strange land" was once again ensconced in familiar surroundings in Chicago, Darrow decided maybe he hadn't been treated so unfairly after all. In a letter dated December 23, 1913, to District Attorney John Fredericks, who by then had decided to dismiss the charges in the Bain case rather than retry it after the hung jury, Darrow wrote:

> *Now that this entire matter is terminated, I wish to say*

> that when I came to California to undertake the defense of the McNamaras, I expected some battle, and I think I know what battles are. But you gave me the battle of my life, and through the case it may be some satisfaction for you to know that I felt and feel now that while your actions were strenuous in the extreme, you were simply doing your duty as you saw it, and that you were absolutely fair, both to me and my clients.[lxxxvii]

If one takes this letter at face value, as sincere, that means Darrow's attacks on prosecutors in both Lockwood and Bain were nothing more than tactics, reeking of falsehoods that he, himself, didn't believe, but that he wanted juries to believe.

This was disingenuous, at best and blatantly dishonest at worst.

But entirely consistent with his character.

Big Business is Being Mean to Me

Darrow repeatedly argued that big business, the antithesis of labor, was out to get him, and that was what the case was all about. Although that might have seemed paranoid, there was certainly a grain of truth to it.

Still, arguing that you are the victim of a witch hunt doesn't address the central issue: Are there any witches? Even a witch hunt might be excused if it actually turns up witches.

One of Darrow's first non-denials, which are discussed below, was made in support of this argument. They're not really after me for supposedly bribing jurors, he said. No, this is all about trying to bring me down because I am a champion for the little guy. This was the metaphorical martyr on the cross argument.

> I am not on trial for having sought to bribe a man named Lockwood. There may be and doubtless are many people who think I did seek to bribe him, but I am not on trial for that, and I will prove it to you. I am on trial because I

> have been a lover of the poor, a friend of the oppressed, because I have stood by labor for all these years, and have brought down upon my head the wrath of the criminal interests in this country. Whether guilty or innocent of the crime charged in the indictment, that is the reason I am here, and that is the reason that I have been pursued by as cruel[23] a gang as ever followed a man.

This might have been a logical place to throw in something like, "Oh, by the way, I didn't do what I'm accused of," but for some reason he felt it was more beneficial to impugn the motives behind the case rather than actually plead his innocence.

He would save that for later.

The industries opposed to the labor movement were out to get him, he said, because of his effectiveness on behalf of labor; specifically, he referred to the Erectors' Association and the Steel Trust. Let he who is without sin cast the first stone, his argument went. Not only did those entities have no interest in actually catching bribers, "almost every dollar of their ill-gotten gains has come from bribery." This was a form of an "unclean hands" defense: their hands are unclean, they're just as guilty, so they can't come after me. But, again, this was not a denial; simply a justification, almost tantamount to an admission.

Darrow poured it on.

> They would stop my voice—my voice, which from the time I was a prattling babe, my father and mother taught me to raise for justice and freedom, and in the name of the weak and the poor.

---

[23] This is an ironic use of a word "cruel" by Darrow. Years later, in the Leopold and Loeb case, where his clients kidnapped a fourteen-year-old boy, bludgeoned him in the head with a chisel, suffocated him by shoving a cloth down his throat, stripped him and poured acid on his body, then stuffed him in a culvert, Darrow argued: "I say that very few murders ever occurred that were as free from cruelty as this." Consistency was not his strong suit.

Blowhard

Recall Luke North's statement in the Foreword of Darrow's published address that Darrow was not a man of "rhetorical flourishes and flights of mere oratory"—or recall his own statement that he strove to make his statements "plain and direct"—then read this passage from his argument and draw your own conclusions:

> *They would stop my voice with the penitentiary. Oh, you wild, insane members of the Steel Trust and Erectors' Association! Oh, you mad hounds of detectives who are willing to do your master's will! Oh, you district attorneys! You know not what you do. Let me say to you, that if you send me to prison, within the gray, dim walls of San Quentin, there will brood a silence more ominous and eloquent than any words that my poor lips could ever frame.*

The paranoia continued for most of his closing argument in Lockwood. Of course, one has to remember Joseph Heller's admonition in *Catch-22*: "Just because you're paranoid doesn't mean they aren't after you." Still, Darrow seemed to carry it to an extreme. On the other hand, this jury would acquit him, so maybe he knew what he was doing.

And he pled it earnestly.

"I am going to tell you the truth this afternoon."

That, of course, might suggest he had not been telling the truth up until then. Earnestly asserting that you are about to tell the truth is unnecessary if you are a habitual truth teller. The admonition to "trust me" is one of the tools of a confidence man. But that truth was, he said, "These men are interested in getting me."

As with the "prosecution is being mean to me" argument, he also repeated this one in the Bain trial.

> *I am not here because they think or because they care whether the allegations of this indictment are true or*

> *false, but because, as* [prosecutor] *Gray says, they want me; because I have committed the unpardonable sin— have dared to oppose the mighty and the strong and speak in defense of the poor and the weak. And I had rather go to the penitentiary and spend the rest of my life convicted of that crime, than to have sold myself to them for gold.*

At least in the Bain case, he was willing to name names, firing up class warfare.

> *It is the men who have reached out their hands and taken possession of all the wealth of the world. It is the owners of the great railroad system. It is the Rockefellers. It is the Morgans. It is the Goulds. It is that paralyzing hand of wealth, which had reached out and destroyed all opportunities of the poor.*

These behemoths of industry really didn't care about bribery, except when "that bribery had been committed for the poor." So this case against him wasn't really about justice, he said.

No, the "real enemies of society are trying to get me inside the penitentiary." And if that should happen, "I can find work to do in prison, such work as I have done, and if I haven't so lived that I could adjust my life to such conditions as fate forces on me, then I haven't lived enough and it will do no harm for this to come."

Serial Non-Denials

Darrow could have denied the bribery allegations while addressing "why" big business, or capital (as he sometimes referred to it), was out to get him, but he didn't. Instead, he raised the rhetorical question, "Suppose I am guilty of bribery, is that why I am prosecuted in this Court?"

Similarly, in his correspondence to his brother, son, and girlfriend, he didn't deny the charges, but justified anything he had done because of the justness of his cause. And while pursuing his paranoia defense, he raised yet another non-denial:

> *Do you suppose they care what laws I might have broken? I have committed one crime, one crime which is like that against the Holy Ghost, which cannot be forgiven. I have stood for the weak and the poor. I have stood for men who toil.*

In perhaps one of his biggest misstatements, echoing his statement in his autobiography, Darrow told the jury, "You will find that I am a plain-speaking man." If so, why not just come right out, up front, and plainly deny the charges? Sure, he issued denials as a witness on the stand, but in closing argument, even when he attempted to deny the charge, he buried it amidst other rhetoric. I don't have a dog, my dog doesn't bite, that's not my dog.

Other non-denials followed. He reiterated that "this is not a case of bribery at all," then almost in the next breath said, "Let me say this, gentlemen, there are other things in the world besides bribery, there are other crimes that are worse. It is a fouler crime to bear false witness against your fellow-man...." This one seems to channel Igor from *Young Frankenstein* as he and the good doctor dig up a corpse in a ghoulish cemetery: "Could be worse; could be raining."

Another non-denial:

> *Suppose you thought that I was guilty, suppose you thought so—would you dare as honest men, protecting society, would you dare to say by your verdict that scoundrels like this should be saved from their own sins by charging those sins to someone else?*

This hearkens back to the unclean hands defense, but again does not deny the charge. It simply argues that the latter crime should be excused because of the former.

He latched onto the notion that bribery is better than lying, again without denying the bribery.

> *Why, gentlemen, if I have to do one or the other, I will go down on Main Street and bribe jurors rather than bear false witness like Ford.*

Ford: his favorite punching bag after the Erectors' Association and Steel Trust.

> *No man, gentlemen, honestly believes that I had anything to do with bribing or attempting to bribe Lockwood down at the corner of Third and Los Angeles streets. Of course, there may be men who think I would do it. Ford thinks so, I guess.*

Here was his first real chance, at least in the structure of his argument—if one could actually find a structure—to deny the bribery. But what he said, instead, was that he had always "played according to the rules of the game" and that "I have played it that way for 35 years, and I have never done anything of this kind nor had to do anything of this kind."

A non-denial, for sure, but also probably not true. Remember the Haywood case. Maybe what he really meant was that he had never been caught at it before.

And while complaining bitterly that the prosecution had advantages not available to the defense, and had acted unethically and even illegally, he said:

> *Of course I did not pass $500 in the elevator, but if I had, I had just as much right to give that $500 for that purpose as I would have to buy $500 worth of hogs, just exactly. I was doing exactly what they were doing....*

Just fighting fire with fire. But again, that sounds like a subtle admission.

It wasn't until roughly a third of the way into his argument (or at the bottom of page 18 of the 59-page published argument) that Darrow finally got around to denying the charge—sort of. He started out with:

> *If I am guilty, which I have told you in every way, under oath and not under oath, that I am not—and I have proven, I believe fortunately by a greater array of honest men and women than are often gathered by a man accused of crime....*

But then he segued from "if I am guilty" to:

> *...is there one man who loves justice and fair play, who will say that I should be singled out from among this mess, and the very crook and thief and spy and informer and traitor in this case get immunity?*

This was a reference to Franklin, who turned State's evidence, but in Darrow's eyes, a traitor was worse than a briber. Again, he muddied the water, which, one supposes, is what good lawyers do.

Guilt Trips

If all else failed, lay a guilt trip on the jury. This was standard Darrow fare. He told them that, if they convicted him, while it:

> *...would place a blot upon my name, it would place one infinitely darker upon the name of every person connected with an outrage like this.*

Even though he made the occasional detour, he was always able to find his way back to the guilt trip.

> *Now, again, gentlemen, in passing judgment on me, you pass judgment upon yourself—that is all there is to it. If you are so kindly, if you are human, if you are decent, if*

> *you love your fellowman, if you believe in him, you will find me innocent; if you feel malicious, if you feel suspicious, if you look upon me as guilty, then find me guilty, I cannot put it any better than that.*

He fired up the steam on the train for a return to the guilt trip in the Bain case, coming around full circle to the "stranger in a strange land" metaphor. All the downtrodden in the country, "men who toil with their hands" and "women, worn and weary, who are sowing at their daily tasks," were praying for him, praying that "they may reach the hearts of those twelve men who hold my fate."

Praying, he said:

> *...that you twelve men will save the life and the liberty of a man who has fought their fight and battled for them.... Gentlemen, it is with you, in the hands of these twelve men, strangers. Strangers in a strange land. After my long career, after my hard fight, after all the bitterness and hatred of the past, I come to you worn and tired and submit my fate, the fate of my family, and the hopes and fears and the prayers of my friends to you.*

In his closing words, Darrow told that jury that untold thousands and millions around the world would be grateful to them if they would just acquit him.

> *...if in your judgment and your wisdom and your humanity, you believe me innocent, and return a verdict of not guilty in this case, I know that from thousands and tens of thousands and yea, perhaps millions of the weak and the poor and the helpless throughout the world will come thanks to this jury for saving my liberty and my name.*

This was a tried and true tactic for Darrow. In the Haywood

case, he told the jury that:

> ...[t]*he eyes of the world are upon you—upon you twelve men of Idaho tonight. Wherever the English language is spoken or wherever any tongue makes known the thoughts of men in any portion of the civilized world, men are talking, and wondering and dreaming about the verdict of these twelve men that I see before me now.*

If you find him guilty, he said in that case, you'll be revered "in the railroad offices" and "amongst the spiders of Wall Street" and banks, "where men hate Haywood because he fights for the poor and against that accursed system upon which the favored live and grow rich and fat." But if you acquit, the common people will "bow their heads and thank these twelve men for the life and reputation you have saved."

> *Out on our broad prairies where men toil with their hands, out on the wide ocean where men are tossed and buffeted on the waves, through our mills and factories, and down deep under the earth, thousands of men, and of women and children—men who labor, men who suffer, women and children weary with care and toil—these men and these women and these children will kneel tonight and ask their God to guide your hearts—these men and these women and these little children, the poor, the weak, and the suffering of the world, are stretching out their helpless hands to this jury in mute appeal for Bill Haywood's life.*

The "guilt trip" tactic survived from Haywood to McNamara, and also for future use, as well. In Leopold and Loeb, he told judge John Caverly, the sole arbiter of punishment for his clients, that:

> ...*if these boys hang, you must do it. There can be no*

> division of responsibility here. You can never explain that the rest overpowered you. It must be by your deliberate, cool, premeditated act, without a chance to shift responsibility.

In the Massie Case, he told the jury:

> Take this case with its dire disasters written all over by the hand of fate, as a case of your own, and I'll be content with your verdict.... You have not only the fate but the life of these four people.

As the Roman playwright Plautus said, "Nothing is more wretched than the mind of man conscious of guilt." Darrow saw his role as ensuring that each juror had such consciousness. Too bad he didn't.

Or maybe, as we'll see shortly, he did.

Does it Make Sense?

Another of Darrow's non-denial defenses actually had some logic to it. He asked the jury to apply their own common sense and ask whether what the prosecution had accused him of actually made sense to them.

Look at me, he seemed to say. Do you really think I would do something like that? And even if you do, do you really think I would do something as stupid as that? Because, as sloppily as it was handled, you'd have to be stupid and surely you don't believe I'm that stupid.

> *If you twelve men think that I, with 35 years of experience, general attorney of a railroad company of the city of Chicago, attorney for the Elevated Railroad Company, with all kinds of clients and important cases—if you think I would pick out a place half a block from my office and send a man with money in his hand in broad daylight to go down on the street corner to pass $4,000,*

> and then skip over to another street corner and pass $500—two of the most prominent streets in the city of Los Angeles; if you think I did that, gentlemen, why, find me guilty. I certainly belong in some state institution. Whether you select the right one or not is another question, but I certainly belong in one of them, and I will probably get treated in one the same as in the other. I say, nobody in their senses could believe that story....

Sometimes he was quite colorful. Nobody ever said Clarence Darrow didn't have a sense of humor.

> Now, I am as fitted for jury bribing as a Methodist preacher for tending bar. By all my training, inclination, and habit, I am about the last person in all this world who could possibly have undertaken such a thing.

The argument has been made, and Darrow was chief among those making it, that he was simply too smart to have fallen into the trap he claimed was laid by the prosecution.

Earl Rogers told him:

> Any intelligent mouse would have sniffed the cheese but you are not a mouse, you are a man of great emotional heat, dedicated, idealistic, selfless.... It is beyond the bounds of reason, probability, possibility that **if you were guilty**, you would arrive on the scene at the moment the crime was committed. [lxxxix] [emphasis in original]

This sounds good, but it overlooks the probability, or at least the serious possibility, that under pressure, people are still human and, brilliant or not, can do incredibly stupid things.

As Lincoln Steffens asked the question: Was it 3:00, when Darrow was a hero for courage, nerve, and calm judgment, or 3:15, when he was a coward for fear, collapse, and panicky mentality? Or, as Adela Rogers put it:

> Twelve men in the jury box wouldn't **know** what Lincoln Steffens had learned from long, intense association with Darrow under fire. Men in great fear, cravens, do the worst thing possible, run into the tiger's mouth, tell idiotic lies, wave their hats and plead clients Guilty [sic].[xc] [emphasis in original]

Sometimes, under the right (or wrong) circumstances, logic, judgment, and sense fly out the window.

Fighting Fire with Fire

One of Darrow's most vehement defenses, which can be seen as inherently compatible with his non-denials, justifications, and unclean hands defense was that he was simply fighting fire with fire.

The prosecution had all the advantages and had even engaged in unseemly conduct, themselves, so if he had stooped to their level—well, he was just giving back what they had dished out, and that should be okay.

He prefaced it this way:

> Now, gentlemen, I am going to be honest with you in this matter.[24] The McNamara case was a hard fight. I will tell you the truth about it; then, if you want to send me to prison, go ahead, it is up to you.[xci]

At that point he launched into a litany of the prosecution's advantages and/or wrongs: they had the grand jury, but the defense didn't; they had organized government backing them, but the defense didn't; they had subpoena power; they had

---

[24] See the discussion above about protesting too much about being honest. The person who starts with "I'm going to be honest with you…" is probably about to try to mislead you.

detectives secretly imbedded in the defense camp ("They had us surrounded by gumshoe and keyhole men at every step"); they had the rich to help them, while the defense was aided only by the poor ("The poor would help me and the rich would help them, but the help of the rich was always of greater avail than the help of the poor") (if one overlooks the financial help of the American Federation of Labor).

Then, echoing his "they're being mean to me" arguments, he said:

> Now let us look at the pitiful thing that they have brought to this jury to have you think badly of me. No matter if I had killed my grandmother, it would not prove that I had sought to bribe Lockwood; it might cause you to have a bad opinion of me, but you could not convict me of bribery on that opinion.

Again, not a denial.

Jury Nullification: So What if I Did It?

This was one of Darrow's more interesting defenses, tantalizingly close, yet again, to an admission.

He seemed to say that, suppose he had bribed jurors, would that have been so bad? Surely you wouldn't convict me, even if I had, because of the way the prosecution acted.

This is tantamount to a jury nullification argument, which says that a jury may overlook the law in order to do the right thing.

This wouldn't be the last time he tried that tack. See the Massie Case discussion.

He said:

> Gentlemen, suppose I did this bribery, suppose I did, then what? Is there any man in whose soul lurks a suspicion of integrity and fair dealing, is there any civilized man on earth who would convict me under circumstances like that?

And, in almost the next breath:

> Will you tell me if anywhere there could be an American jury, or anywhere in the English-speaking world there could be found a jury that would for a moment lend itself to a conspiracy so obvious and foul as this?

Then, in a near confession, "Gentlemen, I could tell you that I did this bribery, and you would turn me loose."

And consider this bit of rhetorical flourish, notwithstanding Luke North's denials, arguing that the fate of the whole country, along with the fate of Clarence Darrow, rested in the jury's hands:

> Suppose you thought I was guilty, suppose you thought so—would you dare as honest men, protecting society, would you dare to say by your verdict that scoundrels like this [the prosecution] should be saved from their own sins, by charging those sins to someone else? If so, gentlemen, when you go back to your homes, you had better kiss your wives a fond goodbye, and take your little children more tenderly in your arms than ever before, because, though today it is my turn, tomorrow it may be yours. This consideration, gentlemen, is more important to orderly government, to the preservation of human liberty, than "to get" any one man, no matter how hard they want "to get" him.

In Luke North's defense, perhaps this was not a rhetorical flourish but was, instead, mere bafflement with bullshit.

The Golden Rule

This was a defense Darrow would hammer in the Massie Case, but he trotted it out here, as well.

Maybe this was just a tune-up for Massie.

Premised upon the Biblical "golden rule" of "do unto others

as you would have them do unto you," in the legal context it asks jurors to place themselves in the shoes of a party and ask themselves: "What would I have done in that same circumstance?"

It's a form of jury nullification, because it essentially requests that the jury exonerate any conduct that they, themselves, might have engaged in. After all, how can it be wrongdoing if you, yourself, would have done it had you been in their shoes?

Here, Darrow utilized a variation on the Golden Rule.

Though he didn't emphasize it as heavily as he did in Massie, it was one of the arrows in his quiver, and he was not shy about shooting any arrow available.

We've already seen a snippet of the variation in the quote above, where Darrow charged the jury with protecting society because, if they "got" him today, they might "get" the jurors tomorrow.

So, by their verdict, they might prevent some unfortunate future from befalling themselves.

> *Gentlemen, don't ever think that your own life or liberty is safe; that your own family is secure; don't ever think that any human being is safe, when under evidence like this and circumstances like these, I, with some influence, and some respect, and some money, am brought here and placed in the shadow of the penitentiary for six long months. Am I dreaming? And will I awaken and find it all a horrible nightmare, and that no such thing has happened?*

Don't Hold What the McNamara Brothers did Against Him

Darrow waxed eloquent to the jury:

> *Oh, you wild insane members of the steel trust. Oh, you bloodhounds of detectives who are willing to do your*

> *master's evil will. Oh you district attorneys, you know not what you do. But if I must drink this cup to the dregs....*

Adela Rogers and her father, Earl, listened in the corridor as Darrow spoke. Rogers was willing to write off the foregoing as merely "a figure of speech," which Darrow had the right to do. But when Darrow launched into oration about how this all "...grew from a social conflict," that this was "...one of those inevitable acts which are part of this industrial war," and that the loss of life was merely "accidental," Rogers was livid—filled with "...a sort of white anger and then acrimonious contempt for the way Darrow had behaved."[xcii]

Twenty people dead, but the crime of the McNamaras was merely a "social crime," Darrow said, not cruel and vicious. After all, they had no control over the oppression of labor in this country, and the crime "grew out of a condition of society for which his clients were in no wise responsible."

They didn't mean to kill anyone, and the jury shouldn't allow the fact that they did, inadvertently, to "work upon your passions for me." Instead, his clients simply wanted to "scare" the newspaper's employees. If they had truly intended to destroy the building or kill anyone, he wrote in his memoir, they would have used more dynamite and placed it inside the building, not merely in an alley behind the building. What happened after that—the fire spreading and sparking an explosion—was purely an accident.[xciii]

Oops!

But, he said, the bombing and the deaths that followed were "paraded before this jury, in the hope that in some way it may awaken a prejudice in your hearts against me."

He reiterated this argument in the Bain case. His clients might have been misguided, even though they "laid their lives upon the altar of what they thought was right," but their actions weren't his, and their conduct wasn't his. In fact, had he known what they were up to, "I would have walked here to have prevented it."

They were truly sorry for the loss of life:

> I have heard them lament the sad, sad consequences that came from the destruction of the Times, which in itself was a great accident in the great sweep of things.

But don't hold that against Darrow. He was simply doing what lawyers do: representing clients. He was doing his duty.

> [W]hatever the facts, they were entitled to their defense. I was bound to them by the law of my profession.... I did what I could to save them. I did it honestly. I did it bravely.

Honestly? Maybe not so much.

Bravely? Well, crying like a baby doesn't necessarily mean you're not brave, does it?

Reminding the jury that he had already been acquitted once, if they needed to be so reminded, he said:

> I have told the story before to twelve jurors. They have heard all this. They went to their room and pronounced me not guilty. That should have ended it.

But it didn't.

They Didn't Mean to Hurt Anyone

As reinforcement for the prior argument, Darrow reiterated the lack of intent by the McNamara brothers to kill—not lack of intent to bomb, just to kill. Darrow would again trot out that "they didn't mean to kill" line in defending four white people accused of killing a young native man in territorial Hawaii in 1932.

It wasn't a valid legal excuse in Massie nor was it here. But that didn't stop Darrow from browbeating the jury with it in both cases *as if it were an excuse*. In the Times bombing:

> [N]one of the perpetrators of this deed was ever morally guilty of murder. Never. No one knows it better than the people who were prosecuting them. Sixteen sticks of dynamite were placed under a corner of the Times building to damage the building, but not to destroy life, to intimidate, to injure property, and for no other reason. It was placed there wrongfully, criminally, if you will, but with no thought of harming human life. The explosion itself scarcely stopped the printing presses. Unfortunately, there was an accumulation of gas and other inflammable substances in the building which ignited, and the fire resulting destroyed these human lives.

That conveniently overlooks the fact that they planted bombs with a reckless disregard for the harm they might cause—and which surely was foreseeable. Blow up a building and someone might get hurt or killed. How could you not figure that out?

In his memoir, Darrow emphasized the "no intent" point with an exercise in semantics. The *Times* building "was not blown up; it was burned down" by a fire started by the dynamite.[xciv]

That is a distinction without a difference. The bomb caused the fire and the fire burned the building; ergo, the bomb caused the destruction of the building and the loss of twenty lives.

He emphasized this point even more heavily in the Bain trial, a fact that many observers believe was why he was nearly convicted, unlike the easy acquittal in Lockwood, because it offended a number of jurors.

In a repetitive bit of redundancy, saying what he had already said before, he argued:

> First, they never morally committed murder. They made a statement which was delivered to the district attorney and is on file in this court that J. B. McNamara placed 16 sticks of dynamite in the alley, about 4 pounds. It would not have destroyed the building and it did not. It did not

even stop the printing presses. But unluckily, he placed it beside some barrels of ink, dropped it down, and it exploded, and it lighted it, and the horrible catastrophe followed. Neither one of these boys would have taken human life, and it was an accident. But under the laws of men, which makes little account of motives, they were guilty of murder. Under the laws of God, which considers motive everything, they were not guilty of murder.[25]

They were Justified because Their Cause was Just

Misguided they may have been and were, but I know that they laid their lives upon the altar of what they thought was right.

And so, Darrow contended, because their cause was just, their motives pure and their reasons sound, they were justified.

This was simply an extension of his arguments in Haywood, which prosecutor William E. Borah attacked in his closing argument on July 25, 1907, when he said that Darrow "justifies murder, coldblooded, deliberate murder, openly in the courts of our country."

In an editorial on August 24, 1907, *Collier's* magazine essentially asserted the same criticisms of Darrow as had Borah.

The plain inference from Mr. Darrow's argument is that he endorses crime so long as the criminal carries a union card, and doesn't tell.[26] In any event, he, a lawyer sworn to uphold the law, argues that crime is just under certain circumstances. Is he, as a citizen, liberal, and loose in his

---

[25] Yes, I know this is remarkably similar to the language quoted on the prior page. Redundancy was a favored Darrow tactic.

[26] The "doesn't tell" is in reference to the testimony of Steve Adams, a union member who flipped and testified for the prosecution, drawing Darrow's ire and condemnation.

logic, to the same degree? ^{xcv}

It also said that Darrow's "long speech before the Haywood jury ought to be printed in full," reference to the fact that the *Collier's* editors believed that, when published in the socialist publication *Appeal to Reason*, Darrow's argument had been edited.

Darrow responded with a letter, published in *Collier's* on September 21, in which he cited a passage from the editorial that purported to be from his argument—"I don't care how many wrongs they commit.... I don't care how many brutalities they are guilty of. I know that their cause is just" [27]—then complained:

> *Your editorial comments infer that this is language in excuse of violence and crime. It has been a long time since I have attempted to answer anything stated by a newspaper in reference to my public utterances. The reason I write this letter is not because your comment is more unfriendly than others, but because it is much less so, and because it bears upon its face your purpose to deal with my language fairly. It does seem to me, however, that any one [sic] who carefully reads the first statement quoted, even though not quoted in full, must see that it is perfectly plain that the language used simply means **that in spite of wrongs and brutalities**, the cause of labor is just. No one who heard it or who carefully reads it could draw any other inference from it.* ^{xcvi} [emphasis in original]

In response, *Collier's* said, "Let us be frank. Mr. Darrow has edited out of his speech, as printed in the 'Appeal to Reason,' all the words of violence; which is well. It would have been better had they never passed his lips." ^{xcvii}

Darrow responded with a letter, dated September 23 but published in the magazine on October 26, denying the

---

[27] This language is cited more fully above.

accusation and referred the editors to the purported text of his published argument.

Darrow wrote, in part:

> Editor of Collier's:
>
> Sir—In your issue of the 21st you published a letter from me in reference to certain portions of my argument in the Haywood case, and then made editorial comment thereon which is justified by neither the letter nor the facts. The argument as published in the 'Appeal to Reason' was not tampered with nor changed in any way—not one word has been cut out of it, nor any violent utterance omitted; there were no words of violence to cut out—these were found only in the newspaper reports.[xcviii]

Upon reviewing the argument in *Appeal to Reason*, though, *Collier's* realized that it was inconsistent with its reporters' notes:

> Regarding Mr. Darrow's candor we have no desire to speak. In his former letter he by distinct implication admitted the accuracy of the quotations made by us, and, instead of denying the words, attempted to explain that they were meant lightly and in the excitement of extemporaneous address.

But, it said, "[t]he worst of these words we do not find in the 'Appeal to Reason,'" even though *Collier's* own notes, from which it quoted, "were taken for us by an expert stenographer."

When *Wayland's Monthly* later published the full argument, a comparison with *Appeal to Reason* put the lie to Darrow's denials. *Collier's* published a brief excerpt from the full argument, including language quoted above that began "I don't care how many wrongs they have committed," then noted that such language had been "cut out" in the *Appeal to Reason*. *Collier's* ended its editorial with: "Our compliments to the 'Appeal to

Reason' and to Mr. CLARENCE DARROW. The question of veracity between them and us is completely settled now." [xcix]

Invoking God

Clarence Darrow was a well-known agnostic, at least by his own assessment, if not an atheist, which he probably was but wouldn't admit. The difference between the two is that an atheist says, "There is no God," while the agnostic says, "I don't know if there is a God—but I have my doubts." Given Darrow's self-label of agnostic, it is interesting to see his willingness to invoke God when it suited his purpose. That was probably because he was playing to an audience of ostensibly God-fearing jurors whom he did not want to alienate. It was something he would also do in the Leopold and Loeb case.

He first invoked God when attacking his own investigator, John Harrington, who testified for the prosecution and whom Darrow blamed for any wrongdoing attributed to the defense team:

> *I know Harrington is not to blame for being a coward. I know God made him a coward, and he cannot help it, and I have spoken of him with this view in mind all the way along.*

Again hearkening to Harrington:

> *Only the infinite God can judge the human heart, and I never tried to judge.*

He acknowledged, though, that he was:

> *...especially bitter against Harrington, but I don't believe in bitterness—as some of you may have suspicioned this afternoon. I have always tried to curb it, all my life.*

Of course, one wonders how else to couch Darrow's attacks upon prosecutor Ford ("cowardly and malicious" and "villainy and infamy") as anything other than bitterness.

And one merely has to cursorily review his scathing remarks against prosecutors in the Leopold and Loeb case and in the Scopes Trial, including his cross-examination of William Jennings Bryan, to see further evidence of bitterness. In Darrow's defense, though, maybe he was just saying that his repentance of bitterness had a sell-by date of 1912, but he wasn't vouching for the future.

When excusing his clients' conduct as a mere "social crime," Darrow suggested that the jurors had no right to judge him, nor let those judgments influence their verdict in the case against him, because that was the province of God (the one he didn't believe in), not man.

> [B]ut judged in the light of his motives, which is the only way that man can be judged—and for that reason only the infinite God can judge a human being—judged in the light of his motives I cannot condemn the man, and I will not.

Perhaps, in subtext, he was also suggesting that judgment for the crimes he, himself, was charged with, should be left in the hands of God, not twelve men in a jury box.

But Darrow wasn't finished invoking the very God whose existence he questioned—unless it suited him. Complaining bitterly of Bert Franklin, who claimed to have passed the bribes on Darrow's instructions, Darrow said:

> I have no feeling against him, he is the way God made him. He can't help it any more than you can help being you, or I can help being I.

But then he went on to say, remarkably, and again redundantly:

> I don't want anybody to think that I would judge him with hardness or bitterness. I have never judged any

human being that way in my life, I never shall.

Finally, near the end of his filibuster, and in an argument that foretold one of his primary defenses in Leopold and Loeb—that those two child-killers were the victims of their genetics and environment, and thus they should not be held accountable for their actions—he invoked God one final time while talking about Jim McNamara.

Not just invoked God; he blamed God.

> *In a way his troubles have come by his own fault. In a way they did not. He did not give himself birth. He did not make his own brain. He is not responsible for his ideas. He is the product of all the generations that have gone before. And he is the product of all the people who touch him directly or indirectly through his life, and he is as he is, and the responsibility rests on the infinite God that made him.*

The "God" defense worked so well that, like other defenses, he trotted it out again in the Bain trial. In a shot at one of the prosecutors, Darrow said that no one is "wholly bad unless it is Gray."

Then he decided it was time to blame God again.

> *Above it all is the God who shapes our brain, the God who shapes us, the great nature that controls us and makes us do her bidding, whether we will or not.*

It was, after all, the "infinite God who molded their skulls and fitted the brain to the skull made them the way they are...."

So it was all God's fault.

Special Defense for the Second Trial

Because the Lockwood jury acquitted him, Darrow had a particularly compelling argument to make in the Bain trial: The prosecution played its best card first—Lockwood—and lost; this one is weaker, so how can you reach a different result?

It made sense.

Many of the same witnesses testified in the Bain trial as in the Lockwood trial, at least as far as those who were turning State's evidence in exchange for plea deals. If the prior jury didn't believe them, why should this one?

In fact, the prior finding of "not guilty" was incredibly fast, "almost without leaving the box" Darrow hyperbolized. Or, as he put it later, the prior jury "vindicated me almost without leaving their seats."

Hyperbole again, but still fast, which just goes to show how poor that jury thought the prosecution's case was—if you overlook the possibility that, as Earl Rogers claimed to have discovered during his mysterious absence, Darrow had bribed jurors again.

Since the Bain case was weaker but the prosecution was proceeding anyway, obviously it was because, Darrow said, "the forces that control in this United States, the great forces of evil, want to destroy me."

He argued:

> *I have been subjected to three months of this, and I have been found Not Guilty. I am subjected to six weeks more, because I have committed the sin of sins—I have defended the poor.*

Besides, he said, you really can't believe the ones who testified against him because they got immunity in exchange for helping the prosecution "get" him.

> *They have raked up every gutter-snipe and sewer-rat they*

could find and bribed them that their masters might get me! Get me! I have fought a brave fight, and if you get me I will try to die a brave death. It has got to come sometime.

If it helped, he wanted the jury to know he would look quite fondly on them if they acquitted him, just as he did the previous jury. He referred to that prior bunch as "the twelve jurors who passed on my case before and for whom I will always feel a kind of affection that I couldn't for other men...."

As we'll soon see, he had such an affection—or something—for at least one of them that he sent him money.

Waxing Poetic

Darrow loved reciting poetry. He found it to be a pretty good distraction from the facts of a case. It was windbaggery at its finest. He relied heavily upon it in Leopold and Loeb, citing the likes of A.E. Houseman and Omar Khayyam. In the Lockwood bribery case, he borrowed from Lord Alfred Tennyson's *The Charge of the Light Brigade* with his own personal twist. Noting that nine detectives had testified against him, he said:

> *Detectives to the right of me,*
> *Detectives to the left of me,*
> *Detective behind me,*
> *Sleuthing and spying.*
> *Theirs not to question why—*
> *Theirs but to sleuth and lie—*
> *Noble detectives!*

In yet another waxing of the poetic, he recited the words of Eugene Fitch Ware.

> *Life is a game of whist.*[28] *From unknown sources*

---

[28] Whist is trick-taking card game that was developed in England and

Blowhard

The cards are shuffled and the hands are dealt.
Blind are our efforts to control the forces
That though unseen are no less strongly felt.
I do not like the way the cards are shuffled,
But still I like the game and want to play
And through the long, long night, I play unruffled
The cards I get until the break of day.

"I have taken the cards as they came," he explained. "I have played the best I could; I have tried to play them honestly,[29] manfully, doing for myself and for my fellow man the best I could. I will play the game to the end, whatever that end may be."

In the Bain trial, he was just as poetic as ever. First came John Neihardt's *Battle Cry*, which had been introduced to him by Olaf Tvietmoe, the San Francisco union leader.

Darrow liked the poem so much that he recited it in his closing as a self-aggrandizing tribute to himself as some kind of noble warrior.

Good ol' Clarence Darrow, fighting the good fight against overwhelming odds.

And when he and others of his ilk are gone, and he is banished to the penitentiary for life, "other men will come to take our places forever and forever until the blind world sees and the dumb speaks."

More than half beaten, but fearless.
Facing the storms and the night.
Breathless and reeling but tearless,
Here in the lull of the fight.
I who bow not but before Thee,
God of the fighting clan,
Lifting my fists I implore Thee,

---

popular in the 18th and 19th Centuries.
[29] There's that word again: honestly.

Mike Farris

Give me the heart of a man.

What though I live with the winners,
Or perish with those who fall?
Only the cowards are sinners,
Fighting the fight is all.
Strong is my foe, he advances!
Snapped is my blade, O Lord!
See the proud banners and lances!
O spare me this stub of a sword.
Give me no pity nor spare me,
Calm not the wrath of my Foe.
See where he beckons to dare me!
Bleeding, half-beaten I go.
Not for the glory of winning,
Not for the fear of the night.
Shunning the battle is sinning,
O spare me the heart to fight!

Red is the mist about me,
Deep is the wound in my side.
"Coward" thou cryest to flout me?
O terrible Foe, thou hast lied!
Here with my battle before me,
God of the Fighting Clan.
Grant that the woman who bore me
Suffered to suckle a Man!

But the bard of the courtroom was just getting warmed up, later launching into an excerpt from *The Garden of Proserpine* by Algernon Charles Swinburne.

It's not entirely clear what point he hoped to make by this poem, which is based on the ancient Greek story of the abduction of the young girl Proserpine by Hades, god of the underworld, and taken to be his queen.

But, pursuant to a deal her mother struck with Hades, she

Blowhard

was permitted to return to the world above each year for one season, Spring, before returning to the underworld.

Setting the context for his recitation, Darrow condemned his enemies for lacking both pity and decency, instead being motivated solely by money. "It isn't fair. I've grown weary and tired, as the poet says."

Then, almost as if impossible to resist, he launched into verse, a bit paraphrased (although it's possible that any variances from the original poem may be the result of stenographer's error).

I am tired of tears and laughter,
Of men who laugh and weep,
For what may come hereafter,
For those who sow to reap.
Weary of days and hours,
Blown buds of vanished flowers,
Desires and dreams and powers
And everything but sleep.

From too much love of living,
From hope and fear set free,
We thank with brief thanksgiving
Whatever Gods may be.

That no life lives forever,
That dead men rise up never,
That even the weariest river
Winds somewhere straight to sea.

There sun nor star shall waken,
Nor any change of light,
Nor sound of water shaken,
Nor any sound or sight.

Nor wintry leaves nor vernal,

Mike Farris

Nor days nor things diurnal,
Only the sleep eternal
In an eternal night.

Then Darrow said, "I am ready for that sleep."
    As was, quite likely, the jury by that point.

Chapter Seven: Did He, or Didn't He?

What do I care if he is guilty as hell?
—Lincoln Steffens

DARROW PLAYED ENOUGH cards in his two bribery trials to qualify as a card shark. Some worked, some didn't, but he obviously held a winning hand in the Lockwood case, in which he was acquitted. And one of Darrow's best cards in the subsequent Bain bribery trial was the prior acquittal.

He argued that the prosecution logically brought its best case first and, if it couldn't win the best, what did that say about the second choice? He played the card often—and why wouldn't he?—even exaggerating the speed with which the Lockwood jury acted.

It was actually closer to thirty minutes, and the jury took three votes: the first was 8-4 in favor of acquittal and the second 10-2 before the unanimous 12-0 decision came in.

Despite the Lockwood acquittal and Darrow's heavy reliance on it as his trump card, he didn't fare nearly as well with the Bain jury. Some historians believe his efforts to sanitize and justify the bombing by his clients may have irritated the second jury.

As noted, he had utilized that argument in the Lockwood

case, but maybe a bit more cautiously. In the Bain case, he felt free to lean on it more heavily, a lapse in judgment. After hearing Darrow's justification for the violence, some of the Bain jurors told reporters that "they were convinced that Darrow would surely resort to bribery, and other illegal acts, to defend or advance his beliefs and clients." [c]

In the Bain case, the jury deliberated for forty hours before announcing it was hung, with an 8-4 vote in *favor of conviction*. If you add the four original Lockwood votes for conviction to the eight in Bain, you get to twelve.

Of course, it doesn't work that way, but ain't it interesting?

Verdicts notwithstanding, the question that has lingered without a definitive answer for more than a century is whether Darrow bribed any jurors, either George Lockwood or Robert Bain or others in the McNamara case. And let's not get started on whether he did so in the Haywood, or any prior or subsequent cases.

Popular Belief that Darrow was Guilty

Attorney Charles Erskine Wood, a close Darrow friend, believed Darrow had bribed jurors in the Haywood case and feared, almost presciently, that he would do so in McNamara.

Other of Darrow's friends believed him not only capable of such behavior, but also willing, or maybe even compelled, to do so if the right circumstances presented themselves. None of them, not even his closest confidants, believed he was ethically pure.

Austin Willard Wright, a noted anarchist and author of the booklet *War's Folly and Futility*, wrote to Wood in 1904 and accused Darrow of having "no principles whatever," and as being a man whose "acts emphasize greed for money equal to that of the most insatiable of millionaires." In a final dagger, he bemoaned that he once had a "fondness approaching affection for Darrow," but that feeling had "shriveled up…and died" due to the "withering blight of [Darrow's] moral bankruptcy…." [ci]

Blowhard

Prior to McNamara, and even prior to Haywood, Darrow had received an on-the-job tutorial in bribing jurors. In 1902, he defended lawyers for the Chicago Union Traction Company who had been charged with bribing jurors in personal injury cases brought against the streetcar company. There is some question whether Darrow ever directly defended company attorney Cyrus Simon, who was perhaps the driving force behind that bribing campaign. He did, however, subsequently hire Simon to work in his office. That would seem to be at least a tacit acceptance of the ethics of Simon's bribery campaign.

Darrow's labor friends were particularly upset by his defense of the lawyers in those cases. Darrow had previously represented socialist Eugene V. Debs, five-time presidential candidate, in his role as leader of the American Railway Union arising out of the Pullman Strike of 1894. William E. Burns (not to be confused with detective William J. Burns), a top aide to Debs during the Pullman matter, criticized Darrow for "defending men who had bribed jurors in cases where crippled children were asking for justice from the traction companies which had injured them." [cii]

Daniel Cruice, head of the Referendum League of Chicago, charged Darrow with a "breach of trust," and other union officials claimed that Darrow "had never done anything for labor unless he was paid an inflated fee." [ciii] That would surely seem to run counter to the Darrow legend as attorney for the underdog, or "attorney for the damned," as Lincoln Steffens dubbed him.[30]

Geoffrey Cowan wrote:

> Darrow always had some glib explanation for taking these cases, but after a while his friends, who were turning into his critics, began to conclude that he had simply become greedy, that he would handle any case for a fee, no matter who was hurt. They were troubled by cases that went

---

[30] Of course, given the reputation of attorneys in popular culture, maybe they really were the "damned," after all.

> *beyond a quest for financial security and seemed to be based on avarice. But it was the cynicism, more than the avarice, that so offended longtime admirers. He defended his work and his increasingly iconoclastic political views by resorting to arguments that were, to put it mildly, sophistic.*[31] *He was a fatalist, he said. No one was responsible for his actions. There wasn't much that one could do to make the world better—the forces of capital were too strong, the impoverished masses were too ignorant and fickle.*[civ]

These criticisms painted a view of Darrow that supported a belief that he was certainly *capable* of bribing jurors. But it takes more than merely a belief that Darrow was capable of bribing jurors to make the leap to his actually having bribed them.

There must be evidence.

Cowan, for one, believed the evidence existed. Perhaps not the "beyond a reasonable doubt" evidence required for a criminal conviction, where life and liberty are at stake. But outside of a courtroom, that lofty standard is not the benchmark.

Historians can only review the historical records, hopefully consisting largely of primary sources, then draw conclusions on what likely happened. Cowan concluded, "On the basis, then, of all the available evidence, it is fair to conclude that Darrow bribed both Lockwood and Bain." [cv] Darrow biographer John A. Farrell concurred. "Did Darrow participate in the bribery scheme? Almost assuredly." [cvi]

Most courtroom observers of the bribery trials, and even friends of Darrow, believed him to be guilty of the charge.

In a letter to Sara Field Ehrgott, Erskine Wood wrote:

> *While Darrow has naturally my human sympathy there*

---

[31] *Merriam-Webster* defines sophistry as "subtly deceptive reasoning and argumentation."

> goes with it the old Greek sense of...justice. He played the game. He made his own code of morals. He took the risk.

And Sara told Wood:

> I don't forgive Mr. D.'s wrong, but I can forgive the man of which it came because from him, from his composite, has come his great good.

In the context, she appears to be referring to bribing jurors as Darrow's "wrong."

Reporter Hugh Baillie wrote that Darrow struck him as someone who "had come to feel that the rules which bound ordinary people were not binding on him" and that "he had few scruples about the procedure to be used in winning so long as he personally believed that the cause was just."

He further wrote:

> I never had any doubts on the subject. In my opinion, Darrow was guilty—on the evidence which included his presence across the street while Franklin was passing the money to Lockwood; on his attitude and appearances during trial; and on the basis of my private conversations with him. [cvii]

Banker-turned-anarchist W.W. Catlin, a long-time acquaintance of both Darrow and Wood, wrote to Wood, after conversations with Darrow in early 1912, that Darrow might well have employed bribery under an ends-justifies-the-means philosophy. Darrow's "course [of conduct]" and his talk, Catlin said, supports "the belief that he thinks such a course right under the circumstances existing."

Another W.W., Robinson, a California lawyer who was a student at the University of Southern California at the time of the trials, later published various works on southern California history, including a pamphlet on the McNamara case and the bribery trials called *Bombs and Bribery*. He reported that attorney Jerry Giesler, who assisted Rogers in Darrow's defense, admitted to him that he believed Darrow to be guilty. Reporter Fletcher Bowron told Robinson that "he believed Darrow was unquestionably guilty of bribery." In fact, Robinson wrote, "...I have been unable to find a lawyer or anyone else directly connected with, or an observer of, the McNamara and Darrow trials who believed in Darrow's innocence."

He reported that Paul Jordan Smith, a friend of Darrow's from Chicago who later relocated to Los Angeles, said that Darrow as much as admitted his guilt in a private conversation at a welcome reception for Darrow upon his return to Chicago. According to Smith, Darrow said, "When you're up against a bunch of crooks you will have to play their game. Why shouldn't I?" [cviii]

Adela Rogers St. Johns wrote, "A press-box vote would have convicted him, that's for sure." She said her father, Earl Rogers, believed that Darrow bribed the jurors. Her "stomach," often looked to by lawyers associated with her father as an "oracle," "howled warnings." She wrote, "Never in my whole life had it been as sure of anything as it was that Darrow was guilty." [cix]

Now, admittedly St. Johns was not a Darrow fan, by any means. While it might seem an overstatement to say that she hated Darrow, she actually acknowledged that, at the time of the bribery trials, she did.

> *Doubtless through the years Darrow redeemed himself. Earned the right to be called the Great Defender. I don't hate him now. Thank God for that. But I did then.* [cx]

But even writing fifty years after the fact, it's probably safe to say she wouldn't give up her seat for him in the lifeboat of a sinking ship. She obviously resented that Darrow downplayed the role her father played in his acquittal. "When Darrow in his autobiography dismissed my father's part in his defense with one line, 'I hired a local lawyer named Earl Rogers to assist me,' he overlooked, or had forgotten, or perhaps never faced the fact that he, Darrow, was the *under-est* dog the West's leading trial lawyer, Earl Rogers, ever defended." [cxi] [emphasis in original]

Interestingly, St. Johns, who later covered the Leopold and Loeb case, blamed Darrow for the growth of the "compulsion" defense for violent juveniles and delinquency run amuck.

> *I did not know then* [at the time of the bribery trials] *that Clarence Darrow would, for the largest fee ever up to then paid a criminal lawyer, defend two very very very rich teen-age delinquents for the brutal blood-and-sex-thrill murder of a nice little boy who wore glasses. That he would hurrah over a big victory when he got them life imprisonment instead of the chair or the asylum, and thus began the theory of compulsion for juvenile delinquents to kill and torture and slay. For if you will check it you will find the juvenile delinquency murder and the school of literature which sold such boys psychiatric pardon in open court began with Darrow's defense of Leopold and Loeb in Chicago. There also began the fear of using the rod, or parental discipline, of standards of conduct and rules of decent behavior. So when I walked into the courtroom and there saw Darrow as chief counsel for Loeb and Leopold, I forgave a little the hardhearted, cruel, high-stomached, overloyal, overbearing teenage girl I had been.*[cxii]

Even her descriptions of Darrow seem to evoke contempt. She noted that, at one meeting with her father, Darrow sat across from him at a table, "with the usual grease spots on his tie and vest, though what they were intended to prove I never knew."[cxiii]

Adela's mother was equally contemptuous, telling Irving Stone, "I never liked Darrow. He always had a hangdog look. He was one of the dirtiest men I ever saw; his nails were dirty; his ears were dirty." And she added, speaking of Ruby Darrow, whom she disliked equally, that Ruby was "putting on a show of poverty." [cxiv] When Rogers forced Ruby to leave his conference room—"put her out"—so he could consult with his client in private, under the umbrella of attorney-client privilege, Adela believed that Ruby always held that against him. "She spent the rest of her life getting even by the things she said about him. *Thank you* was never one of them." [cxv]

When Adela first learned that Darrow had been added to the defense team in the McNamara case, and knowing that Rogers idolized Darrow, she asked her father whether he believed the McNamaras were innocent. Rogers replied, "No." Then she asked whether he thought Darrow might believe they were innocent. After a moment's thought, he answered:

> *A man afire, alight, inspired for and by a cause, can deceive himself as to the facts of a case. He sees with his heart, his blood stream, his bowels of mercy, he is able to see what he wants to see and not to see what he doesn't want to see. Or—he may have accepted that the end justifies the means and be able to believe the crime is justified, and justification is the same as innocence.*

Adela also provided this interesting insight:

> *If the story of Clarence Darrow had ended the day he pleaded James B. McNamara guilty of murder in the Times dynamiting, he would have gone down to his grave a failure, a traitor to his cause, a bumbling poseur. If he had not been acquitted on the odious charge of jury bribery, Darrow would never have had a chance to win the moral victories of the Leopold-Loeb, Scopes, Scottsboro, and Massey [sic] trials, all of which, of course, he lost in court. Let's face it, he would have been disbarred, in the penitentiary, or in his grave. The Great Defender came after and sprang from the acquittal Rogers won for him on*

> *a charge of **which we believed he was guilty**.*[cxvi]
> [emphasis added]

But most significantly, she said that Darrow admitted it.

> *I never had any doubts, not even before one of my father's private conversations with Darrow included an admission of his guilt to his lawyer.*[cxvii]

Ironically, although she admitted to behaving badly around Darrow and his wife, Ruby, and she included several stories of how she resented the two of them, she later wrote that she did so, "not because I always knew he was guilty," but because "I didn't like him, felt that he was a phony...."[cxviii]

Anton Johannsen, a player in the case, stated his belief that Darrow did it "to save his own skin" while one of Darrow's law partners, Francis Wilson, suggested a financial motive. According to Wilson, Darrow had been "lured" by the chance of winning that $50,000 fee quickly, in a few months." But "since he had collected his full fee by late summer, there was an economic incentive to end the case as expeditiously as possible."[cxix]

Lincoln Steffens also appeared to share the belief that Darrow was guilty, although his wording was arguably ambiguous. Writing to his sister Laura on June 25, 1912, he said:

> *When the fight is on, there is a call, not for an umpire, but a friend. That's why I'm here with Darrow. He is scared; the cynic is humbled; the man that laughed sees and is frightened, not at prison bars, but at his own soul. Well, then, what do I care if he is guilty as hell; what if his friends and attorneys turn away ashamed of him and of the soul of Man—Good God, I'll look with him, and if it's any comfort, I'll show him my soul, as black as his; not so naked, but—Sometimes all we humans have is a*

friend, somebody to represent God in the world.

In correspondence with family, Darrow asserted that his "conscience refuses to reproach me," but he didn't specifically deny the bribes. Even his beloved Mary Field appeared to believe him guilty. Years later, writing to her daughter, she said, "I think that if he thought bribery was the only way to keep the boys from being killed, he would have felt justified in using it."

In 1934, she wrote in her diary of:

> ...[d]*ays when I walked through Gethsemane with Darrow, crushed and weighted with the desertion of friend, with betrayal, with the impending doom of jail...bribing a juror to save a man's life...who knows if he did? But he wouldn't hesitate anyway. If men are so cruel as to break other men's necks, so greedy as to be restrained only by money, then a sensitive man must bribe to save.*

For the minority view, Darrow apologists Arthur and Lila Weinberg believed him to be truly innocent. Their verdict, though, is not based on evidence but primarily on the notion that the bribing of jurors had been mishandled and Darrow would have been too smart to make those errors.

"Darrow was a shrewd lawyer who understood personalities and, had he contemplated bribery, would have moved carefully and meticulously." He wouldn't have chosen Franklin as the instrument of the bribes, they say, because he had only recently met Franklin, and he wouldn't have used $1000 bills for the payoff because they were "difficult to exchange and easily traced." He wouldn't have gone ahead with the bribing once McNamara had been settled, and he wouldn't have favored "such unlikely individuals as the fanatically antiunion Bain and the reluctant, righteous Lockwood" to bribe.[cxx]

These sound like opinions, but certainly not evidence. It

might even be wishful thinking. They seem to foreshadow Darrow's argument in Leopold and Loeb that his clients were so brilliant, and the crime so bungled, that negligence in the murder of Bobby Franks was proof of their mental disease. And the argument advanced by the Weinbergs also reflects Darrow's own contention that, if he had done something so stupid, "I certainly belong in some State Institution." Or, as Willie Nelson sang, "I'd have to be crazy, plum out of my mind."

As for the bungled logistics, Darrow might well have been ill-advised in some of the actions he took and personalities he employed. However, as a "stranger in a strange land," not familiar with the terrain and the players, he may simply have been less careful than he should have been.

Secondarily, the Weinbergs offered a reputation defense, that bribing jurors "is totally at variance with Darrow's character and all of his actions up to that time and afterward." They contend that he wouldn't have staked his reputation on "the winning or losing of one case." [cxxi] The truth is that Darrow's character was not nearly as impeccable as the Weinbergs wanted to believe. Look no further than the taint attached to his reputation following the Haywood case that led Erskine Wood, who knew Darrow personally and closely, to distance himself from his friend in the McNamara case.

Another Darrow apologist, Irving Stone, also vouched for him, although he acknowledged that many didn't. According to Stone, Venice police sergeant and longtime Darrow friend Billy Cavanaugh asked Darrow, "Mr. Darrow, why did you have to go on down to the corner and get yourself caught?" Darrow had no response. "[H]ow could he protest to an accuser who had instantly assumed him to be guilty?" [cxxii]

Another of Darrow's "intimates," Dr. Perceval Gerson seemed to acknowledge his guilt while justifying his conduct.

"None of your friends blame you for what you did, Clarence. If you are guilty, what of it? You had to fight the devil with fire." [cxxiii]

Stone wrote that, after Darrow's return to Chicago, many

people blamed him for damaging the city's reputation because of his exploits on the west coast. Even though they were in the minority, Stone said, the damage was nevertheless done.

> *Though the general run of folks believed him innocent of the bribery, the more cynical said, "You know how it is— where there's smoke there's bound to be fire. Even if he didn't pass the bribe he probably knew it was being done." And Clarence Darrow saw confirmed the fear he had felt when he sat in the Los Angeles courtroom and heard Joe Ford accuse him of being worse than Benedict Arnold or Judas Iscariot; if you fling mud at a fence some stains will remain after the mud has dried and fallen off.*[cxxiv]

But, according to Stone, his Chicago brethren in the legal profession, by and large, defended him.

One, Edward Maher, even suggested that the Lawyer's Association of Illinois give a banquet in Darrow's honor. But even as much as he must have appreciated that offer, Darrow, himself, was a bit ambiguous when reflecting, years later, on this chapter of his life. Although he noted that he had taken the stand "denying any knowledge or connection with an attempt to bribe any juror," some of the jurors in the Bain case seemed "hostile." However, they "reported a disagreement" and returned no verdict.[cxxv]

Then, in a vein almost akin to O.J. Simpson's ridiculous *If I Did It: Here's How It Happened*,[32] Darrow wrote:

> *There was only one view that I was sure practically*

---

[32] This was the original title of the book, co-written by Pablo Fenjves for ReganBooks. When a Florida bankruptcy court awarded the rights to the book to the family of Ronald Goldman, who had been murdered along with Simpson's wife, as partial satisfaction of their civil judgment against Simpson, the subtitle was changed from *Here's How It Happened* to *Confessions of the Killer*.

> *everyone would agree on—that, whatever the facts might be, there had been no sordid or selfish motive connected with the affair. They would know that if the charge was true it was because of my devotion to a cause and my anxiety and concern over the fate of some one* [sic] *else.*^{cxxvi}

In other words, *if* he did it, he did it with the purest of motives; therefore, it was okay. This is a corollary to the end-justifies-means; it's the motive-justifies-the-means-which-justifies-the-end.

This goes hand-in-hand with his near-admission to the Lockwood jury that:

> *Of course I did not pass $500 in the elevator, but if I had, I had just as much right to give that $500 for that purpose as I would have to buy $500 worth of hogs, just exactly.*

And now we've come full circle back to "that's not my dog."

Darrow had his own notions of justice, a term he often spoke of with disdain—unless his own personal sense of justice was implicated. And to achieve that so-called justice, he was willing to excuse just about any behavior, whether his or others, that helped achieve that end.

So, it is easy to see how a man who appeared to justify bombing a newspaper building and excuse the resultant loss of life as merely an "accident," could easily justify behavior ranging from bribing jurors and witnesses to kidnapping witnesses and whooshing them away from courtrooms, and even suborning perjury.

Bribing the Bribery Jurors?

Though not directly on point on the issue of bribing McNamara jurors, but relevant to Darrow's willingness and propensity to bribe jurors, a bit of circumstantial evidence arose after the fact—about fifteen years after the fact, to be more specific—that Darrow bribed at least one juror in his own trial.

To explain it requires a bit of context.

During jury selection in the Lockwood case, a potential juror named Fred E. Golding, treasurer and part-owner of a lumber company, expressed prejudice against "unscrupulous labor leaders," but said he would follow the evidence in deliberations if selected to serve on the jury.

This would appear to be a bias sure to draw at least a peremptory challenge from the defense, if not a challenge for cause, but Darrow allowed him to pass onto the jury without objection. The prosecution, of course, was more than happy to accept him, with his unfavorable views of labor, as a juror.

During the trial, Golding was perhaps the most active juror, making himself well-known, and maybe even a nuisance. He registered a complaint with the court that the prosecution had engaged "spies" to shadow the jurors. This led to an inquiry into the conduct of chief bailiff Martin Aguirre, who had been tasked with providing for the needs of the jurors.

Prosecutor Fredericks, for his part, asserted that Aguirre showed favoritism to the defense, even going so far as to disparage prosecutors to the jury. All of the jurors affirmed, however, that Aguirre had not attempted to influence them either way, but Aguirre nevertheless asked that his duties be reassigned to someone else. During discussion the judge held with counsel and the jurors, Golding spoke up on Aguirre's behalf, notwithstanding that it was his complaint that started the investigation.

Although Aguirre was replaced, there was some belief that it was a Pyrrhic victory for prosecutor Fredericks, who had alienated the jury. "Fredericks, the warrior, had won the battle.... But the battle had been won at an incredible cost." [cxxvii]

But more significant was Golding's participation in the trial, itself. Under California law, jurors were permitted to ask questions of witnesses, and Golding took full advantage, often asking questions that appeared favorable to the defense. With

Bert Franklin, the man who paid the bribe to Lockwood, on the stand, Golding jumped in with both feet, asking questions about the bribe money that suggested it was all part of a big frame-up. According to author John A. Farrell, it caused Franklin, the prosecution's star witness, to "respond with an unappealing testiness." cxxviii

Earl Rogers called Lincoln Steffens to the stand on July 18 to testify regarding the settlement of the McNamara case. When Prosecutor Fredericks finished his cross-examination and Judge Hutton invited questions from the jury, Golding (simply identified in the transcript as "A Juror") asked what might today be termed a "softball" question, seemingly beneficial to Darrow and eliciting an exculpatory answer from Steffens.

> A JUROR: *You had several conferences with him [Darrow] that week up to the 26th of November, and after you read that Express article announcing the arrest of Franklin and went to see Darrow. I would like to have a little more information* [about how] *did he appear there? Whether he appeared like a guilty man, frustrated in bribing a juror, or an innocent man. Just how he appeared and what he said. A little more about that.*

When Darrow took the stand on July 29, Golding asked a number of questions, some of which, again, appeared to be favorable to Darrow. He seemed to suggest that many people in the United States had an interest in the outcome of the McNamara case and wished to contribute funds toward their defense, and not just those in labor leadership that the prosecution asserted was providing funds for bribes.

In effect, it was an endorsement of Darrow's character and reputation.

> GOLDING: *Just tell me how many persons in the United States were directly interesting in your handling of the McNamara case, through their contributions to the*

defense fund, through their affiliated unions?

DARROW: *Yes, approximately 2 million.*

GOLDING: *Two million people?*

DARROW: *That is, there were more than that. The total membership of the American Federation of Labor is upwards of two million. When this case started there was to be a call for 25 cents apiece from the membership and I think about a quarter of them paid, upwards of $200,000. Outside of the membership of the unions there were large numbers of people in all walks of life and large numbers of organizations, like the socialistic organization, throughout the country who were interested, and who contributed something, and who were interested in it, but there were at least two million that were directly interested in the way you spoke of.*

Golding then asked a few more questions, ultimately leading to a relevance objection from Fredericks, which was sustained. But his questions spurred Darrow's attorney Earl Rogers to take a new approach.

ROGERS: *One thing suggested to me. Suggested by Mr. Golding's question. I will ask you to state from the people that were actually contributing money, aside from these 2,000,000 men that you have spoken of, is it or not a fact that there were many people interested in the case from one standpoint or another, whether like Mr. Tvietmoe, because he was mentioned concerning it, people who were vitally and materially and personally interested in the matter?"*

DARROW: *Everybody in the United States took sides on that case, and were interested, actively interested.*

Blowhard

When Darrow was acquitted in the Lockwood case, "The first to greet him was Juror Golding, who threw his arms around Darrow and told him how happy he was." [cxxix] John A. Farrell, writing in *Smithsonian Magazine*, asserted that Golding "was Darrow's most outspoken defender on the jury.... He openly suggested that the case was a frame-up orchestrated by California's business interests as part of their infamous scheme (immortalized in the film *Chinatown*) to steal water from the Owens Valley and ship it to Los Angeles." [cxxx] In today's world, that might have marked Golding as a conspiracy nut.

Hugh Baillie said that, at least a week before the jury vote, Golding "caught my eye" several times, would smile, and shake his head, as if sending a message that the jury was not going to convict.

At least that was how Baillie took it.

After the acquittal was announced, Baillie spoke to Golding, who asked, "Did you get my signal, little cub?" He also told Baillie that the jury had decided early on to acquit and didn't even debate the testimony during their deliberations, but simply took their vote.[cxxxi] That conflicts with other reports that the jury actually took three votes, with the number of votes to convict reducing each time until arriving at zero.

With Golding's role now in context, consider this. Golding wrote Darrow in 1913, after the end of the second bribery trial, asking for money. He told Darrow that "[y]ou must not consider that you are under obligation to me, because I stood for what was right and just." We don't have a record of whether Darrow sent Golding money or, if he did, how much, but it is certainly curious, and presumptuous, for a juror to solicit money from an attorney involved in a case in which that juror served.

There is also no record of an ongoing relationship between Darrow and Golding, but on December 16, 1927, fifteen years later, Darrow wrote to his son Paul and said:

> *I want you to send a Draft or Cashiers check to Fred E. Golding on receipt of this Via Air Mail to 608 Central*

Bldg. Los Angeles Cal for $4500. Mr. Golding is one of my dearest friends. He was one of the strongest men on the jury in Los Angeles & seems to need this now. He has considerable property but it is more or less encumbered. I am sure I will get it back in a year but I would send it just as quickly if I knew I would not.

That dollar amount equals about $75,000 in today's money, which Darrow instructed his son to send to one of Darrow's so-called "dearest friends" who doesn't appear in Darrow lore other than that fateful jury service.

Given that Darrow left Los Angeles after the hung jury, not to return, how did he develop such a close friendship with one of his jurors, close enough that he felt compelled to contribute financial aid to the man? Was this the juror he was reputed to have bribed in the bribery trial? Was this what Earl Rogers was referring to when he said of Darrow, "Oh, that son of a bitch has been up to his old tricks again"? Did this juror have that bribery to hold over Darrow's head as blackmail or to extort money from him even long after the trial?

John A. Farrell believes this begs two additional questions: "Did Darrow bribe a juror while on trial for bribing jurors. If so, what does that say about his willingness to join in the McNamara bribery plot?" [cxxxii]

John Brown's Body

Geoffrey Cowan suggests that "Darrow may actually have believed that, under some circumstances, bribery was the right course, the moral course of action." [cxxxiii] That mindset, he says, is reflected in his support of the violent and merciless tactics of the abolitionist John Brown. If he could support Brown's violence, and in turn the violent tactics of labor unions, it's not a great leap to believe that Darrow could also believe in doing whatever he deemed necessary, illegal or not, to win a case.

His end-justifies-the-means mentality certainly suggests that, in his mind, he would be able to justify bribing jurors if it ensured the acquittal of his "victim" clients, the McNamaras, or for that matter, himself. While his views on Brown are certainly not dispositive of the "did he or didn't he" conundrum, they are at least worth looking at.

Unquestionably Darrow believed in the righteousness of the cause of labor in its battle against the forces of capital. In addition to his crusade against the death penalty, he tilted at windmills of big business and their oppression of the working man.

He released a pamphlet in 1904 outlining the evils of the open shop and advocated for the closed shop, the demand for which, he said, "is nothing but the means that experience has shown is essential to protect the liberty labor unions have won and give some vantage ground for other triumphs yet to come."

In 1912, he gave a Labor Day address in San Francisco, in which he continued to justify the conduct of his clients, the McNamaras. "I believe that J.B. McNamara and others of his kind are simply victims in a great industrial conflict, and that their act was not personal, but social and industrial, and for this they are not to blame."

In an address to a union convention in 1922, he discussed the "ideal of a labor union."

Darrow, himself, gave insights into his thoughts on Brown in a speech that he delivered to the Radical Club Forum in San Francisco on December 12, 1912. Brown's mind, Darrow said, was "so strong, his sense of justice so keen, and his sympathies so deep...." Of men of this ilk, he said, "Lucky are the sons of man when these prophets are born upon the earth."

He compared the battle against slavery to the uphill labor battles against overwhelming odds of his own time. "Then, as ever, officials and power and wealth were with slavery, and the dreamer and idealist with liberty." Strong action was necessary. "Guerilla warfare was the order of the day." Anything less, like the underground railroad, while beneficial, was not sufficient. "To John Brown this was like bailing out the ocean with a dipper. This might free a slave, but it would not abolish slavery.

The system must be destroyed."

He even compared Brown to Jesus Christ, yet another example of Darrow's flirtation with tenets of the same Christianity he so despised. While Brown offered up his own life for the abolition cause, the ones for whom he fought "looked blindly on as their masters strangled him to death."

This was an old story, Darrow said, "old as the human race. Ever and ever hangs the devoted Christ upon the cross, and ever with faint heart and dumb mouths and palsied hands, the poor for whom he toiled, stand helpless and watch their savior die." But John Brown, he said, "was right; he was an instrument in the hands of a higher power."

It's easy to see how that justification of the brutality of John Brown might translate into a belief in the ends-justify-the-means methods of Darrow's own cause. What others might see as wrong—like, for example, bribing jurors—was actually just a necessary step on the road to a greater good. It was almost as if he were channeling the future Barry Goldwater, who said, "Extremism in defense of liberty is no vice. Moderation in pursuit of liberty is no virtue."

And in this defense and pursuit, the agnostic/atheist Clarence Darrow argued that he was, essentially, an instrument of the same God he denied.

> *Of all the foolish questions asked by idle tongue, the most childish is to ask if a great work should not have been done some other way.... He who accepts results must accept with them every act that leads to the result. And all who think must accept all results. To deny destiny is to deny God, and all the forces that move the universe of which man is so small a part. To condemn an act as wrong assumes that the laws of justice laid down by the weak minds of man are the same as the laws of the universe, which stretch over infinite matter, infinite time and space, and regards nothing less than all.*

Nearing his conclusion, Darrow quoted scripture out of context, and incompletely. "Long ago it was said, 'By their fruits ye shall know them.' The fruits of John Brown's life are plain for all to see...." While quoting *Matthew* 7:20, Darrow failed to tie it in to *Galatians* 5:22-23 (KJV), which says: "But the fruit of the Spirit is love, joy, peace, longsuffering, gentleness, goodness, faith, meekness, temperance: against such there is no law." Hard to see any of that fruit in Brown's bloody trek across Kansas and other parts of the South, but Darrow apparently saw it as holy.

Cowan summed up Darrow's attitude this way:

> *The illegal and sometimes violent acts of his clients were justified by the importance of their cause, the purity of their purpose, and the power of their oppressors; by analogy, his unorthodox legal strategies were given legitimacy by the abusive power of industry and government.*[cxxxiv]

It's hard to argue with that observation.

"I'm going to kill myself."

The most compelling bit of evidence may be this: Darrow showed up at Mary Field's apartment on Ingraham Street one night in December of 1911.[33] It was raining and, from the pockets of his raincoat, he extracted a bottle of whiskey from one side and a revolver from the other.

"I'm going to kill myself," he said. "They're going to indict

---

[33] One source says it was January 28, 1912 (*American Iconoclast*), but others place it in December of 1911 (*The People v. Clarence Darrow*, *American Lightning*, and *Clarence Darrow: Attorney for the Damned*). Darrow biographers Arthur and Lila Weinberg (*Clarence Darrow: A Sentimental Rebel*) simply refer to it as "[l]ate one rainy evening...." The December 1911 date seems more accurate since Bert Franklin was arrested on November 28, 1911, while Darrow retained Earl Rogers to represent him on January 26, 1912, with the indictment returned three days later.

me for bribing the McNamara jury. I can't stand the disgrace." Drawing on all her powers of persuasion, Mary was able to convince him to spare his own life and fight for his reputation. But suicidal depression followed him thereafter.

At one point, the Darrow-led defense team wanted Larry Sullivan, the detective asked to kidnap John Harrington so he couldn't testify, to destroy evidence harmful to the McNamaras and fabricate favorable evidence.

In Erskine Wood's words, Sullivan was requested "to frame up or carry out a plan looking to the defense and acquittal of the accused men regardless of the facts." [cxxxv] When the prosecution tried to flip Sullivan, he fled to, and hid out in, Mexico under the alias "Malachi." Upon later returning to Los Angeles, he told Wood, in reference to Darrow, "I have never seen a man fall away as fast as has Darrow. I honestly think that Darrow will either plead guilty or commit suicide."

Even correspondence found in the papers of the American Federation of Labor reference Darrow's depression, including one that said, "I know him [Darrow] so well that it would not surprise me to know that he has committed suicide any day, for they surely have the goods on him and he knows it."

A logical conclusion that can be drawn from Darrow's suicidal depression is that he was not so much afraid of being indicted, but rather of being convicted. Given his years of defending those accused of crimes, it seems unlikely that mere allegation of criminal conduct, or even an indictment, would drive him to the brink of despair. It might well be termed "consciousness of guilt."

Notwithstanding his repeated protestations of having a clear conscience, it appears that he actually had a guilty conscience.

If he truly believed he had done nothing wrong, and that the end justified the means, to even contemplate suicide, much less acquire a gun to carry out the deed, is mystifying.

PART THREE:
The Smartest Guys in the Room—Leopold and Loeb

This is a Christian community...and yet they would hang these boys in a Christian community. Let me ask this court, is there any doubt about whether these boys would be safe in the hands of the founder of the Christian religion?
—Clarence Darrow

Mike Farris

Chapter Eight: A Fair Fee

My sympathies always went out to the weak, the suffering, and the poor.
—Clarence Darrow

AS WE MOVE from the earlier cases on Darrow's resume into the wind-up of his career, we see that, while his overt dishonesty, and in fact criminality, may have waned—though it never fully disappeared[34]—his bombastic rhetoric kicked into high gear.

It probably reached its zenith in the twelve-hour argument he made over the course of three days in the Leopold and Loeb case. Several terms immediately leap to mind when considering Darrow's courtroom arguments in that case, as well as in the final chapter of his career, Hawaii's Massie Case—although four hours and twenty minutes in that swan song pales next to Leopold and Loeb.

Merriam-Webster defines windbaggery as "pompous meaningless talk" and blowhard as "an arrogantly boastful or opinionated person." It defines bloviation (the noun form of the verb "bloviate") as speaking or writing "verbosely and windily."

I've already noted that President Warren Harding once

---

[34] As the Bible he rejected says, "[A] leopard cannot change its spots." *Jeremiah* 13:23.

defined it as "the art of speaking for as long as the occasion warrants and saying nothing." William Gibbs McAdoo, son-in-law of President Woodrow Wilson, called it "an army of pompous phrases moving over the landscape in search of an idea."

Paint Clarence Darrow as the poster child for all three terms. Make that four terms: sophistry might also be an apt description. Sophistry is defined as subtly deceptive reasoning that seems plausible on its face, but that is actually unsound, meant to deceive.

Nowhere are all four of these terms more readily demonstrated than in Darrow's three-day, twelve-hour closing argument in the Leopold and Loeb case. It was also a case that challenged several of the basic tenets of the legend that Darrow had fought so hard to create.

Money, Money, Money, Money

In 1924, when Clarence Darrow undertook the defense of Richard Loeb and Nathan Leopold for the so-called "thrill killing" of Loeb's 14-year-old cousin (some sources call him a "distant" cousin, others a second cousin, while at least one disputes any relation) Bobby Franks, his reputation at the time, and largely still today, is that he was a lawyer standing up for the underdogs, even at his own financial expense. We know that was Darrow's reputation because, as I said at the outset of this book, Darrow told us so.

So, imagine my surprise when researching Hawaii's Massie Case for my book *A Death in the Islands*, to find out that Darrow didn't represent the weak and the poor in that case, but instead he defended the powerful and rich, accused of murdering the weak and the poor—a young Hawaiian man—and attempting to dispose of his body in the ocean.

He was paid $40,000, close to a million in today's dollars, for a few months' work. But that was at a time when his own finances had been devastated by the Depression and he was forced to come out of retirement for one last case for financial reasons. He admitted as much in his autobiography, "...the so-called 'depression' had swept away practically all the savings that I thought I had for keeping me comfortable to the end, and I needed the fee." cxxxvi

So, I suppose we can forgive that lapse, right? I mean, after all, he *needed* it.

But let's not forget his fee we discussed earlier in the Haywood case, reputed to be anywhere from $35,000 to $50,000 in 1907 money, approaching a million-and-a-half in today's dollars.

A pretty good payday if you can get it.

And also there was his insistence on a large fee in the McNamara case, demanding that the American Federation of Labor guarantee him a fund of at least $200,000 to finance the defense—plus, apparently, a bribe or two—and allow him to retain at least $50,000 of that as his fee. That last number is about $1.57 million dollars today. Of course, for that one he had to be lured from his comfortable practice in Chicago to again take up the mantel of labor, and it seemed when he accepted the engagement that it might well take a couple of years.

Still, again, a pretty good payday, especially for supposedly acting on principle, alone.

But the Leopold and Loeb case didn't have the same kinds of excuses attached to them as did Massie—or even McNamara, where he contended that he was merely fighting fire with fire. It did have a cause, though: Darrow's passionate opposition to the death penalty and the promotion of his belief that people lacked free will and, thus, shouldn't be held accountable for their actions. And, fortunately for him, the parents of Nathan Leopold and Richard Loeb were especially well-heeled[35] and were able to pay the fee he demanded.

---

[35] Multi-millionaires at a time when a million dollars was a lot of money. According to various sources, Loeb's father was reputedly worth anywhere between $3 million to $10 million, at the time.

He wrote to his son Paul on June 25, 1924, "As to fees I will of course get a fair & substantial fee, as yet I have no idea how much time it will take. The families are fine people and will do what is right & of course you know I will." [cxxxvii] Later, after the fact, he wrote in his autobiography, "I felt that I would get a fair fee if I went into the case," but he protested that "money never influenced my stand one way or the other." [cxxxviii]

It's always nice, though, when the "weak, the suffering, and the poor" have money. Or at least when their parents do. After all, we know that, in Darrow's lexicon, "fair" equates to "substantial," particularly when dealing with "fine people" who will do "what is right."

I Can't Think without my Glasses

So what, factually, was the Leopold and Loeb case all about to draw Darrow's attention?

On the morning of May 22, 1924, Tony Minke, born Antoni Mankowski in Poland before immigrating to the United States and Americanizing his name, finished his night shift at American Maize Products Company and headed across a prairie area surrounding Wolf Lake, near Chicago.

While walking along a drainage ditch between Wolf Lake and Hyde Lake, he spotted what appeared to be a body in a concrete culvert. It was the naked body, lying facedown, of 14-year-old Bobby Franks, who had last been seen the day before with a group of boys playing baseball after classes had let out from Harvard School for Boys in the elite Kenwood area of Chicago.

With the assistance of two railroad workers, Bobby's body was extricated from the culvert and turned over. Ugly gashes marred his forehead, and both his face and genitals appeared rust-colored.

It would later be determined that Bobby had been struck on the forehead with a blunt object, with an additional two skull-penetrating blows to the back of his head. According to the autopsy report, he also bore defensive wounds on his face, shoulders, and buttocks, as if he had struggled with his assailant.

All indications were that the wounds had been inflicted prior to death. The report indicated that these wounds bled, which meant the heart was still pumping when the injuries were inflicted.

The report also indicated that acid had been poured on Bobby's face and genitals, although there was no apparent explanation for its use. However, the report concluded that Bobby had not died from any of those wounds, but rather had suffocated as a result of an ether-soaked rag being stuffed into his throat.

Fumes from the ether discolored his throat and found their way into his lungs. Because there was no water in his lungs, the report concluded that Bobby was dead before being forced, facedown, into the culvert.

The one detail that seemed particularly outrageous, and which led to much speculation that was ultimately never proven, was that Bobby's "rectum was dilated, and would admit easily one middle finger," though there was no sign of "recent forcible dilation." The coroner refused to draw any conclusions one way or the other, asserting that "it is difficult to determine this. Attempts to attack him might have been made, and some forms of attacks accomplished without leaving external evidence of violence." This became an issue at trial when the prosecution strongly implied Bobby had been sexually assaulted, but that any seminal fluid would have been washed away by water in the culvert.

Bookmark the preceding paragraphs in your minds. We'll revisit them when we discuss Darrow's argument that the killing of Bobby Franks was one of the "least dastardly and cruel of any that I have known anything about" because it was "all over in fifteen minutes…and he probably never knew it or thought of it" and he "suffered very little."

Let your outrage fester for a while until we return to this nonsense later.

A pair of eyeglasses was also discovered about thirty feet or so away from the culvert, presumably belonging to the young boy. When police delivered the body to a nearby funeral home, the funeral director, also assuming they belonged to the boy, placed the glasses on Bobby's face. This would initially cause some confusion as to the boy's identity since Bobby Franks, who at this point had been missing since the night before, did not wear glasses.

That prior night, Bobby's parents had been alarmed by his failure to come home after school. He missed dinner, which was unlike him, then still had not been heard from on into the night. His parents called around to several of his friends' homes, but nobody had seen him since earlier that afternoon when he had been playing baseball with some classmates. Well, maybe not playing—he was somewhat slight of build, only five feet tall and one hundred pounds, and not much of an athlete—but instead he was umpiring the sandlot game.

Later, during questioning by police, a classmate named Irvin Hartman, Jr., told of having seen Bobby about a half-block ahead of him, apparently walking home following the baseball game. Irving said he was distracted by shrubs and flowers in a nearby yard when a car blew past him. When he looked ahead again, he no longer saw Bobby.

As night fell, Franks family friend Samuel Ettelson, a lawyer and former senator, arrived shortly after nine. He and Jacob Franks, Bobby's father, retraced the route to the school, even climbing inside an unlocked window at the building and scouring the passageways. At about 10:30 PM, while Jacob and Ettelson were away, the phone rang. Flora Franks answered.

"May I speak to Jacob Franks," a male voice said.

"He's not at home," Flora said. "This is his wife."

"Your son has been kidnapped. He is all right. Further news in the morning."

"Who is it?" a flustered Flora asked.

"George Johnson."

Then the caller hung up.

Upon the return home of her husband and Ettelson, Flora

told them about the call. Ettelson telephoned the phone company and asked for a trace on incoming calls, then he and Jacob went to the police station to report the missing boy and the mysterious phone call.

That same night, about 1:30 in the morning, a watchman on patrol in Kenwood saw a red car—he couldn't tell the make—drive past the intersection of 49th Street and Greenwood Avenue. He heard a loud metallic sound as it passed. Following up, the watchman found a chisel on the street, wrapped on one end with tape, while the other end—the business end—seemed smeared with dried blood.

At 9:00 AM the next day, May 22, Jacob Franks received a special delivery piece of mail. Typed on good quality paper, despite crude handwriting on the envelope, the enclosed letter said:

Dear Sir:

As you no doubt know by this time your son has been kidnapped. Allow us to assure you that he is at present well and safe. You need not fear any physical harm for him provided you live up carefully to the following instructions and such others as you will receive by future communications. Should you, however, disobey our instructions, even slightly, his death will be the penalty.

1. For obvious reasons make absolutely no attempt to communicate with either the police authorities or any private agency. Should you already have communicated with the police, allow them to continue their investigations, but do not mention this letter.

2. Secure before noon today $10,000. This money must be composed entirely of old bills of the following denominations: $2,000 in $20 bills; $8,000 in $50 bills. The money must be old. Any attempt to include new or marked bills will render the entire venture futile.

> 3. The money should be placed in a large cigar box or, if such is impossible, in a heavy cardboard box securely closed and wrapped in white paper. The wrapping paper should be sealed at all openings with sealing wax.
>
> 4. Have the money thus prepared as directed above and remain at home after 1 o'clock p.m. See that the telephone is not in use. You will receive a future communication instructing you as to your future course.
>
> As a final word of warning, this is a strictly commercial proposition, and we are prepared to put our threats into execution should we have reasonable ground to believe that you have committed an infraction of the above instructions. However, should you carefully follow out our instructions to the letter, we can assure you that your son will be safely returned to you within six hours of our receipt of the money.
>
> Yours truly, George Johnson

The ransom letter offered a clue for police. A typewriting expert said that the letter had probably been typed on an Underwood portable, and that it had defects peculiar to it—specifically in the lower case "t" and "f"—that would allow the letter to be matched to a specific machine, if it could be found.

Before the arrival of the ransom demand, though, the only clue seemed to be the pair of glasses discovered near Bobby's body. When Jacob Franks received a call from a reporter who had visited the funeral home to which the body had been delivered, the reporter advised that the boy there, although he fit the general description of Bobby, wore glasses. That greatly relieved Jacob, since his son did not.

Still, he wanted to make absolutely sure, so he dispatched his brother-in-law, Edwin Gresham, to the funeral home to confirm. Upon his arrival, Gresham made the grim discovery that this was, indeed, his little nephew, leaving him with the unfortunate task of informing Jacob, which he did by phone.

Minutes later, the phone rang again at the Franks house. The caller, who identified himself as "Johnson," spoke to Jacob. Although Jacob already knew that Bobby was dead, he kept that information to himself as he listened to instructions from "Johnson."

Johnson told Jacob that a yellow cab would arrive soon at the Franks house to pick him up, along with the ransom, and take him to a drugstore at 1465 East 63rd Street. He was to wait there for another call, this one to the drugstore's pay phone, which would provide him with specific instructions for delivering the ransom.

A screw-up occurred at this stage. Jacob failed to write down the address and, when the cab driver arrived at the Franks household, no one knew where he was supposed to go with his fare. Ettelson asked who had sent him and what his destination was, but the driver was ignorant. Ettelson paid him, and he left without Jacob.

At shortly past three in the afternoon, the pay phone rang at the drugstore—twice. First time, an employee answered. When asked if Jacob Franks was there, he replied that there was "no Mr. Franks here." The second time it rang, the druggist answered. Same question and answer ensued. After all, because Franks had failed to write down the address, he didn't know where to go to receive the call. That might have been traumatic if his failure to take the ransom call led to the kidnappers killing his son, but Franks already knew his son was dead. Ultimately, no ransom was ever delivered, but that failure was of no effect.

A private funeral was held at the Franks home for Bobby on Sunday, May 25, where his body lay in a white coffin in the library. The room overflowed with floral arrangements, but one wreath caught everyone's eye: it consisted of tiger lilies and bore a card that said, "Sympathy from Mr. Johnson." [36]

---

[36] A few years later, a young Japanese man in Hawaii named Myles

By now, police had two decent clues to follow up on, but no identifiable suspects. One was the type on the ransom letters, with the defective "t" and "f," but as of yet they had no typewriter to match it to.

The other, and best, clue was the pair of eyeglasses found at the scene. Once it became apparent that they didn't belong to Bobby, the next logical alternative was to consider that, perhaps, they belonged to the perpetrator and had fallen out of a pocket during the commission of the crime. Although the lenses were a common prescription, the frame turned out to have a distinctive, new-fangled hinge manufactured by the Bobrow Optical Company in Brooklyn.

Only one Chicago firm sold glasses with that particular hinge, Almer & Coe, and it had sold exactly three pairs. One of the purchasers was an attorney, who was away in Europe. The second was a woman who still had hers and showed them to police.

The third was Nathan Leopold, Jr.

You Have the Right to Remain Silent

Leopold, known to his family as "Babe," the son of a Chicago millionaire, had graduated from high school at the age of fifteen, then from the University of Chicago at the age of eighteen, and was planning to attend Harvard Law School later that year.

Considered by many to be a genius, he read multiple languages and was a locally known expert on birds, often leading classes and field trips for ornithology students. At first blush, he seemed an unlikely suspect for the crime—something that

---

Fukunaga would emulate the murder of Bobby Franks by kidnapping and killing 10-year-old Gill Jamieson, son of an executive of the Hawaiian Trust Company. He patterned his crime after the Chicago crime to a tee. That included sending a ransom demand after having already killed the victim and plagiarizing the language of the Franks letter. He emulated the crime right down to using a chisel to bludgeon Gil to death and later sending flowers to his victim's funeral, with the words "With sincere sympathy" on the accompanying card.

would soon change—but the presence of glasses that appeared to belong to him compelled at least some initial questioning.

When police brought Leopold in for questioning, he admitted having similar glasses, but he denied losing them—at first. He also acknowledged that he owned a typewriter, but that it was a Hammond, not an Underwood, and he denied owning a portable typewriter of any sort. As for the evening in question, he claimed to have been out drinking with his friend, Richard Loeb, who just happened to be a cousin to Bobby Franks and who lived across the street from the Franks family.

Loeb, another self-proclaimed genius, was the son of a multimillionaire executive at Sear, Roebuck & Company. He and Leopold had been friends for a few years, with suspicions among classmates that they were "perverts," a common term at the time for homosexuals.

Loeb graduated from the University of Michigan just shy of his eighteenth birthday making him, at the time, the youngest graduate in the university's history. Leopold and Loeb would both place themselves close to the investigation, supposedly offering helpful information, particularly to reporters. At one point, Loeb told reporters, "If I were going to murder anyone, I would murder just such a cocky little son of a bitch as Bobby Franks."

That seemed odd to those who heard it. Soon enough, police and prosecutors would learn more oddities; it would be all they needed to know about this "genius" duo.

Detectives drove Leopold home to produce his eyeglasses, but—wouldn't you know it?—damned if he couldn't find them. All he could produce was an empty glasses case marked "Almer Coe & Co." He reiterated his denial of having a portable typewriter, but the Leopold family maid said that, in addition to the Hammond typewriter, she had seen a portable typewriter in the library just weeks prior.

It would ultimately turn out to be a typewriter Leopold and Loeb had stolen from a fraternity house at the University of Michigan. That burglary was but one of multiple crimes the two would be suspected of but for which they were never charged. A group of those crimes became known as the "ABCD" crimes and included three murders and one abduction and castration of a taxi driver. Newspapers referred to the last one as the "gland robbery."

In searching the house and Leopold's room, police uncovered bottles of strychnine, arsenic, and ether—remember the ether-soaked rag that had been stuffed down Bobby's throat?—as well as a .32 Remington automatic and a .38 Remington. But one of the most bizarre things that came out of the questioning was an answer that Leopold gave to a question posed to him by state's attorney Robert Crowe, who asked if there was any difference between the death of a dog and a man.

"No, sir," Leopold said.

Because Leopold had implicated Richard Loeb, or "Dickie," as he was called, in his alibi, police questioned Loeb, as well, in a separate room from where Leopold was being questioned. But Loeb failed to mention being with Leopold on the day in question, despite Leopold having given his name as an alibi.

Upon driving Loeb home and searching his room, police found something that struck them as exceptionally bizarre. In Loeb's desk, they found two letters written to him from Leopold the prior autumn. After returning from the Loeb house for more questioning of the two, the letters led to this particularly interesting Q and A between Leopold and prosecutor Crowe:

> **Q:** *Did you ever commit any act of perversion on either one of these boys* [Richard Loeb or Dick Rubel]?
> **A:** *No, sir.*
> **Q:** *Or they on you?*
> **A:** *No, sir.*
> **Q:** *You are positive of that?*
> **A:** *I am positive of that.*
> **Q:** *There wasn't any rumor around that you had?*
> **A:** *Yes, sir.*

Q: *Of some act of perversion on Loeb?*
A: *Yes, sir.*

Crowe then followed up on language in one of the letters which said: "I do want to warn you that in case you deem it advisable to discontinue our friendship, that in both our interests extreme care must be used. The motif of a 'falling out of cocksuckers?'"

In other words, Leopold was concerned that, if he and Loeb broke off their relationship, it would be viewed by others as simply a falling out between homosexuals. Leopold told Crowe:

> [T]hat refers to the rumor which was spread about the two of us, as I mentioned in 1921, which was very prevalent, as a result of which Dick and I were very careful when we were alone together for over a year, in fact, we were very seldom alone together, and when we were, we took a chaperon [sic] along.

As Crowe interpreted the letter, Leopold was contending that he and Loeb should merely pretend to be friends, "for appearance's sake."

Leopold confirmed that interpretation. "Otherwise, there would have been a great deal of talk."

"Cocksuckers falling out?" Crowe asked.

"Yes."

Because, Crowe pressed, "There had been rumors that you were a cocksucker?"

"Yes, sir."

The prosecution would later attempt to make much of this "perversion," particularly in light of the autopsy report that suggested the possibility that Bobby Franks had been sodomized. As we shall see, Darrow would latch on to this, as well, in his argument for leniency in sentencing.

It's important to note that this questioning all occurred

without the boys having the benefit of counsel present, but this was an era that preceded key U.S. Supreme Court cases that recognized certain fundamental rights in regard to counsel: *Escobedo v. Illinois*,[37] which held that the right to have counsel present attaches during a custodial interrogation, wasn't decided until 1964, and *Miranda v. Arizona*,[38] which requires that suspects be advised of their rights and that questioning cease if a suspect invoked the right to counsel, came two years after that.

While the two boys were being questioned in separate rooms, Loeb broke first. When questioners confronted him with evidence, such as the glasses belonging to Leopold and the fact that Leopold's handwriting matched the handwriting on the ransom envelope, Loeb cried out, "My God, my God." He burst into tears, crying, "This is terrible." Then he poured out the story of how the two had planned and carried out the crime.

Once Leopold, in the next room, was told that Dickie Loeb was singing like The Mormon Tabernacle Choir, he decided it was time to come clean, himself, a decision likely motivated by a desire to whitewash his involvement in the murder of Bobby Franks. Not to exculpate himself, mind you, but to shift the blame for the actual killing to his companion.

"Well," he said, "if Loeb is talking, I will tell you the real truth."

He then poured out his story.

The two boys told remarkably consistent accounts. They ultimately even directed police to the Jackson Park lagoon, where they had disposed of the Underwood portable typewriter; divers recovered it.

After detailing the logistics of the ransom plan, Leopold said, "The next problem was getting the victim to kill." Though there had been prior discussion—such as whether to pick a girl, an adult, or even one of their own friends—"we decided to take the most likely looking subject that came our way."

---

[37] 378 U.S. 478 (1964).
[38] 384 U.S. 436 (1966).

To Bobby Franks's eternal bad luck, he was that subject.

According to Leopold, he was driving the car they had rented for this purpose—it wouldn't do to be seen in one of their own cars[39]—while Loeb sat in the back seat.

They stopped beside Bobby on the sidewalk and offered him a ride home, but Bobby demurred. Then his cousin told him to get in the car because "I want to ask you about a certain tennis racket." Once Bobby made the fatal mistake of getting into the car, his fate was sealed.

"As soon as we turned the corner, Richard placed his one hand over Robert's mouth to stifle his outcries, with his right beat him on the head several times with a chisel, especially prepared for the purpose. The boy did not succumb as readily as we had believed, so for fear of being observed, Richard seized him, pulled him into the back seat. Here he forced a cloth into his mouth. Apparently the boy died instantly by suffocation shortly thereafter."

Leopold said that they then drove him to the spot where the body was ultimately found, which happened to be an area he was familiar with from having conducted birding expeditions there. "We had previously removed the shoes, socks and trousers of the boy, leaving the shoes and belt by the side of the road, concealed in the grass." Then, after arriving at their destination, "[W]e completed the disrobing; then in an attempt to render identification more difficult, poured hydrochloric acid over the face and body. Then we placed the body into the drain pipe, pushed it in as far as we could. We gathered up all the clothes, placed them in the robe."

And then, the crucial mistake. "Apparently at this point the glasses fell from my pocket." Glasses he ultimately admitted were his, even after his initial denials.

In answering follow-up questions, Leopold denied striking or choking Bobby, though he admitted the "general plan" had

---

[39] Just one of the little "details" that would trip them up when police traced the rental car.

always been to murder him, hide the body, and collect the money. They had to kill him, of course, so "he couldn't expose us." But he placed the onus of the actual killing on Richard Loeb.

For his part, Loeb told a remarkably similar story, with a few variances in minor details. There was, though, a significant variance in one key respect: who actually killed Bobby Franks. According to Loeb's account, he, not Leopold was driving the car and Leopold was in the back seat. After inducing Bobby into the front seat so Loeb could "talk to him about a tennis racket," he turned the corner and "Leopold reached his arm around young Franks, grabbed his mouth and hit him over the head with the chisel. I believe he hit him several times. I do not know the exact number. He began to bleed and was not entirely unconscious, he was moaning."

Leopold then "grabbed Franks and carried him over the back of the front seat and threw him on a rug in the car. He then took one of the rags and gagged him by sticking it down his throat, I believe."

They would hold to their respective stories throughout the case. Years later, after Loeb had been murdered in a prison shower, Leopold continued to advance his version.

With Loeb no longer around to contradict him, he even came up with a reason for why Loeb had steadfastly maintained that Leopold committed the actual murder. In his memoir, Leopold wrote that Loeb said, "I figure it will be much easier for each of our families if they believe the other fellow is the actual murderer. I know [Loeb's mother] feels less terrible than she might thinking you did it." [cxxxix]

In a minor deviation from Leopold, who said that Bobby suffocated "instantly" from the rag being stuffed down his throat, Loeb said that Bobby was merely "unconscious" at this point. By the time they reached the dump site at the culvert, though, "the boy was quite dead when we took him there."

Furthermore, Loeb said, pointing his finger at this partner in crime, "I am fully convinced that neither the idea nor the act would have occurred to me, had it not been for the suggestion and stimulus of Leopold. Furthermore, I do not believe that I would have been capable of having killed Franks."

In a fairly unusual bit of procedure, after each of the two had confessed, police brought them together into the same room and read their respective confessions to the other, to allow them to make any corrections they deemed necessary. Though both of them stuck to most of the details they had already given, the pair went after each other on the key point of who had actually killed Bobby. According to the May 31, 1924, *Chicago Times*, "They cursed each other, shouted hysterical charges and denials and threats."

Leopold leveled the first broadside.

"At the time the Franks boy entered our car, I was driving, not Mr. Loeb, and Mr. Loeb was in the back seat. It was Mr. Loeb struck him with the chisel, and not I." For clarification, if there was any confusion as to whom he was pointing the finger, he added that the whole thing was "his [Loeb's] plan, and it was he who did the act."

When Loeb had his chance to clear up any errors in his compadre's confession, he blamed the whole idea on Leopold. When State's Attorney Robert Crowe asked, "Who hit him [Bobby] with the chisel?" Loeb answered, "Nathan Leopold, Junior."

It was only logical, Loeb said. Bobby was his cousin, and he didn't know Leopold, so he would have gotten into the car next to Loeb. If Loeb had been in the back seat, the logic went, Bobby would have crawled into the back seat with him. But since they both agreed that Bobby got into the front passenger seat, that must mean that Loeb was driving, with Leopold in the rear seat to administer the blows with the chisel.

Not so, Leopold countered, returning Loeb's volley in the debate. See, he said, "I opened the door to let the Franks boy in," who clambered into the passenger seat, but then from the back seat, Loeb "leaned over forward and spoke to the boy from the back. I was driving the car, I am absolutely positive."

In the short run, it really didn't matter who drove and who

Blowhard

struck the first blow. Arrested and charged with the crime, the prosecution asserted that both men were equally culpable for the brutal murder of Bobby Franks and both deserved to be hung.

But Clarence Darrow wouldn't see it that way. In fact, he would later argue that neither one of them was culpable. And it really wasn't even all that brutal a murder, he said. In fact, as quoted above, he would state, "[U]nder all fair rules and measurements, this was one of the least dastardly and cruel of any that I have known anything about."

Tell that to Bobby Franks.

Mike Farris

Chapter Nine: My Kingdom for a Lawyer

Could this scarecrow know much about the law? He didn't look as if he knew anything.
—Nathan Leopold

WHEN CLARENCE DARROW arrived on the scene, he was more than happy to take on the cause of opposing the death penalty.

> *No client of mine had ever been put to death, and I felt that it would almost, not quite, kill me if it should ever happen. I have never been able to read a story of an execution. I always left town if possible on the day of a hanging. I am strongly—call it morbidly, who will—against killing.*[40]

Nathan Leopold described his first meeting in jail with Darrow this way:

> *My first impression was horror. For on the other side of*

---

[40] Except, as we'll see later, he was okay with killing in the Massie Case, where he recognized it as a husband's right to kill anyone who assaulted his wife—even if the assault never really happened.

the bars stood one of the least prepossessing, one of the least impressive-looking human beings I have ever seen. The day was warm, and Mr. Darrow was wearing a light seersucker jacket. Nothing wrong with that, surely. Only this one looked as if he had slept in it.

His shirt was wrinkled, too, and he must have had eggs for breakfast that morning. I could see the vestiges. Or perhaps he hadn't changed shirts since the day before. His tie was askew....

He wore no hat that first day, and his unruly shock of lusterless, almost mousy hair kept falling over his right eye. Impatiently, he'd brush it back with his hand from time to time.

Even his face, that face which I was later to see as majestic—the strong jutting nose, the broad, calm forehead, the rugged contours of cheeks and chin—didn't strike me as majestic then. It took time for the nobility of his appearance to sink in. That first time I saw him I was taken aback. He looked for all the world like an innocent hayseed, a bumpkin who might have difficulty finding his way around the city. Could this be the renowned Darrow (for I had heard much of his reputation in the last twenty-four hours)? It didn't seem possible. Could this scarecrow know anything about the law? He didn't look as if he knew much of anything! [cxl]

Maybe Darrow wasn't exactly happy to take on the case, at least not to hear him tell it. Rather, he saw it more as a duty. At 68 years old, he was "weary" from fighting legal wars, a voice crying in the wilderness, "tired of standing in the lean and lonely front line facing the greatest enemy that ever confronted man—public opinion." [cxli] Furthermore, as he pronounced in his later closing argument, the responsibility for the lives of the two young men "is almost too great for anyone to assume, but we lawyers can no more choose than the court can choose."

That last line is, of course, false. This was not a court

appointment, so he was free to turn down the case if he had wanted.

So how, exactly, did he manage to become ensnared in the case?

You Must Save our Two Boys!

In the early morning of June 2, a group of men, including Richard Loeb's uncle, Jacob, buzzed Darrow's doorbell at his Chicago apartment, rousing him from slumber. Despite Ruby Darrow's protestations that her husband not be awakened, the men insisted on speaking to him.

According to one account, they actually forced their way into his bedroom where "[t]he leader of the group, Richard Loeb's uncle, flung his arms around Darrow's shoulders, exclaiming, 'Thank heavens you are here! No one else can save us. If you had been away we would have been ruined. You must save our two boys!"

Those words were written by biographer Irving Stone in his book *Clarence Darrow for the Defense*.[cxlii] Stone, perhaps better known for his biographies of Michelangelo (*The Agony and the Ecstasy*) and Vincent Van Gogh (*Lust for Life*), certainly had a flair for the dramatic. One can almost imagine the teary-eyed Loeb uncle latching on to the startled and just-awakened attorney for the damned, still beneath the bedding. The pronouncement that "no one else can save us" smacks of melodrama, but the whole scene is perhaps of questionable authenticity.

Although Stone attests that his research for the book included "back files of court reports, congressional reports," he acknowledged that other main sources were "Clarence Darrow's private correspondence, family documents, manuscripts, legal briefs, notebooks and unpublished memoirs sold to me by Mrs. Darrow."

Additionally, he relied upon the "personal contributions of more than two hundred of Darrow's lifelong friends, partners, associates, and the untiring efforts of the Darrow family, in particular Mrs. Clarence (Ruby) Darrow and Paul Darrow

[Clarence Darrow's son], to enrich and authenticate every phase of Clarence Darrow's life."

In other words, the melodramatic account of Darrow's bedroom engagement came from biased sources who were likely intent on either elevating Darrow's memory or polishing his legend since his passing just three years prior to the book's publication. In fact, it probably came from just one source, Darrow's wife Ruby, as no one else was present other than the couple and the visiting entourage.

The men informed the just-awakened Darrow that "Dickie and Babe confessed this afternoon," and they pleaded, "Save their lives! Get them a life sentence instead of a death sentence. That's all we ask of you."

Then one of them said the magic words, which were probably music to Darrow's ears: "We'll pay you anything you ask." [cxliii]

And so he accepted the assignment, presumably with a big sigh.

Oh, what a burden he assumed.

In his courtroom argument, he told Judge Caverly, "I went in, to do what I could for sanity and humanity against the wave of hatred and malice that, as ever, was masquerading under its usual *nom de plume*: 'Justice.'" Clarence Darrow, standing in the breach, with no thought of himself.

As almost a footnote, he said in his autobiography, "I felt that I would get a fair fee if I went into the case, but money never influenced my stand one way or the other." [cxliv]

Quite the superhero, fighting for truth, justice, and the American way without a thought for a dollar. But let's break that "money" thing down a bit.

Affluenza

There was no actual agreement on the fee before trial, which allowed Darrow to argue to the judge that his defense in the case wasn't influenced by money. "We announced to the public that no excessive use of money would be made in this case...."

In fact, he said, the psychiatrists hired to evaluate Leopold and Loeb were receiving only a per diem equal to that paid by the State to its experts, and that he and his co-counsel had agreed to let the Chicago Bar Association set the amount of their fee.

Money was bad, he argued, so he wasn't going to let it be a factor.

> *If we fail in this defense, it will not be for lack of money. It will be on account of money. Money has been the most serious handicap that we have met. There are times when poverty is fortunate.*

This is perhaps the first documented defense using what was later termed "affluenza"—the notion that affluence, and never wanting for anything, numbed the defendants' moral compasses to the extent that they were ineffectual, if not outright broken.[41]

Despite disclaiming that money had anything to do with the case, Darrow nevertheless made repeated references to money and the wealth of his clients' families throughout his twelve-hour

---

[41] A 1997 PBS documentary called *Affluenza* posited the term as an affliction of wealth. In the book *Affluenza: The All-Consuming Epidemic* (Berrett-Koehler Publishers 2001) by John de Graaf, David Wann & Thomas H. Naylor, it is described as "a quasi-illness caused by guilt for one's own socio-economic superiority." In 2013, a Texas teenager named Ethan Couch was indicted, and tried, on four counts of intoxication manslaughter. His attorneys argued that Couch suffered from affluenza, which they described as lack of understanding of ethical and legal boundaries as a result of bad parenting by his wealthy parents. The attorneys argued, much as Darrow did in the Leopold and Loeb case, that he needed rehabilitation, not prison. A Texas judge apparently agreed, sentencing Couch to probation for the four deaths. Not long after that, Couch and his mother fled Texas to Puerto Vallarta in Mexico, though he was subsequently apprehended and returned to Texas to serve prison time, but only two years—six months per death.

argument. Money made for a good villain. For example, he claimed that the only reason Leopold and Loeb were on trial for their lives in the first place, instead of receiving an agreed-to life sentence as might have been expected had a person of lesser wealth pleaded guilty, was "[b]ecause, unfortunately, the parents have money. Nothing else." Later, he argued that they would have already been sent to a psychiatric hospital "had it not been for the wealth" of their parents.

Yet again, he argued that public pressure to hang them was "because everybody is talking about the case, and their people have money." And "[t]his tragedy has not claimed all the attention it has had on account of its atrocity. There is nothing to that. What is it? There are two reasons, and only two that I can see. First is the reputed extreme wealth of these families; not only the Loeb and Leopold families, but the Franks family, and of course, it is unusual."

Then, almost as an afterthought, he clarified the second reason for the attention as being "the fact it is weird and uncanny and motiveless."

He noted that "these two most unfortunate boys" had "every opportunity, with plenty of wealth," but cautioned that:

> *It is just as often a great misfortune to be the child of the rich as it is to be the child of the poor. Wealth has its misfortunes. Too much, too great opportunity and advantage given to a child has its misfortunes, and I am asking Your Honor to consider the rich as well as the poor.*

And:

> *The great misfortune in this terrible case is the money. That has destroyed their lives. That has fostered these illusions. That has promoted this mad act. And, if Your Honor shall doom them to die, it will be because they are the sons of the rich.*

Playing Devil's advocate, one might argue that the great misfortune in this case was actually the murder of Bobby Franks and if the judge sentenced them to die, it would be for that reason.

Darrow argued affluenza at its finest: the "most unfortunate" Leopold and Loeb had too much wealth, too much opportunity, so they couldn't help themselves when they slaughtered Bobby Franks.

But, almost obsessed with the idea of money, he didn't stop there.

> *Excessive wealth is a grievous misfortune in every step of life. When I hear foolish people talking of excessive fees in this case, it makes me ill. That there is nothing bigger in life, that it is presumed that no man lives to whom money is not the first concern, that human instincts, sympathy and kindness and charity and logic can only be used for cash. It shows how deeply money has corrupted the hearts of most men.*

Do you understand what Darrow was saying here? He was upset that people thought he was motivated in this case by money. Why, he protested (too much, perhaps), nothing could be farther from the truth. Of course, at this point, it was a little unclear how that fee arrangement was going to work out, but he still was concerned by public perception.

Though Darrow told Judge Caverly that the defense attorneys had "agreed to take such amount as the officers of the Chicago Bar Association may think is proper in this case," after the punishment hearing was over, he quoted the sum of $200,000 as the "reasonable fee" he thought he was entitled to. The Leopold and Loeb families—the "fine people" he wrote to his son who would do "what is right"—balked.

"Quoted" and "balked" are my words in interpretation of the reported facts. In an editorial note to a compilation of excerpts of various of Darrow's arguments, editor Arthur

Weinberg wrote that Darrow merely "mentioned" the $200,000 amount and that the families were "shocked." [cxlv] Not surprising, since Darrow's representation lasted approximately three months—he bragged about the yeoman's service he provided during that period, telling the Court, "I have stood here for three months as one might stand at the ocean trying to sweep back the tide"—and the value in today's dollars of $200,000 in 1924 is about $3.5 million.

He wanted more than a million dollars a month, to accomplish what would be, as we shall soon see, a foregone conclusion even without Darrow's involvement.

In a biography of Darrow published during Darrow's life, called fittingly, if not a bit on the nose, *Clarence Darrow*,[42] Charles Yale Harrison wrote that Darrow reminded the families of their agreement to submit any dispute on fee to the Chicago Bar Association.

The family protested that they would be at a disadvantage before the Bar since Darrow was, himself, a lawyer and a member of that association. The lawyer and clients ultimately reached a settlement at $70,000 in 1924 dollars, with a present value of over $1.2 million. Harrison reported that Darrow had to split his fees equally with his law firm, and he had to pay $5,000 in taxes, so that he netted a mere $30,000 for his efforts. Not the $200,000 he requested, but still more than a half million dollars in today's money for three months' service. Good work if you can get it.

Let's hear it for the weak, the suffering, and the poor.

Darrow's Bully Pulpit

Darrow used the trial as a platform for his own anti-death penalty and anti-punishment views as much as he did to defend his clients. He wrote in his autobiography that he could not

---

[42] Published by Jonathan Cape & Harrison Smith in 1931. Makes you wonder if Harrison took lessons from Darrow's own on-the-nose title, *The Story of My Life,* for his autobiography.

"imagine why men who think themselves civilized build cells" and that "[p]unishment as punishment is not admissible unless the offender had the freewill to select his course."

Darrow believed that a person's conduct was due to one of two circumstances, natural equipment or training and opportunity. If the cause of wrongdoing "is natural equipment, then surely no credit or blame should attach to the individual. If due to training, the individual is no more responsible for that."[cxlvi]

In other words, no fault either way.

He put it another way in his debate with New York judge Alfred J. Talley on capital punishment, held in the Manhattan Opera House on September 23, 1924, less than two weeks after sentence was pronounced on Nathan Leopold and Richard Loeb:

> *All people are products of two things, and two things only—their heredity and their environment. And they act in exact accord with the heredity which they took from all the past, and for which they are in no wise responsible, and the environment, which reaches out to the farthest limit of all life that can influence them.*

His views on capital punishment were equally as strong as his views on lack of free will.

> *Only one thing is certain about capital punishment or its effect, that it is administered for no reason but deep and fixed hatred of the individual and an abiding thirst for revenge.*

It was not a deterrent, he believed.

> *No one can find any facts to prove that capital punishment has any effect toward preventing killing; no intelligent person disputes that we have more murders and capital punishment than any European land.*[cxlvii]

Blowhard

In his debate with Judge Talley, he said:

> *I am against it* [capital punishment] *because I believe it is inhuman, because I believe that as the hearts of men have softened they have gradually gotten rid of brutal punishment, because I believe that it will only be a few years until it will be banished forever from every civilized country—even New York; because I believe it has no effect whatever to stop murder.*

Having a public pulpit for his beliefs and philosophies was likely one of the main reasons why he undertook representation of Leopold and Loeb in the first place in a case very much in the pubic eye, (in addition to that fee), much as he undertook the Scopes case primarily to use it as a platform for his anti-religion views.

The die was cast.

Mike Farris

Chapter Ten: A Plea in Mitigation

Of course, if they wish me to hang I will plead not guilty and the jury will hang me, or I will plead guilty before a friendly judge and get life imprisonment. Also, there is the insanity plea.
—Nathan Leopold

BY THE TIME Darrow was hired, Leopold and Loeb had already given detailed confessions that varied in only one key point: which of them had actually killed Bobby Franks.

Leopold claimed he was driving the car and that Loeb beat Bobby to death with a chisel, while Loeb told the flip side of that story. Their guilt already a foregone conclusion, Darrow's goal was solely to help his clients escape the death penalty.

And so, in a surprise twist as trial commenced on the morning of July 25, 1924, Darrow made this announcement to a surprised judge and courtroom full of observers:

> *We know, your honor, the facts in this case are substantially as have been published in the newspapers and what purports to be their confession, and we can see we have no duty to the defendants, or their families, or society, except to see that they are safely and permanently excluded from the public. Of course, after this is done, we*

> want to do the best we can for them within these limits. After long reflection and thorough discussion, so long as that is the only issue in the case, we have determined to make a motion in this court for each of the defendants in this case to withdraw our plea of not guilty and enter a plea of guilty.

That meant all that was left to address at trial would be sentencing, to be decided by the judge rather than a jury. Darrow believed a judge would be more lenient than would inflamed members of the community sitting in judgment as jurors; hence, the stratagem.

That also explains one of Darrow's several ethical lapses during the case. Perhaps, though, "lapse" is not the right word. That implies an ethical person temporarily slipping up, but not an attorney with a lack of character who was pretty much bereft of ethics to start with. That means it's not a lapse but simply consistency in a pattern of conduct.

Crazy

Insanity could be a defense to a murder charge and, if asserted, was an issue required by Illinois law to be determined by a jury.

Once his clients switched their pleas to guilty, Darrow had to walk a tightrope between using mental illness or disease as a mitigating factor without falling off on the side of an outright insanity defense, thereby triggering the jury requirement.

Darrow deemed it expedient to suppress his experts' original report that proclaimed his clients insane. He would then, in court, use his experts' carefully coached testimony on mental illness, meticulously avoiding the concept of insanity, to mitigate his clients' conduct.

Authors Greg King and Penny Wilson wrote: "It was a dangerous gamble: if one of [his experts] accidentally mentioned insanity, it would result in a jury trial."

Then Darrow hedged his bets and "arranged to have the report 'stolen,' knowing it would be reprinted in newspapers."

[cxlviii] The idea was to "soften perceptions and portray the killers as mentally ill" to the public. And, of course, prejudice the judge to be predisposed toward leniency.

Although the leaked final report didn't actually deal with the issue of insanity, there apparently was an initial report that did. Alienist[43] (psychiatrist) Dr. Harold Hulbert wrote in his section addressing Richard Loeb, "In conclusion, this man is insane, in my opinion...."

As for Nathan Leopold, he wrote that Leopold suffered from "Dementia Praecox," something we know today as schizophrenia. Although Leopold had an academic knowledge of the difference between right and wrong, Hulbert said that "he is unable to apply this knowledge to modify his conduct. His crimes are due to his insane extreme suggestibility from one who fits in with his insane delusion of 'King and Slave.'"

This is a reference to one of Leopold's oddities, fantasies in which he envisioned himself as the slave of another man, according to King and Wilson:

> Even when Nathan fantasized that he was a slave to a handsome man, he cast himself as exceptional. In these fevered sexual dreams, he pictured himself as endowed with all that he lacked in reality: he was desired, powerful and strong, always selected to do battle against other slaves and always the victor in conflicts. He never envisioned himself as truly submissive. Instead, he had to be the dominant, the silent power controlling the apparent master and skillfully shaping people to his way of thinking.[cxlix]

---

[43] "Alienist" derives from the Latin term *alienatus*, which means "to deprive of reason." Alienists were so-called experts on the issue of whether one suffered from, in effect, a deprivation of reason rendering them mentally incompetent.

Blowhard

Dr. William White wrote of Leopold:

> ...[i]t would seem obvious that under the ordinary conceptions of right and wrong tests he is insane within the meaning of the law. He acted entirely from the influence of motives which estranged him entirely from reality, which made it impossible for him to see right and wrong in any sense comparable to the sense in which it is conceived that the average man sees it.

Dr. William Healy wrote that Loeb was a person with a...

> ...pathological mental life; he is a case of abnormal split personality with an obsessive thought life that has such compulsive force that his acts can be seen to be directly dependent on the diseased elements of his mental life.

As for Leopold, Healy wrote:

> I see no other conclusion possible but that Leopold is a thoroughly unbalanced individual in his mental life, really mentally diseased, of the paranoia or monomaniac type, which has produced so many criminals. He is a socially dangerous person, suffering from a psychosis.

It's important to note that "psychosis" means a mental condition so severe that the person has lost contact with reality.

As noted, Darrow realized that, given the outrage in the community and its likely effect of poisoning the well of potential jurors, he must endeavor to avoid a jury at all costs.

Ironically, Leopold had even foretold the strategy before Darrow appeared on the scene when he told police interrogators, in response to a question about what his potential defense might be at trial, "Of course, if they wish me to hang I will plead not guilty and the jury will hang me, or I will plead guilty before a friendly judge and get life imprisonment." Then he added, "Also, there is the insanity plea."

But when asked if he felt sorry for Robert Franks, he said, "Not at all."

And as for the Franks family?

"I don't give a damn if they would croak this minute."

One wonders if Leopold was already conniving the type of shocking answers that might lend themselves to a deranged personality, to be used in mitigation.

Not Crazy, Exactly; Just Mentally Diseased

With insanity taken off the table, what evidence of mental disease or defect of Leopold and Loeb would be admissible in mitigation of the crime? State's Attorney Robert Crowe argued that no psychiatric testimony should be admitted from alienists.

Once you've pled guilty, he contended, you should no longer be able to rely on any defenses to the crime.

Walter Bachrach, an attorney who had been retained to assist Darrow, got into the act with a ridiculous argument that once the State had presented its case on guilt or innocence, which was essentially established by a guilty plea, then it was "none of the State Attorney's business, in this proceeding, as to what punishment was to be meted out."

Darrow jumped in next, turning on a mixture of charm and sarcasm.

> *Now I understand that when everything has been said in this case from the beginning to the end, the position of the State's Attorney is that the universe will crumble unless these two boys are hanged.... If I thought hanging them would prevent any future murders I would probably be in favor of doing it. In fact I would consent to have anybody hanged, excepting myself, if I thought it would prevent all future murders. But I have no such feeling.*

Darrow was on familiar ground here, arguing against the death penalty, something he fervently opposed. As it turned out, had he simply attacked capital punishment and emphasized the youthfulness of his clients, he would have achieved the same result he ultimately obtained.

But instead, he chose to belittle the seriousness of the crime and attempted to portray his clients as the real victims. As if they had not abducted a 14-year-old boy, clubbed him into senselessness with a chisel, shoved an ether-soaked rag down his throat to suffocate him, stripped his body, poured acid on it, and shoved it into a culvert like a piece of trash.

Darrow launched into what would become one of his major themes in his closing argument, a position he had long championed: the mentally diseased should not be held accountable for their actions. At this early stage in the trial, he was simply advocating the need for evidence of that disease as a mitigating factor, to set up his argument at closing. But he was already starting his tap dance around the edges of a plea of insanity.

"What is a mitigating circumstance?" he asked rhetorically. "Is youth? If so, why? Simply because the child has not the judgment of life that a grown person has. A mental condition, if nothing else."

He pointed out that the law didn't permit minors to enter into contracts, or even to marry without parental consent. "Why? Because they haven't that judgment which only comes with years; because they are not fully responsible."

So why then, he wondered, should they be held legally responsible for any other acts? He compared mental disease to youth, an argument that might appeal to any parent. He noted that mental disease stole the full capacity to exercise judgment just as youth was deemed to.

The parry and thrust of the two sides, solely on the question of what evidence and what witnesses could be introduced, was bitter. Darrow wanted to put on a full array of psychiatric testimony about his clients' mental disability to mitigate their gruesome act. The prosecution, led by State's Attorney Crowe, argued that any such testimony was inadmissible once the plea of guilty had been entered because it was tantamount to a defense against a murder charge that had already been admitted. But, the argument went, once you've pled guilty, you're no longer entitled to introduce a defense to your conduct.

Crowe could see that Darrow intended to use insanity, even if only in subtext, as part of his case.

> *Insanity, if your Honor please, is a defense, just the same as an alibi. Would your Honor tolerate or permit these defendants to enter a plea of guilty in this case, and then put witnesses on the stand to show that when the crime was committed they were in California? Have we got to a point in the law where we can enter a plea of guilty before the court in order to avoid a jury, and then try that plea as a plea of not guilty and put in a defense?*

Judge Caverly wasn't buying the prosecution's argument:

> *The defense hasn't said they are going to put on alienists to show that these men are insane, and I don't think they are going to attempt to show that they are insane.*

State's Attorney Crowe seemed to be champing at the bit to respond. When he took the floor again, he virtually exploded in sarcasm of his own:

> *When the jury returns a verdict, Mr. Bachrach says that the State Attorney ought to leave the court, he ought not to see that judgment is rendered on that verdict and if the verdict is a corrupt verdict he has no business to use the power of his office and the machinery of the law to demonstrate that fact.... Nobody has the right to suggest to your Honor what the punishment should be in this case but the defense.*

Then Crowe levelled a broadside directly at Darrow who, Crowe said, argued that:

> These two men are not men of intellect and men of accountability, they are mere infants wandering around in a 'boyish dreamland.' The State's Attorney ought not be permitted to discuss the gruesome details of the horrible murder in their presence. A kindly old nurse ought to tell them a bedtime story. They did not commit a murder. They broke a jar of jam in the pantry. That is not blood on their hands, that is jam.... Mr. Darrow says put away the judicial slaughter and do not spank these naughty boys, but let their nurse take them out to play.

Darrow ultimately won the point and both sides were permitted to introduce their psychiatric testimony. Darrow's defense focused on testimony of the four alienists who had contributed to the report leaked to the press, while State's attorney Crowe introduced over 100 witnesses of his own. After a month of testimony, it was time for the main event: closing arguments.

In his argument, which would last twelve hours over the course of three days, Darrow continually raised the specter of insanity that he claimed he wouldn't rely on, sometimes overtly, sometimes more subtly.

It might even be deemed subliminal as often as he said the word. "How insane they are, I care not, whether medically or legally," he said. But he did care. He had to care if he was going to successfully navigate the minefield that threatened to, at any moment, explode and send his clients to face a jury.

While decrying some of the boneheaded mistakes his clients made, and the risks they took, Darrow scoffed that, "There is not a sane thing in all of this from the beginning to the end."

Here, he was specifically addressing the fact that Leopold and Loeb had lured Bobby Franks into their car in broad daylight, "in sight of their own homes, and surrounded by their neighbors." They then drove on:

> ...a populous street, where everybody can see, where eyes may be at every window as they pass by. They hit him over the head with a chisel and kill him, and go on about their business, driving this car within a half block of Loeb's home, within the same distance of Franks's home, drive it past the neighbors that they know, in broad daylight.

Why, he exclaims, they could have been discovered with the body in their car upon the occurrence of even the "slightest accident, the slightest misfortune, a bit of curiosity, an arrest for speeding."

His conclusion drawn from this?

Well, only the madness of King Lear rises to the same level of this carelessness that, itself, proved their mental defect. "The mad acting of the fool in *King Lear* is the only thing I know of that compares with it." Yet, he scoffed, "doctors will swear that it is a sane act. They know better."

Then he caught himself. Perhaps he realized he had used the "s" word—sane—injudiciously. If he went overboard, he might argue himself right into a jury and the possibility of the death penalty. So, not insane, exactly, he said; rather, it's the act of "a diseased brain."

But what about the intricate planning of the crime? Didn't that show a rational thinking mind? "Well, what does that mean?" Darrow said. "A maniac plans, an idiot plans, an animal plans, any brain that functions may plan; but their plans were the diseased plans of the diseased mind."

For a while, then, he stayed on track—or at least not off-track onto the insanity shoulder—before slipping up again. At a later point, arguing the lack of proper training by their parents, he said that Leopold and Loeb were seized by strong feelings and passions, "when the call of sex is new and strange...at the time boys grow insane, at the time crimes are committed."

Later, Darrow discussed the influence on Nathan Leopold

of Friedrich Nietzsche, not to mention the possible homosexual urges Leopold experienced.[44]

Leopold was obsessed with the philosophies of Nietzsche and the idea of an *Übermensch*—a superman—to whom the laws of mere mortals did not apply.

"He," meaning Leopold, Darrow said, "did it obsessed of an idea, perhaps to some extent influenced by what has not been developed publicly in this case, perversions that were present in the boy. Both signs of insanity, both, together with this act, proving a diseased mind."

Windbaggery on Display

But let's shift from his flirtation with insanity and consider Darrow's argument while pleading for imprisonment rather than hanging for his clients. Apparently Darrow was, himself, mindful of his own windbaggery. On at least three occasions, he seemed to acknowledge it to the judge. When complaining of Christian society demanding blood, he said, "Your Honor, I feel like apologizing for urging it so long."

Talking about heredity and its role as culprit for his clients' crime, he said, "Your Honor, I wish I knew when to stop talking about this question that has always interested me so much."

Goodness! I, too, wish he knew when to stop.

And as he, at last, approached the end of his twelve-hour filibuster, he said, "Now, I must say a word more and then I will leave this with you where I should have left it long ago," and shortly after that, "I feel I should apologize for the length of time I have taken." Do I hear an "amen"?

Multiple accounts of Darrow's filibuster describe tears streaming down faces, including that of Judge Caverly. Far be it for me to be skeptical, and maybe it's because I didn't hear his wonderful oratory in real time, but reading the transcript, it's hard to imagine that his words swayed any but those who were

---

[44] Think back to the "falling out of cocksuckers" portion of the police interrogation.

already persuaded of his point in the first place. It was a master compendium of windbaggery, bloviation, sophistry, and melodrama.

Once you consider the following arguments that he made in an effort to mitigate the effect of the murder, you might agree that perhaps the most outlandish thing he said throughout the twelve-hour ordeal of his argument was this:

> *I mean to argue this thoroughly, and it seems to me that there is no chance for a court to hesitate upon the facts in this case. I want to try to do it honestly and plainly and **without any attempt at frills or oratory**; to state the facts of this case just as the facts exist, and nothing else.* [emphasis added]

Arguments in Mitigation

Leopold and Loeb were the Real Victims

Darrow often painted his clients as the actual victims in cases. Here, it was Leopold and Loeb who were victims, he said, not the young boy they murdered.

He referred to them several times as "unfortunate boys," once calling them "most unfortunate boys," ones whose lives have been "imperiled, with the public aroused." It would be "an unheard-of thing for any court, no matter who, to sentence these boys to death." The press, he said, and the prosecutors have whipped up the public into a "frenzy of hate…planning and scheming, and contriving and working to take these two boys' lives."

Ladling in a dose of his patented "they couldn't help themselves" argument, he contended that Leopold and Loeb were victims of their own heredity—"because someone in the past has sinned against them"—and were simply "two immature boys of diseased mind."

As a result, the State wanted to take "two boys, one eighteen and the other nineteen, irresponsible, weak, diseased, penning them in a cell, checking off the days and the hours and the minutes until they will be taken out and hanged."

At one point he referred to Loeb as "this poor boy," at another time as "poor Dickie Loeb," and Leopold was "this poor fellow." He asked that the judge "not visit the grave and dire and terrible misfortunes of Dickie Loeb and Nathan Leopold upon these two boys."

In other words, don't hold them accountable for their act.

And, toward the end of his filibuster, presumably breathless by then, he told Judge Caverly that he stood there "not merely for the lives of these two unfortunate lads, but for all boys and all girls; for all of the young, and, as far as possible, for all of the old."

Then he closed with this:

> *If I can succeed, my greatest reward and my greatest hope will be that I have done something for the tens of thousands of other boys, for the countless unfortunates who must tread the same road in blind childhood that these poor boys have trod; that I have done something to help human understanding, to temper justice with mercy, to overcome hate with love.*

To Darrow's credit, he did on a couple of occasions refer to "poor" Bobby Franks, but his effusive lavishing of victimhood on Leopold and Loeb left those perfunctory references in the cold. He diminished the crime committed against Bobby and his family, almost dismissing it in a what's-done-is-done throwaway.

His cavalier attitude about the real victims, and by that I include the Franks family, is unforgiveable.

> *Robert Franks is dead, and we cannot call him back to life. It was all over in fifteen minutes after he got into the car, and he probably never knew it or thought of it. That does not justify it. It is the last thing I would do. I am*

sorry for the poor boy. I am sorry for his parents. But it is done.

What Would Jesus Do?

Remarkably, while decrying the public outcry to hang Leopold and Loeb, the agnostic/atheistic Darrow invoked a "what would Jesus do?" argument. His agnosticism, which he defined as a belief that one can never actually know whether God is real, would later be on full display in the Scopes Monkey Trial.

While Darrow examined William Jennings Bryan on the witness stand, Bryan protested a ruling against him on an admissibility of evidence objection with this:

> *Your Honor, they have not asked a question legally, and the only reason they have asked any question is for the purpose, as was the question about Jonah asked, for a chance to give this agnostic an opportunity to criticize a believer in the Word of God; and I answered the question in order to shut his mouth so that he cannot go out and tell his atheistic friends that I would not answer his question.*

In his autobiography, Darrow wrote, while discussing the concept of divine design and purpose behind creation:

> *They* [life forms] *are not made for any purpose; they simply grew out of needs and adaptations; in other words, they happened. Just as God must have happened, if he exists at all.*[cl]

Writing about the uselessness of prayers to God, he wrote:

> *Nature brings hordes of insects that settle over the land and destroy the farmer's crops. Who are the objects of the glorious design: the farmers who so patiently and laboriously raise the crops or the grasshoppers that devour*

> them? It must be the insects, because the farmers hold prayer meetings and implore their God to kill the bugs, but the pests go on with their deadly work unmolested.[cli]

Lest there be any doubt, on March 12, 1929, after Leopold and Loeb but before the Massie Case, Darrow spoke at a symposium in Columbus, Ohio, along with a rabbi, a Protestant bishop, and Catholic judge. Darrow's topic was "Why I Am an Agnostic."[clii] He said:

> I would say that belief in at least three tenets is necessary to the faith of a Christian: a belief in God, a belief in immortality, and a belief in a supernatural book.... I am an agnostic as to the question of God. I think that it is impossible for the human mind to believe in an object or thing unless it can form a mental picture of such object or thing.... No such image comes, or can come, with the idea of a God who is described as a force.

He concluded his remarks by elevating agnosticism over faith.

> The fear of God is not the beginning of wisdom.[45] The fear of God is the death of wisdom. Skepticism and doubt lead to study and investigation, and investigation is the beginning of wisdom.

Writing in *The Forum* in October of 1928, also after Leopold and Loeb but before Massie, he attacked faith, while addressing the issue raised by the second tenet mentioned at the symposium quoted above:

> Upon what evidence, then, are we asked to believe in

---

[45] A frontal assault on *Proverbs* 9:10: "The fear of the LORD is the beginning of wisdom, and the knowledge of the holy is understanding." (King James Version)

immortality? There is no evidence. One is told to rely on faith, and no doubt this serves the purpose so long as one can believe blindly whatever he is told.

And as for life in heaven after death? In that same *Forum* paper, he wrote:

There are those who base their hope of a future life upon the resurrection of the body.[46] *This is a purely religious doctrine. It is safe to say that few intelligent men who are willing to look obvious facts in the face hold any such belief.*

Yet, as we have seen, Darrow repeatedly invoked God while pleading for his own freedom in the McNamara matter in which he was charged with bribing jurors. And in Leopold and Loeb, he certainly knew his audience in Chicago and knew enough about the tenets of Christianity to appeal to them when it suited his purpose.

This is a Christian community…and yet they would hang these boys in a Christian community. Let me ask this court, is there any doubt about whether these boys would be safe in the hands of the founder of the Christian religion?

That last sentence was perhaps the first "WWJD" argument of its kind: Jesus wouldn't hang these boys, so you shouldn't either. If so, Darrow was ahead of his time.

---

[46] It's not surprising that Darrow misstated the concept of heaven and resurrection of the *soul* and not the physical body. That little distinction would not have served his thesis, so he chose to distort this tenet of faith. To his credit, though, he does mention it in an offhand remark ("Some of those who profess to believe in the immortality of man—whether it be of his soul or his body….") though he doesn't really address it.

Bobby Franks Might Never Have Amounted to Much

This is my own paraphrase of Darrow's remarks, but I think it's true to his actual words. Responding to assistant prosecutor Joseph Savage's argument that the 14-year-old victim would never have a chance to grow up and accomplish things with his life, Darrow callously disregarded the notion.

> Of course, I cannot say with the certainty of Mr. Savage that he [Bobby] would have been a great man if he had grown up. At fourteen years of age I don't know whether he would or not. Savage, I suppose, is a mind reader, and he says that he would. He has a fantasy, which is hanging. So far as cruelty to the victim is concerned, you can scarce imagine one less cruel.

Darrow also seized the moment to ridicule prosecutor Savage for his name. Personal attacks on opposing counsel were a Darrow trademark.

> ...I only say it now because my friend Mr. Savage—did you pick him for his name or his ability or his learning?—because my friend Mr. Savage, in as cruel a speech as he knew how to make, said to this court that we pleaded guilty because we were afraid to do anything else.

A bit later, he attacked Savage again:

> I marveled when I heard Mr. Savage talk I do not criticize him. He is young and enthusiastic. But has he ever read anything? Has he ever thought? Was there ever any man who had studied science, who has read anything of criminology or philosophy—was there ever any man who knew himself who could speak with the assurance of which he speaks?

Good thing Darrow wasn't going to criticize him. Later, in a particularly callous diatribe about Bobby, Darrow said:

> *Mr. Savage told us that Franks, if he lived, would have been a great man and accomplished much. I want to leave this thought with Your Honor now. I do not know what Bobby Franks would have been had he grown to be a man. I do not know the laws that control one's growth. Sometimes, Your Honor, a boy of great promise is cut off in his early youth. Sometimes he dies and is placed in a culvert. Sometimes a boy of great promise stands on a trap door and is hanged by the neck until dead. Sometimes he dies of diphtheria. Death somehow pays no attention to age, sex, prospects, wealth or intellect.*
>
> *It comes, and perhaps—I can only say perhaps, for I never professed to unravel the mysteries of fate, and I cannot tell; but I can say perhaps—the boy who died at fourteen did as much as if he had died at seventy, and perhaps the boy who died as a babe did as much as if he had lived longer. Perhaps, somewhere in fate and chance, it might be that he lived as long as he should.*

And so, in order that "the death of poor little Bobby Franks should not be in vain," spare the lives of Leopold and Loeb, he pleaded.

> *Would it mean anything if on account of that death, these two boys were taken out and a rope tied around their necks and they died felons?.... No, Your Honor, the unfortunate and tragic death of this young lad should mean something.*

Maybe Leopold and Loeb actually did young Bobby a favor, right? His number was up and the two geniuses simply carried out the hand of fate. So now let's all join hands, sing *kumbaya*, and use Bobby's death as an impetus to "appraise children, to understand the emotions that control them, to understand the ideas that possess them, to teach them to avoid the pitfalls of life."

Leopold's and Loeb's Youth

Darrow argued that the youth of his clients should work to their favor. Since they weren't even able to legally enter into contracts for themselves—"two children, who have no right to sign a note or make a deed"—Darrow found it despicable that they should be on trial for their lives.

He went on to say that, if the youth of the victim is to be taken into account, so, too, should the youth of the killers. "It may be that the state's attorney would think it particularly cruel to the victim because he was a boy. Well, my clients are boys, too, and if it would make more serious the offense to kill a boy, it should make less serious the offense of the boys who do the killing."

To Darrow, this killing was simply "a senseless act of children." The scheme of committing a perfect crime arose in Loeb's mind, he said (though Loeb accused Leopold of envisioning the plot), "[n]ot due to any wickedness of Dickie Loeb, for he is a child." It was a "childish scheme growing up in these childish minds." So the killing of Bobby Franks was really nothing more than an act of juvenile delinquency. Some madcap escapade as a young boy, like breaking windows or stealing candy, or maybe even stealing a car for a joyride. "It developed as a child just as kleptomania has developed in many a person."

> Youth is hard enough. The only good thing about youth is that it has no thought and no care; and how blindly we do things when we are young! Where is the man who has not been guilty of delinquencies in youth? How many men are there today—lawyers and congressmen and judges, and even state's attorneys—who have not been guilty of some mad act in youth?

Oh, Darrow pleaded with Judge Caverly, remember what it was like when you were a young boy. Only then can you truly judge what was done. It's a variation on the Golden Rule argument (put yourself in the shoes of the defendant and decide how you would have acted).

> *We might as well be honest with ourselves, Your Honor. Before I would tie a noose around the neck of a boy I would try to call back into my mind the emotions of youth. I would try to remember what the world looked like to me when I was a child. I would try to remember how weak and inefficient was youth in the presence of the surging, controlling feelings of the child. One that honestly remembers and asks himself the questions and tries to unlock the door that he thinks is closed, and calls back the boy, can understand the boy.*

So bludgeoning another child to death with a chisel, shoving an ether-soaked rag down his throat, dousing him with acid, and shoving his body into a culvert is just, you know, mischief.

Boys will be boys. Come on, judge; be a sport!

The Murder was Not Particularly Cruel or Cold-Blooded

This is, perhaps, the most remarkable and outrageous of Darrow's arguments. Were it not so tragic, it would be laughable. Darrow contended that not only was the killing of Bobby Franks not cruel or cold-blooded, it would be worse to punish Leopold and Loeb for killing him.

As you read this, you may think this is an exaggeration of Darrow's argument or blowing his words out of proportion. We'll see.

For starters, Darrow attacked the prosecutors for even suggesting that the crime was cruel or cold-blooded, language he dismissed as rhetorical hyperbole, an arrow in every prosecution's quiver.

Blowhard

> *I have never yet tried a case where the state's attorney did not say that it was the most cold-blooded, inexcusable, premeditated case that ever occurred.*

It's all about bragging rights for prosecutors, he said.

> *Why? Well, it adds to the credit of the state's attorney to be connected with a big case. This is one thing they can say. 'Well, I tried the most cold-blooded murder case that ever was tried, and I convicted them, and they are dead.*

Besides, he continued, that sort of rhetoric is persuasive with juries.

> *...these adjectives always go well with juries; bloody, cold-blooded, despicable, cowardly, dastardly, cruel, heartless—the whole litany of the state's attorney's office goes well with a jury.*

But, to:

> *...stand them [Leopold and Loeb] up on the trap door of the scaffold, and choke them to death...will be infinitely more cold-blooded—whether justified or not, than any act that these boys have committed or can commit.*

So, let's revisit the crime before we analyze Darrow's take on what is or is not cold-blooded. Just as a reminder, Leopold and Loeb enticed Bobby Franks into an automobile on the pretext of giving him a ride home, bludgeoned him in the head with a chisel and, when that didn't kill him quickly enough, stuffed an ether-soaked rag down his throat that he suffocated on, then stripped his body, poured acid over it, and stuffed it into a culvert.

Darrow argued that, because it was over so quickly, Bobby

hardly had much of a chance to feel fear or pain, so the crime really wasn't that bad, certainly not as bad as hanging his clients would be.

Don't believe me? Read Darrow's own words yet again:

> *I insist, Your Honor, that under all fair rules and measurements, this was one of the least dastardly and cruel of any that I have known anything about.... I say that very few murders ever occurred that were as free from cruelty as this.*[47]

He outlined his personal standards for measuring the cruelty of a crime, then applied those standards to his case. First, he said, consider the "sufferings of the victim," or the "degree of pain to the victim." Here, "[p]oor little Bobby Franks suffered very little.... It was all over in fifteen minutes after he got into the car, and he probably never knew it or thought of it." This is where he added the obligatory "I'm sorry" for Bobby's death "[b]ut it is done."

Next, "I would put the attitude of those who kill." By that, he meant that, "In order to make this the most cruel thing that ever happened, of course they must have a motive."

Well, there really was no good reason for the killing so, he contends, the absence of motive mitigates the severity of the crime. Here's how he unraveled that bit of sophistry. Start with this question: "What was there in the conduct of these two boys which showed a wicked, malignant and abandoned heart beyond that of anybody else who ever lived? Your Honor, that is simply foolish."

No, "this is a senseless, useless, purposeless, motiveless act of two boys."

Furthermore, stripping off Bobby's clothes and stuffing his body in a culvert was, in effect, a non-event. He was already

---

[47] I realize I have repeated this quote several times, but it bears repeating, no matter how often.

dead, "past pain, when no harm can come to him." The only relevance of desecrating the dead body was to "shock the fine sensibilities of the state's counsel."

But, he asked, want to know something even more shocking? One...

> ...that makes this pale into insignificance. I can think, and only think, Your Honor, of taking two boys, one eighteen and the other nineteen, irresponsible, weak, diseased, penning them in a cell, checking off the days and the hours and the minutes until they will be taken out and hanged.

Oh, the horror!

But as far as Bobby's death went, by Darrow's reckoning, quick death plus lack of motive equals the "least dastardly and cruel" act of any and, thus, not cold-blooded or cruel. It's total nonsense. When you're the victim of a violent crime, fifteen minutes (by Darrow's calculation) isn't quick, particularly if it's a bloody and painful fifteen minutes.

And the lack of motive actually makes the crime worse.

The dictionary definition in *Merriam-Webster* of cold-blooded is "done or acting without consideration, compunction, or clemency." In the legal sense, *Black's Law Dictionary* defines it simply as a "state of mind characterized by a pre-meditated intent to commit a murder." Planning a kidnapping and murder for no reason other than to prove you can do it and get away with it fits the definition without taking into account the brutality of the crime. That brutality fits the dictionary definition of cruelty, which *Merriam-Webster* defines as "disposed to inflict pain or suffering; devoid of humane feelings" or "causing or conducive to injury, grief, or pain."

Ironically, Darrow, himself, later argued the very definition of cruelty when he said, "Why did they kill little Bobby Franks? Not for money, not for spite, not for hate. They killed him as they might kill a spider or fly, for the experience."

But, he said, the State should overlook that and "set an example in consideration, kindheartedness and tenderness...."

Bobby's Parents are to be Envied

Though Darrow claimed to have sympathy for the parents of Bobby Franks, his own words suggest he wasn't really all that sorry for the Frankses.

It was the Leopolds and the Loebs, instead, who commanded his sympathy.

> *I know that any mother might be the mother of a little Bobby Franks, who left his home and went to his school, and who never came back.... But when you are pitying the father and mother of poor Bobby Franks, what about the fathers and mothers of these two unfortunate boys [Leopold and Loeb], and what about the unfortunate boys themselves, and what about all the fathers and all the mothers and all the boys and all the girls who tread a dangerous maze in darkness from birth to death?*

While any mother might be the mother of Bobby, so, one supposes, the mothers of dead children are a dime a dozen, but "these two [Mrs. Leopold and Mrs. Loeb] are the victims." After all, they had to live with knowing that the gene that led their sons to commit the act might have been passed down through them, asking themselves, "How came my children to be what they are? From what ancestry did they get this strain? How far removed was the poison that destroyed their lives? Was I the bearer of the seed that brings them to death?"

And not just the mothers, but the Leopold and Loeb families as a whole also would have to live with the disgrace caused by poor little Babe and Dickie. "[W]e are dealing in the future fate of two families. We are talking of placing a blot upon the escutcheon of two houses that do not deserve it."

While he had singled out mothers earlier, Darrow next talked about other family members, like Mr. Leopold. "It is a hard thing for a father to see his life's hopes crumble into dust." And Loeb's "faithful uncle and brother, who have watched here day by day, while Dickie's father and his mother are too ill to stand this terrific strain...."

The stain of disgrace would almost be too much to bear:

> Your Honor, why their proud names and all the future generations that bear them shall have this bar sinister written upon them?... And I ask Your Honor, in addition to all that I have said, to save two honorable families from a disgrace that never ends, and which could be of no avail to help any human being that lives.

This is the flip side of the Biblical tenet that the "Lord...[visits] the iniquity of the fathers upon the children unto the third and fourth generation." *Numbers* 14:18.

Darrow seemed to be saying the iniquity of the children is visited upon their parents.

While Darrow had sympathy for the Loebs and the Leopolds, and while he dismissed the sorrow of Bobby's mother, what about the rest of Bobby's family? To hear him tell it, they actually got off easy compared to the Leopold and Loeb families.

> I am sorry for the bereavement of Mr. and Mrs. Franks, for those broken ties that cannot be healed. All I can hope is that some good may come from it all. But as compared with the families of Leopold and Loeb, the Franks are to be envied—and everyone knows it.

Pity the Mothers. Again. Except Flora Franks.

In an argument that foreshadowed his bloviation a few years later in the Massie Case, Darrow waxed eloquent about the wonders of motherhood—at least as relates to his clients' mothers—and how they should be pitied—except Flora Franks, who should be "envied."

After bemoaning how dreadful it must be for Mrs. Loeb and Mrs. Leopold to have to wonder whether they were responsible for passing the psychopathic murder gene to their offspring ("Was I the bearer of the seed that brings them death?"), he launched into this:

> *I am sorry for all fathers and mothers. The mother who looks into the blue eyes of her little babe cannot help musing over the end of the child, whether it will be crowned with the greatest promises which her mind can imagine or whether he may meet death upon the scaffold. All she can do is to rear him with love and care, to watch over him tenderly, to meet life with hope and trust and confidence, and to leave the rest with fate.*

Compare that with his 1932 argument on behalf of Grace Fortescue in a Honolulu courtroom in the Massie Case while glossing over the pain of murder victim Joe Kahahawai's mother:

> *To them* [mothers] *there is one all-important thing and that is a child that they carried in their womb*[48].... *Everything else is forgotten in the emotion that carries her back in time when this was a little baby in her arms which she bore and loved.*

Dickie and Babe

The prosecution took offense at Darrow referring to his clients by their nicknames, "Dickie" for Richard Loeb and "Babe" for Nathan Leopold. The obvious concern was that Darrow was trying to soften his clients in the eyes of the judge by

---

[48] In Leopold and Loeb, Darrow also decided that referring to the "womb" was a good ploy. "What influence, let me ask you, will [hanging] have for the unborn babes still sleeping in their mother's womb?"

personalizing them. It would seem like a minor point and it's not totally clear why prosecutors made the objection because it simply emphasized the point to Judge Caverly.

It also gave Darrow something to use as a bludgeon, much as his clients had used a chisel. Settling on "Dick" and "Nathan," to avoid running afoul of the objection, Darrow then occasionally "slipped."

> ...then poor little Dickie Loeb—I shouldn't call him Dickie, and I shouldn't call him poor, because that might be playing for sympathy, and you have no right to ask for sympathy in this world; you should ask for justice, whatever that may be; and only state's attorneys know.

He repeatedly slipped again thereafter; in fact, he spent more time calling them Dickie and Babe than Dick and Nathan. He knew exactly what he was doing. The more he did it, the more he "apologized," the more he made his point. Talking about "Babe" Leopold, he said:

> I call him Babe, not because I want it to affect Your Honor, but because everybody else does. He is the youngest of the family and I suppose that is why he got his nickname. We will call him a man. Mr. Crowe thinks it is easier to hang a man than a boy, and so I will call him a man if I can think of it.

If I can think of it. Pretty much a clue that he was going to continue to try to lead the judge to think of both his clients as boys which, in fact, is exactly what he did.

After all, one of his prominent arguments was that they should not be sentenced to hang due to their young age. It was his best argument. "If Your Honor can hang a boy of eighteen, some other judge can hang him at seventeen, or sixteen, or fourteen." As it turned out, it was his only really effective argument. The prosecution would have been better off leaving the "Dickie" and "Babe" issue alone.

The Senselessness of the Crime Proved the Disease of the Minds

Darrow claimed, in his autobiography, that his sole goal was to save the lives of his two clients and that "we did not even claim or try to prove that they were insane." [cliii] As we have seen, he walked a mighty fine line on that issue, and occasionally fell off on the wrong side. Still, "We did believe and sought to show that their minds were not normal and never had been normal."

It was a defense of mitigation, not justification, he said. His goal wasn't to justify the killing of Bobby Franks but to mitigate the punishment. His theory was that "there is no sort of question that these boys were mentally diseased.... [the crime] can be accounted for only on the theory of the mental disease of these two lads."

And because of that mental disease, their degree of culpability should have been less. This mustn't be confused with his other mitigation argument, discussed below, that they had no control over their actions because of their heredity and, thus, were not responsible, at all, for their conduct.

It's interesting to note that one of the prime evidences Darrow relied upon to show the diseased minds was the mindlessness and depravity of the crime, itself—the same crime he said was neither cold-blooded nor cruel.

For starters, as has already been mentioned, there was no clearly identifiable motive. It wasn't money, even though they sent a ransom demand, because both were from wealthy families and didn't need money. There was no question of hate, no question of revenge. Instead, as quoted above, Darrow said they simply killed him "as they might kill a spider or a fly, for the experience."

So, if there was no motive, no reason for the killing, he concluded that proved that this was clearly a senseless act of a diseased mind. "[T]here is no sort of question that these boys were mentally diseased.... [this case] can be accounted for only on the theory of the mental disease of these two lads."

The notion that there was no motive is simply not true.

Although it may not have been a conventional motive, and it may not have been one society at large could understand or identify with, it was still a motive: they did it for the sheer thrill of committing a "perfect" crime and getting away with it.

During Nathan Leopold's interrogation by prosecutors Robert Crowe and Joseph Savage, and the State's psychiatrists, at which Richard Loeb was also present and interrogated, he was asked "what was your incentive?"

Leopold responded:

> *There is no question of being swayed by momentary excitement at all; I am sure, as sure as I can be of anything that is, as sure as you can read any other man's state of mind, the thing that prompted Dick to want to do this thing and prompted me to want to do this thing was a sort of pure love of excitement, or the imaginary love of thrills, doing something different; possibly, as the Doctor here suggested, the satisfaction and the ego of putting something over, as the vernacular has it. The money consideration only came afterward, and never was important, the getting of the money was a part of our objective as was also the commission of the crime, but that was not the exact motive, but that came afterwards.*

Richard Loeb concurred. Explaining why he didn't have much remorse, he said:

> *I felt sorry about the thing, about the killing of the boy— oh, well, that very night. But then the excitement, the accounts in the paper, the fact that we had gotten away with it and that they did not suspect us, that it was given so much publicity and all that sort of thing, naturally went to the question of not feeling as much remorse as otherwise I think I would have.*

Whether Darrow could accept that as a motive or not, it was still a motive, though to him it was simply proof of diseased minds.

The two killers were quite likely sociopaths and he believed that their sociopathy mitigated their conduct, even though they both fully understood, and admitted, that they knew their conduct was wrong. Loeb admitted that he had the "power of will and choice" to decide whether to kill Bobby or not. Leopold confirmed that the crime had long been in the planning stage, going back "as long ago as last November [1923]."

That the two were quickly caught due to careless mistakes, and that they ran unnecessary risks, was also something that Darrow pointed to as proof of their diseased minds.

Reciting the specifics of the scheme, he argued:

> *I submit, Your Honor, that no one unless he had an afflicted mind, together with youth, could possibly have done it.*

That argument presupposes that the only crimes not driven by afflicted minds are those that are risk-free, with clear and identifiable motives, and during which no errors, small or large, are committed by the criminals. Prisons are full of stupid and/or careless criminals who made stupid and/or careless mistakes, as well as smart criminals who made stupid and/or careless mistakes.

Stupidity and carelessness are neither defenses nor mitigating factors.

They Couldn't Help Themselves

This is where Darrow really goes off the rails, but it was this pet theory, along with a hate for capital punishment, that enticed him to the case in the first place.

And money, of course.

He elaborated at length in his autobiography how forces

beyond our control, sometimes inherent in our genes and other times embedded in us due to our upbringing, compel our behavior and absolve us of responsibility for our actions.

> *It is perfectly plain that at birth any two children are equally good or bad, if one is so senseless as to use those words. No one is either good or bad; still, two boys may start apparently alike, and in a very few years one may be in the penitentiary and the other in Congress. What has caused this difference in results? There can be but two causes: one, natural equipment; the other, training and opportunity.[49] If it is natural equipment, then surely no credit or blame should attach to the individual. If due to training, the individual is no more responsible for that.*

He addressed both natural equipment and training in his argument, arguing that either of them fully absolved his clients of responsibility for what they had done.

We'll cover the latter in the next chapter but focus here on the former.

To expand on language quoted above, here is Darrow's complete thought:

> *Why did they kill little Bobby Franks? Not for money, not for spite, not for hate. They killed him as they might kill a spider or a fly, for the experience. They killed him because they were made that way. Because somewhere in the infinite processes that go to the making up of the boy or the man, something slipped, and those unfortunate lads sit here hated, despised, outcasts, with the community shouting for their blood. Are they to blame for it?.... It is one of those things that happened; that happened, and it*

---

[49] A third possibility might be that the criminals in Congress have simply not been caught or their actions have been overlooked or excused by partisan politics.

> *calls not for hate but for kindness, for charity, for consideration.*

Now let's break that down and examine the full rationale behind Darrow's argument that the State's desire to "hang two boys" is something that flies "in the face of science."

He hinted at it when addressing Mrs. Leopold and Mrs. Loeb as the "victims," when it came to the mothers, because they would be left to wonder, "How came my children to be what they are? From what ancestry did they get this strain?... Was I the bearer of the seed that brings them to death?"

Darrow believed that all people were the product of their ancestry and heredity, not just in terms of skin, hair, and eye color, but also predisposition to engage in certain acts. This is that "natural equipment" he referred to in his autobiography.

There was a reason for the very crime being prosecuted, the murder of Bobby Franks, and that reason preexisted Nathan Leopold and Richard Loeb.

> *I do not know what it was that made these boys do this mad act, but I do know there is a reason for it. I know they did not beget themselves...someone in the past has sinned against them.*

Early in his filibuster, Darrow laid a guilt trip on Judge Caverly, noting that since there was no jury, "Your Honor, if these boys hang, you must do it.... It must be by your deliberate, cool, premeditated act, without a chance to shift responsibility."

He later piled on, claiming that justice (though his concept of justice was nebulous) could only be meted out by one "[w]ho knew the origin of every cell that went into the body, who could understand the structure and how it acted."

In other words, you must buy into my "original sin" theory before you can legitimately dispense justice. And if you buy it, then tread lightly on punishment.

That, essentially, was what Darrow's argument was all

about: original sin. That was an interesting concept for the atheist in him to embrace and champion, particularly because it arose out of the Christian concept that all humans are predisposed to sin because of their descent from Adam and Eve.

Of course, he had his own particular slant.

For him, it wasn't about the taint of the original sin, which was more about proclivity to sin, but rather of some defective gene somewhere in the past that made its way from parent to child, from parent to child, down to the present. It ultimately manifested itself in Leopold's and Loeb's emotional lives, without their having a say in it, thereby compelling their conduct.

That meant, he concluded, they had no control over their conduct because it was embedded in their very natures. They were predestined to commit this particular act. Thus, if they had no control, they bore no responsibility.

> *I know what causes the emotional life. I know it comes from the nerves, the muscles, the endocrine gland, the vegetative system. I know it is the most important part of life. I know it is practically left out of some.*

***

> *Is Dickie Loeb to blame because out of the infinite forces that conspired to form him, the infinite forces that were at work producing him ages before he was born, that because out of these infinite combinations he was born without it? If he is, then there should be a new definition for justice. Is he to blame for what he did not have and never had? Is he to blame that his machine is imperfect? Who is to blame?*

Presumably Darrow actually believed what he was saying. If true, it absolves all persons of any crimes or moral wrongs they commit. That seemed to be the point Darrow was making.

Lest it have been lost in subtlety, he continued to hammer on it, stretching credulity while asking the judge to suspend disbelief.

> *I know that one of two things happened to Richard Loeb: that this terrible crime was inherent in his organism, and came from some ancestor; or that it came through his education and his training after he was born.... To believe that any boy is responsible for himself or his early training is an absurdity that no lawyer or judge should be guilty of today. Somewhere this came to the boy.... I do not know what remote ancestors may have sent down the seed that corrupted him, and I do not know how many ancestors it may have passed until it reached Dickie Loeb.*

As he told the prisoners in the Cook County Jail:

> *I really do not in the least believe in crime.... I do not believe that people are in jail because they deserve to be. They are in jail simply because they cannot avoid it on account of circumstances which are entirely beyond their control and for which they are in no way responsible.*

As that sage of The Three Stooges, Curly, said, "I was a victim of circumstances."

Do it for All Children Everywhere

At last, his supply of nonsense running low, Darrow lapsed into an appeal that patted himself on the back for his selfless efforts. "I have stood here for more than three months as one might stand at the ocean trying to sweep back the tide."

He told Judge Caverly that his plea wasn't really just about the teen-aged Leopold and Loeb, but it was for "all boys and all girls; for all of the young, and as far as possible, for all of the old."

Apparently, however, it was not for Bobby Franks.

Blowhard

This hearkens back to an earlier foray into back-patting when he said, "I am not pleading so much for these boys as I am for the infinite number of others to follow, who perhaps cannot be as well defended as these have been."

You know, those who cannot afford the brilliant Clarence Darrow to defend them.

Returning to the guilt trip he laid on Judge Caverly at the start, he said that if the judge sentenced the two killers to hang, "you are making it harder for every other boy who, in ignorance and darkness, must grope his way through the mazes which only childhood knows. In doing it you will make it harder for unborn children."

But please do the world a favor, he argued. Spare their lives, because "you may save them and make it easier for every child that sometime may stand where these boys stand. You will make it easier for every human being with an aspiration and a hope and a fate."

The future of the world is in your hands, Judge. "I am pleading for the future; I am pleading for a time when hatred and cruelty will not control the hearts of men, when we can learn by reason and judgment and understanding and faith that all life is worth saving,[50] and that mercy is the highest attribute of man."

Then he started working himself up for his grand finale:

If I should succeed in saving these boys' lives and do nothing for the progress of the law, I should feel sad, indeed. If I can succeed, my greatest reward and my greatest hope will be that I have done something for the tens of thousands of other boys, for the countless unfortunates who must tread the same road in blind childhood that these poor boys have trod; that I have done

---

[50] Ironically, in the Massie Case, he seemed content to argue that his clients were justified in killing Joseph Kahahawai. Why wasn't Joe's life worth saving?

Mike Farris

something to help human understanding, to temper justice with mercy, to overcome hate with love.

At last, after twelve hours, Darrow decided to rest with one last spasm of pretension by reciting a verse from Omar Khayyam. Or maybe he just liked reciting poetry; he had already twice recited from Khayyam ("The Moving Finger writes...." and "But helpless pieces in the game He plays..."), as well as twice from A.E. Houseman, *The Culprit* ("The day my mother bore me she was a fool and glad, for all the pain I cost her") and *Nothing But the Night* ("In all the endless road you tread there's nothing but the night.")

Or maybe Darrow was simply the forerunner of the cartoon character Bullwinkle who would stand in Poetry Corner and recite various poetical works.

So I be written in the Book of Love,
I do not care about that Book above.
Erase my name or write it as you will,
So I be written in the Book of Love.

Blowhard

Chapter Eleven: Someone Else's Fault

If you could kick the person in the pants responsible for most of your trouble, you wouldn't sit for a month.
—Theodore Roosevelt

IN ADDITION TO using his clients' ancestors and endocrine glands as grounds for mitigation, Darrow also pointed the finger of actual culpability at them—and other factors, as well.

That shouldn't have been a surprise.

Truth is, Darrow never lacked for others to blame for the murder of Bobby Franks. Because he cast his net far and wide, it was only natural that it scooped up everyone remotely related to the case—ranging from his clients' parents to governesses and even extending to the parents of the murder victim—and everything, whether related to the case or not—ranging from World War I to money—*except for* his own clients.

Darrow needed the judge to agree with him that other persons and things were to blame, not just to mitigate the conduct, but to exculpate Leopold and Loeb.

After all, if someone or something else was to blame, how could you hold those two most unfortunate boys accountable?

Consider the culprits he blamed.

Pointing Fingers—The Wealth of his Clients' Families

Swedish pop sensation ABBA had a huge hit in 1982 with "Money, Money, Money." Pink Floyd deducted two moneys in their 1973 hit, "Money," while the O'Jays added a fourth in the opening line ("Money money money money") of their hit "For the Love of Money," released the same year as the Pink Floyd smash.

There is an oft-misquoted *Bible* verse in the *New Testament* that says, "For the love of money is the root of all evil." 1 *Timothy* 6:10 (KJV). In the Leopold and Loeb case, Darrow seemed to buy into that misquotation, which omits the phrase "the love of" and settles blame solely on money, itself.

He took his swings at money, not just as a mitigating factor but also as the miscreant centrally responsible for the crime, though he didn't put his words to music. It is perhaps surprising, though, that he didn't recite poetry about money.

Alongside the irresistible compulsion caused by heredity, his number one whipping boy was the wealth of the Leopold and Loeb families. As mentioned before, he eased into the money issue by trying to convince the judge that money paid to the lawyers and psychiatrists was irrelevant.

> *We announced to the public that no excessive use of money would be made in this case, neither for the lawyers nor for psychiatrists, nor in any other way.*

In other words, please understand that the parents of Leopold and Loeb are not trying to buy their sons' escape from the noose.

But that didn't mean that the issue of money, itself, was irrelevant, as far as Darrow was concerned. "Money has been the most serious handicap that we have met. There are times when poverty is fortunate." Or, stated another way, "Your Honor, it is just as often a great misfortune to be the child of the rich as it is to be the child of the poor. Wealth has its misfortunes."

Or yet another way: "They [the parents] might have done better if they had not had so much money. I do not know. Great wealth often curses all who touch it."

And he pleaded with Judge Caverly not to hold that wealth against his clients by pointing out the cloud such action would suspend above his own head. "And, if Your Honor shall doom them to die, it will be because they are the sons of the rich."

This was all about the affluenza defense, not just in mitigation but as the actual culprit. "The boys had been reared in luxury, and they had never been denied anything; no want or desire left unsatisfied; no debts; no need of money; nothing."

They were so spoiled, the argument went, so used to getting whatever they wanted, that they perceived no boundaries to their conduct. Money was to blame, not the two killers, themselves. "Too much, too great opportunity and advantage given to a child has its misfortunes, and I am asking Your Honor to consider the rich as well as the poor."

Yes, money made for a great villain, but that was a particularly ironic argument given Darrow's overarching belief that the number one cause of crime in this country was the *lack* of money. He told the prisoners in the Cook County Jail: "First and last, people are sent to jail because they are poor." It was what motivated crime, he said.

"Crime is born, not because people are bad...but because they see a chance to get some money out of it," and that "[m]ost all of the crimes for which we are punished are property crimes."

Money: damned if you have it; damned if you don't.

He did exploit that Leopold and Loeb family wealth, though, to try to prove that the ransom money wasn't a motive for the crime since they already had access to all the money they wanted. Classic Darrow, using both sides of the coin to his advantage.

I suppose that is no more than any lawyer might do under

the circumstances, and if it were an isolated instance of hypocrisy, we might overlook it. But hypocrisy pervaded much of his rhetoric.

Coloring outside the lines, he repeatedly contended that the only reason so much attention had been directed at the case had to do with money, as well. "We are here with the lives of two boys imperiled, with the public aroused. For what? Because, unfortunately, the parents have money. Nothing else."

Later, "But they must be hanged, because everybody is talking about the case, and their people have money."

And still later, as one of the reasons the case claimed so much attention: "First is the reputed extreme wealth of these families."

In fact, he said, ordinarily there would be no dispute that his clients' minds were diseased, but the "question is raised only because their parents have money."

If it weren't for money, he said, they would already have been sent to the "psychopathic hospital." But, because the boys were from wealthy families, there was a demand that they be treated differently.

Hang the rich bastards!

Darrow discounted the possibility, no matter how remote—or not remote—that the public was, instead, aroused by the brutality of the crime, which he discounted almost to nothingness.

This was not the only occasion in which he trivialized the murderous act of his clients to the courtroom.

He did his level best to deflect from the crime at every turn, and money was his favorite target, another irony (or hypocrisy) in light of how much he ultimately demanded as payment for his services.

Carrying his argument to the absurd, he blamed "not only the [wealth of] the Loeb and Leopold families, but the Franks family...."

Leopold's and Loeb's Parents

Recall that Darrow had specifically identified two primary causes for crime: natural equipment (or heredity) and training.[51] Both of those can be traced to parents, with the former going back deeper into other generations as well.

We have discussed heredity in the prior chapter, but training, or upbringing in the home, fits better in this chapter. It allowed Darrow to directly blame the Leopolds and the Loebs for not only their money, but also for their parental malpractice in raising sociopathic sons.

This was another fine line he had to tread.

If he was going to get paid, he couldn't offend or alienate the payors.

At least not upfront. Finesse was required.

His argument about heredity wasn't something to directly blame the parents for; after all, they were just as excused from guilt for passing along the killer gene from their ancestors as their offspring were from receiving it. And even when he began to ease into the assault on the parents, he couched it primarily in terms that excused bad parenting by blaming it on their wealth.

He started with a disclaimer, not to mention the aforementioned appeal to motherhood. "I seem to be criticizing their parents. They had parents who were kind and good and wise in their way." Then he lowered the boom. "But I say to you seriously that the parents are more responsible than these boys."

He tried to soften the blow, however, by circling back to that old bugaboo, money.

> *I say this again, without finding fault with his parents, for whom I have the highest regard,[52] and who doubtless did the best they could. They might have done better if*

---

[51] Three causes, if you include the lack of money he argued to the prisoners at the Cook County Jail.
[52] Particularly as long as they were holding on to those checkbooks.

> *they had not had so much money. I do not know. Great wealth curses all who touch it.*

And...

> *The great misfortune in this terrible case is the money. That has destroyed their lives. That has fostered these illusions. That has promoted this mad act. And, if Your Honor shall doom them to die, it will be because they are the sons of the rich.*

Children, he said, aren't born with any inherent knowledge of right and wrong. It's up to the parents and educators to teach that.

> *Gradually his parents and his teachers tell him things, teach him habits, show him that he may do this and he may not do that, teach him the difference between his and mine. No child knows this when he is born.*

Darrow apparently believed—or at least wanted the judge to believe; let's not confuse Darrow's actual beliefs with what he felt he needed to say to advance his positions—that was where the Leopolds and Loebs went off-course. "[I]f he had been trained as he should have been it [the murder of Bobby Franks] would not have happened."

So there it was.

The parents didn't teach their sons right and wrong, and this crime was the inevitable result. After all, unless your parents have so instructed you, by the time you are a teenager going on into your twenties, you have no idea if it is right or wrong to bludgeon and suffocate a young boy to death. And since you just have no way of knowing, it must be the fault of your parents; it's certainly not yours.

Trying to placate the parents again, he said of his clients, "They had parents who were kind and good and wise in their way. But I say to you seriously that the parents are more responsible than these boys. And yet few boys had better parents." In common parlance, this is called "speaking out of both sides of your mouth." But there was yet a glimmer of hope for the conundrum of blaming the parents who would write the check. Maybe there was someone else he could blame for deficient training and upbringing besides the parental Loebs and Leopolds.

But who?

Richard Loeb's Governess

Well, in Richard Loeb's case, he spent much of his formative years in the care of a governess. So, let's blame her. Even though Darrow said, "Now, I am not criticizing the nurse," he damn sure was.

He complained that the governess, into whose care Loeb had been placed, was overly ambitious for her charge and pushed him too hard. He said that she was "intellectual, vigorous, devoted, with a strong ambition of the welfare of this boy." That "ambition was that he should reach the highest perfection." So, she "pushed" him, "as plants are forced in hothouses. He had no pleasures, such as a boy should have, except as they were gained by lying and cheating."

In other words, in order to thwart her lofty ambitions for him, he was forced to learn deceit and, ultimately, murder. Her fault, of course. She insisted that he read "the best books," but he rebelled by reading, in secret, detective stories.

According to Darrow, there was a statute in Illinois that prohibited minors from reading detective stories because, the legislature believed, "it would produce criminal tendencies in the boys who read them." And so, if Loeb developed such statutorily predicted tendencies from reading them, that was apparently the governess's fault for making him resort to reading them in secret instead of the higher forms of literature she foisted on him.

And all the while, he was "scheming and planning as healthy

boys would do, to get out from under her restraint." Putting that lying and cheating to good use, no doubt. Darrow didn't explain at what point that "healthy boy" developed his diseased mind.

Instead, he seemed to be simply saying that Loeb's mind was agile enough to actually plot his way around his governess; ergo, anything nefarious he did was her fault.

Detective Stories

Darrow contended that those banned detective stories, that Loeb wouldn't have read but for the governess, produced criminal tendencies in him just as the Illinois legislature feared they would. It was these stories that were the genesis of the ultimate crime.

He read them day after day and, early on, developed this capacity, in his formerly healthy but now diseased little mind, to be a detective, employing ways to trail...

> ...some unfortunate individual through devious ways until his victim is finally landed in jail or stands on the gallows. They all show how smart the detective is, and where the criminal himself falls down.

But, instead of identifying with the detective, Loeb apparently found himself wanting to be the criminal and getting away with the crime.

One of his role models was whoever kidnapped and killed little Charley Ross in Philadelphia in 1874—and got away with it, despite the involvement of the Pinkerton National Detective Agency. Little Charley, who was four-years-old at the time, was snatched from his front yard and never seen again, even though a $20,000 ransom demand was sent to his father.

One arrest was made, of former Philadelphia policeman William Westervelt, but with no evidence to tie the suspect to the crime, Westervelt was acquitted at trial. This was one of the first kidnappings to become national news in the media and is still unsolved today. Charley's father, Christian, wrote a book about the case in 1876, called *The Father's Story of Charley Ross, the Kidnapped Child*, and the story attracted Loeb's attention. Darrow said:

> *This boy early in his life conceived the idea that there could be a perfect crime, one that nobody would ever detect; that there could be one where the detective did not land his game—a perfect crime. He had been interested in the story of Charley Ross, who was kidnapped. He was interested in these things all his life. He believed in his childish way that a crime would be so carefully planned that there would be no detection, and his idea was to plan and accomplish a perfect crime. It would involve kidnaping and murder.*

And just a scant three years later, the kidnapping and murder of Bobby Franks would inspire a Japanese youth living in Hawaii, Myles Fukunaga, to kidnap and kill 10-year-old Gill Jamieson, emulating the Leopold and Loeb crime right down to the weapon of choice (a chisel) and plagiarizing the language in the ransom note.

Fukunaga was also a big reader of detective stories, filling his head with not only fictional detectives like Philo Vance and real-life stories, such as Leopold and Loeb, but also the case of Edward Hickman, who kidnapped and killed twelve-year-old Marion Parker in Los Angeles and then, after her death, sent a ransom demand.

Maybe the Illinois legislature was on to something.

Lack of Proper Training

This went hand-in-hand with blaming the Leopold and Loeb parents, though it was broader than just the household. Still, that was where it started, and that was on the parents. "No one chooses his parents or early environment in the first years which are all-determining after birth." [cliv]

Furthermore, as Darrow said in his autobiography, "There are but few, even among idiots, who cannot fairly well fill some useful position if rightly trained." [clv]

While the scheme that resulted in the death of Bobby Franks may have been initially inspired by those detective stories that Richard Loeb read, it also "grew from the lack of proper training until it possessed him. He believed he could beat the police. He believed he could plan the perfect crime."

But it was the homelife that drew Darrow's sharpest attack. Dickie Loeb "needed more of home, more love, more directing.... Had these been given him, he would not be here today."

Let this be a lesson to all you parents out there.

Youth

Just as Darrow argued that youth of the two boys should have mitigated the consequences for the murder, he also directly blamed youth as the actual cause of the crime.

Youth, both as mitigation and culprit, was probably Darrow's best and most effective argument, that the crime could both be blamed on youth and excused by youth. It was the ultimate factor the judge relied upon for withholding capital punishment, something he would have done that no matter what Darrow said.

It suggests that all Darrow really needed to do was to make a brief argument against the death penalty, point out the ages of his clients, who were eighteen (Loeb) and nineteen (Leopold) at the time of the killing, and then throw them on the mercy of the court. The result would have been the same and everyone could have been spared twelve hours of Darrow's overwrought oratory.

Darrow's sin, however, at least as far as this author is concerned, was in creating a false equivalency between the recklessness of youth and a brutal murder. We've discussed this above, so I won't belabor the point (too much more) here.

But in directing a finger of blame in the direction of youth,

Blowhard

he also rolled it into a complaint about lack of training.

> ...it is the dreams and the hallucinations of childhood that are responsible for his conduct. There is not an act in all this horrible tragedy that was not the act of a child, the act of a child wandering around in the morning of his life, moved by the new feelings of a boy, moved by the uncontrolled impulses which his teaching was not strong enough to take care of, moved by the dreams and hallucinations which haunt the brain of a child.

The deficiencies of youth are why the legal system makes distinctions based upon the age of majority, which varies in various categories: *e.g.*, age to buy liquor, age to vote, age to serve in the military, age to get married, age to make legal contracts, and age to be tried as an adult in criminal courts.

Immaturity and inexperience are taken into account. And Darrow is correct that there are many occasions when conduct is the result of a "youthful indiscretion." As he noted vociferously here, Leopold and Loeb were not even old enough to make contracts, yet there they were being tried as adults with the gallows hanging in the balance.

And so, to argue mitigation based upon youth was logical and reasonable. But to blame youth entirely, and thereby excuse the conduct, or to minimize the crime by analogizing it to simple youthful indiscretions—boyhood pranks and mischief; at one point he compares it to kleptomania, as if it were no worse than shoplifting, a "childish scheme growing up in these childish minds"—was out of bounds.

But Darrow deliberately conflated excuse and mitigation in the same way he conflated the diseased minds argument with youth...

> ...it was the senseless act of immature and diseased children, as it was; a senseless act of children wandering around in the dark and moved by some emotion that we

still have not the knowledge or the insight into life to understand thoroughly.

Darrow drew a particularly ridiculous analogy at one point while attacking Dr. William O. Krohn, a prosecution psychiatrist who testified in support of the death penalty. Darrow excoriated him as providing his testimony in exchange for cash. "One was the mad act of a child; the other the cold, deliberate act of a man getting his living by dealing in blood."

Interestingly, and apparently without a trace of irony, Darrow also attacked Krohn for his speechifying. "Krohn is not an alienist. He is an orator." Of all of Clarence Darrow's positive attributes, self-perception was not one.

His clients, he was saying, were children incapable of making informed choices and thus should be excused by their childhood. Or, as he restated it later, it was the act of "two immature boys of diseased mind...." At this point came one of his stabs at Omar Khayyam, using it to support the notion that "nature is strong and she is pitiless" and that, in boyhood, "we are her victims. We have not much to do with it ourselves. Nature takes this job in hand, and we play our parts."

> *But helpless pieces in the game He plays*
> *Upon this checkerboard of nights and days;*
> *Hither and thither moves, and checks, and slays,*
> *And one by one back in the closet lays.*

Later, still commingling "natural equipment" and youth as culprits, the murder of Bobby Franks was all, as far as Darrow was concerned, some "act of immature and diseased brains, the act of children. Nobody can explain it any other way. No one can imagine it in any other way." And so, he said as if leading to a logical conclusion for the argument, "it would be monstrous to visit upon them the vengeance that is asked by the State."

To reiterate his point, he launched into another discussion of age and youthfulness, as if bringing it up for the first time. "I want to discuss now another thing which this court must consider and which to my mind is absolutely conclusive in this case. That is, the age of these boys."

As noted before, youth was likely his best and highest argument.

So, one wonders, why did he save it for near the end of his filibuster? That was kind of like burying the lede, wasn't it?[53] Could it be that he didn't really believe it himself? Or was it simply that he wanted his own pet arguments against capital punishment and free will to take precedence?

It would not be the only time he subordinated his client's position to his need to spotlight his own philosophies. Just see the Scopes Monkey Trial.

Puberty and Sexuality

Leopold and Loeb were reputed to have been gay lovers, something that led to the "falling out of cocksuckers" letter that they were questioned about in their interrogation. Prosecutor Crowe referred to them as "perverts," which was a common view of homosexuality at the time. Without confirming or denying the rumor, Darrow seized upon it, or at least the idea of it, as yet another culprit.

> *From the age of fifteen to the age of twenty or twenty-one, the child has the burden of adolescence, of puberty and sex thrust upon him. Girls are kept at home and carefully watched. Boys without any instruction are left to work the period out for themselves. It may lead to excess. It may lead to disgrace. It may lead to perversion. Who is to blame? Who did it?.... And yet there are men who say that for what nature has done, for what life has done, for what training has done, you should hang these boys.*

---

[53] The "lede" is the introduction to a journalistic article. To "bury the lede" means to hide or obscure the most important part of a story.

But regardless of whether Darrow accepted the relationship as true, one of his own alienists, Dr. William Healy, provided testimony to support it. He described a compact between Leopold and Loeb that included permitting homosexual conduct between the two.

> *This compact, as was told to me separately by each of the boys on different occasions, and verified over and over, consisted of an agreement between them that Leopold, who has very definite homosexual tendencies, which have been a part of his makeup for many years, was to have the privilege of* [performing homosexual acts on Loeb].

Healy was quite explicit in his testimony, stating that the permitted conduct included experimentation with "mouth perversions." In keeping with Darrow's blaming of youth, he described it as...

> *...a childish form of perversion. There are many kinds of perversion. But, as far as that goes, there are many children, very innocent children of fine people who get into many things of that sort.*

Prosecutor Crowe sought to make something of this issue during his closing argument, obviously hoping to outrage Judge Caverly. The autopsy report on Bobby Franks noted that, in addition to his body being nude, his "rectum was dilated, and would admit easily one middle finger."

It did not, though, report any signs of "recent forced dilation" and declined to conclude there had been any sexual assault. However, the fact that Bobby had been stripped, coupled with the bare reference to rectum dilation and testimony of "perversion," was all Crowe needed. Judge Caverly shut him down after Darrow and co-counsel Benjamin Bachrach objected.

Blowhard

MR. CROWE: *I want to tell your honor, bearing in mind the testimony that was whispered into your ear, one of the motives in this case was a desire to satisfy unnatural lust. They first wanted a little girl so that Leopold could rape her and then they decided on a little boy. What happened? Immediately upon killing him they took his trousers off. How do you undress a child? First the little coat, the collar, the tie, the shirt, and the last thing is his trousers. Yet, immediately after killing this poor little boy, his trousers alone came off, and for three hours that little dead boy, without his trousers but with all his other clothes on him, remained in that car, and they did not take the balance of the clothes off until they pushed the body into the culvert. You have before you the coroner's report.*

MR. DARROW: *Well, now—*

MR. B. BACHRACH: *If the court please, I take exception to that statement. The coroner's report said there was no sign of recent dilation.*

MR. CROWE: *Your honor has the report.*

MR. BACHRACH: *Your honor will look at the report.*

MR. CROWE: *And I want to call your honor's attention to the fact that this little naked body lay in the water all night long with running water going over it, and that is why there wasn't any other evidence.*

After leaving the subject for a while, Crowe continued his argument, but when the subject came up again, Bachrach objected that "this is the first time it has been charged in this case that the committing of an immoral act was the purpose of this crime on the part of this boy."

After argument about what the coroner's report did or did not show, or imply, portions of the report were re-read. Darrow said, "This is the evidence of the coroner and certainly conclusive and we will let it rest with what the coroner says."

Then Crowe put his own button on it.

> The evidence is that these two defendants are perverts, and when they took the body of the boy in, the first thing they took off was his trousers.[clvi]

Society

Although he did not elaborate much, Darrow took a swipe at society as a culprit. It appeared to be the proverbial throwing anything and everything against the wall to see what sticks. "Society, too, should assume its share of the burdens of this case, and not make two more tragedies...."

Friedrich Nietzsche

Nathan Leopold was enamored with Friedrich Nietzsche, a 19th Century German philosopher with worldwide influence.

Nietzsche was a nihilist, a philosophy that basically rejected societal norms and concepts of morality. He championed the notion that "God is Dead," and advocated a belief that certain people were above such basic human constraints as morality and right and wrong. Apparently one of those who fell under his spell, likely because he was searching for a philosophy that would absolve him for his own unnatural wants and desires, was Nathan Leopold.

He was an avid reader of Nietzsche's work and an advocate of the concept set forth by Nietzsche's notion of the "*Übermensch*"—translated as "Superman," from his book *Thus Spoke Zarathustra*.

Oversimplified, the "Superman" was a being who had achieved a status of intelligence for whom "the laws of good and evil do not apply."

Leopold, unquestionably highly intelligent, believed he fit

that mold. Or, at least, that was what he wanted to believe because it would validate his notion that he could decide right and wrong for himself and act accordingly, without any constraints. The Apostle Paul seemed to anticipate this very behavior in his second letter to Timothy in the *New Testament*.

> *For the time will come when men will not put up with sound doctrine. Instead, to suit their own desires, they will gather around them a great number of teachers to say what their itching ears want to hear.* 2 Timothy 4:3. (New International Version)[54]

Darrow described the so-called "Superman" this way: "[T]he man has no obligations; he may do with all other men and all other boys, and all society, as he pleases...." Leopold was an impressionable "boy who never should have seen it at that early age," but he was "obsessed with it." Darrow went on to say that "He [Leopold] and Dickie Loeb were the supermen. There might have been others, but they were two, and two chums. The ordinary commands of society were not for him."

Darrow claimed that Leopold "could not have believed it excepting that it either caused a diseased mind or was the result of a diseased mind."

> *Here is a boy who by day and by night, in season and out, was talking of the superman, owing no obligations to anyone; whatever gave him pleasure he should do, believing it just as another man might believe a religion or philosophical theory.*

Nietzsche, himself, became insane for fifteen years prior to his death, and Darrow asserted that "[h]is very doctrine is a species

---

[54] The King James Version has it this way: "For the time will come when they will not endure sound doctrine; but after their own lusts shall they heap to themselves teachers, having itching ears."

of insanity."

Interestingly, Harrison Otis, owner of the *Los Angeles Times*, whose building was destroyed by a bomb Darrow's clients, the McNamara brothers, were responsible for, was also a follower of Nietzsche.

And Darrow became somewhat of a Nietzsche expert in the aftermath of his bribery trials. Following his departure from Los Angeles, he wrote to Charles Erskine Scott Wood on May 19, 1913, of an upcoming talk he was scheduled to give. "I am to speak on Nietzsche next Sunday & have been reading him industriously. I am getting quite enamored of him & he is doing me good...." [clvii]

Books [Part Two]

Darrow had already blamed detective stories and now he blamed libraries that were full of books about Nietzsche, the man of whom he had, himself, become enamored.

> *If this boy is to blame for this, where did he get it? Is there any blame attached because somebody took Nietzsche's philosophy seriously and fashioned his life on it? And there is no question in this case that it is true. Then who is to blame? The university would be more to blame than he is. The scholars of the world would be more to blame than he is. The publishers of the world—and Nietzsche's books are published by one of the biggest publishers in the world—are more to blame than he. Your Honor, it is hardly fair to hang a nineteen-year-old boy for the philosophy that was taught to him at the university.*

But then Darrow seemed to backpedal on blaming universities and their libraries. Perhaps he realized that wouldn't pass the smell test. "I do not believe that the universities are to blame. I do not think they should be held responsible. I do think, however, that they are too large, and that they should keep a closer watch, if possible, upon the individual."

Nice save: schools and libraries are simply too big, so let's not blame Babe and Dickie.

World War I

Darrow contended that the war, as do all wars, cheapened the value of life and desensitized people to death. Even though in the case of this particular war, he "believed in it," it still had a deleterious impact on people that somehow led Leopold and Loeb to kill Bobby Franks.

> *For four long years the civilized world was engaged in killing men.... We read of killing one hundred thousand men in a day. We read about it and we rejoiced in it—if it was the other fellows who were killed. We were fed on flesh and drank blood.... War is a part of it; education is a part of it; birth is a part of it; money is a part of it— all these conspired to compass the destruction of these two poor boys.*

While it certainly might have taught some "to place a cheap value on human life," he didn't mention the millions of others who were similarly impacted by the effects of the war but who did not degenerate into killers, themselves. He also dismissed, or ignored, the time element: the war had been over for six years, and Leopold and Loeb were thirteen and fourteen when it ended. Would it really have impacted them at the time, in an age where the war's violence was not broadcast over the Internet or social media?

Perhaps anticipating the question, Darrow invented his own statute of limitations: "It will take fifty years to wipe it out of the human heart, if ever. I know this, that after the Civil War in 1865, crimes of this sort increased marvelously."

And, he contended, the war certainly impacted his clients.

> *I know it has influenced these boys so that life was not the same to them as it would have been if the world had not*

been made red with blood.

Just like any other boys in the fifty years after any other war who didn't commit grisly crimes like the murder of Bobby Franks.

Happenstance

Darrow argued, and many historians agree to some extent, that this particular crime—the murder of Bobby Franks—might never have happened but for the fact that two sociopaths happened to find each other.

A match made in hell.

It makes for a pretty good argument, though there is some belief that at least Richard Loeb had committed other crimes, including murder, on his own.

King and Wilson questioned: "Did they recognize a certain darkness in the other that mirrored their own secret malignancies?" They wrote that "Loeb had swept into Nathan's drab, ordered world like a ray of gleaming sunshine, breathing life into his grim existence." [clviii]

As early as 1921, the two began committing crimes, but more serious than the types of petty crimes in which Loeb had previously been involved. "Once Nathan entered the picture, things accelerated. Richard needed more excitement and Nathan was eager to please." [clix] Soon, "[t]he relationship became a way to test their own limits, their devotion to each other, to see how far they could carry their subversive acts." [clx]

Darrow certainly seemed to buy into the theory, as if the two, if they had never met each other, would have otherwise been model citizens.

> *These boys, neither one of them, could possibly have committed this act excepting by coming together. It was not the act of one; it was the act of two.... Their parents happened to meet, these boys happened to meet; some sort of chemical alchemy operated so that they cared for each other, and poor Bobby Franks's dead body was found in*

the culvert as a result.

It seems like a leap to conclude that two sociopaths, acting alone, could not possibly have committed atrocities on their own. It also seems to undercut his arguments that they were fated by heredity to be killers, that they were doomed by their families' wealth to be killers, that Nietzsche and detective stories compelled them to be killers, that poor training and bad nannies caused them to be killers, that youth caused them to be killers, that their diseased minds caused them to be killers, the war caused them to be killers, and so on.

But even assuming the validity of the theory, it's hard to fathom how it could possibly justify the acts the two committed. It might give rise to brand new defense to crimes committed by multiple criminals—gee, I never would have done it had I not met John Doe, so give me a pass.

Spared from the Gallows

Various newspaper accounts reported that, by the time Darrow finished his argument, tears were streaming down the faces of many spectators, as well as the of the judge.

His speech passed muster with his clients.

Leopold said:

> *It is a masterpiece of English prose. It is much more. It is a deep treatise on philosophy, yet so simply told that a child can understand it. It is moving oratory, moving because the man who delivered the oration was moved, deeply moved.*

He added, perhaps a bit blasphemously:

> *[I]f I were asked to name the two men who, in my opinion, came closest to preaching the pure essence of love—love for the human race—I think I'd feel compelled to name Jesus of Nazareth and Clarence Darrow.*[clxi]

But prosecutor Crowe wasn't having any of it, seeing through Darrow's arguments for the nonsense they were.

> ...my God, I am glad that I do not know of any lawyer who would get on the witness stand and under oath characterize an unnatural agreement between these two perverts as a childish compact.

Referring to Darrow's alienists as the "Wise men from the East," he debunked their "distorted theories," which Darrow put forth as mitigating circumstances. His argument reeked of sarcasm. Noting Darrow's plea to treat his clients with mercy and charity, Crowe said:

> ...they are as much entitled to the sympathy and mercy of this court as a couple of rattle snakes [sic], flushed with venom, coiled and ready to strike. They are entitled to as much mercy at the hands of Your Honor as two mad dogs are entitled to, from the evidence in this case.

In addition to referring to the defendants as "perverts," Crowe also called them "egotistical young smart alecks," and devolved into Darrow-esque sarcasm.

> Why, when they murder a boy they ought to be treated with kindness and consideration. If they had taken a little tot, a little girl, debauched and raped her, I suppose we ought to have given each a medal and told them to go their way. My God, what are we coming to in this community?

They were a "disgrace to their honored families and they are a menace to the community." All that should be left to them in this life, he said, is to "go out of life and go out of it as quickly as possible under the law."

Then came this interesting attack on Darrow's philosophy,

itself. Crowe claimed that Darrow was concerned about his own alienists' testimony, so he put on one to testify "about certain glands, ductless and otherwise." Then, he said, "the grand old man of the defense, Clarence Darrow, seeing how absolutely absurd it all was, discarded all their testimony and substituted as a defense in this case his peculiar philosophy of life...."

Crowe characterized Darrow as being "in a day dream [sic] and indulging in fantasies" and that Darrow, when presented with evidence establishing that the two killers carefully planned the crime, debunked it as "just the mad act of mad boys, wandering around in the dark, looking for a teddy bear."

Toward the end of his argument, Crowe tore into Darrow's "dangerous philosophy of life." He reminded the judge that Darrow claimed not to be pleading just for Leopold and Loeb, but that he was looking into the future, at future young boys who might commit crimes.

Darrow, he said, "has preached in this case that one of the handicaps the defendants are under is that they are rich, the sons of millionaires." Pointing out the irony of that, Crowe had noted earlier that had it not been for the wealth of his clients' families, Darrow wouldn't even have been there in the first place.

> Take away the millions of the Loebs and Leopolds, and Clarence Darrow's tongue is as silent as the tomb of Julius Caesar. Take away their millions, and the "Wise men from the East" would not be here, to tell you about phantasies [sic], and teddy bears, and bold, bad boys who have their pictures taken in cowboy uniforms. Take away their money, and what happens? The same thing that has happened to all the other men who have been tried in this building who had no money.

In the end, Judge John R. Caverly spared Leopold and Loeb from the gallows, sentencing them to life plus 99 years—life for murdering Bobby Franks, 99 years for kidnapping him.

It appears, though, that he didn't buy into Darrow's twelve

hours of windbaggery and bloviation. In his sentencing memorandum, he wrote that all of Darrow's analysis could just as easily apply to any other person charged with a crime and that it is "in no wise peculiar to these individual defendants." He concluded, "The court is satisfied that his judgment in the present case cannot be affected thereby."

So why did Judge Caverly spare their lives?

The ages of Leopold and Loeb, pure and simple.

> *In choosing imprisonment instead of death, the court is moved chiefly by the consideration of the age of the defendants, boys of eighteen and nineteen years.*

Leopold later wrote:

> *If Judge Caverly meant literally what he said in his opinion, the whole elaborate psychiatric defense presented in our behalf and the herculean efforts of our brilliant counsel were to no avail. The only thing that influenced him to choose imprisonment instead of death was our youth; we need only have introduced our birth certificates in evidence.*[clxii]

But a blowhard will always be a blowhard.

Chapter Twelve: Bye Dickie; Hello New and Improved Babe

Today, Nathan Leopold might be very willing to cooperate again in further examination and study of his life. This cooperation would undoubtedly contribute to our understanding of abnormal and normal psychology.

—Meyer Levin

WHAT HAPPENED TO Bobby Franks was a tragedy, but the trial was a travesty. Darrow argued that the former would not have occurred had not Nathan Leopold and Richard Loeb come together: two sociopaths, one a manipulator and one a malleable personality, combined to snuff the life out of a young boy for the sheer experience.

The latter half of the equation, the travesty, was simply an extension of that match made in hell: the two sociopaths met up with an ethically challenged egotist for an attorney, and suddenly the killers became the victims. "most unfortunate boys," "two unfortunate lads," who had no control over their actions, subject to the vagaries of genes and endocrine systems.

It was their ancestors' fault; it was their parents' fault; it was society's fault; it was the war's fault; it was Nietzsche's fault; it was the nanny's fault; it was the detective stories' fault;

it was the educational system's fault.

Heck, it was even Bobby Franks's own fault, "cocky little son of a bitch" that Loeb said he was. But it was never "Babe" Leopold's and "Dickie" Loeb's fault.

Bless their hearts!

And therein lies the travesty.

There is likely some truth to the notion, as Darrow argued, that it was the union of Leopold and Loeb that led to the inevitable thrill killing. Most historians seem to concur with this idea. In *Nothing But the Night*, one of the most recent takes on the whole affair, authors Greg King and Penny Wilson write: "Individually, Richard and Nathan were damaged but probably not dangerous. It was their coming together that proved deadly." [clxiii]

That, then, begs the question: which of the two was the driving force behind the crime?

King and Wilson noted that conventional historical wisdom had put Loeb behind the metaphorical steering wheel, a perception that Leopold later perpetuated, using his own paintbrush to color himself as "helplessly in thrall to Richard, completely subservient to his desires."

However, these authors believe, and argue convincingly, that the leadership mantle actually must fall on the shoulders of Nathan Leopold. According to their argument, conventional wisdom had been unduly influenced by Leopold's ability to reshape the narrative after Loeb was brutally slashed to death in the prison shower by an inmate named James Day in 1936.

The Violent Demise of Dickie Loeb

According to Day's account of the killing, Loeb had made numerous homosexual advances toward him and, on the fateful day, razor in hand, attempted to sexually assault him in the shower.

Day resisted and, when Loeb dropped the razor, Day retrieved it and used it to slash Loeb in self-defense.

Reporter Edwin A. Lahey of the *Chicago Daily News* led his

report with this line: "Richard Loeb, a brilliant college student and master of the English language, today ended a sentence with a proposition."

The evidence suggested, however, that Day had been the aggressor, that Loeb had defensive wounds on his hands and arms, and that his throat had actually been slashed from behind. However, Day was acquitted at trial of the killing. His lawyer claimed that Day had the right to defend himself, even if that meant killing Loeb in self-defense.

The verdict turned Day into somewhat of a celebrity as an avenger (of sorts) of Bobby Franks. The *Chicago Tribune* reported that those in the courtroom applauded when the not guilty verdict was announced, apparently content that one-half of the homicidal duo of Leopold and Loeb had been dispatched.

Day later wrote, or had ghostwritten for him, several articles about the episode, including one published in *True Detective* magazine titled "Why I Killed Richard Loeb."

He latched onto his fifteen minutes of fame.

Clarence Darrow told reporters that death benefitted Loeb over Leopold, who was still confined to prison.

"He's better off dead," he was reported in the *Chicago Daily News* as saying. Leopold bemoaned the loss of his friend this way: "I missed him terribly—all the more so since all the years in prison we shared everything and planned everything together. I was very lonely." [clxiv]

But Loeb's death actually posed a distinct advantage, and presented a golden opportunity, for Leopold, notwithstanding his self-proclaimed loneliness and Darrow's pronouncement that he was worse off.

With his murderous mate gone, Leopold now had *carte blanche* to rewrite history, including his role in the Franks murder. King and Wilson say he did just that. They suggest that Leopold may even have been behind the murder of Loeb, by paying James Day to accomplish the deed.

Both Leopold and Loeb were serving the same sentence, life plus ninety-nine years, with an admonition from the judge that the department of public welfare should never parole either of them.

However, the possibility, if not probability, existed that one of them—and only one of them—might well be paroled someday. For Leopold to grab that brass ring, though, it just wouldn't do if he was the perceived mastermind behind the murder of Bobby Franks.

Instead, "he needed to become the sole narrator of his own story, to present himself as an unwilling victim, under Richard's malignant domination and unable to resist his magnetic personality, without objection from his former partner." [clxv]

Repairing Fine China

Abraham Lincoln said, "Reputation is like fine china: Once broken it's very hard to repair." But apparently that was one of the things Leopold worked on to make prison tolerable, rehabilitating his reputation to try to set himself up for parole.

That would be a prime motive, indeed, for silencing Loeb, whom Leopold had actually threatened to kill on several occasions in 1923. King and Wilson wrote: "....money talked at Statesville [Prison]: it isn't impossible that Nathan might have arranged the attack on Richard with the promise of financial reward." [clxvi]

Regardless of whether Leopold was behind Day's murder, something we'll likely never know, the end result was that:

> Death deprived Richard of the redemption story Nathan soon claimed for himself. History—and increasingly Nathan—would portray Loeb as a malicious mastermind who had corrupted an adoring Leopold and led him to murder. In the coming years Nathan seized the opportunity to remake himself and revise his history, free from fear that Richard would contradict him, in an effort to enhance his own shattered image at the expense of his "best pal." [clxvii]

Blowhard

Leopold worked on that redemption by vilifying the now-dead Loeb in his memoir. Though he praised Dick as full of charm:

> [T]here was that other side to him. In the crime, for instance, he didn't have a single moral scruple of any kind. He wasn't immoral; he was just plain amoral—unmoral, that is. Right and wrong didn't exist. He'd do anything—anything. And it was all a game to him. He reminded me of an eight-year-old all wrapped up in a game of cops and robbers. Dick, with his brilliant mind, with his sophistication.[clxviii]

He also speculated at Loeb's motive for the killing of Bobby Franks:

> Dick's basic motive, I think, must be sought in his basic personality—in what he was, in how he had been conditioned. Primarily, I think, it was a kind of revolt—an over-reaction against the strictness of the governess who had had charge of him until he was fifteen. A basic feeling of inferiority, maybe; a desire to show that he could do things and bring them to a successful end on his own.[clxix]

And Leopold's motive? "My motive, so far as I can be said to have one, was to please Dick."[clxx] Master-slave, with Dick the master and Nathan his slave.

Leopold used that revamped narrative to obtain a parole in 1958, a parole that presaged the so-called "Son of Sam" laws with an addendum that forbade him to "voluntarily participate in any publicity activities or personal appearances on stage, radio, motion pictures, television, or any other publicity media."

But while those laws in a later era would impose a full-scale prohibition on convicted criminals from profiting from publicity for their crimes, the parole document excepted his memoirs.

In a letter from Darrow to Leopold dated September 20,

1924, Darrow encouraged him write a book about birding, which he had aspired to. Darrow said, "I have had a good deal of pleasure, or rather forgetfulness in writing books which no one reads, & [sic] I want you to write one which will be read." [clxxi] It wasn't the birding book, but while in prison Leopold did write his memoir, *Life Plus 99 Years,* for which he had already obtained a publisher. It did not meet with the success he expected.[55]

In a *Rutgers Law Review* article, Professor Edward J. Larson wrote that, following Loeb's death, Leopold worked actively to "...remake his public image," including writing his memoir that "...portrayed him as a model prisoner," part of his effort to establish himself as "...a celebrity in the eyes of the general public..." and to "...rehabilitate his image." [clxxii]

After 1936, there was, conveniently, no Richard Loeb around to contradict him.

Compulsion

Once published, Leopold's memoir was a commercial failure. Few people want to see a sociopath make money off of his sociopathy. And it was that lack of success at gaining wealth from his book that probably led Leopold to later litigation, after his parole, involving the book *Compulsion*,[clxxiii] written by author Meyer Levin, and its adaptation to the movie screen.

Levin attended the University of Chicago with, and knew, both Leopold and Loeb at the time.

In fact, he covered the case as a cub reporter for *Chicago Daily News*, and even broke a scoop or two about the case. More than thirty years later, after a distinguished career as a journalist and novelist, he penned *Compulsion*, based on the Leopold and Loeb case.

In a style that may have paved the way for later works based on true crime, such as *In Cold Blood* by Truman Capote, Levin made no secret that his book was based on fact, although

---

[55] Although it initially sold well, sales tapered off quickly and the book was remaindered, leaving Leopold disappointed.

fictionalized to some extent. In the book's Foreward, he wrote:

> *In using an actual case for my story, I follow in the great tradition of Stendhal with* The Red and the Black, *of Dostoevski [sic] with* Crime and Punishment, *of Dreiser with* An American Tragedy.... *I follow known events. Some scenes are, however, total interpolations, and some of my personages have no correspondence to persons in the case in question. This will be recognized as the method of the historical novel. I suppose* Compulsion *may be called a contemporary historical novel or a documentary novel, as distinct from a roman à clef.*[56]

The 1959 movie *Compulsion*, based on the novel, starred Dean Stockwell as Judd Steiner and Bradford Dillman as Artie Straus, characters based on Leopold and Loeb respectively. A paperback reissue of the book stated that the novel was "based upon the Leopold-Loeb case" and that it "is a spellbinding fictionalized account of one of the most famous and shocking crimes of our age—the Leopold-Loeb case."

The movie version sought to downplay the link to actual events with this disclaimer contained in promotional materials:

> *It should be made clear emphatically that* Compulsion *is not an effort to reproduce the crime of Leopold and Loeb, nor their trial. The screenplay was taken from a recognized work of fiction "suggested" by the Leopold-Loeb case, but neither the author of the book nor the producer of the film has attempted anything but to tell a dramatic*

---

[56] *Roman à clef* is French for a novel that is purportedly fiction but which depicts real life events and actual persons, although using fictitious names. Levin seems to be saying that his book differs from a *roman à clef* in that it does not even pretend to be fiction—he acknowledges the non-fiction foundation of his story over which he has spread his interpretations and suppositions.

> story.... The picture is in no way a documentary and its makers have attempted only to translate the book into terms of good dramaturgy.[57]

Leopold decided that, if his book wasn't the moneymaker he had hoped for, he might at least share in the riches from *Compulsion*.

He filed a lawsuit in state court in Chicago, accusing the powers-that-be behind the book and the movie, as well as of a play based on the book, of illegally appropriating his name for commercial purposes and invading his privacy.

Although he initially won in the trial court, obtaining summary judgment on the liability claim with the amount of damages to be decided later, it was that "later" that did him in. A new judge presiding over the damages question reconsidered his predecessor's finding in Leopold's favor on liability and dismissed the claims.

Leopold made a direct appeal to the Illinois Supreme Court.

He lost.[58]

The Illinois Supreme Court noted that Leopold agreed that "a documentary account of the Leopold-Loeb case would be a constitutionally protected expression, since the subject events are matters of public record." However, he argued that "the constitutional assurances of free speech and press do not permit an invasion of his privacy through the exploitation of his name, likeness, and personality for commercial gain in 'knowingly fictionalized accounts' of his private life and through the appropriation of his name and likeness in the advertising materials."

In other words, Leopold recognized that Levin had the right to talk about the sordid details of a brutal crime, including Leopold's role in it, but not the right to make up stuff.

---

[57] *Merriam-Webster* defines "dramaturgy" as "the art or technique of dramatic composition and theatrical representation."

[58] *Leopold v. Levin*, 45 Ill. 2d 434 (Ill. 1970).

The Court didn't buy it. Not under these facts, anyway. Even though other lower Illinois state courts had recognized the existence of a right of privacy, it was a case of first impression for the state's highest court. It noted that even among those rulings that recognized the privacy right, they nevertheless found that its application was a "limited one in areas of legitimate public interest, as where there is a legitimate news interest in one's photograph or likeness as a public figure."

So, the case was going to turn on whether Nathan Leopold was a "public figure" as opposed to a purely "private person." Just as the "later" did him in at the trial court level, this private/public issue did him in at the state's highest appellate court.

The Court said that "we must hold here that the plaintiff did not have a legally protected right of privacy." It based its decision on, among other factors, "the enduring public attention to the plaintiff's crime and prosecution, which remain an American *cause célèbres*; and the plaintiff's consequent and continuing status as a public figure."

The Court noted that Leopold "certainly did not appear to seek retirement from public attention" and even published his own autobiographical account of the crime and his subsequent life, which "unquestionably contributed to the continuing public interest in him and the crime."

In a hand-slap, it added, "He cannot at his whim withdraw the events of his life from public scrutiny."

Then the Court addressed the core complaint. Leopold had contended that, while a non-fiction account might be constitutionally protected, the "fictionalized" account didn't merit that same constitutional protection because it "caused the public to identify the plaintiff with inventions or fictionalized episodes in the book and motion picture which were so offensive and unwarranted as to 'outrage the community's notions of decency.'"

As opposed, one supposes, to the actual crime of bludgeoning and suffocating a young boy to death, stripping him of his clothes, pouring hydrochloric acid on his face and private parts, and then stuffing his naked body in a culvert.

Surely that wouldn't outrage anyone's notion of decency, would it?

Whatever Leopold's reasons for being disturbed by any fictionalizations, the Court didn't buy this argument, either.

> *However the core of the novel and film and their dominating subjects were a part of the plaintiff's life which he had caused to be placed in public view. The novel and film were derived from the notorious crime, a matter of public record and interest, in which the plaintiff had been a central figure. Further, as the trial court appeared to do, we consider the fictionalized aspects of the book and motion picture were reasonably comparable to, or conceivable from, the facts of record from which they were drawn, or minor in offensiveness when viewed in the light of such facts.*

The lawsuit actually seemed a bit of a surprise, given an apparent reconciliation of sorts between Leopold and Levin after the book's release. Leopold complained in his memoir that when Levin diverged from the historical record, the book was "pure fiction—pure moonshine." He particularly complained that it depicted his family members poorly, that they were "slightly handled."

And as for the portrayal of Judd/Leopold and Artie/Loeb?

> *The insidious, devastating thing about the book, as I see it, is Mr. Levin's consummate artistry. He has taken a large amount of fact and to it he has added an even larger amount of fiction—of pure balderdash. And he has done it in such a superbly artistic fashion that the seams don't show. No general reader can possibly know what is true and what is contrived. I confess that I, on several occasions, had to stop and think hard to be sure whether*

certain details were true or imaginary. That's what hurts.

Then came the gravamen of his complaint, that it "diminished my own hopes for release." [clxxiv]

And there it was. Leopold still held out a belief that he might obtain parole, and he feared the success of *Compulsion*, which introduced the murder of Bobby Franks to a new generation, would be detrimental to those hopes.

It surprised him that many, including Levin, himself, believed that *Compulsion* might actually be beneficial to his hope for parole. Levin wrote a letter to the editor of *Life* magazine after an interview and close-up of Leopold that was published in the March 4, 1957, issue.

According to Leopold, in the letter Levin said that he was shocked:

> ...to learn that I was unhappy over the appearance of Compulsion. He had not intended it to hurt my chances for freedom. He strongly believed that I should be released. And, further, he did not think that his book had hurt my chances. Quite the contrary. Everyone to whom he had talked agreed with him that it actually helped my chances. [clxxv]

Levin even wrote an article that was published in the May 1957 issue of *Coronet* magazine titled "Leopold Should Be Freed!" Leopold was "overwhelmed" and "most grateful" to Levin for the article, so he sent him a one-word message: "Thanks."

He said in his memoir, "I hope [Levin] knew how sincerely I meant it. If he didn't, I hope he reads this book."

Yet several years after that *kumbaya* moment, and while he was out on parole, Leopold sued Levin over the book. Regardless of what he said in his memoir, it's a good bet that Leopold's complaint had more to do with Levin's frank portrayal in *Compulsion* of him and Loeb as homosexual lovers, even though that was explicitly addressed at trial under the guise of "perversion," than the murder of Bobby Franks or the "slightingly handled" portrayals of his family members.

Or maybe it was because, even though Leopold had been released on parole, *Compulsion* portrayed him as the driver of the crime, which ran afoul of his continuing efforts to rehabilitate his image.

For example, *Compulsion*'s narrator, the intrepid cub reporter based on Levin, recounted how a fellow student blamed Judd Steiner (the Leopold character) for a different incident involving Judd and Artie Straus (the Loeb character).

That student said, "Hell, you know Artie—he'll try anything just for the hell of it. He's happy-go-lucky, but Judd, there's something that gives you the shivers about him."

Our intrepid narrator reflected on what his classmate said:

> *Artie would try anything once, and Judd was capable of anything at all, and if Artie was in trouble Judd had dragged him into it. And suddenly I saw why Artie had held back from admitting he had been with Judd on Wednesday. For if they had been together, they could have been together committing the crime! Judd was capable of anything. Why not even murder?* [clxxvi]

And, when Judd/Leopold was told that Artie/Loeb was confessing, he exclaimed, "Oh, the weakling," and then vowed to his interrogators, "I shall reveal the true purpose and meaning of the deed." [clxxvii]

Then, when our narrator informed a fellow student of Judd/Leopold's confession, and she seemed sympathetic to his plight, the narrator exclaimed, "Why keep sympathizing with him? He's a plain monster! It was he who instigated the whole thing; he even dominated Artie in the whole affair."

Compulsion even addressed the possibility that each perpetrator was equally responsible for the crime, though that begged the question of why each, in his confession, tried to punt the actual murder to the other.

As noted before, their confessions meshed almost perfectly except in one critical regard: Loeb said he drove the car while Leopold killed Bobby, but Leopold said he drove the car while Loeb killed Bobby.

As noted above, Leopold offered a supposed explanation from Loeb, that it made the crime more palatable for their respective families if they believed the non-family member committed the actual murder.

> To this day, the crime has been thought of as a deed in which they were organically joined, like Siamese twins. This may be true as to legal guilt. But understanding will never come through such an assumption. And if we see them as two beings who became wedded in the deed, then it does become momentous that one, here, had been telling the truth while the other had been lying.[clxxviii]

Babe's Final Chapter

After his parole, Leopold continued to try to rehabilitate his image. He moved to Puerto Rico, where he worked as an X-ray technician, then obtained a master's degree in social work from the University of Puerto Rico.

He later became involved in research toward a vaccine for leprosy and, in 1961, took a wife, Gertrude ("Trudi") Garcia de Quevado, an American widow who had previously been married to a Puerto Rican doctor.

But, according to Trudi, who was planning a book of her own, Leopold continued the pursuit of homosexual relationships and really hadn't changed from the man he was in 1924 when he and Loeb killed Bobby Franks.

In a master's thesis at the College of William & Mary, John Carl Fiorini wrote:

> In April and May 1971, respectively, Trudi and Nathan each told someone they were considering divorce. Trudi accused Leopold of having been a lifelong homosexual who

> carried on affairs in both Stateville [Prison] and Puerto Rico, including throughout their marriage.... Leopold had built the normality narrative in part on the idea that his sexual development was arrested during his relationship with Loeb, and that his maturation away from it was an important step in his rehabilitation. A book from his wife denouncing their marriage as a sham and alleging that "he isn't one bit different than he was in 1924" would have devastated Leopold's image of acquired heterosexuality and normality.[clxxix]

Leopold died in Puerto Rico in 1971, thirteen years after he was paroled. Having previously been told by his brother that the Leopold family did not want him buried in the family plot at Rosehill Cemetery in Chicago, he willed his body to the University of Puerto Rico for medical research.

Meanwhile, Back at the...Darrow

One last bit of information is worth noting. Ostensibly for purposes of publicly printing his closing argument for sale to the public, Darrow borrowed the court transcript.

On September 8, 1924, two days before Judge Caverly issued his decision, he wrote to his friend Frank Walsh and said, "My argument will be out in pamphlet form in a few days and will send you one. I am hopeful of winning."[clxxx]

It is interesting, but perhaps not surprising, that Darrow thought highly enough of his argument that he wanted to publish it, regardless of the case's outcome.

But, he failed to return all of the transcript to the court. The Clarence Darrow Digital Collection at the University of Minnesota contains this note regarding "Trial Transcript 6: August 15 and September 9, 1924": "Pages 3937 to 4115 are missing because after the hearing Clarence Darrow borrowed the part of transcripts that contained his closing argument from the court clerk but he never returned these pages. No library or archive appears to have these missing pages."[clxxxi]

Blowhard

According to historian Simon Baatz, in his note on manuscript sources, Darrow "rewrote his speech, cutting out long passages, correcting his syntax, and streamlining his argument, and published the amended version as a pamphlet. Darrow's speech in the courtroom was ponderous, disorganized, prolix, [59] and often tedious...." [clxxxii]

The authors of *Nothing But the Night* assert that, as hard as it might be to believe, the published version of Darrow's closing that is dissected in this book "was not Darrow's actual closing, but instead a carefully edited version." [clxxxiii]

> *Darrow's actual closing was disorganized, jumping back and forth from one subject to the next, dangling arguments and then neglecting to follow up on them. In his stream-of-consciousness rambles, Darrow repeatedly interrupted his own narrative, reiterated the same points multiple times, and left many in the courtroom confused.* [clxxxiv]

---

[59] Defined by *Merriam-Webster* as "unduly prolonged or drawn out; too long; marked by or using an excess of words."

Mike Farris

PART FOUR:
A Barrel of Monkeys— The Scopes Trial

The Dayton trial was only a moment of a long and, I hope, useful life. Nonetheless, in many minds I'll always be John T. Scopes, the Dayton, Tennessee, teacher who was the defendant in the Monkey Trial, despite the fact that I taught for only one year and have been a geologist for the years since.
—John T. Scopes

Chapter Thirteen: An Act Prohibiting

Democracy is the art of running the circus from the monkey cage.
—H. L. Mencken

THERE IS A POP culture perception about the Scopes Monkey Trial that defies facts and flaunts legend. Accordingly, it is widely accepted. Hearkening back to *The Man Who Shot Liberty Valance*'s "print the legend" maxim, the monkey trial legend might very well top the Darrow list.

That legend was largely shaped by *Inherit the Wind*, a play that debuted in Dallas in early 1955, produced and directed by Margot Jones after having been rejected by multiple Broadway producers. Following its success in Texas, it opened on Broadway that spring, reversing the usual procedure of Broadway first and then the hinterlands.

The production starred Paul Muni as Matthew Harrison Brady (based on William Jennings Bryan) and Ed Begley as Henry Drummond (based on Clarence Darrow), with Tony Randall as reporter E.K. Hornbeck (based on H.L. Mencken) and Karl Light as Bertram Cates (based on John T. Scopes).

Inherit the Wind ran for more than two years on Broadway. The play was later adapted for the movie screen in 1960, starring Spencer Tracy as Drummond/Darrow, Fredric March as Brady/Bryan, and Gene Kelly as Hornbeck/Mencken, while Dick York played the role of schoolteacher Cates/Scopes.

York would later achieve fame in the television series *Bewitched*, opposite Elizabeth Montgomery (who portrayed Samantha Stephens, the good witch) as Samantha's first husband, Darrin. After leaving the series a few years later, he was replaced by Dick Sargent, which spawned many an argument over who was the better Darrin, though probably not quite rivaling the Ginger or Mary Ann debates about *Gilligan's Island*.

The Scopes legend proffered that in 1925, a poor, beleaguered biology teacher in Tennessee risked his career, and even his liberty, by defying a criminal law forbidding the teaching of evolution in schools.

When William Jennings Bryan, a former three-time presidential loser (running as a Democrat in 1896, 1900, and 1908), stepped in as champion for organized religion and the anti-evolution forces to defend the law in a courtroom in the small town of Dayton, none other than Clarence Darrow galloped into town on his white horse to challenge Bryan and to defend academic freedom.

Makes for a good legend, but it doesn't comport with the facts. In reality, while Bryan did view himself as the premier spokesperson for Christianity and defender of the Bible, Darrow didn't really give a damn about academic freedom. His principal interest was to assail Christianity and antagonize his nemesis Bryan. H.L. Mencken of the *Baltimore Sun* reportedly was one of the first to encourage Darrow's participation in the case, saying, "Nobody gives a damn about that yap schoolteacher. The thing to do is to make a fool out of Bryan." [clxxxv]

That sounded good to Darrow.

> *At once I wanted to go. My object, and my only object, was to focus attention of the country on the programme of Mr. Bryan and the other fundamentalists in America.* [clxxxvi]

And, as he wrote, in hindsight, to Mencken a month after the trial, his intent had been to "show the country what an ignoramus [Bryan] was...." [clxxxvii]

So how did the Scopes Monkey Trial come to pass?

What really brought Clarence Darrow and William Jennings Bryan together in rural Tennessee in the summer of 1925?

And why Dayton, of all places?

Divine Creation v. A Lower Order

Ever since publication of Charles Darwin's *Origin of Species* in 1859, which advanced a theory of natural selection that seemingly debunked Biblical creationism, controversy raged over the issue.

Religious fundamentalists believed in the literal truth of the creation account in *Genesis*, including six twenty-four-hour days to accomplish it, while the world of science believed modern man was a product of evolution over millions of years, and not instant creation.

Pulitzer Prize winner Edward J. Larson described the conflict this way:

> *Some secular scientists in that era of romanticism and transcendentalism attributed the successive new creations of species to a vital force within nature. Christian geologists, in contrast, saw the hand of God directly at work in these creative acts. Both groups, however, accepted a long geologic history and the progressive appearance of new life forms. For Christians, this posed a conflict with the account in Genesis, which declared that God formed the heavens, the earth, and all kinds of living things in six days, culminating in the creation of Adam and Eve as the forebears of all human beings.* [clxxxviii]

Following World War I, the controversy escalated, and it was only a matter of time before theological, philosophical, and scientific debates would influence statutes. After the first anti-evolution laws were passed in 1923 in Oklahoma and Florida—a bill had been proposed in Kentucky in 1922 but it failed, by a single vote in the House of Representatives, to pass—the next state to fall in line was Tennessee, which would ultimately host a battle royale over the issue and focus the world's eye on the tiny town of Dayton.

The statute in question was the Butler Act (named for John W. Butler, who introduced it in the Tennessee House of Representatives), sometimes scoffingly referred to as the "Monkey Law," which said in pertinent part:

> *Section 1. Be it enacted by the General Assembly of the State of Tennessee, That it shall be unlawful for any teacher in any of the Universities, Normals[60] and all other public schools of the State which are supported in whole or in part by the public school funds of the State, to teach any theory that denies the story of the Divine Creation of man as taught in the Bible, and to teach instead that man has descended from a lower order of animals.*
>
> *Section 2. Be it further enacted, That any teacher found guilty of the violation of this Act shall be guilty of a misdemeanor and upon conviction, shall be fined not less than One Hundred ($100.00) Dollars nor more than Five Hundred ($500.00) Dollars for each offense.*

Interestingly, before the law's passage, Tennessee state senator John Shelton sought input on the bill from William Jennings Bryan, which led to Darrow's somewhat hyperbolic claim at the Scopes trial that Bryan was "responsible for this foolish mischievous and wicked act."

Shelton invited Bryan to address a joint session of the legislature, but Bryan declined the invitation. He did, however, advise that no penalty provision should be included. He wrote to

---

[60] "Normals" were schools or colleges that trained teachers.

Shelton that, because opponents of the bill would not be able to voice meritorious opposition to the law, itself, they would try to "find something that will divert attention, and the penalty furnished the excuse...." [clxxxix]

Had the Tennessee legislature listened to such sound advice from the man Darrow branded as the prime force behind the Butler Act, we might never have had the Scopes Monkey Trial, or at least not in the circus-like atmosphere in which it ultimately presented itself. As Larson explained:

> *With no penalty, of course, there would be no martyrs to the cause of freedom—and no Scopes trial—simply obstinate teachers flaunting the public will.*[cxc]

But the Butler Act ultimately included a penalty provision (the $100-$500 fine), contrary to Bryan's suggestion, and was approved by the Tennessee House of Representatives on January 27, 1925, by a vote of 71-5. The Tennessee Senate passed it on March 13, by a vote of 24-6, and Governor Austin Peay signed it into law on March 21.

Given the national attention that focused on the law's passage, and the controversy raging at the time, it was really no surprise that it took only a few months for the inevitable circus to descend somewhere in Tennessee.

That "somewhere" turned out to be the tiny town of Dayton. Less certain was that it would become the subject of a spectacle that would dramatically rewrite, at least as far as popular culture was concerned, the Darrow legend and his part as one of the ringmasters of the circus.

He that Troubleth his own House...

The playwrights of *Inherit the Wind*, Jerome Lawrence and Robert E. Lee, expressly disclaimed its historicity, although they conceded that the events of the Scopes Monkey Trial "are clearly the genesis of this play."

However, they continued, "Inherit the Wind" does not

pretend to be journalism. It is theatre."

In short, it is part of our popular culture. It is perhaps ironic that, given Darrow's role as a debunker of the Bible, and particularly the *Old Testament*, the title derived from that which he debunked. "He that troubleth his own house shall inherit the wind: and the fool shall be servant to the wise of heart." *Proverbs* 11:29 (KJV)

In the play, a courageous schoolteacher named Bertram Cates is arrested and charged with violating Tennessee's law against teaching evolution in public schools. As Bert recounts in dialogue, his conduct, which the State called a crime, was intentional.

> *I know why I did it. I had the book in my hand, Hunter's Civic Biology. I opened it up, and read my sophomore science class Chapter 17, Darwin's Origin of the Species. All it says is that man wasn't just stuck here like a geranium in a flower pot; that living comes from a long miracle, it didn't just happen in seven days.*

For that, he faced the wrath of his town, possibly the loss of his teaching job, and potentially a fine and jail sentence. What was worse, none other than the inimitable Matthew Harrison Brady, champion of the common man and the Word of God, was going to lead the charge against him.

But much to Bert's surprise, and delight, he learns that he will be defended by none other than Henry Drummond, whose own reputation preceded him, though his tactics were treated in the small town with nothing but scorn.

Townspeople scoff at him as "Henry Drummond, the agnostic," who "got those two Chicago child murderers off just the other day," a dramatic reference to the Leopold and Loeb case.

One of the citizens complains, "A man was on trial for a most brutal crime. Although he knew—and admitted—the man was guilty, Drummond was perverting the evidence to cast the guilt away from the accused and onto you and me and all of society."

Even Brady castigates Drummond. "He'll try to make us forget the lawbreaker and put the law on trial." And when Drummond first appears in the little town? A "terrified" townswoman screams, "It's the Devil!" and runs off.

Drummond's goal in the trial?

"All I want is to prevent the clock-stoppers from dumping a load of medieval nonsense into the United States Constitution," a reference to his later attack on the *Old Testament* prophet Joshua's battle in which "the sun stood still." *Joshua* 10:13 (KJV).

At trial, Brady introduces testimony from one of Cates's students as to what he actually taught in the classroom. "Well," the boy says, "he said at first the earth was a mite too hot for any life. Then it cooled off a mite, and cells and things began to live.... Little bugs like, in the water. After that, the little bugs got to be bigger bugs, and sprouted legs and crawled up on the land."

The play offers a particularly dramatic scene when Cates's girlfriend Rachel, daughter of a crusading fundamentalist preacher, describes the point when Cates made his turn away from Christianity. Following the drowning death of one of his eleven-year-old students, Rachel testifies that her father, the Reverend Brown, preached that the boy "didn't die in a state of grace, because his folks had never had him baptized...."

Cates exclaims from the defendant's table in the courtroom, "Tell 'em what your father really said! That Tommy's soul was damned, writhing in hellfire.... Religion's supposed to comfort people, isn't it? Not frighten them to death."

The dramatic centerpiece of the play is Drummond's cross-examination of Brady, who testifies as an expert on the Bible, just as in the real Scopes trial, Darrow did that very thing to Bryan who, in turn, did that very thing.

In the play, the dramatic Drummond examined the dramatic Brady on the literalness of the Bible, just as the real

Darrow did with the real Bryan. His questions, as did Darrow's, focused on whether a whale really swallowed Jonah and whether the sun actually stood still. In the end, the jury finds Cates guilty and imposes a one hundred dollar fine, with no prison time, after which Brady keels over dead while making final remarks in the courtroom.

Very dramatic indeed, with some vestiges of truth. But not quite what really happened.

Something is Afoot at the Drugstore

When first passed, the Butler Act sent leaders of the ACLU into a tizzy. They viewed it not only as an attack on the First Amendment's religion clauses but also on the guarantee of free speech, particularly as it related to academic freedom for educators.

But for the publicity-seeking Daytonians, the ACLU's outrage afforded an opportunity.

In mid-1924, less than a year before passage of the Butler Act, the ACLU had issued a public statement staking out its position on academic freedom. In the spring of 1925, upon learning of the Act's passage in Tennessee, it drafted a press release in which it offered to defend any teacher who might be prosecuted under it. The release ran in the *Chattanooga Times* on May 4 and stated:

> *We are looking for a Tennessee teacher who is willing to accept our services in testing this law in the courts. Our lawyers think a friendly test case can be arranged without costing a teacher his or her job. Distinguished counsel have volunteered their services. All we need now is a willing client.*

Think of the brazenness of the release. We have money and lawyers at the ready; all we need is a client. Have lawsuit, will travel.[61]

So where would the ACLU find that client?

Well, as luck would have it, one small Tennessee town was desperately looking for some publicity—something that would put it on the map—and it just might have a schoolteacher to put in play.

Dayton was a small town with a population just under 2,000 that served as the county seat of Rhea County in the Cumberland Valley, between Chattanooga and Knoxville. Journalist Marquis Jones of *The New Yorker* pegged the population at exactly 1,903, and said that "the fundamentalists outnumber the modernists, though perhaps not more greatly than 1,890 to 13. These figures include the foreign element which comprises three Jews, one Greek and a family of Roman Catholics." [cxci]

Population had once been around 3,000, but it dwindled as jobs dwindled, and town leaders were desperate for a way to highlight their town and stoke renewed interest in its businesses. When town leaders saw the announcement in the Chattanooga newspaper, it was as if they had received a sign from God. The ACLU press release offered promise and publicity on the ACLU's dime. All Dayton needed was a teacher willing to be arrested. And Dayton had just such a teacher.

Enter John T. Scopes. That was when, as Scopes later wrote in his memoir, "...a series of circumstances brought me directly into conflict with the new statute and left my name infrangibly linked with the new testing of the Butler Act." [cxcii]

After graduating from the University of Kentucky, Scopes was a man in search of a teaching job. When the football coach in the Rhea County schools in Dayton, Tennessee, suddenly resigned in the late summer of 1924, a job opened up, even for someone who had no college athletic experience.

He had, however, played basketball in high school and was qualified to teach algebra, physics, and chemistry. So, when

---

[61] With apologies to TV hero Richard Boone's Paladin in *Have Gun, Will Travel.*

Rhea County offered Scopes a job, he jumped at it. He signed a contract for the school year of September 1, 1924, through May 1, 1925, at a salary of $150 per month.

Then 1925 rolled around, the spring of his first year as a teacher. Let's hear about it in Scopes's own words.

> *In 1925 women's skirts went up a couple of inches, to the knees. Waists went down. Florida real estate boomed. Brigadier General Billy Mitchell had been demoted as the result of his fight for a unified air service. Moon Mullins, The Gumps, Winnie Winkle the Breadwinner, and Mutt & Jeff entertained Americans in the comic strips. Advertisements told how to make "cloudy teeth" whiter— quickly!—with Pepsodent tooth paste [sic]. Bookstores displayed An American Tragedy by Theodore Dreiser, Gentlemen Prefer Blondes by Anita Loos, and The Man Nobody Knows by Bruce Barton, the advertising man. In Johannesburg, Professor Raymond A. Dart had discovered, late in 1924, the latest missing link in man's evolution, and by 1925 scientists were busily discussing the manlike ape Australopithecus Africanus. Closer to home, in February, Floyd Collins had been found dead in a cave in Kentucky.*[62]
>
> *There was nothing about 1925 to suggest that I would become embroiled in one of the most dramatic confrontations of the year and, possibly, of the century.*[cxciii]

---

[62] Floyd Collins was a spelunker who became trapped in Kentucky's Great Crystal Cave, later renamed Sand Cave, while seeking an alternate way to access Mammoth Cave. Nationwide attention focused on rescue efforts that ultimately failed following a collapse of rock that sealed the entrance to the cave, shutting down efforts to reach him. He died from a combination of hunger, thirst, and hypothermia after two weeks, and his body was not recovered until two months later. His tombstone dubbed him the "Greatest Cave Explorer Ever Known."

While playing tennis with some students at the school one afternoon in May, a young boy summoned the professor to Robinson's Drugstore to meet with Fred E. "Doc" Robinson, its proprietor.

A few other town leaders were there, as well, including George W. Rappelyea who managed mining properties in the area; a Mr. Brady who owned the town's other drugstore; a man named Wallace Haggard; an unnamed man who worked at the post office; two attorneys; and Sue Hicks (one of the Hicks brothers, well known attorneys in town. At least one account holds that Sue Hicks was the model, at least in name, of "A Boy Named Sue," written by Shel Silverstein and popularized by Johnny Cash).

According to Scopes, Rappelyea asked him if it was possible to teach biology without teaching evolution. Scopes grabbed a copy of George William Hunter's *A Civic Biology*, the same book taught by *Inherit the Wind*'s Bert Cates, which was on a nearby shelf. Robinson's Drugstore supplied textbooks to the local schools. *A Civic Biology* had been in use in the schools since 1909 and had been adopted by the Tennessee textbook commission in 1919. The five-year contract with the State had expired August 31, 1924, and no replacement had as yet been selected.

During the later trial, Darrow would point out the irony of criminalizing the teaching of a state-adopted textbook that was sold in a drugstore owned by a member of the school board. That led chief prosecutor Tom Stewart to quip, "The law says teach, not sell."

Though he was not the school's regular biology teacher— that was Mr. Robertson, who was also the school's principal— Scopes had temporarily filled in for him during an illness and used the book for review purposes. After taking the volume from a shelf in the drugstore, he opened it to a chart and text on evolution, which he showed to those gathered. "Rappelyea's right," Scopes said, "that you can't teach biology without teaching evolution. This is the text and it explains evolution."

"Then you've been violating the law," Robinson said.

As the discussion progressed to the main event—what to do with the ACLU's offer about the Butler Act—somebody asked Scopes, "Would you be willing to stand for a test case? Would you be willing to let your name be used?"

Scopes later wrote in his memoir: "I realized that the best time to scotch the snake is when it starts to wiggle. The snake already had been wiggling a good long time." He said, "If you can prove that I've taught evolution, and that I can qualify as a defendant, then I'll be willing to stand trial." [cxciv]

The truth was that Scopes doubted whether he had actually taught evolution. Although he had used the book for final exam review, he figured the most likely person to have taught the section on evolution was the teacher for whom he had substituted. But that didn't matter to the others, who "apparently weren't concerned about this technicality. I had expressed willingness to stand trial. That was enough." [cxcv]

At that point, Robinson called the *Chattanooga Times*. Identifying himself as the chairman of the school board in Dayton, he said, "We've just arrested a man for teaching evolution."

Let the circus begin.

"Why," Scopes later mused, "had I volunteered to be prosecuted for teaching evolution in a public school, thereby violating the criminal code of Tennessee?" He proclaimed his role to merely be a "passive one that developed out of my willingness to test what I considered a bad law.... I did not think the state of Tennessee had any right to keep me from teaching the truth." [cxcvi]

Even if he may never have actually taught evolution.

In fact, he later wrote that the regular biology teacher should have been the most logical defendant but, when asked, refused since he was married with children and had family responsibilities. "After him, I was the next logical defendant," Scopes wrote. "I was a bachelor." [cxcvii]

Marquis James, writing in *The New Yorker*, said that the

"hustling druggist," as he dubbed Fred Robinson, denied that the lawsuit had been "arranged," but that it was simply a matter of chance that Scopes was in the drugstore at the opportune time, overhearing a conversation, and things proceeded from there.

"That's a good joke," says the hustling druggist. "Publicity stunt! Started right in my store here and I didn't know enough to send it to the *Chattanooga Times* and I'm their local correspondent. This thing just happened. Four young fellows around a table there. Just happened...like most big things, when you get right down to it. They just happen. We had no idea.... Of course, eventually we did expect a little notice in the papers. Testing the law and all. Maybe make the *Literary Digest*. But nothing like you see. We're as surprised as anybody."

To this day, there is still a little uncertainty as to the true story.

One book described it this way:

> The exact order of events that followed over the next few days, and even details of the events themselves, have been retold, reinterpreted and spun to the point where no definitive account clearly emerges from the historical mist.[cxcviii]

The most probable "real" story, the one that Scopes verified in his memoir, was actually first broken by Nellie Kenyon of the *Chattanooga Times*, though Marquis James said that, while it was a local sensation, it wasn't picked up by outside papers.

"The orthodox version will pass into history, like the fable of Washington and the cherry tree," James wrote. To again quote *The Man Who Shot Liberty Valance*, "When the legend becomes fact, print the legend."

According to Kenyon's reporting, "[The arrest of Scopes] didn't grow out of a desultory debate in the store of the 'hustling druggist'.... The trial was carefully planned." The real architect of the scheme was George Rappleyea, who, Kenyon wrote, "conceived and planned" the affair.

Rappleyea sent a telegram to the ACLU, which read:

> *Prof. J.T. Scopes, teacher of science Rhea Central High School, Dayton, Tennessee, will be arrested charged* [sic] *with teaching evolution. Consent of superintendent of education and chairman of the board of education for test case to be defended by you. Wire me collect if you wish to cooperate and arrest will follow. G.W. RAPPLEYEA*

The ACLU agreed to cooperate, Scopes was arrested, and on May 25, was indicted.

The curtain was about to go up in Dayton.

Blowhard

Chapter Fourteen: Under the Big Top

Two months ago the town was obscure and happy. Today it is a universal joke.
—H.L. Mencken

THE *ST. LOUIS POST DISPATCH* printed an editorial that asked the question, "Why Dayton, of all places?"

The town answered with a promotional brochure, published by Fred E. "Doc" Robinson, Marquis James's and Nellie Kenyon's "hustling druggist," bearing that question as its title and responded, "Of all places, why not Dayton?" [cxcix]

Robinson noted that "She [Dayton] steps to the rostrum keenly mindful of her diminutive stature and of the supercilious smiles directed at her from those in high places." But, before launching into a full-scale promotion of the town's virtues, he reminded readers on both sides of the evolution issue that, to coin a phrase, big things come in small packages.

History was replete, he wrote, with grandly significant events that transpired in, and persons who hailed from, small, obscure places. It was the event, he argued, not the venue, that impacted the world.

What happened, not where it happened. You had to look no further than the Bible.

You champions of the survival of the fittest, you followers of the lowly Nazarene! If the consciousness of a plunging, seething race has been aroused by this mountain town's act, if the maddening rush of mankind had been arrested, even though momentarily by the shout from Main Street to halt, will you slight it and pay it less respectful attention because the cry arose from the fields, the forests, the rivers, the mines, and the factories? Not when the evidence is in, we feel sure. If you are concerned over the questions involved in the Dayton Evolution Case you are ever seeking the light and fighting for the right, and you will not forego an opportunity just because it emanated from a country drug store, to take up the challenge thus afforded and do for your posterity what your ancestors failed to do for you under similarly favorable circumstances long, long ago.

***

You are listening in on Dayton today because the principles of evolution which Aristotle anticipated and which he stoutly voiced amid the echoing hills of Ancient Greece lay dormant for centuries after him. Did his deliberations fall flat because he failed to embrace a popular idea that a responsible principle must originate only in a seat of learning? You are listening in on Dayton today because the lonely Cross of Calvary has looked too desolate and burdensome for countless of its worshipers to bear it to exalted and sublime heights. Would it have appeared more inviting had it been erected in front of the Forum in Rome? [cc]

The brochure included pictures of the "main actors," including Doctor George W. Rappelyea, "who Swore out the Warrant" and Constable Perry Swafford "who Served the Warrant," and even a photo of the classroom "where Prof. John Thomas Scopes

Taught Evolution." It recounted Robinson's version of the happenstance at his drug store that triggered everything into motion.

> *Main Street was scanning the papers in a few days and came across a little line or two to the effect that a New York society would finance an effort to test the constitutionality of the new Tennessee law. Main Street could discourse on the affair with unction and assumed assurance, and ventured the notion that for "just two-cents" they'd start something and maybe it would be interesting and stir up a little confab in Rhea County. Just then the county school pedagogue, belated from having enjoyed a tennis game, strolled into the drug store and heard the comment. Well, it was his opinion that anyone who was teaching the text books was doing so in violation of the law. He could show 'em the very place that could not legally be taught and the textbook itself was handed him from the shelves that contained the supplies for the schools, for of course, Main Street's drug store is an emporium for such goods. Pointing to the passage and admitting that he used it in his instruction work brought forth the half playful, half serious threat that he was breaking the laws of this state and that a warrant should be served on him for his immediate arrest. With a little sparring, a little side-stepping, the hats were in the ring, and the whole world has done its bit to hold up the stage to public view.*[cci]

Dayton's role in "parading a so-called circus," the brochure said, "was done without malice or aforethought of its culminating in an [sic] universal chatter to prove or disprove the world's a menagerie." [ccii] Rather, it was all about garnering a little publicity for their fair burg.

> *If this is an age of commerce (and there is cumulative*

> *proof that it is) and if it is to continue to be an age of progress (and the contrary has yet to be proven) Dayton would be woefully remiss in her duty to herself not to grasp this hour of her lime-light incandescence and make of it an occasion for self-aggrandizement with some incontrovertible facts about her products and natural resources.* [cciii]

The Great Commoner and the Attorney for the Damned

Press reports announced that the prosecution was acting under the "auspices" of the ACLU in bringing the case, and that the ACLU even helped "defray" the prosecution's expenses, though that may not be clearly established.

Still, this was not quite lining up as the David versus Goliath match-up of legend. But one place where legend and fact melded was the battle of giants the case created between William Jennings Bryan and Clarence Darrow.

Bryan was once lauded as the "Boy Orator of the Platte," though detractors liked to point out that the Platte River was only six inches deep and a mile wide at the mouth—i.e., shallow and with a big mouth. However, never one to let opportunity or publicity elude him, Bryan leaped at the chance to represent the State of Tennessee in defending its law and the right of a popular majority to dictate what could and could not be taught to their children in schools.

Edward J. Larson wrote that it didn't make sense for Bryan, sometimes called the Great Commoner for his persona as a champion for the common man, to take the case. At least not as a lawyer. He hadn't practiced law in more than thirty years and, with three failed presidential runs in his record, was now making his mark championing political causes from monetary reform to anti-evolution legislation.

To Bryan, this was more than a courtroom challenge to a statute. It was, instead, an opportunity to seize a platform for his personal philosophies, a platform inadvertently provided for him

Blowhard

by his philosophical and constitutional opposite, the American Civil Liberties Union.

> In a stroke, the ACLU lost control of what it initially conceived as a narrow constitutional test of the statute. With Bryan on hand, evolution would be on trial at Dayton, and pleas for individual liberty would run headlong into calls for majority rule.[cciv]

No one knew it at first, but the ACLU was about to lose even more control, to someone who should have been a huge ally. In a somewhat similar vein to, and rationale as, Bryan, Clarence Darrow, who also possessed a keen eye and nose for self-aggrandizement opportunities, volunteered his *pro bono* services to Scopes, who eagerly accepted.

And with that, the "ACLU's plan for a narrow test case promptly suffered a second setback...." [ccv] With Bryan and Darrow on board, "the ACLU never regained control of events."[ccvi]

Gee, it seemed like such a good idea at the time.

Unlike the legend, Darrow didn't ride in on his white steed, tilting at the First Amendment windmills of free speech and freedom of religion, not to mention academic freedom.

Rather, he hijacked the case to advance his own agenda of debunking religion and, as a personal perquisite, humiliating Bryan. Darrow had made a name for himself in court, of course, but also on the lecture circuit attacking religion and questioning the existence of God.

Just two years prior, Darrow had published a paper called *Absurdities of the Bible*, which he intended to highlight at the Scopes trial, even if it was not directly at issue in the case. Rather than address the validity of the anti-evolution statute, Darrow's assault in the courtroom would be against the Bible, with Bryan as its spokesperson.

For his part, Scopes was more than happy to accept Clarence Darrow as his counsel, and who could blame him? He understood why Darrow wanted the case, and that it had very little to do with Scopes and his criminal charges.

He wrote, "Darrow probably wouldn't have offered his services if Bryan hadn't entered the case and changed the focus from law to religion." [ccvii]

There was initially significant opposition from the ACLU, itself, to Darrow's participation, for the reasons already stated. Additionally, there were arguments that "he [Darrow] was too radical, that he was a headline hunter, that the trial would become a circus, that with Darrow in the case there would be no chance of getting it into the Federal courts." [ccviii]

But when Scopes, as the defendant, was asked to speak to the issue, he said simply, "I want Darrow." [ccix] Though there was still no shortage of controversy to follow, the issue of defense counsel was decided and Darrow was on board.

And so, the stage was set for two legal behemoths to face off on an issue the ACLU, originator of the whole shebang, had originally neither contemplated nor intended, nor even desired. Though there was probably nothing it could have done to prevent Bryan's appearance, Darrow's was another story.

Larson wrote that ACLU counsel Wollcott H. Pitkin confided to Felix Frankfurter, "In my belief, a great mistake had been made at the start in accepting the services of Mr. Darrow, thereby allowing fundamentalists to present the issue as a clash between religion and anti-religion." [ccx] But that was the Faustian bargain the ACLU had made, and it would have to live with it.

Which, of course, is exactly what Darrow wanted as he subordinated his client's interests to his own. On April 27, 1925, just a few weeks prior, The Memphis *Commercial Appeal*, addressing Darrow's previous performance in the Leopold and Loeb case, had editorialized:

> *The fact that* [this] *and others of his cases were personal victories for himself does not by any means connote that they were also victories for the majesty and efficacy of the law.*

Past is prelude, and it was as if the *Commercial Appeal* had a crystal ball.

Dayton was ripe for a two-ring circus with dueling ringmasters, motivated by opposing ideologies, each determined to elevate his platform on a national, if not international stage, their clients be damned.

The die was cast.

View from the Fourth Estate

The national press got the message out and the world focused its attention on tiny Dayton. No member of the press was more instrumental in spreading the word than *Baltimore Sun* reporter H.L. Mencken, himself an atheist.

Mencken was one of the most well-known writers of his day, as a journalist and essayist, as well as a satirist and critic. Mencken was particularly close to Darrow and reportedly even counseled Darrow on whether the lawyer should involve himself in the Scopes matter in the first place.[ccxi] Mencken's columns and articles about the trial for *The Baltimore Sun* were later compiled and reprinted in a single volume.[ccxii]

Mencken, like Darrow, reveled in ridiculing a faith neither of them shared nor fully understood. After having helped persuade Darrow to take up the mantel of challenging the Butler Act, he traveled to Dayton to provide his eyewitness account and accompanying scathing commentary on the spectacle. He, in effect, served as Darrow's accomplice in the assault on organized religion. Or maybe he was more like the little demon who perched on Darrow's shoulder and whispered in his ear, appealing to his darker angels. Assuming, of course, that one believed in the existence of angels.

It was Mencken who first called the Scopes case the "Monkey Trial," and who also coined the term "booboisie," a reference to the ignorant middle classes. An admirer of Friedrich Nietzsche, although not to the same extent as Nathan Leopold, with each keystroke his dispatches from the Monkey Trial front fairly oozed his self-perceived superiority to the subjects of his articles. He teamed with Darrow for a full-frontal assault on not only the aforementioned booboisie, but also on the religious fundamentalists they held in such contempt. Nowhere is that more readily apparent than Mencken's likening of the whole affair to a "religious orgy."

Nellie Kenyon wrote that, when she first saw Mencken in the Aqua Hotel lobby, "There was no mistaking him. He had that round smooth face I had seen in pictures. He relished a cigar and his mischievous blue eyes drank the scene." [ccxiii] Mencken even asked her to take him to a "Holy Roller" meeting that night so that he might get a taste of the local religious frenzy flavor in order to ridicule it in print. He wrote about it a few days later in an article dated July 13, 1925, entitled "Yearning Mountaineers' Souls Need Reconversion Nightly." His account of the Holy Rollers, whom he said numbered about 20,000, was decidedly uncomplimentary. As the preacher preached, Mencken observed the listeners.

> *A young mother sat suckling her baby, rocking as the preacher paced up and down. Two scared little girls hugged each other, their pigtails down their backs. An immensely huge mountain woman, in a gingham dress cut in one piece, rolled on her heels at every "Glory to God." To one side, but half visible, was what appeared to be a bed. We found out afterward that two babies were asleep upon it.*
>
> *The preacher stopped at last and there arose out of the darkness a woman with her hair pulled back into a little tight knot. She began so quietly that we couldn't hear what she said, but soon her voice rose resonantly and we could follow her. She was denouncing the reading of books. Some wandering book agent, it appeared, had come to her cabin and tried to sell her a specimen of his wares. She refused to touch it. Why, indeed, read a book? If what was in it was true then everything in it was already in the Bible. If it was false then reading it would imperil the*

soul. Her syllogism complete, she sat down.

There followed a hymn, led by a somewhat fat brother wearing silver-rimmed country spectacles. It droned on for half a dozen stanzas, and then the first speaker resumed the floor. He argued that the gift of tongues was real and that education was a snare. Once his children could read the Bible, he said, they had enough. Beyond lay only infidelity and damnation. Sin stalked the cities, Dayton itself was a Sodom. Even Morgantown had begun to forget God. He sat down, and the female aurochs[63] in gingham got up.

She began quietly, but was soon leaping and roaring, and it was hard to follow her. Under cover of the turmoil we sneaked a bit closer. A couple of other discourses followed, and there were two or three hymns. Suddenly a change of mood began to make itself felt. The last hymn ran longer than the others and dropped gradually into a monotonous, unintelligible chant. The leader beat time with his book. The faithful broke out with exultations. When the singing ended there was a brief palaver that we could not hear and two of the men moved a bench into the circle of light directly under the flambeaux. Then a half-grown girl emerged from the darkness and threw herself upon it. We noticed with astonishment that she had bobbed her hair. "This sister," said the leader, "has asked for prayers." We moved a bit closer. We could now see faces plainly and hear every word.

What followed quickly reached such heights of barbaric grotesquerie that it was hard to believe it was real. At a signal all the faithful crowded up the bench and began to pray—not in unison but each for himself. At another they all fell on their knees, facing us, their arms over the penitent. The leader kneeled, facing us, his head alternately thrown back dramatically or buried in his

---

[63] A species of extinct cattle.

hands. Words spouted from his lips like bullets from a machine gun—appeals to God to pull the penitent back out of hell, defiances of the powers and principalities of the air, a vast impassioned jargon of apocalyptic texts. Suddenly he rose to his feet, threw back his head and began to speak in tongues—blub-blub-blub, gurgle-gurgle-gurgle. His voice rose to a higher register. The climax was a shrill, inarticulate squawk, like that of a man throttled. He fell headlong across the pyramid of supplication.

A comic scene? Somehow no. The poor half wits were too horribly in earnest. It was like peeping through a knothole at the writhings of a people in pain.

Chapter Fifteen: Send in the Clowns

Now the clowns turn out to be armed, and have begun to shoot.
—H.L. Mencken

THE INDICTMENT RETURNED against Scopes on May 25, 1925, provided:

> That John Thomas Scopes, heretofore on the 24th day of April 1925, in the county aforesaid, then and there unlawfully did wilfully teach in the public schools of Rhea County, Tennessee, which said schools are supported in part, or in whole by the public school fund of the State, a certain theory or theories that denied the story of the divine creation of man as taught in the Bible, but did teach instead thereof, that man is descended from a lower order of animals, he, the said John Thomas Scopes, being at the time, and prior thereto, a teacher in the public schools of Rhea County, Tennessee, as aforesaid, against the peace and dignity of the State.

An effort was made by the defense to move the case to federal court, with an end game of ultimate appeal to the United States Supreme Court as the goal, but it failed. The case remained in

Judge John Raulston's 18th Circuit Court and started on the morning of Friday, July 10, 1925.

Trial and Error

As a trial, *State of Tennessee v. John Thomas Scopes* left much to be desired. Of the eight days' duration, less than a day was spent presenting evidence to the jury.

In fact, the jury wasn't even in the courtroom for the bulk of the trial. Better than half of the first day was spent picking the jury, which was promptly "retired" for the legal proceedings and arguments that followed hard on its heels. When the floor of the courtroom was turned over to the lawyers, they, as lawyers are prone to do—particularly these lawyers—talked. And talked. And talked. As H.L. Mencken wrote in the *Baltimore Sun* on July 14, "Now the clowns turn out to be armed, and have begun to shoot."[ccxiv]

The second day was spent with counsel arguing, seemingly endlessly,[64] the defense's motion to dismiss and quash the indictment. That spilled over to the third day, again outside the presence of the jury, for continued argument over the motion. That was followed by a new motion by Darrow, this one objecting to opening each day's session with prayer, followed by more argument, which, in turn, spilled over to the fourth day. It was as if the courtroom were a bucket and each lawyer was a spigot from which rhetoric flowed like water, but the bucket was too small to contain it.

It might seem surprising that Darrow waited until the third day to make his objection to prayer, since both preceding days had been so opened. But his concern was its possible prejudicial effect on the jury, which wasn't yet present for any of the proceedings other than the initial day of jury selection. So, no harm, no foul.

On the morning of the fourth day, Judge Raulston read

---

[64] Plenty of windbaggery to go around.

aloud his lengthy opinion[65] denying the motion to quash the indictment. The actual presentation of evidence commenced that afternoon, finally giving the jury something to do besides spit and whittle, but not before defense counsel Dudley Field Malone delivered a lengthy statement of the defense theories for the record.

Ironically, Malone had served as Third Assistant Secretary for Willliam Jennings Bryan during Bryan's tenure as President Woodrow Wilson's Secretary of State, and now they were opposing each other in the courtroom. Further ironically, given the presence of Clarence Darrow and William Jennings Bryan as the main attractions, it was widely felt at the time, and confirmed by this author's reading of the transcript, that the less heralded Malone provided perhaps the most eloquent and persuasive speech of the trial. But, since it was merely a warm-up act for the headliners, it is not usually given its due.

Malone made a commonsense argument that the Bible must be read and interpreted based upon the time in which it was written, which excluded much scientific truth. The creation account in *Genesis* was not inconsistent with evolution, he said, but it had to be considered in the context of its time.

How do you talk about evolution in *Genesis* when no study had ever been done of the issue at the time it was written by Moses? And evolution, he emphasized, wasn't the only science *not* mentioned in the pages of *Genesis*.

> *Moses never heard about steam, electricity, the telegraph, the telephone, the radio, the aeroplane* [sic], *farming machinery, and Moses knew nothing about scientific thought and principles from which these vast accomplishments of the inventive genius of mankind have been produced.*

He denied that the defense was part of a conspiracy "to destroy

---

[65] More windbaggery, this time from the bench.

the authority of Christianity or the Bible." Instead, he said:

> [t]*he narrow purpose of the defense is to establish the innocence of the defendant Scopes. The broad purpose of the defense will be to prove that the Bible is a work of religious aspiration and rules of conduct which must be kept in the field of theology.*

In other words, theology and science were like the proverbial oil and water—they don't mix. Or, at least, they shouldn't mix.

Following Malone's statement, the jury was led in and the prosecution's witnesses finally took the stand. School superintendent Walter White testified that Scopes had used *A Civic Biology*, which contained a chapter on evolution, as part of a review for final exams during the weeks he substituted for the regular biology teacher.

A copy of the book was admitted as Exhibit 1.

White's testimony was interrupted by an effort by the defense to offer the Bible into evidence, which was admitted as Exhibit 2.

That made sense.

After all, the element of the Butler Act that had been allegedly violated was teaching a theory that man descended from a lower order of animals, as outlined in *A Civic Biology*, in denial of the story of divine creation of man as taught in the Bible. Both books were clearly relevant.

The Bible said, "So God created man in his own image…" (*Genesis* 1:27, KJV), while *A Civic Biology* said that "…animal forms may be arranged so as to begin with very simple one-celled forms and culminated with a group that contains man himself…" and that "…simple forms of life on the earth slowly and gradually gave rise to those more complex and that thus ultimately, the most complex forms came into existence." [ccxv]

After much discussion among the lawyers, it was decided that the King James Version was the iteration the legislature likely referred to in passing the Butler Act, so that was the version admitted into evidence as Exhibit 2.

Specifically, it was "Holman's Pronouncing Edition of the Holy Bible, containing the Old and New Testaments. Translating—Text conformable to that of 1611 known as the authorized or King James version."

The first chapter of *Genesis* had been read to the grand jury on the first day, in connection with the reindictment of Scopes (see discussion below). After all, if the Butler Act made it illegal to teach any creation theory that conflicted with the Bible, a record needed to be made as to what the Bible said about creation.

Later, Chapters 1 and 2 of *Genesis* would be read aloud to the trial jury. Chapter 1 describes the first six days of creation, and Chapter 2 provides more detail on the creation of man.

Two students, Howard Morgan and Harry Shelton testified, confirming that Scopes had taught from *A Civic Biology*. This testimony was critical because, under the indictment, the prosecution had to prove that Scopes had actually taught:

> ...a certain theory or theories that denied the story of the divine creation of man as taught in the Bible, but did teach instead thereof, that man is descended from a lower order of animals.

When he had been drafted for the test case, Scopes had agreed, provided, as he wrote in his memoir, they could "prove that I've taught evolution, and that I can qualify as a defendant."

In a 1960 radio interview with Pulitzer Prize winning writer and broadcaster Studs Terkel, in connection with the movie release of *Inherit the Wind*, Scopes clarified what he meant by that statement. He said that he meant they would need to prove he taught evolution *without requiring him to commit perjury*.[ccxvi] As he wrote in his memoir, "To tell the truth, I wasn't sure I had taught evolution," so he wasn't willing to say, under oath, that he had. It became necessary, then, for someone other than Scopes to provide evidence of his teaching evolution.

Hence, the testimony of Superintendent White and the two students.

Through leading questions, Darrow obtained admissions from the boys that hearing about evolution from Scopes had not "hurt you any," that Scopes did not tell them "anything else that was wicked," and that they "didn't leave the church when he told you all forms of life began with a single cell."

Then F.E. Robinson, the "hustling druggist" owner of Robinson's Drug Store, and a member of the school board, testified and admitted that he sold *A Civic Biology* in his store for use in the school.

Two other students, Morris Stout and Charles Hagley, were lined up to testify, but their testimony was dispensed with when the prosecution acknowledged that it would be the same as that of Morgan and Shelton. At that point, the state rested its case. The jury was removed from the courtroom, again, and the remainder of the fourth day was spent examining expert witnesses on science, followed by the fifth day spent arguing over whether that expert testimony should be admitted.

On the afternoon of the fifth day, Bryan delivered a passionate speech, during which he responded directly to several personal attacks by Darrow.

> *The principal attorney has often suggested that I am the arch-conspirator and that I am responsible for the presence of this case and I have almost been credited with leadership of the ignorance and bigotry which he thinks could alone inspire a law like this.*

Part of Bryan's response also included dragging, for some reason, the Leopold and Loeb case into the record. We can only speculate as to his purpose, but it is not unreasonable to assume that it was because of the scorn with which Darrow was treated for his defense of the two thrill killers in that case in Chicago. Perhaps, Bryan wanted to tar him with the "he defends child killers" brush in Dayton. To quote the *Old Testament,* "be sure your sin will find you out." *Numbers* 32:23 (KJV).

Bryan said that Darrow argued to excuse Leopold and Loeb because of Leopold's adherence to Nietzsche's theory of the superman—the *Übermensch*—and that Darrow said that the doctrine, and the universities that taught it, were to blame for the murder of Bobby Franks. It was a logical extension, Bryan said, of the theory of evolution, as Darwin had been an admirer of Nietzsche.

Darrow objected.

> *Your honor, I want to object; there is not a word of truth in it. Nietzsche never taught that. Anyhow, there is not a word of criticism of the professors, nor of the colleges in reference to that....*

How soon Darrow forgot. He had, in fact, argued in the Leopold and Loeb case that, if Leopold "took Nietzsche's philosophy seriously and fashioned his life on it," then "[t]he university would be more to blame than he is. The scholars of the world would be more to blame than he is. The publishers of the world...would be more to blame than he is."

Holding up a copy of Darrow's closing argument from that case—the published version that resulted from Darrow's "borrowing," and never returning a portion of, the trial transcript, then editing his filibuster-like argument in order to publish it for sale—Bryan said, "I will read you what you said in that speech here."

Darrow, perhaps with a flash of sudden memory of what he had previously said, objected to "injecting any other case into this proceeding, no matter what the case is." A legitimate relevance objection, to be sure. And maybe he simply wanted to head off his words from that case being brought up in this trial.

When Judge Raulston intimated that he would sustain the objection, Bryan said, "If I do not find what I say, I want to tender an apology, because I have never in my life misquoted a man intentionally."

"I am intimating that you did," Darrow shot back.

After the bickering settled down, Darrow noted that "The fellow that invented the printing press did some mischief as well as some good." Bryan informed the spectators that the published argument was on sale in Dayton (possibly at Robinson's Drug Store, though Bryan didn't specifically say), that he had purchased four copies, himself, for two dollars—fifty cents apiece. "I will pay $1.50 for yours," said co-defense counsel Dudley Field Malone.

Bryan then read the passage quoted above about universities, scholars, and publishers. In response, Darrow borrowed the copy from Bryan and read his remarks just a paragraph later from the passage read by Bryan, in which he tried to have it both ways.

> *I do not believe that the universities are to blame. I do not think they should be held responsible. I do think, however, that they are too large, and that they should keep a closer watch upon the individual.*

And when Bryan insisted that Darrow return the copy he loaned Darrow to read from, Darrow replied, "I'll give you a new one autographed for you."

On the morning of the sixth day, Judge Raulston issued a lengthy statement excluding the defense's experts.

At the heart of his ruling was his opinion that the court did not need to determine whether either the Biblical story of creation or Darwin's theory of evolution was correct. That was not the court's province, he reasoned. The issue was simply whether a validly passed law had been violated.

> *...under the provisions of the [Butler Act], it is made unlawful to teach in the public schools of the state of Tennessee the theory that man descended from a lower order of animals. If the court is correct in this, then the evidence of experts would shed no light on the issues.*

Darrow accepted the ruling with his typical sarcasm, perhaps the first steps along his road to being held in contempt the following Monday for comments he would make later that afternoon. "Don't worry about us. The state of Tennessee don't rule the world yet."

On the seventh day—avoiding the temptation to write that God rested; *Genesis* 2:2—in addition to Judge Raulston holding Darrow in contempt for his remarks in the prior court session, along with Darrow's apology for those remarks, statements were entered into the record of what the defense's experts *would have said* had they been allowed to testify.

There was also a fight over a banner in the courtroom, a Hebrew copy of the Bible was admitted into evidence, then came Darrow's examination of Bryan as an expert on the Bible—all outside the presence of the jury—making the seventh day an eventful one.

And on the eighth day, the case finally went to the jury and a verdict was returned.

Motions and Speeches and Prayers—Oh My!

The preceding section offers a brief day-by-day summary of events as they played out in the courtroom. This section will delve a bit more deeply into some of the specifics of those days.

Outside of the actual presentation of evidence, much "speechifying" and pontification filled most of the trial days. Therein lay Darrow's trademark windbaggery on full display, although, in his defense, it wasn't just limited to Darrow. It seemed as if most, if not all, of the lawyers brought their windbags and their A-games with them.

The first day of trial, Friday, July 10, opened with prayer by Reverend Cartwright. A fairly lengthy prayer, as far as opening prayers go—apparently the good reverend had a little windbag in him, as well. He requested "that the power and the presence of the Holy Spirit may be with the jury and with the accused and with all the attorneys interested in this case."

Although Darrow did not object that morning to an

opening invocation, he was keeping his powder dry for later.

For technical reasons, and out of a concern that the indictment might be invalid, Judge John Raulston convened a new grand jury, which he charged essentially the same way the prior jury had originally been charged.

Because the Butler Act criminalized the teaching of any theory that denied the Biblical account of creation, Judge Raulston read the entire first chapter of *Genesis* from the King James Version to the jury so it might compare the *Genesis* story of creation with that "descended from a lower order of animals" part of the Act.

This actually created a fairly interesting, somewhat technical, dilemma in the case. If evolution was not inconsistent with the creation story in Genesis, and there were many Christian evolutionists who believed the two were actually compatible, then teaching evolution did not violate the first part of the Butler Act ("...teach any theory that denies the story of creation as taught in the Bible") though it still might violate the second part ("...and to teach instead that man has descended from a lower order of animals").

The conjunction "and" arguably created an ambiguity in the statute. That would actually be part of Dudley Field Malone's statement of the defense case, mentioned above, that he made on the afternoon of the fourth day.

In that statement, Malone said, "The defense contends that to convict Scopes, the prosecution must prove that Scopes not only taught the theory of evolution, but that he also, and at the same time, denied the story of creation as set forth in the Bible." However, "we believe there is no conflict between evolution and Christianity." In fact, he said:

> *We maintain and we will prove that Christianity is bound up with no scientific theory, that it has survived 2,000 years in the face of all the discoveries of science and that Christianity will continue to grow in respect and influence if the people recognize that there is no conflict with*

science and Christianity.

But Mr. Malone's wisdom wouldn't be imparted until a few days after the reindictment, and this second grand jury did not have the benefit of what he would say. It promptly returned a new indictment like the first.

With a banner on the courthouse wall that admonished folks to "Read Your Bible Daily," the afternoon session that first day was spent in *voir dire*, or jury selection, which saw several interesting exchanges between Darrow and potential jurors. One involved J.P. Massingill, who identified himself as a "minister" in Rhea County with appointments to pastor four churches in rural areas of the county.

DARROW: *Ever preach on evolution?*

MASSINGILL: *I don't think so, definitely; that is, on evolution alone.*

DARROW: *Now, you wouldn't want to sit on this jury unless you were fair, would you?*

MASSINGILL: *Certainly, I would want to be fair; yes, sir.*

DARROW: *Did you ever preach on evolution?*

MASSINGILL: *Yes. I haven't as a subject just taken that up in connection with other subjects. I have referred to it in discussing it.*

DARROW: *Against it or for it?*

MASSINGILL: *I am strictly for the Bible.*

DARROW: *I am talking about evolution. I am not*

talking about the Bible. Did you preach for or against evolution?

MASSINGILL: *Is that a fair question, judge?*

JUDGE RAULSTON: *Yes, answer the question.*

MASSINGILL: *Well, I preached against it, of course.*

The transcript shows that there was applause at this answer. Darrow immediately asked that the judge "have anybody excluded that applauds."

"Yes," Raulston replied, "if you repeat that, ladies and gentlemen, you will be excluded. We cannot have applause. If you have any feeling in this case, you must not express it in the courthouse, so don't repeat the applause. If you do, I will have to exclude you."

The minister Massingill said that he had a "fixed opinion" based upon newspaper reports that Scopes had "taught a theory contrary to the theory of the Bible as to the creation of man," and Darrow inquired whether that would "have any weight with you or any bearing with you in the trial of this case if you were selected as a juror?"

Massingill said he believed himself to be "fair and honest enough to lay aside things and give a man justice."

On further questioning from Darrow, he admitted he currently had an opinion that "evolution is contrary to the Bible" and that Scopes had taught evolution, but that he could change his opinion if he heard enough evidence to base it on. Nevertheless, Darrow objected and requested that Massingill be excused for cause, which the judge granted.

Much of the *voir dire* questioning proceeded the same way, with the same types of questions. The defense elicited from most potential jurors whether they were church members, though not everyone was asked.

After the jury was seated, Darrow noted that he had failed

to ask that question of the first juror, W.F. Roberson, who had already been accepted on the jury. He requested an opportunity to ask it at that late time, but he said that he would not challenge the juror regardless of the answer; he just wanted to know.

Judge Raulston permitted it, leading to one final question and answer.

DARROW: *Are you a member of the church?*

ROBERSON: *No, sir.*

With the jury seated, court broke for the weekend, to resume Monday morning, July 13. Court again opened with prayer, this time by the Reverend Moffett, who included requests for "blessings upon this Court" and that "Thy blessings might guide the presiding judge," as well as blessings for the jury, the lawyers on each side of the case, the principles in the case, and even "these newspaper men as they take reports and interpret the facts throughout the world." Almost like Tiny Tim's "God bless us, everyone," in Charles Dickens's *A Christmas Carol*.

Again, Darrow stayed silent on the prayer. After all, who could object to Tiny Tim? He did not stay silent, though, in arguing on behalf of the defense's motion to quash the indictment as unconstitutional. He cited Section 3, Article 17 of the Tennessee constitution, which provided that "no preference shall ever be given, by law, to any religious establishment or mode of worship." The Butler Act and the indictment under it, Darrow argued, violated that clause because they gave "preference to the Bible."

Chief prosecutor Tom Stewart denied the claim.

He asked Darrow, "What is there in this [Act] that requires you to worship in any particular way?" He then added, speaking directly to the judge, "If your honor please, the St. James Version of the Bible is the recognized one in this section of the country."

Presumably he meant the *King* James version. It was, after

all, King James I of England who had commissioned, in 1604, the version that was first published in 1611 for the Church of England, and not James, brother of John, the son of Zebedee, who was one of Jesus's twelve disciples and who, along with his brother John, were surnamed "the sons of thunder." *Mark* 3:17 (KJV)

But let's not quibble with Stewart (who is referred to in the transcript as "General" Stewart) and his grasp of the Bible.

Speaking of titles, on that second day, after the judge had several times referred to Darrow as "Colonel," Darrow responded, "I shall always remember that this court is the first one that ever gave me a great title of 'Colonel' and I hope it will stick to me when I get back north."

"I want you to take it back to your home with you, colonel," Judge Raulston replied.

After that, Colonel Darrow launched into high gear in attacking the Bible and not merely the Butler Act. That, after all, was why he was there—not just to defend John Scopes, or really even to challenge the constitutionality of the law, but to attack the Bible and its spokesman William Jennings Bryan. It wasn't a hidden agenda; rather, it was his stated intent.

A couple of years earlier, he had published a pamphlet, edited by E. Haldeman-Julius, titled *Absurdities of the Bible*, which he had prepared as a response to a list of questions Bryan had submitted through the press.

Bryan ignored them then, so now Darrow saw this trial as his opportunity for a face-to-face confrontation. He essentially used that paper as his outline for later questioning Bryan on the witness stand.

It was clear from the beginning that Darrow didn't take the trial seriously. At least not as a trial. He admitted as much in his memoir.

> *I try never to take things too seriously; if I did, I would have been wiped out long ago. As to the Dayton case, from the beginning it seemed to me a joke. And I was*

> *satisfied that it would be only that if we could get the world to see it in its right light, which we did.* [ccxvii]

To Darrow, the case was a sure loser, something he already knew. He was banking on a higher court to ultimately rule, but the trial gave him a platform, with the eyes and ears of the nation—if not the world—on him, to make his pet arguments and advance his personal views while at the same time humiliate an adversary.

He hoped to ridicule the Bible, Christianity, and organized religion in one fell swoop, and to make them seem lesser in the eyes of the world.

He also aimed to destroy Bryan in the process.

Lest you think that last line is hyperbole, note that he amply demonstrated, in his memoir, his contempt for Bryan, upon whom he freely heaped ridicule. On the first day of trial that hot, southern July morning, he described his nemesis this way:

> *Down below, at a long table, near the judge's bench, sat William Jennings Bryan, wearing as few clothes as possible. So few, indeed, that had he seen some girl so arrayed he would have considered her a bad sort, and straightway turned his head the other way.* [ccxviii]

Bryan, he said, sat there "fanning himself, looking limp and martyr-like between assaults upon the flies that found a choice roosting-place on his bald, expansive dome and bare, hairy arms." [ccxix]

Darrow's observations of the courtroom were no more complimentary. He noted the presence, in multiple locations, of "Read Your Bible" banners and thought "[i]t looked as though there might have been a discount for ordering a wholesale lot." [ccxx] He claimed that one of his first actions was to ask that the banners be removed, though that order of things is not reflected in the transcript; his request was actually not made until near the end of the trial.

His first real argument, his first opportunity to make one of his preselected speeches, was the motion to quash the indictment, which was argued on the second day, outside the presence of the jury. Judge Raulston ordered the jury excused, since it was purely a legal motion for the court to consider, but Darrow objected to the jury being removed.

He didn't state his reasoning. He simply objected and was overruled, but it's safe to presume he wanted the jury to hear his brilliance during his initial frontal assault on the Bible and its story of divine creation.

John Neal, one of his co-counsel, offered a weak justification for keeping the jury in the courtroom—"The jury has got to be the judge of the law and the facts of this case...."— but the judge disagreed. "It may become necessary for the court to make inquiries from you gentlemen during the arguments," Judge Raulston said, "from which the jury might infer that the court had certain opinions as to the facts and so the court will be more at ease with the jury not present."

"We will be less at ease," Darrow said, a forerunner to later exchanges that ended with Darrow cited for contempt of court.

When it came his time to argue in favor of quashing the indictment, Darrow began by directly attacking Bryan. Not by name, but everyone knew who he was talking about when Darrow referred to "another who is prosecuting this case, and who is responsible for this foolish mischievous and wicked act...."

He also acknowledged his contempt for the entire proceeding, when he said, "I am going to argue it as if it was serious...." He then attacked the Butler Act as being "as brazen and as bold an attempt to destroy learning as was ever made in the middle ages, and the only difference is we have not provided that they shall be burned at the stake, but there is time for that, Your Honor." So much for arguing it as if it was serious.

The brunt of his attack, however, was not on the statute,

but was on the Bible, which he also clearly held in contempt. "I have read it myself," he said. "I might read more or more wisely. Others may understand it better. Others may think they understand it better when they do not. But in a general way I know what it is."

By attacking the Bible, he was also, by extension, attacking those who believed in it. By way of disclaimer, he recognized that millions of people used the Bible to "derive consolation in their times of trouble and solace in times of distress," and that "I would be pretty near the last one in the world to do anything or take any action to take it away." But, he cautioned, "I feel just exactly the same toward the religious creed of every human being who lives."

So whose religion, he pondered, should get the imprimatur of government? None, he said. The Bible is not one book, but it was made up of sixty-six books (thirty-nine in the *Old Testament* and twenty-seven in the *New Testament*), and "...it is a book primarily of religion and morals. It is not a book of science."

Then, after a brief divergence to actual legal matters, arguments on the clarity or ambiguity of the Butler Act, he moved back to his initial thrust that the Bible was better left to religion and not to government. It might have been a legitimate point, but there was that "by extension" assault on believers to contend with.

> [T]*here is nothing else, Your Honor, that has caused the difference of opinion, of bitterness, of hatred, of war, of cruelty that religion has caused. With that, of course, it has given consolation to millions.*
>
> *But it is one of those particular things that should be left solely between the individual and his Maker, or his God, or whatever takes expression over him, and it is no one else's concern.*

Give Me that Old-Time Religion

Probably the most common description of the Scopes Monkey Trial was that it created a circuslike atmosphere. There's a lot to be said for that, what with Mencken's armed clowns shooting and all, but it could be argued that, within the courtroom itself, the atmosphere was more akin to an old-fashioned tent revival, with an almost evangelistic fervor.

And that was one of the things that Darrow railed against, albeit not quite as vociferously—or punctually—as he would have you believe.

Each day's session was opened with prayer, and the courtroom was festooned with banners, including at least one to the side of the jury box that proclaimed *Read your Bible*.[66] On the first day of trial, the session was opened with a prayer led by a Reverend Cartwright, whom Darrow sarcastically referred to as "Brother Twitchell."

His default for those he disagreed with or simply misunderstood was contempt. He wrote, "This was new to me. I had practiced law for more than forty years and had never before heard God called in to referee a court trial."[ccxxi]

Darrow wrote that, after court was adjourned for the day, he approached Judge Raulston and told him the defense believed it was unfairly prejudicial to open the day with prayer. "[A]t best it was an unfair weapon to introduce, particularly as the case had a religious aspect."[ccxxii]

The prosecution was shocked at his objection, he said. He claimed that at the beginning of the next session, he made his objection on the record. "The people assembled looked as though a thunderbolt had stunned them, and the wrath of the Almighty might be hurled down upon the heads of the defense."[ccxxiii]

It was actually the third day before Darrow raised a formal

---

[66] In Darrow's memoir, he wrote that the banner said *Read your Bible daily*, but the trial transcript has it at *Read Your Bible*.

objection. The nature of the case involved a "conflict between science and religion," he said, reasonably, and "there should be no part taken outside of the evidence in this case and no attempt by means of prayer or in any other way to influence the deliberation and consideration of the jury of the facts in this case."

Again, reasonable.

He concluded by asking the reporters in attendance "to take down the prayer" so he could "make specific objections again to any such parts as we think are especially obnoxious to our case." He told the judge directly, "I do object to the turning of this courtroom into a meeting house in the trial of this case. You have no right to do it."

In his memoir, he wrote that when he made his objection:

> ...the people assembled looked as though a thunderbolt had stunned them, and the wrath of the Almighty might be hurled down upon the heads of the defense. None of them had ever heard of anyone objecting to any occasion being opened or closed or interspersed with prayer. That there should be no dearth of preachers, the court had appointed a committee of church members to keep us supplied, so that there would be a new one at every session of the trial. [ccxxiv]

Judge Raulston overruled the objection, stating that he had specifically instructed the ministers who would be leading opening prayers "to make no reference to the issues involved in this case."

Darrow objected again the following day, was overruled again, and finally asked for, and was given, a running objection to opening prayer. This is a common practice in trials when everyone knows an objectionable (at least by one party's perception) question or subject will come up repeatedly so that the trial is not constantly interrupted with an objection and adverse ruling.

For the most part, the praying ministers followed the judge's instruction to refrain from referencing issues in the case. At least not directly, although there were perhaps subtle mentions, or maybe even subtext, in some of their prayers.

For example, on that very morning that Darrow first formally raised his objection and was overruled, Dr. Stribling included a request in his prayer that "there be in every heart and in every mind a reverence to the Great Creator of the world." Seems like "Great Creator" was a reference to the very theme of the case—divine creation versus evolution.

On the fifth day, Dr. J.A. Allen, pastor of Glensley Avenue Church of Christ in Nashville (apparently there weren't enough preachers in Dayton, so preachers had to be imported to pray) asked for divine guidance upon the "deliberations of this court, to the end that Thy Word may be vindicated, and that Thy truth may be spread in the earth."

Again, asking for vindication of the "Word" might be interpreted as a prayer for validation of the Biblical account of creation. On the sixth day, Reverend Dr. C.G. Eastwood prayed for "Thy divine guidance in the things that shall be done and the decisions that shall be made."

The subtext appears to be: It's your Word; lead the jury to decide correctly in its favor.

And on the fateful eighth day, when the jury verdict was returned against Scopes, Reverend Standefer mentioned that God had constantly been "seeking to invite us to contemplate higher and better and richer creations of Thine, and sometimes we have been stupid enough to match our human minds with revelations of the infinite and eternal."

Perhaps it's just subtext, but it sounds like he may have been calling the evolutionists "stupid." It's certainly understandable why Darrow might have felt the deck was being stacked against him.

The banner by the jury box was another matter altogether. Darrow claimed that he had not made an issue of it before since the jury had been excluded from the courtroom while various motions were argued *ad nauseam*. But when the jury was finally brought in, he objected to the banner. He wrote in his memoir that it was clear that the purpose of the banner was to influence the jury, and so it should be removed. "Every one [sic] paused in awe at the audacity, but it was not a rainy day so that I was taking no chance with lightning." [ccxxv]

The transcript shows, however, that the jury was finally brought in on the fourth day, when the prosecution presented its witnesses and made its case, but Darrow didn't object to the banner at that time.

In fact, the only thing that happened immediately upon bringing in the jury was that the foreman, J.R. Thompson, requested electric fans for the jury box. He prefaced his query with "If it ain't out of order," and explained that it was a unanimous request from the jury because "this heat is fearful."

The judge agreed.

Darrow would also complain in his memoir about the heat, but apparently he didn't get an electric fan, though there were many in the courtroom.

> *All those fans were set to cool the fevered feelings of the judge, the jury, the prosecution and the different distinguished natives invited from day to day to sit alongside "His Honor." And all their friends, the flower of Dayton, and Mr. Bryan and his friends sat in social state as cool and comfortable as possible over in the shady section, opposite our sun-scorched side. As Southern gentlemen, they must have been sorry that there were not enough fans to go around, nor one wee socket left for "the defense."* [ccxxvi]

It wasn't until the jury was to be brought back in on the seventh day that Darrow finally got around to objecting to the banner.

It's not clear if he simply hadn't thought about it on those few prior occasions when the jury was in the box, or perhaps he was too preoccupied with the prayer issue. Or maybe there was some ulterior motive for waiting, but he suggests in his memoir that he did it before the jury was brought in the first time, which is not correct.

There was passionate argument on both sides about the banner. One of the prosecutors, Gordon McKenize, son of Ben McKenzie, a retired attorney on the prosecution team, agreed that it should be taken down while others on his team—including his father—opposed that, leading Dudley Field Malone, one of Darrow's co-counsel, to quip, "The house is divided against itself."

But then McKenzie the younger changed his mind, seemingly angered by arguments from the defense.

> *I want to withdraw my suggestion in regard to removing the sign "Read Your Bible," for this reason: I have never seen the time in the history of this country when any man should be afraid to be reminded of the fact that he should read his Bible, and if they should represent a force that is aligned with the devil and his satellites, finally I say when that time comes that then is the time for us to tear up all of the Bibles, throw them in the fire and let the country go to hell.*

It's no surprise that the defense objected to McKenzie's language, which Judge Raulston sustained. He instructed the court reporter to expunge that part of Mr. McKenzie's statement from the record where he said, "if you were satellites of the devil."

Not exactly an accurate restatement of what McKenzie said—he actually said that the defense represents a "force that is aligned with the devil and his satellites"—but it was close enough.

Remarkably, Darrow remained relatively silent after making his initial objection and request. At least until Bryan weighed in. At that point, Darrow could stay silent no longer. Just like he couldn't help but get involved in the case, even over the objections of the fee-paying ACLU, once he learned of Bryan's participation.

Bryan pointed out that the defense had argued that evolution was not necessarily contrary to the Bible, since Christian evolutionists believed that it could, in fact, be reconciled with scripture. "If their arguments are sound and sincere, that the Bible can be construed so as to recognize evolution, I cannot see why 'Read Your Bible' would necessarily mean partiality toward our side."

Still, he said, invoking the doctrine of the weaker brother (a Christian doctrine that says Christians should not engage in conduct that can cause weaker Christians to stumble in their faith), "[I]f leaving that up there during the trial makes our brother to offend, I would take it down during the trial."

That was too much for Darrow, even though Bryan had conceded the main point. He wanted to win the issue on the merits, not on Bryan's condescending version of Christianity.

> *We might agree to get up a sign of equal size on the other side and in the same position reading 'Hunter's Biology' or 'Read your evolution.' This sign is here for no purpose and it can have no effect but to influence this case.*

Judge Raulston ultimately ruled that "If the presence of the sign irritates anyone, or if anyone thinks it might influence the jury in any way...I will let the sign come down."

And the banner, like the walls of Jericho in the Old Testament, came down.

"Your Honor has the right to hope."

A very basic rule of courtroom conduct is to act with respect for the process, including respect for the judge and opposing counsel.

As hard as it sometimes is for lawyers in the heat of battle, and even when "fighting fire with fire," as Darrow claimed during the McNamara case, that respect is supposed to extend to the very lawyers on the other side that they sometimes despise or view with disdain.

The American Bar Association had promulgated its Canons of Professional Ethics in 1908, which included the following:

> The Duty of the Lawyer to the Courts.
> *It is the duty of the lawyer to maintain towards the Courts a respectful attitude, not for the sake of the temporary incumbent of the judicial office, but for the maintenance of its supreme importance....*
>
> Ill Feeling and Personalities Between Advocates.
> *All personalities between counsel should be scrupulously avoided. In the trial of a cause it is indecent to allude to the personal history or the personal peculiarities and idiosyncrasies of counsel on the other side. Personal colloquies between counsel which cause delay and promote unseemly wrangling should also be carefully avoided.*

Darrow was consistently disrespectful of his opposing counsel, particularly Bryan, whom he considered a nemesis and, perhaps worse, an idiot.

But he didn't let it stop there.

He also showed his disrespect for Judge Raulston, which—never mind rules or canons of ethics—flaunted a basic rule of lawyerly common sense: Don't piss off the judge. It's hard to know whether Darrow's disrespect for Judge Raulston harmed his cause, since it seemed a foregone conclusion from the opening day, if not even before, that he was going to lose.

But it did result in his being held in contempt of court, which he claimed was a first in his career as a lawyer. And, but for the grace of a forgiving judge, it might have landed him in jail. Interesting that, while contempt of court might have been a first, he failed to mention two prior indictments for bribing jurors.

Seems like the latter is worse.

The contemptuous conduct occurred near the end of the sixth day of trial, Friday, July 17, just prior to Darrow's examination of Bryan the following Monday.

The contempt ruling was made on that Monday, in the morning before the Bryan testimony. To set the stage, one must remember that Darrow had numerous scientific experts lined up to testify on evolution, but the prosecution had objected on the grounds that expert testimony was irrelevant to the issues before the court. Darrow asked for the opportunity to make an offer of proof, in the form of a bill of exceptions.

What he was asking for was the right to put his experts' statements into the record, even though they would not be presented to the jury, so a higher court, on appeal, would know what the statements were and could make an informed decision whether the judge had properly excluded them.

Bryan asked for the right to cross-examine those witnesses on their statements, which Darrow, rightly, objected to.

> What we are interested in, counsel well knows what the judgment and verdict in this case will be. We have a right to present our case to another court and that is all we are after. And they have no right whatever to cross-examine any witness when we are offering simply to show what we expect to prove.

The judge, however, ruled that, if the experts presented their testimony, he would permit the prosecution to cross-examine. Darrow was justifiably peeved at this and "excepted" to the ruling.

"Always expect this court to rule correctly," Judge Raulston said.

"No, sir, we do not," Darrow replied, to laughter in the courtroom. A rare two-fer. He had disrespected the judge, and he had subjected the judge to ridicule.

Darrow then asked for the opportunity to have his experts put their statements in writing, which could be entered into the record without testimony and cross-examination, solely for purposes of the bill of exceptions for review by an appellate court. When he asked for the rest of the day to draft the statements, the judge denied the request, saying that would take too much time.

A clearly exasperated Darrow then had this exchange with the judge, which directly led to the contempt citation.

> DARROW: *We want to make statements here of what we expect to prove. I do not understand why every request of the state and every suggestion of the prosecution should meet with an endless waste of time, and a bare suggestion of anything that is perfectly competent on our part should be immediately overruled.*
>
> JUDGE RAULSTON: *I hope you do not mean to reflect upon the court.*
>
> DARROW: *Well, your honor has the right to hope.*
>
> JUDGE RAULSTON: *I have the right to do something else, perhaps.*
>
> DARROW: *All right; all right.*

Judge Raulston didn't immediately cite Darrow for contempt, but instead gave it the weekend before ruling. He would later say the delay was in order to avoid making a rash ruling inflamed by passion, but it more likely simply allowed him to stew over the weekend.

After the morning prayer the following Monday, and without the jury in the courtroom, the judge made the following statement before reading into the record the transcript of the critical exchange with Darrow from the previous Friday:

> *In the trial of a case there are two things that the court*

should always endeavor to avoid: First, the doing of anything that will excite the passions of the jury, and thereby prejudice the rights of either party. Second, the court should always avoid writing passion into his own decrees.

After the crucial exchange was read, Judge Raulston continued. Noting that he had deliberately withheld ruling for the weekend, "until passion had time to subdue," he lectured Darrow. "He who would unlawfully and wrongfully show contempt for a court of justice, sows the seeds of discord and breeds contempt for both the law and the courts."

Furthermore, he added, "Men may become prominent, but they should never feel themselves superior to the law or to justice." Given what he felt was "an unjustified expression of contempt for this court and its decrees," Raulston issued a "show cause" order for Darrow to post a bond and to appear the next morning to face the contempt charge and "say why he should not be dealt with for contempt," the penalty for which could be jail time.

Darrow, to his credit, handled the matter quite nicely that afternoon by apologizing, ostensibly sincerely, for his remarks. He said that things had overtaken him the Friday before and that he didn't realize until hearing the transcript read back that morning how bad it might have looked. He had been practicing law for forty-seven years, he said, and "never yet in all my time had any criticism by the court for anything I have done in court."

Again, not taking into account two bribery indictments, though I suppose he was technically correct—the bribe payments didn't actually occur "in court," even though they related to courtroom proceedings.

He thanked the citizens of Dayton who, he said, had treated him "better, kindlier and more hospitably than I fancied would have been the case." Then, directly addressing Judge Raulston, he admitted that he had overstepped and that "I do not see how your honor could have helped taking notice of it and I have regretted it ever since on my own account and on account of the profession that I am in." In concluding, he said, "I want to apologize to the court for it."

Judge Raulston, being the good Baptist that he was, accepted the apology as an act of Christian principle.

> *My friends and Col. Darrow, the Man that I believe came into the world to save man from sin, the Man that died on the cross that man might be redeemed, taught that it was godly to forgive and were it not for the forgiving nature of Himself I would fear for man. The Savior died on the cross pleading with God for the men who crucified him. I believe in that Christ. I believe in these principles. I accept Col. Darrow's apology.... I feel that I am justified in speaking for the people of the great state that I represent when I speak as I do to say to him that we forgive him and we forget it and we commend him to go back home and learn in his heart the words of the Man who said: "If you thirst come unto Me and I will give thee life."*

Raulston then came down from the bench and posed with Darrow for photographers, shaking hands. With great applause, the saga of the contempt was over.

Until later, when Darrow had a chance to reflect back on the whole thing. In a lengthy telegram to the *Chicago Daily News* dated August 11, 1925, less than a month following the Scopes trial, and apparently in response to an appearance by Judge Raulston at a conference hosted by the Illinois Christian Fundamentals Association on August 10, he wrote:

> *Judge Raulston was elected on a fluke and is now campaigning for reelection this fall. The trial was part of his campaign. He called the grand jury and asked them to indict Scopes in a hurry so the case could be tried in his district. The indictment was illegal, as it was brought too soon after convening of a special grand jury, so the judge*

> *had him reindicted a month later, on the day of the trial.*
>
> *On Sunday, three days before the case was closed, Mr. Bryan spoke twice in Dayton. Raulston was present at both meetings and sat on the platform at one. He paraded his fundamentalism all through the trial and has given the people of Chicago a chance to see what sort of trial could have been had before him.*
>
> *It was perfectly proper to call Mr. Bryan as a recognized expert on the Bible, to testify as to meaning of [the] story of creation. The questions asked him were perfectly civil, but when the examination had only commenced the judge came in to court in the morning and took Mr. Bryan off the stand without any motion being made in court to that effect.*
>
> *The judge may be glad he has a limited education. One cannot always avoid being ignorant, but few boast of it.*
>
> *The incident citing me for contempt is absurd. I did feel a contempt for his unfairness. I did show it, as often happens by lawyers in court. I did apologize as I should have done. This constantly happens in court and the judge knows it, although it never happened to me before.* [ccxxvii]

Still later, he would write in his memoir:

> *Judge Ralston, not easily daunted, achieved some further glory through speech-making in fundamentalist churches on the evolution question as he saw it. He was eminently qualified. He had never read a line on the subject and very little on any other. And had held that to teach evolution was a criminal offense in Tennessee and therefore presumably wicked everywhere.* [ccxxviii]

Mike Farris

Chapter Sixteen: The Sun Stood Still

It was plain to everyone, when Bryan came to Dayton, that his great days were behind him—that he was now definitely an old man, and headed at last for silence.
—H.L. Mencken

PROBABLY THE MOST memorable part of the trial, and the event most highlighted in the Scopes legend, particularly in *Inherit the Wind*, was Clarence Darrow's examination of William Jennings Bryan on the witness stand, with Bryan testifying as an expert on the Bible.

It didn't arise in a vacuum, however.

In fact, it would be a surprise if that wasn't Darrow's ultimate goal all along: to actually put Bryan on the stand, not just to duel with him in arguments to the court, but to embarrass, if not humiliate, him. He had tried to force Bryan to respond to a series of questions just two years earlier about the Bible, but Bryan had ignored him.

Now, however, he thought he could get him where he wanted him: in a courtroom, under oath, with no escape hatches.

Although Judge Raulston had already excluded the defense's scientific experts on evolution, the religious angle—

proving the Bible—tapped into Bryan's ego. It was likely a foregone conclusion that Bryan would agree to testify, even though his testimony wasn't actually relevant to any issue in the trial and probably should have been excluded before the first question was even asked.

But Bryan believed himself to be the savior of fundamentalist religion in the country—or, as Dudley Field Malone referred to him, the "evangelical leader of the prosecution," although the defense denied that he was an "authorized spokesman for the Christians of the United States"—and that was why he was there in the first place.

So, even though others on the prosecution team objected when he was called as a witness, Bryan simply said, "Where do you want me to sit?" He even offered to be sworn in. "I can say 'So help me God, I will tell the truth.'"

Darrow demurred.

"No, I take it you will tell the truth, Mr. Bryan."

With Bryan's acquiescence, if not eagerness, to testify, Judge Raulston allowed the drama to continue. And so it began, albeit outside the presence of the jury, since the judge would have to rule later, again, on whether expert testimony, or at least whether *this* expert testimony, was actually relevant and admissible.

To fully understand Darrow's game plan, you have to step back and review the booklet he had published a couple of years prior called *Absurdities of the Bible*, ostensibly to respond to Bryan's questions in the press and also to answer his own question, "Why am I an agnostic?"

Much of what he said in that booklet he would repeat in the courtroom in Dayton. He started with the origin of man from Adam and Eve, and questioned whether it was "a fact or a myth" that God took a rib from Adam to make Eve. Was there really a literal snake, "who presumably spoke to her [Eve] in Hebrew" and, when Eve "fell for it," were she and Adam driven from the Garden of Eden?

And was it literally true that, thereafter, "Adam was cursed to work" and "Eve and all of her daughters to the end of time were condemned to bring forth children in pain and agony"?

He wrote, "I do not think any God could have done it and I wouldn't worship a God who would." From there, he attacked other specifics of the Bible, including the battle described in *Joshua* in which God ordered the sun to stand still, casting ridicule on any miraculous event in the Bible that was inconsistent with science. Of course, that's pretty much what any miracle is: an act of divine intervention that defies science. And if your starting point is that there is no deity, it's nearly impossible to make the intellectual leap to divine intervention.

"I am an agnostic," he wrote, "because I trust my reason.... I am an agnostic because no man living can form any picture of any God, and you can't believe in an object unless you can form a picture of it. You may believe in the force, but not in the object."

It's not surprising that this formed the basis of his examination of Bryan at the Scopes trial. Their exchanges revealed the massive egos of each. Those exchanges were sometimes funny, but were more often malignant and mean-spirited, particularly on the part of Darrow.

"A Lot of Fellows who are Profusely Ugly..."

With Bryan on the stand, Darrow led him through his credentials to qualify as an expert on the Bible. Bryan testified that:

"I have studied the Bible for about fifty years or sometime [sic] more than that" and "I believe that everything in the Bible should be accepted as it is given there; some of the Bible is given illustratively." As an example of the latter, he referred to a verse that says "Ye are the salt of the earth." Obviously, he said, "I would not insist that man was actually salt...."

Darrow then launched into his attack, through leading questions, on specific narratives within the Bible. When the whale swallowed Jonah, he asked, "How do you literally interpret that?"

Blowhard

After correcting Darrow that the Bible actually refers to a "big fish" and not a "whale," [67] he answered the question as asked. "I believe in a God who can make a whale and can make a man and make both of them do what He pleases."

When pressed by Darrow on miracles of the Bible, Bryan said, "When you get beyond what man can do, you get within the realm of miracles; and it is just as easy to believe the miracle of Jonah as any other miracle in the Bible."

Jonah and the whale/big fish might have been a standoff, so Darrow moved on to Joshua and the sun standing still.

In *Joshua* 10, the story is recounted of Joshua leading a victory over enemies of the Children of Israel, but the sun was setting before the victory could be complete. Responding to the request of Joshua, God commanded the sun and the moon to "stand thou still...." Verse 13 (in the King James Version, of course) says:

> *And the sun stood still, and the moon stayed, until the people had avenged themselves upon their enemies. Is not this written in the book of Jasher? So the sun stood still in the midst of heaven, and hasted not to go down about a whole day.*

Again scorning the possibility of a miracle, Darrow relied on science for his scathing attack. Bryan conceded that the earth revolved around the sun and not the other way around, so if anything was stilled, it would have been the earth, not the sun. The anonymous author of the book of *Jonah*, though, was simply writing in terms that could be understood at the time, Bryan said, when people believed that the earth was the center of the universe.

Darrow pounced.

---

[67] Bryan was correct, according to the King James Version. "Now the Lord had prepared a great fish to swallow up Jonah." *Jonah* 1:17 (KJV).

So the Bible is subject to "construction" or "interpretation"?

"Well, I think anybody can put his own construction upon it," Bryan said, "but I do not mean that necessarily is a correct construction."

Darrow established his own understanding of Bryan's position when he said, "But it was the language that was understood at that time, and we now know that the sun stood still as it was with the earth."

When Bryan agreed, Darrow pounced again. "Have you ever pondered what would naturally happen to the earth if it stood still suddenly?... Don't you know it would have been converted into a molten mass of lava?"

In other words, there are natural laws at play that would have prevented such a thing from happening. Like, for example, the molten mass of lava bit. Again, trying to put a human spin on a miracle, discounting the possibility of God, to discredit it.

But Bryan pulled out an illustration he had used before about overcoming laws of nature.

> *I can take a glass of water that would fall to the ground without the strength of my hand and to the extent of the glass of water I can overcome the law of gravitation and lift it up. Whereas without my hand it would fall to the ground. If my puny hand can overcome the law of gravitation, the most universally understood to that extent, I would not set power to the hand of Almighty God that made the universe.*

Darrow responded dismissively. "I read that years ago." Obviously he had heard about this example from Bryan before and was, in effect, saying, "Yeah, yeah, yeah."

The back-and-forth on this topic from *Joshua* led to a particularly humorous exchange, at least as far as the courtroom audience was concerned, regarding the lengths of both the questions and the answers. When Darrow cut off a Bryan answer with "Can you answer my question?" Bryan responded, "When you let me finish the statement."

"It is a simple question," Darrow said, "but finish it."

"You cannot measure the length of my answer by the length of your question," Bryan said.

"No, except that the answer be longer."

Other Biblical topics on which the two jousted included the age of the earth, the flood, and the Tower of Babel. At one juncture, the two men bickered with each other like children leading to an admonishment from the judge to both of them.

> BRYAN: *These gentlemen [defense lawyers] have not had much chance—they did not come here to try this case. They came here to try revealed religion. I am here to defend it, and they can ask me any question they please.*
>
> JUDGE RAULSTON: *All right.*
>
> [Applause from the court yard][68]
>
> DARROW: *Great applause from the bleachers.*
>
> BRYAN: *From those whom you call "yokels."*
>
> DARROW: *I have never called them yokels.*
>
> BRYAN: *That is the ignorance of Tennessee, the bigotry.*
>
> DARROW: *You mean who are applauding you?*

---

[68] Because of the stifling heat in the courtroom, as well as concerns that the structure of the courthouse was not able to withstand the weight of the mass of spectators and might collapse, the trial was moved outdoors to the courtyard. After "forgiving" Darrow for contempt, Judge Raulston said, "I think the court should adjourn downstairs. I am afraid of the building. The court will convene down in the yard." The transcript reflects: "Court thereupon adjourned to the stand in the courthouse lawn...."

BRYAN: *Those are the people whom you insult.*

DARROW: *You insult every man of science and learning in the world because he does not believe in your fool religion.*

JUDGE RAULSTON: *I will not stand for that.*

DARROW: *For what he is doing?*

JUDGE RAULSTON: *I am talking to both of you.*

By the time court ended for the day, the biggest revelation, or perhaps admission, was Bryan's concession that the creation story in Genesis didn't necessarily mean that God created the world in six twenty-four-hour days.

Chief prosecutor Tom Stewart, apparently realizing that this undermined the creationist view of a literal interpretation of the Bible, objected.

"What is the purpose of this examination?" he asked.

Bryan answered his own co-counsel's question with a jab at Darrow. "The purpose is to cast ridicule on everybody who believes in the Bible, and I am perfectly willing that the world shall know that these gentlemen have no other purpose than ridiculing every Christian who believes in the Bible."

Not so, said Darrow. "We have the purpose of preventing bigots and ignoramuses from controlling the education of the United States and you know it, and that is all."

Bryan responded, to prolonged applause, "I am simply trying to protect the word of God against the greatest atheist or agnostic in the United States. I want the papers to know I am not afraid to get on the stand in front of him and let him do his worst. I want the world to know."

But questioning circled back around to Bryan's concession that the creation days were not twenty-four-hour days. "My impression is they were periods," Bryan said. And those periods might have gone on for a long time. "It might have continued for millions of years."

This appeared to be an admission that could reconcile Biblical creationism with evolution, but no one on the prosecution side was about to admit it. That was going a bit too far. If creation might actually have taken millions of years, then it was possible that man wasn't instantly created as a whole man but might well have evolved from something lesser. That was dangerous ground for the prosecution to tread.

Along those lines, and during an earlier argument between Darrow and prosecutor B.G. McKenzie over whether evolution contradicted the Biblical account, the question arose whether Adam was created first as a "complete man" or whether Adam developed from "a single cell of life." Darrow attacked the verse in *Genesis* 1:27 that proclaimed that "God created man in his own image, in the image of God created he him; male and female created he them."

Darrow asked, "When it said, 'in His own image,' did you think that meant the physical man?"

"I am taking the Divine account—'He is like unto me,'" McKenzie said.

"Do you think it is so?" Darrow asked.

McKenzie responded, "I say that, although I know it is awfully hard on our Maker to look like a lot of fellows who are profusely ugly, to say he favored the Master."

The heavyweight battle between Darrow and Bryan ended with a final bickering session between the witness and his chief antagonist.

> BRYAN: *Your honor, I think I can shorten this testimony. The only purpose Mr. Darrow has is to slur at the Bible, but I will answer his question [as to whether he believed in the rainbow after the flood]. I will answer it all at once, and I have no objection in the world, I want the world to know that this man, who does not believe in a God, is trying to use a court in Tennessee—*

DARROW: *I object to that.*

BRYAN: *—to slur at it, and while it will require time, I am willing to take it.*

DARROW: *I object to your statement. I am exempting you on your fool ideas that no intelligent Christian on earth believes.*

JUDGE RAULSTON: *Court is adjourned until 9 o'clock tomorrow morning.*

Darrow later described his view of his examination of Bryan in a very self-congratulatory way.

> *Mr. Bryan left the grounds practically alone. The people seemed to feel that he had failed and deserted his cause and his followers when he admitted that the first six days might have been millions of ages long. Mr. Bryan had made himself ridiculous and had contradicted his own faith. I was truly sorry for Mr. Bryan. But I consoled myself by thinking of the years through which he had busied himself tormenting intelligent professors with impudent questions about their faith and seeking to arouse the ignoramuses and bigots to drive them out of their positions.*[ccxxix]

Find the Defendant Guilty

In the end, it was the judge who wasn't willing to take any more of it. On the morning of the eighth and final day of the trial, he ruled that the "testimony of Mr. Bryan can shed no light upon any issues that will be pending before the higher courts."

The issue, he said, is whether Scopes taught evolution in the public schools and not "whether God created man as all complete at once" as opposed to "the process of development and growth." Accordingly, and over Darrow's objection, who was champing at the bit to continue his examination of Bryan that morning, he expunged Bryan's prior testimony and ruled that "it will not be further considered."

That didn't sit well with Darrow, particularly expunging the testimony from the record, but he at least had the satisfaction of knowing that the press had recorded the prior days questions and answers.

Then Darrow ended matters, depriving Bryan of the chance to make any grandiose closing arguments to the jury. The defense had no witnesses, Darrow said, and no other proof to offer other than what was already in the record. So, he asked the court "to bring in the jury and instruct the jury to find the defendant guilty."

This apparently had been a part of Darrow's strategy all along. Darrow wrote that his entire goal in taking on the case was "to focus attention of the country on the programme of Mr. Bryan and the other fundamentalists in America," and that Bryan "did not represent a real case; he represented religion, and in this he was the idol of all Morondom." [ccxxx]

Darrow knew the case was a loser, he knew he needed a shot at an appellate court to address the real reasons he got involved, and he knew one other thing.

William Jennings Bryan had planned to make a full-blown speech on the evils of evolution as his closing argument to the jury. But, by waiving his own closing argument and asking the court to instruct the jury to return a guilty verdict, Darrow did away with any closing arguments, which were unnecessary at that point.

> I made a complete and aggressive opening of the case. I did this for the reason that we never at any stage intended to make any [closing] arguments in the case. We knew that Mr. Bryan was there to make a closing speech about "The Prince of Peace" and the importance of "The Rock of Ages" above the "age of rocks" and that the closing address he meant should thrill the world was doubtless prepared

> *for the press in manifold copies before he left Florida, and that it would be for the consumption and instruction of those who knew nothing about either "The Rock of Ages" or "the age of rocks." We knew that such of the assembled multitudes as had the capacity to understand would refuse to learn. By not making a closing argument on our side we could cut him out.*[ccxxxi]

The judge did as Darrow requested and the jury returned its guilty verdict after deliberating a mere nine minutes. One wonders what took so long. That beautiful closing argument of Bryan was thus left out of the official court record and was relegated to publication as an undelivered argument. The arrangements for publication were apparently made mere hours before his death five days after the end of the trial.

The penalty provision of the Butler Act called for a fine between $100 and $500. Judge Raulston, in a fateful move, entered the minimum amount of $100. Scopes was required to post a $500 bond pending an appeal, which amount was paid by the *Baltimore Evening Sun*, the paper for which reporter H.L. Mencken worked.

And on the Eighth Day, the Court Rested

As parting shots, the judge allowed the lawyers to address the jury one last time, ostensibly to offer their thanks for being kept cooped up away from the goings-on in the courtroom for the better part of eight days.

Bryan spoke first, noting that...

> *...here has been fought out a case of little consequence as a case, but the world is interested because it raises an issue, and that issue will some day be settled right, whether it is settled on our side or the other side.*

The "some day" for that issue wouldn't come for more than four decades and would be settled by the United States Supreme

Court for "the other side." [69] Bryan downplayed his and Darrow's roles in the case, saying that:

> ...the world little cares for man as an individual. He is born, he works, he dies, but causes go on forever, and we who participated in this case may congratulate ourselves that we have attached ourselves to a mighty issue.

Darrow was less gracious, continuing to take shots at Bryan. "I want to say in thorough sincerity that I appreciate the courtesy on the other side from the beginning of this case, at least the Tennessee counsel...."

Notably, Bryan hailed from Florida for the trial, not Tennessee. To laughter, Darrow thanked Judge Raulston for being lenient with him on the contempt citation. "I appreciate the kind, and I think I may say, general treatment of this court, who might have sent me to jail, but did not."

Then he offered this comparison of the battle of science against anti-evolutionists and fundamentalist Christians:

> I think this case will be remembered because it is the first case of this sort since we stopped trying people in America for witchcraft because here we have done our best to turn back the tide that has sought to force itself upon this modern world, of testing every fact in science by a religious dictum. That is all I care to say.

Judge Raulston closed with a speech praising the town of Dayton and its hospitality, then told the out-of-town lawyers, "We are glad to have you with us."

Arthur Garfield Hays, counsel for the ACLU, which was footing the expensive bill for Scopes's defense, inquired of Judge

---

[69] *Epperson v. Arkansas*, 393 U.S. 97 (1968).

Raulston, "May I, as one of the counsel for the defense, ask your honor to allow me to send you the *Origin of the Species and the Descent of Man* by Charles Darwin?"

The judge accepted the offer over laughter and applause from those in attendance.

Following a benediction from Dr. Jones—"May the grace of our Lord Jesus Christ, the love of God and the communion and fellowship of the Holy Ghost abide with you all. Amen."—Judge Raulston adjourned court.

The great Scopes Monkey Trial was at an end.

Chapter Seventeen: Folding the Tent

God aimed at Darrow, missed, and hit Bryan instead.... We killed the son-of-a-bitch.
—H. L. Mencken

AFTER THE STATE rested its case, and with the exclusionary rulings made by the judge, Darrow knew any further effort in the trial court was fruitless.

> *Every one [sic] had been informed that a body of men and women were seeking to make the schools the servants of the church and to place bigotry and ignorance on the throne. It was some satisfaction to know that in this organization were very few scholars or men of intelligence, and that the great mass of their following was mostly illiterate.*[ccxxxii]

He entered this case, he wrote:

> *...solely to induce the public to stop, look, and listen, lest our public schools should be imperiled with a fanaticism founded on ignorance. We believe that unless the public could be awakened soon, it would be too late.... And in spite of an unpleasant notoriety, we accomplished this*

result.^{ccxxxiii}

On July 26, five days after the end of the trial, tragedy struck William Jennings Bryan. Noted as a man with a prodigious appetite, he offered the morning prayer at a church service in Dayton before enjoying a large lunch.

He then lay down for his afternoon nap, from which he never awoke. Bryan was buried in Arlington National Cemetery, in recognition of his service as a colonel in the Nebraska militia during the Spanish-American War, though he didn't see any military action. "He kept the Faith" is engraved on his tombstone.

Nellie Kenyon interviewed Bryan shortly after the trial had ended, likely one of the last interviews of his life. According to her report, Bryan, seeming "troubled," asked her whether she thought "they believed me." She wrote, "Some say he believed until his dying breath that he had won a great victory over Clarence Darrow." [ccxxxiv]

Kenyon also interviewed Darrow, who she believed "had more religion than he would admit."

When she had asked him, in her first interview with him, whether he believed in Jesus Christ, he answered, "I've never seen the time when I wouldn't like to have him on the jury." [ccxxxv]

Kenyon's suspicions about his religious beliefs seem in keeping with Darrow's repeated invoking of God during his impassioned plea on his own behalf during his bribery trials, not to mention his "What Would Jesus Do?" argument in Leopold and Loeb.

After the Scopes trial, in his final interview with Kenyon, though, he continued his assault on organized religion.

> Country preachers ought to be exported. They are all over the South and most of the West. The church can't last without hell. They usually don't believe in it, but are scared out of their boots. A God like that would be a devil.

> *And people like that don't believe in God—they believe in the devil.*[ccxxxvi]

The Sleep of the Just

As for Bryan, Darrow alternated between scorn and sympathy for his nemesis. When a reporter suggested to him that Bryan died of a broken heart because of Darrow's examination of him at trial, Darrow is reported to have said, "Broken heart nothing; he died of a busted belly."[ccxxxvii]

But later he would lament, when describing the funeral train that transported Bryan's body to Arlington and the throngs of mourners that lined its route, "I am sincere in saying that I am sorry that he could not have seen all this devotion that followed him to his resting place."[ccxxxviii]

Then he shifted back to scorn and derision:

> [Bryan's] *speculations had ripened into unchangeable convictions. He did not think, he knew. His eyes plainly revealed mental disintegration.... He had reached a stage of hallucination that would impel him to commit any cruelty that he believed would help his cause. History is replete with men of this type and they have added sorrow and desolation to the world.*[ccxxxix]

One can't help but wonder if he recognized the irony in complaining of Bryan's "cruelty" to "help his cause" in light of his verbal cruelty to the family of Bobby Franks in the Leopold and Loeb case while excusing the brutal actions of his clients.

In a fit of mean-spiritedness, he also wrote, almost gleefully, that Bryan's friends had failed in their efforts to raise money for a monument in Washington, D.C. honoring Bryan, complete with bells to chime every hour. "But the money was never raised, and the building and tower never adorned Washington, and the chimes never disturbed the sleep of the just who live in Washington."[ccxl]

He noted that an effort had been mounted to build a

college in Dayton, Tennessee, named in Bryan's honor, with a library containing his books, donated by the Bryan family.

As of the time Darrow's memoir was first published (it would later be republished with an addendum chapter about the Massie case added), sufficient funds had not been raised, so "they had dug a hole, perhaps a hundred feet wide and two hundred feet long and ten or fifteen feet deep. And this was what there was of Bryan University." [ccxli]

And, in one final jab, reflecting his pettiness, he wrote that "Bryan's books would be a total loss for any real university" and that "[b]igotry and opposition to learning are not a good foundation for any university in these modern times." [ccxlii]

Despite Darrow's dismissal of the efforts to build the school, William Jennings Bryan University was chartered in 1930 and enrolled its first class in the fall. Later called William Jennings Bryan College, in 1993, its name was shortened to simply Bryan College. Bryan College currently exists as a "regionally accredited,[70] liberal arts college in Dayton, Tennessee, dedicated to educational excellence with a foundation in biblical principles."[ccxliii] With an enrollment of approximately 1,400 students, its motto is "Christ Above All."

Its statement of "Core Values" says, in part:

> *We believe that God is the author of truth; that He has revealed Himself to humanity through nature, conscience, the Bible, and Jesus Christ; that it is His will for all people to come to a knowledge of the truth; and that an integrated study of the liberal arts and the Bible, with a proper emphasis on the spiritual, mental, social, and physical aspects of life, will lead to the balanced development of the whole person.*[ccxliv]

A final note about Bryan's namesake college is worthy of mention. In an article published September 26, 2023, *Forbes*

---

[70] Accredited by the Southern Association of Colleges and Schools.

Magazine included Bryan College in its list of "Best Online Master's in Human Services of 2023." [ccxlv] The Great Commoner would have been proud.

A mean-spirited H.L. Mencken was not nearly so schizophrenic as Darrow in his post-death assessment of Bryan, but instead seemed to revel in his demise. He reportedly said, "God aimed at Darrow, missed, and hit Bryan instead.... We killed the son-of-a-bitch." [ccxlvi]

In a column published in the *Baltimore Evening Sun* on August 10, 1925, he wrote that, with Bryan's death, the anti-evolution forces had lost their loudest voice.

> With Bryan alive and on the warpath, inflaming the morons and spreading his eloquent nonsense, the battle would have been ten times harder. But Bryan was unique, and can have no successor. His baleful rhetoric died with him; in fact, it died a week before his corporeal frame. In a very true sense, Darrow killed him. When he emerged from that incredible cross-examination, all that was most dangerous in his old following deserted him. It was no longer possible for a man of any intelligence to view him as anything save a pathetic has-been. [ccxlvii]

John Scopes was more magnanimous than either Darrow or Mencken.

He wrote that "[n]o fair man can judge Bryan's place in history by his actions at Dayton, alone; he deserves better." He elaborated that, while "some called him a martyr" and "Mencken and others called him a buffoon" because of the Monkey Trial, "[a] fairer label would be based upon all the years of his life rather than those at the end when the flame flickered out of a core of hardened dogma...."

Like everyone, he wrote, Bryan "contributed both good and bad," and that the "fair man would pity him for the bad he brought to the world, and love him for the good." [ccxlviii]

The Judgment Must Accordingly be Reversed

Nearly a year later, arguments were finally heard in front of the Tennessee Supreme Court in the case of *John Thomas Scopes v. The State of Tennessee*.[71] It wasn't the United States Supreme Court, as Clarence Darrow had hoped, but still it was a court of last resort, albeit in the state, and not the federal, court system.

The court filed its opinion on January 17, 1927, first addressing the question of the statute itself. It started by noting that Scopes had been convicted of a violation of the Butler Act "for that he did teach in the public schools of Rhea county [sic] a certain theory that denied the story of the divine creation of man, as taught in the Bible, and did teach instead thereof that man had descended from a lower order of animals."

The court then took up interpretation of the statute, itself. It said that the law was carelessly drafted, but that "nevertheless there seems to be no difficulty in determining its meaning." The "popular significance" of evolution was that it "has been understood to mean the theory which holds that man has developed from some pre-existing lower type," and that is the "sense" by which evolution was used in the Act. No ambiguity, the court said, so there could be no argument that its terms couldn't be understood and, thus, inadvertently violated.

The court then devolved into an arcane discussion of whether the Act mandated a particular teaching of evolution or simply prohibited one. It recognized a difference between stopping a teacher from teaching something as opposed to requiring a teacher to teach something.

With the Butler Act, the court said, it seems "plain that the Legislature in this enactment only intended to forbid teaching that men descended from a lower order of animals," but that it "*requires* the teaching of nothing." [emphasis in original]

So, the court concluded, since the statute did not impose an affirmative duty upon teachers, the statute did not run afoul

---

[71] 152 Tenn. 424, 278 S.W. 57 (Tenn. 1927).

of the First Amendment.

It's not necessary to review the history of the First Amendment protections of religion (both the prohibition against the establishment of religion and against restraining the free exercise thereof) to see the fallacy in the court's reasoning. It would take yet another forty years for the United States Supreme Court to actually rule on the question.

In reality, though, none of it turned out to be relevant to the Tennessee court's ultimate ruling, which hinged on a technicality.

The Butler Act required that, for violations, a minimum fine of $100 be leveled, with a maximum allowable of $500. A provision in the Tennessee Constitution required that any fine in excess of $50 had to be assessed by a jury.

In the Scopes case, however, Judge Raulston had imposed a $100 fine. The Supreme Court held that:

> [s]ince a jury alone can impose the penalty this Act requires, and as a matter of course no different penalty can be inflicted, the trial judge exceeded his jurisdiction in levying this fine, and we are without power to correct his error. The judgment must accordingly be reversed.

Then, to top it off, because Scopes was no longer teaching in Rhea County, or at any public school anywhere in Tennessee, for that matter, the court added, "We see nothing to be gained by prolonging the life of this bizarre case."

Based on that, it recommended that the claim be dismissed by the prosecution, which it was.

In the aftermath of the trial and appeal, Darrow's biggest complaint reflected his bruised ego, lamenting that "in only a limited number of the papers did we get the credit we deserved." [ccxlix]

Mike Farris

Whatever Happened to John T. Scopes?

Scopes's subsequent history is interesting. After the end of the school year at issue in the trial, he entered the University of Chicago to pursue an advanced degree in geology. His graduate education was funded by a scholarship raised for him by the expert witnesses that Darrow had retained, but who had been denied the opportunity to testify at trial.

While at the university he was nominated for a fellowship that, if granted, would allow him to complete his PhD after the prior scholarship funds had been depleted. However, his hopes were dashed by a meeting with the university's president who administered the endowment for the fellowship.

According to Scopes, the president (whom Scopes graciously declined to name in his memoir) told him, "Your name has been removed from consideration for the fellowship. As far as I am concerned, you can take your atheistic marbles and play elsewhere." [ccl]

Instead of completing his PhD, Scopes accepted a job in Venezuela with Gulf Oil of South America. "Venezuela," he wrote, "was a refuge where notoriety could not easily follow me. In South America I would be just another Yankee oil hunter; to the Americans there I would be another geologist. In many ways it was perfect." [ccli]

As for his legacy in the Monkey Trial, he wrote:

> Whether my little part has been a successful one or not, the public view of any such defendant is almost certain to be distorted. There seems to be no way out of it; in the public mind there is only that part of his life that gained him his fame or notoriety. The rest is so much gloss. The Dayton trial was only a moment of a long and, I hope, useful life. Nonetheless, in many minds I'll always be John T. Scopes, the Dayton, Tennessee, teacher who was the defendant in the Monkey Trial, despite the fact that I taught for only one year and have been a geologist for the

years since.

A man's fate, shaped by heredity and environment and an occasional accident, is often stranger than anything the imagination may produce.[cclii]

Whatever Happened to the Butler Act?

Following the Scopes Monkey Trial, the Butler Act lurked quietly in the shadows for a few decades before briefly rearing its head in 1955, coinciding with the first performances of the play *Inherit the Wind*.

At that time, the ACLU got involved again and sought repeal of the Act, but the office of Tennessee Governor Buford Ellington asserted that it was a "dead law;" i.e., it wouldn't be enforced. Because neither the Tennessee legislature nor the governor had any appetite for a political fight, the issue was dropped.

But on April 13, 1967, Gary L. Scott, a teacher at Jacksboro High School, was fired for violating the "dead law" by teaching evolution. Aided by the National Science Teachers Association, he filed a lawsuit challenging the Butler Act.

Within a matter of scant days of his filing suit, the law was repealed and, in response to negative publicity, Scott was reinstated in his teaching post.

The following year, forty-plus years after Scopes was finally decided and thirty years after Darrow's death, the constitutional issue of teaching evolution in public schools finally reached the United States Supreme Court.

In the case of *Epperson v. Arkansas*,[72] the Court addressed a 1928 Arkansas law, a contemporary of the Butler Act, that forbade teaching in public schools and universities "the theory or doctrine that mankind ascended or descended from a lower order of animals." Compare this language with the Butler Act, which forbade teaching "any theory that denies the story of the Divine Creation of man as taught in the Bible, and to teach

---

[72] 393 U.S. 97 (1968).

instead that man has descended from a lower order of animals."

In this case, Susan Epperson, a high school biology teacher in Little Rock, upon seeing a new textbook in her school which had a chapter on evolution (i.e., "the theory about the origin...of man from a lower form of animal"), faced a dilemma: "[S]he was supposed to use the new textbook for classroom instruction, and presumably teach the statutorily condemned chapter; but to do so would be a criminal offense, and subject her to dismissal."

Epperson filed a lawsuit that asked the court to declare the Arkansas statute void and to enjoin the State of Arkansas or the Little Rock school system from firing her if she taught the forbidden chapter. The lower court found that the law violated freedom of speech and thought under the First Amendment because it "...tends to hinder the quest for knowledge, restrict the freedom to learn, and restrain the freedom to teach."

The U.S. Supreme Court, however, addressed the case on First Amendment religion grounds. It found that the law was intended to prevent teachers from teaching anything contrary to the belief that *Genesis* must be the exclusive source of doctrine as to the origin of man and, by so doing, violated the Establishment Clause (which prohibits any law "respecting an establishment of religion").

The Court held, "It is clear that fundamentalist sectarian conviction was and is the law's reason for existence," but said that "[t]here is and can be no doubt that the First Amendment does not permit the State to require that teaching and learning must be tailored to the principles or prohibitions of any religious sect or dogma."

Noting that no argument was made, or even could be made, that the law "may be justified by considerations of state policy other than the religious views of some of its citizens," the Court concluded:

> *The overriding fact is that Arkansas' law selects from the body of knowledge a particular segment which it proscribes*

> *for the sole reason that it is deemed to conflict with a particular religious doctrine; that is, with a particular interpretation of the Book of Genesis by a particular religious group. Government in our democracy, state and national, must be neutral in matters of religious theory, doctrine, and practice.*

Tennessee and other states tried end runs around Epperson with laws ostensibly intended to place the *Genesis* story of creation on an equal footing with evolution and thereby evade the establishment clause restrictions, sometimes called "equal time laws."

A biology professor at David Lipscomb College in Nashville, Russell C. Artist, who was a member of the Creation Research Society (CRS), met with the Tennessee State Textbook Commission in 1970 in an effort to persuade the commission to include a CRS textbook, called *Biology: A Search for Order in Complexity*, in public school curriculums.

When that failed, his next move was to find a sponsor, which he did in state senator Milton H. Hamilton, for what became known as The Genesis Bill. The Genesis Bill essentially required that science classrooms that discussed evolution must give equal time to other theories "including, but not limited to, the *Genesis* account in the Bible." It was passed and signed into law in spring of 1973, although even a number of fundamentalists opposed it as reducing God to "theory" alongside the theory of evolution.[ccliii]

The Genesis Bill failed two judicial tests, one in Tennessee state court, which held that it violated both the Tennessee and United States Constitutions, and one in federal court, where it flunked the First Amendment freedom of religion clause.

United States District Judge Frank Gray, Jr., wrote: "Every religious sect, from the worshippers of Apollo to the followers of Zoroaster has its belief or theory. It is beyond the comprehension of this court how the legislature, if indeed it did, expected that all such theories could be included in any textbook of reasonable size."

The "equal time" cases, a variation on the Butler "monkey law," reached the U.S. Supreme Court a couple of decades after *Epperson* in *Edwards v. Aguillard*.[73]

Louisiana's Balanced Treatment for Creation-Science and Evolution-Science in Public School Instruction Act (also known as The Creationism Act) provided that, if you taught evolution in any given public school, you also had to teach creation, and *vice versa*. In other words, a school didn't have to teach either, but if it decided to teach one, then it had to teach the other, as well.

A group of parents, teachers, and religious leaders challenged the constitutionality of the law, and a federal district court, affirmed by the Fifth Circuit, invalidated it for violating the Establishment Clause "either because it prohibited the teaching of evolution or because it required the teaching of creation science with the purpose of advancing a particular religious doctrine." [74]

The Supreme Court agreed, finding that, "[b]ecause the primary purpose of the Creationism Act is to endorse a particular religious doctrine, the Act furthers religion in violation of the First Amendment."

In order to justify the law, the Court said, the Louisiana legislature needed to articulate some clear secular purpose to justify infringing on fundamental rights. The legislature had argued that the law was designed to protect academic freedom, a particularly ironic argument since it had once been advanced by evolutionists in the long ago.

However, the Court said, the Act, by its very terms, undermined that stated goal. The district court had found that "the Louisiana Legislature's actual intent was 'to discredit evolution by counterbalancing its teaching at every turn with the teaching of creationism, a religious belief.'"

---

[73] 482 U.S. 578 (1987).
[74] *Aguillard v. Treen*, 634 F. Supp. 426 (E.D. La. 1985)

The Supreme Court agreed with the district court, and even ridiculed the so-called "clear secular purpose" articulated by the legislature. It said that:

> *The goal of providing a more comprehensive science curriculum is not furthered either by outlawing the teaching of evolution or by requiring the teaching of creation science. While the court is normally deferential to a State's articulation of a secular purpose, it is required that the statement of such purpose be sincere and not a sham.*

The Court concluded that the stated purpose was a sham based in part on the fact that the State made available research services for teachers, but only for the teaching of creation science and not for evolution science, and only creation scientists served on the board that supplied the resources.

> *The prominent purpose was clearly to advance the religious viewpoint that a supernatural being created humankind.*

In reaching its holding, the Court applied the three-prong *Lemon*[75] test for determining whether a law or other governmental action is established for an improper purpose, and concluded:

> *Teaching a variety of scientific theories about the origins of humankind to schoolchildren might be validly done*

---

[75] *Lemon v. Kurtzman*, 403 U.S. 602 (1971) held that a statute must meet three criteria in order to satisfy compliance with the Establishment Clause of the First Amendment: "First, the statute must have a secular legislative purpose; second, its principal, or primary, effect must be one that neither advances nor inhibits religion; finally, the statute must not foster an 'excessive government entanglement with religion.'"

with the clear secular intent of enhancing the effectiveness of science instruction. But because the primary purpose of the Creationism Act is to endorse a particular religious doctrine, the Act furthers religion in violation of the First Amendment.

Clarence Darrow would have been proud.
    Or maybe he was just ahead of his time.

PART FIVE:
Aloha Oe—Massie

I felt I should scrub my hands afterwards, even though the jury recommended leniency.
—Hawaii Territorial Governor Lawrence M. Judd

Mike Farris

Chapter Eighteen: "I Better Go to Hawaii"

[T]*he so-called 'depression' had swept away practically all the savings that I thought I had for keeping me comfortable to the end and I needed the fee. This was not at all large, but it was sufficient.*
—Clarence Darrow

In the introduction to *A Death in the Islands*, I wrote:

> *In the wee hours of the morning on Sunday, September 13, 1931, two events occurred nearly simultaneously in Honolulu which, although reported separately to police, set in motion a series of events that included lies, deception, mental illness, racism, revenge, murder, and one of the greatest miscarriages of justice in United States history. It nearly tore apart the peaceful islands of Hawaii as it reverberated from the tenements of Honolulu to the hallowed halls of Congress, and right into the White House. And it ultimately left a stain on the legacy of one of the greatest legal minds of all time.*[ccliv]

The Massie Case was actually the bookend to a prior case in the Territory of Hawaii commonly known as the Ala Moana Case, a two-act tragedy of injustice set in motion on that fateful September night. Darrow was not involved in the first but was the star attraction in the second, though an understanding of the former is necessary to a fuller understanding of the latter.

"I Needed the Fee"

In his closing argument at his trial for bribing juror George Lockwood in the McNamara Brothers Case, Darrow said, "I shall spend the rest of my life as I have that which has passed, in doing the best I can to serve the cause of the poor."

Notwithstanding that and numerous other hollow protestations Darrow made over the course of his career that his reasons for taking on cases and causes were ideological and not money-based, dire financial straits trumped his ideals yet again.

Upon accepting engagement in the Massie Case to defend privileged whites accused of killing a native Hawaiian, he justified his decision by blaming the "so-called 'depression'" that had "swept away practically all the savings that I thought that I had for keeping me comfortable to the end, and I needed the fee."

Same song; next verse.

The fee turned out to be a healthy $40,000, plus an additional $10,000 for attorney George Leisure to assist him. In today's money, that equals roughly a million dollars, sufficient for comfort by any definition, for what would turn out to be just a few months of work. It's nice when the "cause of the poor" ends up being the cause of people of means, though that sometimes requires manufacturing the ideological justification out of whole cloth. More about that later.

Darrow acknowledged that he had been reading about the case in the newspapers, and that not only had it aroused his curiosity, but destiny seemed to be summoning him. Almost compelling him to the case, or so he said. "[T]he more I thought of those islands in the Pacific that I had so long wanted to see, and the more I investigated the strange and puzzling case, the more I felt that *I had better go*." [emphasis added]

Ahh, the siren song of the islands. And let's not underplay that generous fee providing harmony. Sometimes destiny speaks (or sings) in a language best understood by bankers.

So, what was the Massie Case and why had it aroused the interest of the impecunious Darrow? Its predecessor, the Ala Moana Case, involved a claim by Thalia Massie, the wife of a navy lieutenant, that five Hawaiian "boys" had abducted and raped her in the wee hours of a September morning on Honolulu's Ala Moana Road.

Following arrest and trial of five impoverished young men who would become known as the Ala Moana Boys, and who had been dubiously identified by Thalia as her assailants, a hung jury was declared after nearly 100 hours of jury deliberation.

Pending a retrial, the Ala Moana Boys were allowed out on bond. The very thought of them freely walking the streets of Honolulu outraged the military and elite *haole* (white) communities.

Thalia's husband (Lt. Thomas Massie) and mother (Grace Fortescue, a socialite from the mainland's east coast), along with two sailors, Albert Jones and Edward Lord, abducted one of the Boys, Joe Kahahawai, and in the process of attempting to coerce a confession, killed him. They were caught while *en route* to dump Kahahawai's body in the Pacific Ocean and were charged with second degree murder, setting up part two, the Massie Case.

Enter Clarence Darrow.

Based on the cursory facts stated above, and the descriptive tag applied by Steffens of "attorney for the damned," followers of the Darrow legend might well assume that he provided his legal services to the "cause of the poor," the Ala Moana Boys charged with a sex crime for which they had been, in all likelihood, falsely accused.

That, in fact, is an error made by author Julie Checkoway in her otherwise wonderful book *The Three-Year Swim Club: The Untold Story of Maui's Sugar Ditch Kids and Their Quest for Olympic Glory*.[cclv]

Blowhard

She wrote that the Massie case:

> ...hinged on a white woman's accusation that a group of native boys had brutally raped and beaten her, charges so inflammatory that none other than Clarence Darrow—he of the Scopes trial—came to town to defend the boys.

But no, in this case the old war horse took on the defense of the privileged whites accused of killing the native boy. Even Darrow himself recognized the contradiction.

He initially declined the case, writing on March 5, 1932, to sociologist and historian Harry Elmer Barnes that:

> I had so long and decidedly been for the Negro and all so-called 'foreigners' that I could not put myself in a position where I might be compelled to take a position, even in a case at variance with what I felt and had stood for.[cclvi]

But then there was that fee! Oh, that fee!

Those more familiar with the facts behind the Darrow legend would probably not be surprised to learn that he changed his mind and actually sold his services at a high price to defend the privileged whites accused of murdering Kahahawai. Given the tenor of the times and the racial unrest in Hawaii, there were no underdogs on his stable of clients in the Massie Case.

In another letter to Barnes, he justified it this way:

> [O]f course I have occasionally in the past represented people of wealth, and there have always been criticisms when I have done so; especially was this true in the Loeb-Leopold case. I don't know what I would have done if now and then a fairly well-to-do client had not come my way; the ravens have never called on me.[cclvii]

As O.N. Hilton, who preceded Darrow as counsel for the McNamara brothers in the *LA Times* bombing, told a *Denver Post* reporter about that prior case:

> Mark my words, you will see that Darrow has not acted in good faith. There isn't a man who has once been associated with him in the profession of law that will not tell you the same thing. Not one of them cares to associate with him again.

High-Minded, Honest, Kindly, and Sympathetic Clients

Although Darrow claimed he "investigated" the Hawaii case prior to accepting engagement, that investigation apparently consisted of no more than reading news accounts in the mainland press, hardly a substitute for any real investigation.

Although hindsight can be a notoriously unreliable twenty-twenty, history shows that the mainland media failed to present an accurate assessment of either the actual facts of the case or of the parties involved.

As the story was inaccurately reported, a horrible injustice had occurred by the failure to convict in the Ala Moana Case.

According to stories that flooded the mainland, native Hawaiian youths roamed the islands and viciously preyed on chaste young white women. A New York tabloid referred to natives as "the new menace." Another ran a picture of Thalia Massie under the heading "Victim of Hawaiian Attack," which presupposed the guilt of the Ala Moana Boys.

It referred to the killers of Kahahawai as Thalia's "avenging kin," suggesting righteousness in their murderous actions.

Darrow wrote:

> The story of the tragedy for which my clients were indicted has been widely published, and in various forms has been spread broadcast over the world. Despite all this, there was little chance to be deceived regarding the facts.[cclviii]

And yet he managed to be deceived, perhaps willfully so. Or

maybe he just rewrote the facts in his own mind to justify his participation on the side he ordinarily would have opposed.

After accepting engagement, Darrow likely got a further whitewashed account of the Ala Moana Case facts from his unimpeachable (at least by his reasoning) clients. He later described them as being "as high-minded, honest, kindly, and sympathetic as it is possible to find." [cclix] At least as far as it was possible to find amongst those willing and capable of putting a bullet into an unarmed man and then watching him die, over an alleged sexual assault that, more likely than not, was a figment of the supposed victim's imagination.

Prosecutor John Kelley would later put it this way in his closing argument in the Massie Case: "Three able men and a cold calculating woman let a man bleed to death in front of them.... They dragged him into the bathroom and let him die like a dog."

High-minded, honest, kindly, and sympathetic, indeed!

As a lawyer, Darrow should have known better than to rely solely upon media accounts, particularly in light of his fervent criticism of the press in many of his earlier cases, and the biased version of events provided by his desperate clients. After all, clients almost always paint themselves as heroes in the retelling of their stories. And God forbid that he actually obtain, and read, a copy of the trial transcript from the Ala Moana Case.

An old Russian proverb made famous by Ronald Reagan, *doveryai no proveryai*—"trust but verify"—might have stood Darrow in good stead here. But many a lawyer's qualms about a case have been assuaged by an appropriate payment, and Darrow was certainly not immune to money's therapeutic powers. As he said, and I repeat, "I needed the fee."

I said in the above-quoted Introduction to *A Death in the Islands* that Darrow's conduct in the case left a stain on his legacy. At the time I wrote it, I was, unfortunately, ignorant of other parts of Darrow's career.[76] After digging more deeply into

---

[76] An ignorance I hope I have now cured with my research for this book.

his past and his conduct in other cases leading up to this last hurrah, and which have been discussed in this book, I have reached the inescapable conclusion that, rather than an aberration, Darrow's lapses in the Massie Case were simply consistent with his ethical misconduct in prior cases.

Darrow's misconduct in Massie didn't leave a stain; it darkened an already-existing discoloration.

To understand why I say that requires us to study the Ala Moana and Massie cases a bit further. It is only by grasping the details of the Ala Moana Case that one can fully understand how vacuous Darrow's defense was in the Massie Case.

It was a defense built upon a foundation of sand,[77] and that foundation had its inception in the Ala Moana Case.

---

[77] The *Bible* tells us that the wise man built his house upon the rock, but the foolish man built his upon the sand. *Matthew* 7:24-27. Draw your own applications to Darrow.

Chapter Nineteen: The Ala Moana Case

From this beginning were to come blasted careers, ruined lives, tragedy and death.... Before the case was closed, I wished devoutly that I was back in private business, or could change place with a carefree motorman on one of the open-sided tramcars that clanked from Honolulu to Waikiki.
—Hawaii Territorial Governor Lawrence M. Judd

AT ABOUT 12:35 AM on September 13, 1931, a young man of Japanese descent named Horace "Shorty" Ida blasted a 1929 Ford Model A Touring Car along Liliha Street in downtown Honolulu and into the intersection at King Street.

It was actually his sister Haruya's car, but Horace had taken it for a fateful evening on the town with some of his buddies that included a visit to a luau at a friend's house, followed by a stop at a public dance at Waikiki Park.

With him in the car were Joseph Kahahawai, a native Hawaiian, and Henry Chang, a Chinese-Hawaiian. Earlier that night, those three had been joined by Ben Ahakuelo, another Hawaiian, and David Takai who, like Horace, was of Japanese descent. All were in their twenties. All were desperately poor.

And all their lives were about to take a dramatic, and tragic, turn based on a lie.

Horace approached the intersection just after Homer Peeples entered it in a 1924 Hudson. Homer, a *haole*—or white—man, and his Hawaiian wife Agnes were searching for an open diner after an evening spent drinking with friends. Horace's Ford lunged into the intersection, its driver apparently oblivious to the Hudson already occupying it.

Seeing the danger, Homer accelerated and spurted past the nose of the Ford just as Horace belatedly braked. The respective drivers screeched their vehicles to a stop mere feet from each other in the middle of the intersection.

1931 was a more innocent time than the 21st Century, and the term "road rage" was still more than half-a-century from entering the American vocabulary. Automobile drivers of that day were unlikely to be equipped with firearms, ready to instantly avenge traffic grievances, real or imagined, they had with other drivers.

An exchange of words was usually about it, and maybe the occasional fisticuffs. Fatalities were virtually unheard of.

Agnes Peeples engaged in the time-honored custom of verbally berating the reckless driver of the Ford, but one of its passengers took offense, notwithstanding Agnes's righteous, though inartfully delivered, position.

Joe Kahahawai, a muscular, athletic young man, got out of the back seat of the Ford and approached the Hudson. Fueled by inebriated bravado, Agnes exited the Hudson, ready to defend the honor and driving skill of her husband, who was fumbling beneath his seat for a tire iron he kept handy.

As Joe neared, Agnes thrust out her hands into his chest and shoved him away, but he retaliated with a right-handed punch to her left ear. While it's unclear whether Joe struck with an open or closed fist, no one would later dispute that Joe delivered a blow of some sort.

Cooler heads prevailed about the time that Homer successfully retrieved and brandished that tire iron in defense of his wife. Discretion seemed the better part of valor for Joe, who returned to his vehicle. Agnes did likewise and the operators of the respective vehicles drove away.

But not before Agnes got the license plate number of the Ford Touring Car: 58-895.

Within 10 minutes, she reported the confrontation, complete with a recounting of the horrors of her assault by a young Hawaiian man and a bleeding ear as proof, and the license number to Cecil Rickard, official radio announcer at the Honolulu Police Station. Although Agnes incorrectly reported that the car was a Chevrolet, she had gotten the correct license plate number, and the police confirmed that it was actually a Ford Phaeton [touring car].

At 12:50 AM, Rickard put out a radio call and broadcast the license plate number in connection with an "assault on a woman."

These words fueled much of the confusion that followed.

Assault on a Woman

While Agnes Peeples was reporting her assault to Cecil Rickard, across town to the east, a good ten or fifteen minutes drive away, Eustace Bellinger, his wife, and their friends the Clarks were traveling down Ala Moana Road on their way to Waikiki for a late night snack.

At approximately 12:50 AM, just as Rickard was putting out the radio call about the assault on Agnes Peeples, the Bellinger car's headlights fell across a young woman walking in the road, about 100 yards from an old animal quarantine station.

She wore a green dress that stretched to her ankles and had a strange, almost hunched, posture as she walked. She waved her arms to flag them down. When she neared the car, other injuries became visible, including a swollen lip and a mark on her cheek that looked as if it might have been caused by a ring worn on a striking hand. George Clark, Sr., later testified that "her face was all puffed up at the mouth, as though someone had beaten her up."

George Clark, Jr., in the front passenger seat, rolled down his window when she approached. She peered inside, squinting, as if unable to see clearly.[78] "Are you white people?" she asked. When Eustace answered in the affirmative, she said, "Thank God" then, without invitation, opened the passenger door, got in, and sat in George Jr.'s lap.

She instructed Eustace to drive to her home at 2850 Kahawai Road in Manoa Valley. This strange young woman was Thalia Massie, who would be the centerpiece in both the Ala Moana and Massie cases and whose rapidly evolving story would lead to tragedy.

Earlier that evening, Thalia had been at the Ala Wai Inn, a nightclub on the north side of Kalakaua Avenue, just west of the Ala Wai Canal. Saturday night at the Ala Wai was "Navy Night," and the place was filled with military personnel from nearby Pearl Harbor. Thalia hadn't wanted to go, but her husband, navy Lieutenant Tommie Massie, insisted. And, he had something to hold over her head to coerce her attendance with him.

Thalia was not well-liked by other navy wives and was maybe liked a little too much by some navy men who, it was rumored, made overnight stays at the Massie house when Tommie was away on maneuvers.

University of Hawaii Professor David Stannard wrote that she had a volatile personality, was rumored to be "'running around with various men—in fact, with almost any man who looked prosperous and clean,'" according to one naval officer, and that she had once been a patient at a sanitarium.[cclx]

Russell Owen, who later covered the Massie Case for *The New York Times*, described her as "a brooding, silent, and not particularly companionable woman."[cclxi]

And those were her good points.

Tommie and Thalia's marriage was not the most stable in

---

[78] Thalia was afflicted with Graves' disease, an immune system disorder that often results in what is known as Graves' ophthalmopathy, which affects the eyes and results in their bulging—a condition known as exophthalmos—along with light sensitivity and vision loss.

the world, and Thalia was not the most stable woman. Professor Stannard wrote that she had a "custom of coming to the front door or walking around in the yard half naked." She was known to freely hurl insults at Tommie and others, and "would occasionally attack Tommie in front of guests, sometimes 'grabbing his arm and biting him viciously.'" [cclxii]

Tommie "was almost perpetually drunk" and the police frequently had to be called to the house in response to disturbances. On at least one occasion, Tommie followed Thalia, who was riding in a car with another naval officer. When he caught up to them, "Tommie punched the other man, then slapped Thalia and dragged her away." [cclxiii]

The preceding descriptions are violently at odds with Darrow's rose-colored-glasses assessment of Thalia during his brief tenure in Hawaii. He wrote in his autobiography, "No one who knew her had ever criticised [sic] her conduct, or had the slightest reason for suspicion about her." [cclxiv]

Maybe he just hadn't talked to the right people. This was neither the first, nor the last, detail he got wrong about Thalia. The question is whether he knew it and simply whitewashed it, in order to paint her sympathetically to the jury in the Massie Case as a poor innocent young thing ravished by fiends and then righteously avenged by a grieving husband, or whether he really believed that an angelic version of Thalia Massie existed, even if only in his own head.

In retrospect, given Thalia's behavior in the Ala Moana and Massie cases, it could almost be argued that Stannard and Owen portrayed the warm-and-fuzzy views of her. A colder, more calculating, arguably more evil Thalia would later emerge.

In her defense, she may well have been mentally ill.

Following the two cases, she tried—and failed—on several occasions to cause her own demise. The first suicide attempt, by swallowing poison, came less than two years after the trial in the Massie Case, on the day her divorce from her husband was finalized.

That same year, she tried again by slashing her wrists and

then attempting to jump from the bridge of a cruise ship. The latter attempt led to a month-long stay in a sanitarium in Genoa, Italy. Off the radar for more than a decade, she resurfaced as a notorious drunk in Los Angeles, facing multiple intoxicated in public or while driving charges.

Her pregnant landlady even accused Thalia of physically beating her. Thalia finally succeeding in taking her own life with a fatal overdose of barbiturates on July 2, 1963.

But this particular night in September of 1931, Tommie held a hole card. The Massies had a written agreement between them that, in effect, provided that Thalia was one strike away from divorce.

Professor Stannard described it this way:

> *It was now August...and then Tommie announced that they were through. He wanted a divorce. Thalia pleaded with him, saying she would do anything to keep their marriage together. At last they agreed to a compromise. In good military fashion—and in a manner that revealed his judgment of his wife's immaturity—Tommie drew up a formal written plan that placed Thalia on "probation" for three months. During that time, as friends who witnessed the document recalled, Thalia had to "mend her ways, or be sent home to her family."* [cclxv]

So, it was to avoid the humiliation of divorce that led Thalia to accompany Tommie to the Ala Wai Inn that night, like a good little navy wife, along with two fellow officers, Jerry Branson and Tom Brown, and their wives Jean and Mary Ann.

Later, after their arrival, Thalia separated herself from Tommie and their friends. She was last reported seen at the Ala Wai around 11:30 PM. and, at about midnight, she left.[79]

---

[79] She will later lie about when she left. She originally told the police she left at midnight, but when she testified at trial, she moved the time up to 11:30 PM. That was ostensibly to plug a hole in the timeline of

She'd had a spat with someone, she told the Clarks and Bellingers when they picked her up, and she needed to get some air.

As it turns out, "spat" was an understatement and not at all inconsistent with her typical behavior.

What actually happened, according to witnesses, was that Thalia had argued with Ralph Stogsdall, skipper of submarine S-26, whose wife's name was Josephine. Thalia insulted his wife by saying, "Oh, Mrs. Stogsdall; Josephine without brains."

No one else thought it was funny. A drunken Stogsdall went to the men's room and, when he returned, found that Thalia was in his chair and wouldn't relinquish it. That led to the "spat," in which a drink was thrown, names were called, and a face—Stogsdall's—was slapped.

What followed after she left the Ala Wai, as Thalia related it to her rescuers, was a terrible tale of woe. It was also all probably a lie.

Shortly after leaving, a car pulled up behind her on John Ena Road. Two men jumped out and grabbed her, punched her in the mouth, and then dragged her into the car. The men continued to hit her as the driver turned onto Ala Moana Road and pulled off near an abandoned animal quarantine station where she was dumped from the car, which sped away.

When pressed for details, her memory was hazy[80]—there were perhaps five men in the car, but she couldn't be sure; she never saw any faces but could tell from their voices that they were all Hawaiians; they were all dark-complected; she didn't know the make or model of the car; didn't see the color of the car; and never got a glimpse of the license plate number.

The sole facts she could recall about the car were that it was old and that there was a flapping noise, as if the convertible top was torn and blowing in the wind.

---

events that night involving the Ala Moana Boys, but that lie was ineffectual.

[80] Later retellings would reveal it to be less hazy and more evolving.

The story seemed odd to her spellbound listeners. Dragged into an automobile and punched only to be unceremoniously dumped a few minutes later? It didn't make sense. But when pressed, she insisted that the men didn't do anything other than strike her and push her from the car. She became angry when her rescuers suggested going to the police station, insisting that they take her home, which they did. They arrived at her house in Manoa at about 1:20 or 1:25 AM.

Within a few minutes of Thalia's arrival at home, Tommie called from a friend's house in the neighborhood, where he and Jerry Branson had gone upon leaving the Ala Wai around 1:00. Branson promptly fell asleep while Tommie phoned home. Thalia answered the call and, when she heard her husband's voice, told him to come home immediately. "Something terrible has happened," she said.

Tommie left a sleeping Jerry Branson behind and rushed home.

At 1:48 AM, Police Captain Hans Kashiwabara received a call at the Honolulu station from a man who, he would later testify, "spoke to me very calmly."

The man didn't give his name, but simply said, "Will you please send a police officer to 2850 Kahawai Street, Manoa, a woman was assaulted by a man."

Captain Kashiwabara had previously been told of the "assault on a woman" reported by Agnes Peeples and of the 58-895 license plate in connection with that assault. Now a second assault on a woman had been reported. What were the odds that two unrelated assaults on women might happen on the same night? Not great, he concluded.

Since the previous report had arisen from a traffic altercation, it hadn't been given a high priority, but this second assault raised things up a notch. Kashiwabara telephoned Detective John Jardine in his upstairs office with the news, who ordered it broadcast to all patrol cars.

Jardine then came downstairs and, as Kashiwabara said, "called my attention to make every effort to pick up automobile

58-895."

Detective George Harbottle and radio patrol officer William Furtado were the first responders to the report of the Massie assault. They had previously heard the broadcast of the assault on Agnes Peeples and, though they didn't respond to that call, Furtado had made a note of the license plate number in his notebook. But after hearing the broadcast of a second assault on a woman, things took on a new urgency for cops on the streets just as they did for officers at the station. All now operated under the assumption that the same men were likely responsible for both attacks.

Jerry Branson awoke to find himself alone, so he wandered outside in search of Tommie. Unfortunately for him, police traffic patrol officer William Simerson and "merchant patrol" (private security guard) William Gomes, who were patrolling around Manoa, spotted him just down the street from the Massie house, on lower East Manoa Road.

Branson was stumbling around with his coat off, shirt open, hair mussed and "his trousers all open," after apparently relieving himself in a flower bed. Branson refused to answer questions, so they hauled him to the closest police box, where a direct phone to the police station was located for patrol officers' use.

While Simerson was calling in, a radio patrol car arrived, occupied by Harbottle and Furtado on their way to the Massie house. Furtado told Simerson that "there was a rape case in Manoa...." Seeing Branson with his trousers open, he added: "Maybe we can use that man" and "put him in this car." Harbottle and Furtado arrived at the Massie house at 2:00 AM, followed by Simerson.

It had been slightly more than thirty minutes since Tommie Massie arrived home in response to the entreaty from his wife.

What happened at the Massie house over the course of the half hour or so between Tommie's arrival and the subsequent arrival of police officers is anybody's guess.

The only thing for sure was that a new detail was about to

be added to the story she had told her original rescuers, the Bellingers and the Clarks.

Tommie Massie met the officers out front, then led them inside to the living room, where Thalia lay on a couch. The officers noticed a mark on her lip and a black and blue mark on her neck, but no other apparent injuries.

She was crying and continued crying throughout the interview. It also appeared that she had been drinking. Despite that, she was, according to their police report, lucid, though Harbottle described her as hysterical and nervous. Tommie, on the other hand, was clearly drunk.

Thalia repeated the same story she had told the Bellingers and Clarks: she had been attacked by a gang of boys on John Ena Road; she could not describe her attackers; she knew from their voices that they were Hawaiians—not *haoles* and not Asians. The officers questioned her about the car but she offered nothing helpful there, either. She said it was an open car with the top flapping; it might have been a dark, possibly black, Ford or Dodge, but she couldn't be sure because there was very little light and she got only occasional glimpses of it as she was being beaten. When pressed about the license plate number, she came up empty again, and she repeated that she could hear the top flapping, as if it was torn.

But then came a dramatic new plot twist that would make any writer of crime fiction proud: She had been raped, she said, perhaps as many as six or seven times.

Detectives George Nakea and Frank Bettencourt joined the party about twenty minutes later. Thalia, trouper that she was, repeated her story almost verbatim to the new arrivals, still with the added rape plot twist. She continued to insist that she never saw the license plate number but reiterated that all her assailants were Hawaiians.

Bettencourt specifically asked whether she could identify the boys if they were apprehended and about the license plate.

He later testified, "She says no; she says all she knew they were Hawaiians. Then I asked her if she took the car number down. She says 'No, I didn't take any car number down.'"

At some point, Furtado took Tommie Massie aside and told him that they already had suspects. He told him about the Peeples altercation and the car they were tracking. He may even have told Tommie the license plate number of the car, though that has never been firmly established.

At some point, Detective John Jardine arrived at the Massie house. He, like the other officers, believed there must be some connection between the car involved in the Peeples altercation and the assault on Thalia Massie.

He stayed only briefly but suggested that Thalia be taken to the hospital. She refused at first. By some reports, she even became hysterical before Tommie persuaded her she needed to go.

The Massies, along with an escort of police officers, arrived at Honolulu's Emergency Hospital around 2:35 AM, where Thalia was seen by Dr. David Liu, assisted by Nurse Agnes Fawcett. Dr. Liu inquired of her what had happened, and she was remarkably consistent in her story as supplemented by the rape allegation. According to Dr. Liu, she was sobbing and crying, but "she didn't seem to show any emotion outside of crying."

Thalia again denied being able to describe the car or its license plate number. It was no wonder she was initially consistent on this point because, as the Pinkerton Detective Agency would later report, she couldn't give information about the car to the authorities "because she did not possess it at the time she was questioned...."

But she was soon to deal another plot twist to the story, changing the whole course and urgency of the investigation, as well as the mournful fates of the Ala Moana Boys.

License Plate 58-805—Close Enough

While Thalia was with Dr. Liu and Nurse Fawcett, the license plate number of the Ford touring car driven by Horace Ida—58-895—was audibly broadcast over police radios on cars parked just outside the louvered windows of the examining room. According to Officer Furtado, it was broadcast "about two or three times" and, as Officer Simerson corroborated, people could hear it clearly.

A.W. Mackenzie, one of the naval personnel gathered outside the hospital, said that after Thalia was brought out of the hospital to a patrol car, "Mr. Massie came out and told us what had happened and one of the detectives standing there said they had the number of the car they were looking for that had assaulted another woman." Mackenzie recalled that the detective mentioned the actual number to Tommie.

Dr. Liu later testified that while he examined Thalia, there were a number of naval personnel, whom he described as the "Massie party," on the porch outside and talking audibly about the car. Then, about 3:00 AM, a broadcast reported that the car with that number had been picked up by Officer John Cluney.

When combined with the possibility that Furtado had also given the license plate number to Tommie back at the Massie house, Thalia's time at the hospital offered multiple additional opportunities to either "refresh her memory," or have it refreshed for her, as to the license plate number she claimed multiple times to never have seen.

It's also important to note here that, while Dr. Liu did not do a particularly thorough exam of Thalia, he and Nurse Fawcett both concluded that, notwithstanding Thalia's assertion that she had been raped multiple times, there were no indications of even a single rape, much less multiple.

Dr. Liu's report stated there was no apparent trauma below her waist and that he found no semen in her vagina. The latter could have been explained by the fact that, as she told him, she douched before coming to the hospital. But as regards the former, his report concluded: "Vaginal examination of hymen was old, lacerated at five and seven o'clock position. No other abrasions or contusions noticeable."

Nurse Fawcett added that an examination of the vaginal area showed that Thalia was "clean as a new pin." The Pinkerton

Agency later reported that it was unable to find "what in our estimation would be sufficient corroboration of the statements of Mrs. Massie to establish the occurrence of rape upon her."

Having identified the owner of the touring car involved in the Peeples altercation as Haruya Ida, Officer Cecil Rickard assigned Detective John Cluney and his partner, Thurman Black, to head out to the Ida house on Cunha Lane, on the fringe of a part of town known as Hell's Half Acre.

Rickard told them that, in addition to the Peeples assault, the car might have something to do with a rape case. With some urgency now, the detectives retrieved Horace Ida and brought him back to the police station, followed by Horace's sisters, Haruya and Chiyono, in the Ford touring car.

Cluney had just led Horace into Inspector McIntosh's office around 3:15 AM, when the Massies and their entourage arrived from the hospital. McIntosh decided to interview Thalia first, so Cluney led Horace away before she was brought to the inspector's office. As Thalia gave her statement to McIntosh, she stuck to several key points—several, but not all—that she had been saying all along.

But then came the sea change. Though she still could not give a description of the car that had picked her up, when McIntosh asked, "What was the license plate number, do you know?" she answered, "I think it was 58-805. I would not swear to that being correct. I just caught a fleeting glance of it as they drove away."

You can imagine the effect of that answer on McIntosh, who apparently had no prior knowledge of Thalia's multiple denials of having seen the plate. He probably had to struggle to conceal his excitement as he wrote the number on the blotter on his desk, then summoned Cluney. He told Cluney not to say anything but to show him the number of the Ida car. Cluney produced a piece of paper from a pocket and handed it to McIntosh: 58-895.

It wasn't perfect, off by one digit, but McIntosh and Cluney thought Thalia could be forgiven a faulty memory on one digit. As far as they were concerned, though, 58-805 was close enough to 58-895 to cinch the deal.

McIntosh instructed Cluney to retrieve Horace Ida. As soon as Horace walked in, McIntosh pointed at Thalia's face and said, "Now look at your beautiful work."

Thalia, *sans* glasses and almost legally blind, had just a few minutes earlier told McIntosh that her assailants were all Hawaiian—one of the few consistencies in her story, at least up until then. But now she looked at Ida, who was obviously Japanese, and nodded her head a couple of times, which McIntosh took as a positive identification. Then she asked Ida, "Where are the other boys?"

It was only a matter of time until those other boys—Henry Chang, Joe Kahahawai, Ben Ahakuelo, and David Takai[81]—would be apprehended, all based on a sudden flash of new knowledge from Thalia Massie: a license plate number she had repeatedly claimed never to have seen.

This was just the first of many previously unknown details that would soon crystallize in Thalia's memory after coaching from police and prosecutors.

Before the Ala Moana Case was over, Thalia would: (1) positively identify four of her five alleged attackers, even though they were not all Hawaiian, and she would never point the finger at David Takai; (2) know the specific order in which they raped her; (3) know that Henry Chang raped her twice; (4) know the color and make of the automobile; (5) know who sat where in the car; (5) know that it was Joe Kahahawai who punched her in the face; (6) know the color of Horace Ida's jacket; and (7) know that Ben Ahakuelo had a gold tooth.

Events were now set in motion that would ultimately lead the impecunious Clarence Darrow out of retirement and across the Pacific because he needed a fee.

---

[81] Remember that Thalia originally claimed that all of her attackers were Hawaiian, but only Kahahawai and Ahakuelo were Hawaiian. Ida and Takai were Japanese; Chang was Chinese.

Chapter Twenty: Hung Jury

We have found nothing in the record of this case nor have thru [sic] our own efforts been able to find what in our estimation would be sufficient corroboration of the statements of Mrs. Massie to establish the occurrence of rape upon her.
—Pinkerton Detective Agency

THE RAPE TRIAL of the so-called Ala Moana Boys commenced on November 16, 1932, and was presided over by Judge Alva Steadman, a 1922 Harvard Law School graduate.

Steadman had married into the Cooke family of Castle & Cooke, one of the Big Five corporations that pretty much controlled Hawaii. The others were Alexander & Baldwin, American Factors, Castle & Cooke, C. Brewer & Co., and Theo H. Davies & Co.

Although Steadman held publicly-known racist views, he was considered a fair and honest judge—as if that was even possible given the racial tensions in the Islands and the *haole* v. native confrontation that would play out in his court.[82]

---

[82] Just a few years earlier, in 1928, Steadman had presided over the trial of a notorious murder case in Honolulu in which a 19-year-old Japanese man named Myles Fukunaga was charged with kidnapping and murdering the 10-year-old son of an officer with the Hawaiian

The prosecutor was the inexperienced Griffith Wight, who had participated along with Captain John McIntosh in the interrogations of the Ala Moana Boys.

Wight was a latecomer to lawyering, earning his law degree only four years prior from Stanford at the age of 37. Admiral Yates Stirling of the United States Navy, who bore an outsized presence and influence in Honolulu, considered Wight unqualified for the prosecution. He may have been right, but that's a topic for another discussion.

An avowed racist who had overseen a reign of terror on the native population in the Philippines in the early part of the century, Stirling pressured Honolulu's political leaders to hire a team of private attorneys for the job. As a practical matter, Stirling had already pre-judged the Ala Moana Boys as guilty, so he didn't really see the need for a trial at all. But, if there was going to be a trial, he damned sure wanted there to be a conviction. He said, "Our first inclination is to seize the brutes and string them up on trees."

He went even further in his memoir, writing, after the fact:

> *The trial in my opinion and many others was a stupid miscarriage of justice which could have been avoided if the Territorial Government had shown more inclination to sympathize with my insistence upon the necessity of a conviction.... The defendants were not men who might be given the benefit of a reasonable doubt. All were of shady character as their records showed.*[cclxvi]

God bless him, at least he didn't hide behind any pretense.

Wight, to his credit—and perhaps the only credit I will give him[83]—refused to buckle to Stirling's pressure campaign

---

Trust Company.

[83] Wight's ethics almost made Darrow look good by comparison. Notice I said "almost."

and resign, and the government was loathe to so blatantly pander to the military.

So, Honolulu and the U.S. Navy struck a compromise: Wight would prosecute with assistance from the territory's attorney general, Henry Hewitt, a more seasoned attorney. He would also receive confidential behind-the-scenes help from private attorney Eugene Beebe, of the prominent Honolulu firm of Thompson, Beebe & Winn, for a retainer of $2,500—a little over $46,000 in today's money.

As we'll soon see, Beebe would later be involved in the lead-up to the events precipitating the Massie Case, and not in a good way.

On behalf of the defendants, Princess Kawananakoa, a symbol of the deposed Hawaiian monarchy,[84] arranged for Ben Ahakuelo, Joe Kahahawai, Henry Chang, and Horace Ida to be represented by William Heen, a graduate of Hastings Law School in San Francisco.

In 1917, President Woodrow Wilson had appointed Heen as a judge of Hawaii's First Circuit Court, making him the first non-*haole* to serve. He resigned two years later to return to private practice. At the time of the Ala Moana trial, he was also the only elected Democrat in the territorial senate. The half-Chinese and half-Hawaiian Heen enlisted the assistance of William Pittman, a *haole*—a southerner, no less, originally hailing from Vicksburg, Mississippi—with his law degree from Washington and having practiced in Nevada and California before arriving in Honolulu in 1915.

David Takai, who had never been identified by Thalia as one of her attackers—and was charged only because he and all the defendants acknowledged that he had been with them that

---

[84] With the backing of U.S. troops from the *U.S.S. Boston*, Queen Lili'uokalani and the Hawaiian monarchy were overthrown in 1893. For five years thereafter, Hawaii existed as the Republic of Hawaii, before being annexed as a U.S. territory in 1898. The Hawaiian people have never forgotten.

night—had his own attorney, a court-appointed lawyer named Robert Murakami, a locally-born Japanese lawyer with a law degree in 1925 from the University of Chicago.[85]

Takai had refused money to flip and testify for the prosecution, insisting that none of the Ala Moana Boys had been involved in the alleged assault. Not even the promise of money, he said, would entice him to lie against his friends.

When he refused the deal, his prior attorney had withdrawn and was replaced by Murakami.

Thalia Takes the Stand

On the first day of trial, things got strange.

Quickly.

Thalia Massie took the stand as the prosecution's star witness and, on direct examination from prosecutor Griffith Wight, now testified, notwithstanding her prior statements, that: (1) she left the Ala Wai Inn shortly after 11:30, and not at midnight as she previously told police; (2) the lighting on John Ena Road was "not very dark" because "there were some street lamps nearby," again in contradiction to what she had told police; (3) she was positive that Henry Chang, Horace Ida, Joe Kahahawai, and Ben Ahakuelo were her assailants, despite her initial steadfast refusal to identify anyone other than to say she knew they were all Hawaiians—however, she again failed to identify David Takai; (4) despite initially being unable to identify Ben Ahakuelo, she now recognized him because "[h]e turned around several times and grinned and I saw his face; I also saw he had a gold tooth;" and (5) she saw Horace Ida's face clearly on

---

[85] Murakami had been prominently involved in the Fukunaga case mentioned in an earlier footnote. Though Murakami did not represent Fukunaga at trial—interestingly enough, that duty was performed by Eugene Beebe, who was assisting the prosecution in the Ala Moana Case—he did handle Fukunaga's futile appeals that ended at the United States Supreme Court, which cleared the way for Fukunaga's execution by hanging.

Ala Moana Road, even though it wasn't as well lighted as John Ena Road, but "it was light enough for me to see his coat[86] and face when he turned."

Thalia also added another new detail, this one regarding Joe Kahahawai, which would play into later events; Darrow would latch onto it in an effort to generate outrage in the Massie Case jury to justify the killing of Kahahawai:

> He [Kahahawai] *knocked me in the jaw; I started to pray and that made him angry and he hit me very hard; I cried out 'you've knocked my teeth out' and he told me to shut up. I asked him please not to hit me any more.*

And yet another new detail.[87] She now knew how many times she had been raped: "[F]rom 4 to 6 times. I think Chang assaulted me twice because he was standing near me and he said he wanted to go again. The others said all right and a little later he assaulted me."

The only consistency between Thalia's trial testimony and her prior statements was her estimate of the attack having lasted about twenty minutes in duration.

But that created a problem for her story.

Using twenty minutes as the length of the attack, and the time she first told police she had left the Ala Wai Inn, midnight,[88] the defense attorneys constructed a timeline that, by any honest interpretation, conclusively established that the Ala Moana Boys couldn't possibly have been involved because there was no available twenty-minute window.

And that assumed there even was an attack.[89]

---

[86] A coat he had not been wearing that night.
[87] She was a marvelous storyteller, the plot points consistently evolving.
[88] Midnight was corroborated by other witnesses.
[89] Something the Pinkerton Detective Agency would later call into serious question.

12:00 AM: Time Thalia first told police she left Ala Wai Inn.
12:05-12:10 AM: Witnesses place Ala Moana Boys near Waikiki Park
12:05-12:15 AM: Witnesses place Thalia on John Ena Road.
12:15-12:45 AM: Only possible time during which rape could have occurred.
12:15-12:20 AM: Witnesses place Ala Moana Boys driving along Beretania Street, several miles away from alleged attack.
12:30 AM: Witnesses place Ala Moana Boys at luau at Correa home, several miles away from alleged attack.
12:35-12:40 AM: Confrontation between Ala Moana Boys and Agnes Peeples, several miles away from alleged attack.
12:50 AM: Thalia picked up on Ala Moana Road.

This timeline, alone, should have been devastating to the prosecution's case, and should have led any serious prosecutor to question whether he truly had a case. Other evidence, as well, revealed serious holes in whatever tatters of a case remained. In hindsight, it's hard to believe this was ever brought to trial. Political pressure and pressure from the United States Navy probably had as much to do with that as anything.

Here are other serious issues with the case:

When Detective Cluney picked up Horace Ida at his house, Horace put on a brown suede jacket to accompany him to the police station. He was wearing that jacket when McIntosh set up the confrontation with Thalia Massie for her to identify him. Though she nodded her head that night, as if to acknowledge him as one of her assailants, she failed to identify him the next day.

But then later, when the Ala Moana Boys were brought to Thalia's hospital room one at a time to be identified, her third confrontation with Horace, he wore that same brown jacket. He was instructed to sit on the edge of the bed, with his back to Thalia, to recreate the view of a car driver from the back seat. Before identifying him, Thalia reached out and felt his jacket, which turned out to be key to her so-called identification of

Horace as one of her attackers—she knew him by his jacket.

But Horace had not been wearing the suede jacket on the night of the alleged assault. He had put it on only when Cluney picked him up to bring him to the station. In separate questioning sessions, the other Ala Moana Boys all said either that Horace had not been wearing it or that they couldn't remember if he had. During the trial, it was revealed that when Griffith Wight presented the typed statements of the defendants for them to sign, he included a sentence in Joe Kahahawai's statement that Horace had been wearing the brown jacket that night. Joe, however, marked through the sentence before he would sign.

Dr. John Porter, of the U.S. Navy, who testified at trial as to Thalia's injuries, said that he gave her "several opiates" when he first saw her at her home, and continued to keep her on those drugs while she was at the hospital. He concluded that, during those first few days, when she was flip-flopping on identifying her alleged assailants, "she probably didn't know just what she was doing...."

Just like their failure to disclose the contradictory statements made by Thalia the night of the supposed assault, the prosecution also failed to disclose this to the defense (although there were no Brady requirements[90] at the time), but the defense lawyers discovered it on their own by speaking with Dr. Liu.

There's a lesson here about being thorough in cross-examination. Although at trial the defense got Dr. Porter to compromise Thalia's ID of the defendants, several questions went unasked that could have been devastating to the prosecution.

Porter later said, *after* both trials, but was never asked *during* the Ala Moana trial, that he believed Thalia was lying

---

[90] In 1963, the U.S. Supreme Court held that prosecutors must disclose any exculpatory evidence to the defense. *Brady v. Maryland*, 373 U.S. 83 (1963).

when she said she was raped, that she definitely was lying when she said she was pregnant, and that she could not possibly have seen her assailants' faces or the license number of the car because she was nearly blind without her glasses.

Had those facts been brought out, it might possibly have undercut the emotional impact of Darrow's arguments in the Massie Case that Thalia had become impregnated by the attack.[91]

Shady Tactics

Officer Claude Benton testified that police found tire tracks at the crime scene that perfectly matched the Ida car. Prosecutor Wight directed him to sketch a diagram of where those tracks were found and led Benton to testify that he had driven the Ida car to the site "the next morning" to compare tracks and found that they were identical.

What Benton apparently thought, but what Wight probably knew, was that, although the intent of the question was to ask about Monday morning when Benton took the car to the site, the impression it created was that it was Sunday morning. The significance is that, by Monday morning, when Benton actually took the car up to the site, Captain McIntosh had already been there the day before in the same car and created tire tracks in the mud.

Other officers were aware of that fact, including a photographer who refused a direct order to photograph the Ford's tracks on Monday because he knew they had been left by McIntosh the day before.

Detective John Cluney testified that on the night Ida was brought in, he protested, unprompted, that he had nothing to do with the "white woman." This was tantamount, Cluney said, to a confession that Ida at least knew of the existence of an assaulted

---

[91] Darrow would argue, in closing: "Here is a man—his wife—she is bearing inside of her the germs of—who? Does anybody know? Not he, but someone of the four ruffians who assaulted her and left a wreck of her."

white woman, which begged the question: How could you have known about that unless you had been involved?

On cross examination, Cluney acknowledged that he thought this was important at the time, but he hadn't included it in his report nor had he told anyone else about it at the time.

When pressed by attorney William Heen as to why he didn't include it, this exchange occurred:

> **Q:** *Didn't you think it was important at that time—that that evidence was important at that time?*
> **A:** *I knew it was important evidence.*
> **Q:** *And you didn't put it into your report?*
> **A:** *I did not. I was instructed to keep that under cover.*
> **Q:** *Who instructed you to keep that under cover?*
> **A:** *I had a conversation with Mr. Wight.*
> **Q:** *Did you put it into that report you made to Mr. McIntosh?*
> **A:** *I did not.*
> **Q:** *Did Mr. Wight tell you why you should keep that under cover?*
> **A:** *He said it was good stuff.*
> **Q:** *To hide?*
> **A:** *I don't know what his intentions were.*[92]

On its face, this testimony seemingly supported the prosecution's case so, so an argument could be made that it wouldn't have benefited the defense, in any event, to know about it.

But as any good lawyer will tell you, you can't prepare for what you don't know about. Had the defense known, they could have girded themselves to deal with it at trial. They might even have been able, with a little investigation, to discover how Ida came to blurt that supposedly damning admission in the first place.

---

[92] Are you starting to see the ethical issues with Griffith Wight?

Ida had been left to wait in the detectives' assembly room at the police station, under the watchful eye of dispatcher Cecil Rickard, while the detectives who brought him went in search of Captain McIntosh. Rickard asked Horace whether he had attacked a white woman on Ala Moana.

Horace denied it, but now he knew about it *because he had been told by a police officer.*

During the trial, it was the defense lawyers, and not the prosecution, who called officers Bettencourt, Nakea, Harbottle, Simerson, and Furtado to the stand. Those officers testified about the inconsistencies in Thalia's so-called identification of the Ala Moana Boys, such as the fact that the license plate number of the Ida car had been repeatedly broadcast over the radio, including on occasions when it was audible to the Massie party.

The last officer to testify, Detective Luciano Machado, testified that after Thalia had already failed once to identify Ben Ahakuelo, she got a second chance. This time the prosecuting attorney and police captain were ready to ensure an identification. When Ben was brought into Thalia's hospital room, Griffith Wight asked her, "This is Bennie? Do you know that this is Bennie?" Before she could answer, Captain McIntosh whispered to Thalia, "yes," who then answered, unsurprisingly, "yes."

The Pinkerton Detective Agency would later uncover even more evidence that established that the Ala Moana Boys were almost certainly innocent, much of it suppressed from the defense. Yet somehow Clarence Darrow would write in his autobiography that Thalia was "shocked by the jury's disagreement" in the Ala Moana Case. And with a straight face, he argued to the Massie Case jury "no one raised even a doubt" about Thalia's story. It was, he said, "[a] strange circumstance, indeed, that the jury disagreed in this case. I don't know, I don't see why."

He must have been blindfolded.

And yeah, about that disagreement.

Six to Six

At about nine o'clock on Wednesday night, December 2, the Ala Moana Case was finally given to an all-male jury, made up of two Chinese, two Japanese, one Portuguese, one "American" (meaning white Anglo-Saxon) and six who were a mixture of Hawaiian and *haole*. All were employed either by corporations or by the city of Honolulu; one was a retired police captain; three worked for Big Five corporations.

At 10:05 PM. on Sunday, December 6, after 97 hours of deliberation, Judge Steadman declared a mistrial, with the jury deadlocked 6-6. The first vote taken had been 6-6. In between, despite dozens of votes, it never swayed more than 7-5 one way or the other.

Judge Steadman said in a later interview that he, personally, wanted the jurors to return a guilty verdict, which is why he kept them out as long as he did. He admitted, though, that while he would have voted guilty, "I would never have felt entirely right about it."

Reading between the lines, the judge's attitude seemed to be that he was willing to put expendable defendants in prison just to try to lessen the pressure on the powder keg that threatened to blow up Honolulu.

The hung jury did, in fact, set off a firestorm in the Islands. There was an immediate push for a second trial, and Admiral Stirling tried to get the judge to deny bond to the defendants pending the retrial, but they had already been released. After all, they had been out on bond before the trial and, since the hung jury meant they had not yet been convicted, the bond terms still applied.

Incidents of violence, mostly minor at first, broke out all across Honolulu between civilians and navy men, but it was just a matter of time until things escalated.

On Saturday, December 12, the *Honolulu Times* hit the streets with a banner headline: *The Shame of Honolulu*. And the powder keg was lit. As hundreds of sailors prepared to hit the streets, Admiral Stirling got wind of trouble brewing and canceled shore leaves—but it was too late. Honolulu was already swarming with navy men and, before the night was over, eight riot calls had been turned in to police headquarters.

At about 9:30 that Saturday night, a group of sailors spotted Horace Ida talking with friends outside a bar on Kukui Street.

As the sailors scrambled from their cars, Horace's friends took off, but he wasn't so lucky. Forced at gunpoint into a car, he was driven to the far side of the Pali Lookout, where he was dragged out and brutally beaten with fists, feet, and belts. His assailants demanded a confession, but he refused.

He was finally knocked unconscious, then dragged into the bushes and left for dead.

Things were headed in a decidedly ugly direction.

Chapter Twenty-One: The Murder of Joe Kahahawai

Life is a mysterious and exciting affair, and anything can be a thrill if you know how to look for it and what to do with opportunity when it comes.
—Phony summons to Joe Kahahawai

DESPITE THE FAILURE to obtain a confession from Horace Ida, Thalia's family and friends continued to scheme. Someone pointed out that a confession from Ida would have been meaningless, anyway, because the goal was to obtain a confession without leaving a mark on the confessor. Anything else would taint the confession as coerced.

It was time to find another one of the Boys to try to crack.

Tommie Massie had been told that Joe Kahahawai was the most likely to buckle under pressure. Thalia's mother, Grace Fortescue, spoke to the court clerk and learned that, as a condition of their bond, the Boys had been ordered by Judge Steadman to report daily, but at separate times, with Joe scheduled to report at 8 AM.

Grace and Tommie dummied up a piece of paper to look like a summons, complete with a seal in the lower right corner that had been cut from a diploma that Tommie had received from the Chemical Warfare School in Maryland. For the text in the middle of the page, Grace cut a paragraph from the *Honolulu Advertiser* and pasted it in. The language made no real sense, but it seems strangely evocative given what was about to happen:

> *Life is a mysterious and exciting affair, and anything can be a thrill if you know how to look for it and what to do with opportunity when it comes.*

On the morning of Friday, January 8, Grace stood outside the courthouse shortly after eight, with a newspaper photo of Joe pinned to her purse so she would recognize him. As Joe left from his morning meeting, accompanied by his cousin, Eddie Uli'i, a man in a dark suit approached, showed Joe the summons, and told him that Major Ross, the sheriff, wanted to see him.

The man then forced Joe into the rear of a dark Buick sedan driven by a man wearing goggles. As the Buick drove away, Eddie, who had been left behind, realized that the car was headed the wrong way to be going to Major Ross's office, so he ran back into the judiciary building to report what had happened.

The man with the summons was navy machinist's mate Albert O. "Deacon" Jones who, along with Fireman First Class Edward J. Lord, had helped plan the abduction; Lord was waiting nearby in a Durant Roadster for Grace.

The driver of the Buick carrying Joe, disguised by the goggles and, by some reports, a fake mustache, was Tommie Massie. Tommie turned into the driveway of the house Grace was renting in Manoa Valley at just prior to nine o'clock; Grace and Lord arrived a few minutes later.

Neighbors later reported that they heard what sounded like a single gunshot a little after nine.

By now, thanks to Eddie Uli'i's report, Joe's kidnapping had already been broadcast to patrol officers, who were told to be on the lookout for a blue Buick sedan driven by a man dressed as a chauffeur. Detective George Harbottle, who had been one of the first to arrive at the Massie house after the alleged rape, was standing outside his police car on Wai'alae Avenue, talking to another officer, Thomas Kekua, when they saw a car that fit the description go by, driven by a woman and with two men inside.

The window shade on the rear window was pulled down—very unusual in Honolulu—so the two officers jumped in Harbottle's car and gave chase.

A Bundle in the Back Seat

Harbottle later reported that he "could see through the windshield of my car the mirror of the car ahead and that the woman was watching us, and on account of this fact it aroused my suspicion all the more."

As Wai'alae Avenue became the Kalaniana'ole Highway, hugging the coastline on the way to the Halona Blowhole, the Buick picked up speed. Harbottle waved at another police car coming the other way to U-turn and join the chase, then he accelerated past the Buick and pulled over to cut it off. Officer Kekua said that, as they passed, he saw "something white wrapped in a bundle" in the back seat.

When the Buick blew past them, Harbottle pulled out his revolver and fired several shots at it before giving chase again.

This time he was successful in forcing the Buick to pull over. Gun drawn, he ordered the occupants from the car. Out stepped Grace Fortescue, Tommie Massie, and Edward Lord.

When Harbottle opened the back door, he saw the "something white" that Officer Kekua had noticed, a bundled bed sheet, soaking wet with water and blood. When they unwrapped the sheet, the officers discovered the nude body of Joe Kahahawai, with a bullet hole in his chest.

Grace and Tommie exhibited some bizarre behavior here as they waited for a paddy wagon to pick them and the body up. It might seem irrelevant to the case but is indicative of the nonchalant and arrogant attitude they exhibited, convinced of their moral superiority.[93]

At first, Grace stood off to the side of the road, almost detached, but when a newspaper reporter with a photographer in tow showed up, she smiled at the camera as if posing. Then, when she saw Officer Percy Bond, she walked over to shake his hand. "Haven't I met you somewhere before?" she asked. "Didn't you come down from the coast about two months ago, the same time I did?"

Bond said "no" and turned away.

Spotting Harbottle standing near Tommie, he said, "Good work, kid." But Tommie, apparently thinking the compliment was aimed at him, congratulating him for killing Kahahawai, grabbed his left hand in his right and pumped it up and down, as if shaking hands.

Then, mimicking Grace, he said, "Hello big boy, haven't I seen you at the police station?"

Detectives searched Grace's home and found two handguns, an Iver Johnson .32 revolver buried inside a basket of eggs in the kitchen, a .45 hidden beneath a couch cushion in the living room, and a steel-jacketed .32 caliber bullet on the dining room table. They also found a coil of rope that matched that binding Joe's body, a man's brown cloth cap, and a woman's purse with a newspaper clipping folded to show Joe's picture, as well as a wet mop in the bathroom, blood stains on the floor, and a blood-soaked towel with the monogram USN.

What they didn't find at first was the .32 owned by Albert Jones that would later be determined to have fired the fatal shot. It was ultimately found hidden in a box of sanitary napkins that had been buried by Thalia's sister, Helene, who had accompanied Grace to Honolulu.

Admiral Stirling refused to allow the Honolulu police to

---

[93] One wonders if Darrow might have been interested had he known of their attitudes and maybe even willing to turn down the case. On the other hand, there was that fee!

keep his people in custody, so he commandeered them and placed them in very generous quarters aboard the USS *Alton*, a decommissioned ship in permanent dry dock, at Pearl Harbor.

Stirling, bless his heart, was also very concerned about the welfare of the Ala Moana Boys, and implored Territorial Governor Lawrence Judd to lock them up "for their own safety," of course.

And lock them up is exactly what Judd did, although he allowed them out to attend Joe Kahahawai's funeral two days later.

Convening the Grand Jury

Judge Albert Cristy, son of a Congregational minister and Harvard Law-educated, presided over the grand jury that convened on Thursday, January 21, to consider indictments against Grace, Tommie, Jones, and Lord for the murder of Kahahawai.[94]

Prosecutor Griffith Wight—the notorious Griffith Wight of the rape trial—presented the evidence. About ninety minutes after Cristy turned the case over to the jury to deliberate, the

---

[94] Cristy had involvement a few years earlier in the Fukunaga case, the abduction and murder of a young boy in a crime that emulated the Leopold and Loeb case. Although Cristy did not preside over the trial in that case, he handled the post-trial motion for new trial, which he denied with a blistering opinion ridiculing the defense's claim of newly discovered evidence following Fukunaga's conviction. A U.S. Navy psychiatrist named Thompson came forward after the trial to volunteer an opinion that Fukunaga was insane, though he had not offered his opinion before trial despite being fully aware of the ongoing trial and the insanity defense that was lodged. Judge Cristy dismissed the dilatory opinion out of hand, referring to Thompson as a "very modest violet hidden in the sands of Pearl Harbor," presenting himself as a "super-human person, whose opinion should be subjected to the weight of throwing out the window of everything that has been done, after he has waited until the defendant is about to receive his punishment."

jurors sent out a note with some fairly basic questions for the judge. Cristy determined that they needed further instruction, which he gave them Friday afternoon:

> *Let me again remind you in a cool, unimpassioned fashion, without any desire to interfere with your discretion as representatives of the community, let me remind you of those things in your oath, that you should present [indict] no one through envy, hatred, or malice, and, on the other hand, you should leave no one unpresented through fear, favor, affection, gain, reward, or hope therefor.*

At 3:15, the grand jury took a vote—nine to indict, twelve not to indict. Jury foreman Harry Franson went to tell Judge Cristy while the others began packing up to leave. Franson returned about ten minutes later accompanied by Cristy, who refused to accept their vote.

He said:

> *The Court at this time is not prepared to receive a report, but is going to ask each one of you jurors that whatever proceedings you have had before you, and whatever you have considered, that you take that matter with yourselves, with the usual caution of disclosing the same to others, and reflect upon it, and reflect upon the consequences of any actions on your part.*

Cristy gave additional instructions, including that "if there is any juror who cannot conscientiously carry out his oath of office, he should resign immediately from the grand jury."

One of the jurors, Edward Bodge asked: "Do I understand you are not accepting this report?"

"Nothing has been presented to me," Cristy responded. "The court refuses to accept any further report until the Grand Jury deliberates further upon matters of serious import to the

Territory." Cristy then adjourned the jury until the following Tuesday morning at 10:00 AM.

When the Jury re-convened on that Tuesday morning, Judge Cristy admonished the jurors that he had reason to believe that:

> [O]ne or more of you entered upon the Grand Jury session in the matters now pending with your minds so fixed and determined on personal views of the law and fact that you were prepared to prevent any indictment in matters now pending so far as you are able to, notwithstanding what the evidence might be and notwithstanding what the court should advise the jury the law might be.

He added that "under the laws of the Territory the taking of human life by private citizens, in the nature of a lynching or its equivalent, is prima facie murder."

At 10:55, he returned to the grand jury room to give yet further instructions. By now, this may have been the most-instructed grand jury in the history of jurisprudence. Cristy told them:

> You are all religious men, as I know, and God has not left this world for an instant, and if you sit with your God and your conscience under the evidence, your duties will clarify themselves in your own minds.

At 3:10 PM, by a vote of 12 to 8, the jury returned an indictment for second degree murder.

Judge Cristy accepted the report, along with resignations of two outraged jurors who had been on the losing side of the vote. He then set bail in the amount of $50,000 each for the four defendants but, after much anguish and impassioned argument, he lowered it to $5,000 for Grace and $2,500 for each of the others. Amfac, or American Factors, one of the Big Five corporations that controlled Hawaii, put up the bail money, and the defendants were returned to their quarters on the *USS Alton*.

But that was far from the end of the story of Judge Cristy and the grand jury. Defense attorney Montgomery Winn, of the Honolulu firm of Thompson, Beebe & Winn—Beebe being Eugene Beebe, the same attorney whose advice, as we'll see, may well have precipitated the demise of Joe Kahahawai—promptly filed a motion to quash the indictment the very next morning.

The reason, he said, was:

> *Because the Honorable A.M. Cristy, Second Judge of the Circuit Court of the First Judicial Circuit, Territory of Hawaii, on Friday, the 22nd day of January, 1932, did arbitrarily and without justification of law refuse to accept the report of the Territorial Grand Jury that it, the said Grand Jury, had returned a no bill against each of the four above named defendants on the bills charging said defendants with first degree murder in connection with the alleged kidnapping and killing of one Joseph Kahahawai....*

Judge Cristy denied the motion. Despite the controversy, he had to be gratified to later receive a hand-delivered letter from the president of the Hawaii Bar Association that concluded:

> *It is with great pride that the Bar Association recognizes that you rose to the occasion and enforced the fundamental idea that this is a government of laws and not of men.*

Just as the military and others of the *haole* elite wanted to strengthen the prosecution team for the Ala Moana Case, there was now a move afoot to strengthen the team of lawyers for the defendants.

Grace's brother, Robert Bell, arrived in Honolulu and almost immediately decided that, notwithstanding the excellent law school credentials of lawyers and judges involved in the case,[95] his sister needed a high-powered attorney from the mainland—and he had one in mind.

The local attorneys, Franklin Thompson and Montgomery Winn, agreed, apparently fearful of the backlash that would befall if they lost.

A High-Powered Attorney Who Needed the Fee

A cable was sent from Honolulu to the home of Clarence Darrow in Chicago, inquiring as to his availability to handle the case.

Darrow, although at the age of 74 was retired, had suffered reverses in the stock market and found himself in need of money.

Grace's brother-in-law, Julian Ripley, did the negotiating and reached an agreement with Darrow for the fee, which Darrow said was "not at all large...." [cclxvii]

The $40,000 Massie fee is just shy of $900,000 in today's dollars, for what would amount to less than two months of work. It's hard to see how $450,000 per month is "not at all large."

Grace's friends on the mainland raised the money and Darrow was hired. He couldn't have been happy, though, with his clients.

For starters, prior to Darrow's engagement, Grace had given an interview to Russell Owen of *The New York Times*, in which she basically admitted to the killing and said their only mistake was "pulling down the shade in the car. I should not have done that.... Now, of course, I realize that we bungled dreadfully, although at the time I thought we were being careful."

Owen said this about his conversation with Grace:

---

[95] Credentials included law degrees from Stanford and Harvard, among others.

> *I asked her why she felt what had happened was justified, and she said that she came from the South and that in the South they had their own ways of dealing with "niggers." She said many other things which I will not recall now, but that one word "niggers," if I had ever revealed it, would have made her position much more unpleasant in Hawaii. Hawaiians are not related to the Negroes, and the designation would have been devastating.*
>
> *When I went back to her attorney[96] I told him all the things which she had told me, except the word "niggers." I did not feel that I should repeat that, as I knew the racial hatreds which were underneath the trial. But I did tell him that she thought her mistake was in pulling down the curtains, and several other things which were rather incriminating. Much to my surprise, he did not ask me not to use them. The only thing he said was that he would give five thousand dollars to be out of the case.*[cclxviii]

Notwithstanding that "not at all large fee," Darrow apparently had his own second thoughts about taking on the case, initially declining it, primarily because of his reputation as an attorney for underdogs and the very racial aspect that reporter Owen was reluctant to print or even reveal to the defense lawyers.

Darrow wrote to his friend, educator and historian Harry Elmer Barnes, on March 5, 1932, initially to justify rejecting the case, because it seemed to champion the elite on the wrong side of the "race issue."

> *Before receiving your letter I had gone over the subject fully and already within that I felt that I could not go into the case and gave my reasons for it. I knew practically nothing about it except that such a case was to be tried in Honolulu, and I really wanted to go. Without expressing any opinion on the matter I learned that*

---

[96] A pre-Darrow lawyer.

> one…could scarcely avoid discussing race conflict in the trial of the case. I had so long and decidedly been for the Negro and all so-called "foreigners" that I could not put myself in a position where I might be compelled to take a position, even in a case at variance with what I felt and had stood for. In the mean time, I got all the "news papers" [sic][97] that I could and knew how the case would inevitably line up.[98] The defendants are entitled to counsel who could not be handicapped by his opinions and former statements and I felt that I might handicap them by former trials and opinions. So, I shall not be in the case and have so written them. They will have the letter in their hands by the time this is written. Won't you please keep this confidential, as it will no doubt be known before you receive this, and I do not want to seem to express any views that could possibly effect [sic] the defendants.[cclxix]

By the time he wrote a subsequent letter to Barnes on March 12, he had changed his mind, apparently tantalized by the "not at all large fee" that was dangled in front of him, and for which he was now content to take the very positions he previously blathered that he could not take. In fact, as subsequent events would show, he was even willing to break the law to support those positions. Barnes was apparently unhappy with Darrow's decision, a fact reflected in Darrow's closing lines:

> Still—I am sorry that it pains you, as you know that my affection for you is genuine and deep. I want you to watch the case and see if you can criticize anything I do in the matter. And I do want you to keep your faith in me.

His apologists readily supported his accepting the case. Irving Stone wrote that Thalia Massie provided Darrow an interesting

---

[97] Apparently the full extent of his investigation.
[98] Because newspapers are, of course, inerrant.

psychological study and that was enough to justify it. Darrow himself wrote, "It was a study in psychology beyond any question, and such cases have always interested me." [cclxx]

Besides, Stone quoted Darrow, "they said I was through as a lawyer, and I wanted to show them that a man in his seventies was keener than a younger person." [cclxxi]

The Weinbergs, Arthur and Lila, acknowledged that Darrow "had difficulty explaining his motives" but that part of his legend was that "he never defended a case in which he was not interested in the principle." Still, a lawyer's got to get paid, right?

Pulling from the April 4 edition of the *Honolulu Advertiser*, they quoted Darrow as saying, "A lawyer would not get along very well who barred clients who could pay their bills. I do not remember having told anyone that I didn't accept fees for my work." [cclxxii]

Those fees, he argued, were exactly what permitted him to take on other cases for no fee. Others were not as forgiving of Darrow as Darrow was of himself, or as the apologists were. Andrew E. Kersten wrote that, in the Massie case, "Darrow chose a fee over principles." [cclxxiii]

Darrow tried out other justifications, as well, some a bit more altruistic than money. Theon Wright quoted Darrow as saying that he was in Hawaii "to heal old wounds, not to make new ones." [cclxxiv] Boy, did he miscalculate that one. Furthermore, Wright says that Darrow told reporters that "I'm down here to defend four people who have been accused of a crime that I do not believe was a crime." [cclxxv]

The bottom line, though, was that he needed the money—and perhaps there was just a bit of wanderlust involved as well. As he later wrote in his memoir: "[T]he more I thought of those islands in the Pacific that I had so long wanted to see, and the more I investigated the strange and puzzling case, the more I felt that I had better go." [cclxxvi]

It might have been better for all had he stayed at home—although it would have deprived me of this section of the book.

Chapter Twenty-Two: Darrow's Final Trial

So, altogether, loafing is not so ideal as it seemed to one who was anxious to welcome it as a dear dream come true. Four years of freedom from work, seemingly doing as I pleased, gradually grew monotonous and dreary. I was tired of resting.
—Clarence Darrow

WHILE THE DEFENDANTS awaited the arrival of Clarence Darrow, two other very significant things occurred.

On March 9, the local attorneys filed a motion asking that the case be transferred from Judge Cristy to "any judge whom you shall select."

In other words, they wanted anyone but Judge Cristy. In doing so, they invoked a statute of Hawaiian laws, Act No. 292 of the Session Laws of 1931, that provided that, when any party to a suit or other action makes an affidavit that the judge has a personal bias or prejudice against him or in favor of an opposing party, "such judge shall be disqualified from proceeding therein."

Under this law, a party gets only one bite at the apple, but it's not discretionary. Transfer is mandatory provided the magic words are used, even if there is no basis in fact.

Attorney Montgomery Winn filed affidavits from all four

defendants—Grace Fortescue, Tommie Massie, Albert Jones and Edward Lord—each of which recited that:

> [T]he Honorable A.M. Cristy, Second Judge of the Circuit Court of the First Judicial Circuit, Territory of Hawaii, has a personal bias or prejudice against [him/her] and the other three defendants in said cause and matter, and for that reason seeks that he be disqualified from further proceeding therein.

Recognizing that the defendants, obviously motivated by anger at the heavy hand Cristy used to secure their indictments, had technically complied with the statute, Judge Cristy transferred the case on March 17 to Judge Charles S. Davis, Cornell, Harvard, and Stanford educated, but a native of Honolulu.[99]

The second event was the culmination of debates in the territorial legislature to convert the prosecutor's job in Honolulu from an elective position to one appointed by either the territorial governor or mayor.

One has to wonder if it was a move designed to oust Griffith Wight as prosecutor. Walter Dillingham, business magnate and the most influential man in the Territory, had lobbied to have the appointment made by the governor, over whom he had a great deal of influence, but the role ending up falling on the mayor.

The local Bar Association recommended John Carlton Kelley for the job, which paid $7,500 a year.[100] The mayor concurred, and so Kelley replaced Wight, a definite step up in competence.

Born the son of a copper miner in Butte, Montana, the forty-six-year-old Kelley received his undergraduate and law

---

[99] Davis had been the prosecutor in the Fukunaga case.
[100] Roughly $167,000 in today's money. Not a bad annual salary but compare that with the $40,000 fee Darrow commanded for what would turn out to be roughly two months of work.

degrees from the University of Michigan.

He spent some time wandering the globe after leaving the mainland, chased away by a serious drinking problem, living in China, Australia, and Fiji, before finally landing in Hawaii. He was considered honest, politically independent, and a bulldog in the courtroom.

The local United States attorney described him as one of the best trial lawyers he had ever seen, with a "terrific 'jury personality' when he was sober." [cclxxvii]

Picking a Jury

Darrow arrived in Honolulu on March 24, 1932, and jury selection began on April 4 in Cause Number 11891, *The Territory of Hawaii v. Grace Fortescue, Thomas H. Massie, Edward J. Lord, and Albert O. Jones.*

Kelley anticipated that Darrow would invoke the "unwritten law," or "honor killing," as a defense, and he sought a way to defuse it during *voir dire*. The "unwritten law" was essentially "jury nullification," and it asked a jury to ignore, or nullify, the law and return a verdict based on its own sense of justice.[101]

Here, it meant that the jury would be asked to overlook the killing of Joe Kahahawai and find it to be justified because of what Joe had allegedly done to Thalia Massie. It's a defense as old as time, or at least as old as the "Old West"—a variation on the "he needed killing" defense.

If Kelley could succeed in keeping the Ala Moana Case out, it would gut Darrow's defense. During *voir dire*, he inquired of potential juror Kenneth Bankston: "Are you willing to return a verdict, understanding that the guilt or innocence of Joseph Kahahawai in the Ala Moana case has nothing to do with this present trial?"

In other words, regardless of whether Joe was guilty of assaulting Thalia or not, can you apply the law of murder in this

---

[101] As we have seen, justice was a very nebulous concept for Darrow.

case?

Darrow bounced up immediately.

After all, he needed the jury to know about what Thalia had claimed happened to her, and the outrage of a hung jury at the Ala Moana trial, to provide the justification for his clients' acts.

His assumption was, however, that the Ala Moana Boys were guilty of the crime, notwithstanding the hung jury and overwhelming evidence to the contrary. If they were innocent, the outrage over a failure to convict faded, and with it any justification for killing Joe.

Darrow needed to convince the judge to let in the fact of the assault while limiting the prosecution's ability to cast doubt on Thalia's account.

"If I have anything to do with it," Darrow said, "the Ala Moana case will certainly have something to do with this case. I hardly think counsel should ask the jurors to ignore that matter." An ironic statement given Darrow's own ignorance about the facts of that case.

"Wrong," Kelley said. "As a matter of law, Joseph Kahahawai could be as guilty as any man could be, and still that does not provide an excuse for killing him."

For his part, Darrow insisted on asking questions of jurors about the rape trial, with repeated objections asserted by Kelley. And so it went, with Judge Davis pretty much allowing the questioning to proceed as the lawyers wanted without sustaining objections from either side.

At one point, assistant prosecutor Barry Ulrich responded to an objection from Darrow by turning to the judge and stating: "May it please the court, this jury should be selected on the assurance that no appeal can be made to anything but the law itself."

Darrow responded, "That isn't the law." That response foreshadowed, one supposes, his intent to appeal to emotion, bias, and, of course, the unwritten law—Darrow trademarks over a long and distinguished career. Anything and everything except the law, because he knew that reliance upon the actual law would torpedo his case.

As he later wrote in his autobiography:

> *Of course, all the attorneys for the prosecution, and those for the defense, as well as the judge, knew that legally my clients were guilty of murder. Yet, on the island, and all across the seas, and around the earth, men and women were hoping and praying and working for the release and vindication of the defendants. As in similar cases, everyone was talking about "the unwritten law." While this could not be found in the statutes, it was indelibly written in the feelings and thoughts of people in general. Which would triumph, the written or the unwritten law, depended upon many things which in this case demand the most careful consideration.*[cclxxviii]

Among the "many things" upon which it would ultimately be decided would be whether Darrow could bludgeon the jury into submission with his words.

Law be damned!

Ultimately a jury was seated and an overview of its make-up suggested a jury far more sympathetic to the prosecution than to the defendants, at least in Darrow's estimation.

It was certainly not the all-white jury he had hoped for.

Notwithstanding his claim in his letter to Harry Elmer Barnes that "I had so long and decidedly been for the Negro and all so-called 'foreigners,'" he didn't trust the non-whites to be open and honest like whites could.

He wrote in his memoir: "What about 'race prejudice'? I found none. Certainly none among the whites against the brown people." Then he trotted out a version of the old "some of my best friends are [fill in the blank]," when he wrote: "Many of the best-known and most intelligent whites have married members of other races in the South Seas."[cclxxix]

His good friend Barnes might have found something to

criticize there.

Darrow also wrote, "If there is no prejudice on the part of the white people against the brown, how about the attitude of the brown toward the white? This is a very different matter, which I was bound to consider in the trial of the case."

Returning to the topic again later, he wrote: "I knew that the white men had no prejudice against the brown ones, nevertheless the brown men were prejudiced against the white."
cclxxx

So, Darrow was quite distressed to end up with a mixed jury of seven whites (including one Portuguese), three Chinese, and one Hawaiian, and one, a man named Walter Napoleon, who was a mixture of Hawaiian, French, Tahitian, Irish, and Scottish. When asked what that made his nationality, Napoleon answered, "League of Nations."

It was an educated jury, with half of the jurors having attended or graduated from college (including Stanford and Princeton) at a time when only one in eight Americans went to college.

Four were employees of Big Five corporations; two more worked for companies owned by Walter Dillingham, a powerful business leader in Hawaii; one was employed by a company that contracted legal services to Thompson, Beebe & Winn—Eugene Beebe's firm—and the foreman, John Stone, was a mainland college graduate and an executive of Castle & Cooke, a Big Five company.

The Trial Begins

The trial started on the morning of Monday, April 11, when John Kelley gave his forty-seven-minute opening statement, speaking entirely without notes.

Darrow reserved his opening statement, so Kelley then went right into the presentation of his evidence, starting with Joe's cousin, Eddie Uli'i. Next came Joe's probation officer, whom Joe had seen the morning he was abducted, followed by the arresting officers and a photographer who had taken pictures of the defendants and the arrest scene on the cliff near Hanauma Bay.

He introduced Joe's clothing, including his undershorts with the buttons ripped off as the defendants had stripped his body, and his blood-spattered shirt with a bullet hole. Darrow either passed cross-examination or did very little questioning, and the evidence moved quickly.

That, of course, was Darrow's plan. Since he wasn't contesting the shooting, the sooner these witnesses got on and off the stand, and no one dwelt on the horror of the crime, the better.[102]

On Tuesday, Kelley introduced the rope that had bound Joe's body in the bloody sheet, blood-stained USN towel, and .32 caliber steel-jacketed bullet that had been removed from Joe's body.

Kelley also examined Dr. Robert Faus, who had performed the autopsy on Joe's body. Dr. Faus testified that the bullet had been fired from the front and off to one side, in a downward course into the left side of Joe's chest—the downward trajectory suggested Joe had been seated and the shooter standing—finally lodging to the right of the seventh dorsal vertebra. "The chest was filled with blood, four or five liters, and the cause of death was hemorrhage from a bullet wound penetrating the left pulmonary artery."

On April 14, Kelley presented Esther Anito, Joe's mother, as his last witness, to identify her son's clothing. Russell Owen reported in the *New York Times*, "She did not become hysterical or cry noisily, but held herself with dignity...." Her appearance on the stand produced what was maybe the second most

---

[102] This was similar to a tactic followed in the Fukunaga case, in which the defense stipulated that Myles Fukunaga had killed Gil Jamieson, then objected to introduction of bloody clothes, which might inflame the passions of the jury tasked with determining whether to apply the death penalty. The theory was that, since the killing was admitted, it wasn't necessary to introduce evidence to prove it.

dramatic moment of the trial when Esther testified that she was divorced and that she had had four children, but two of them died at an early age.

"Only two are now living," she said, "Joseph and Lillian."

"Is Joseph alive?" Kelley asked, shocked.

Esther corrected herself before he could even finish his question. "No. No—he is dead."

Crazy—Leopold and Loeb Redux

After the morning recess, the defense started by putting Tommie Massie on the stand. After some introductory questions, Darrow arrived at the Ala Wai Inn the past September. Kelley interrupted, objecting that what happened that night could only be relevant to an insanity defense. Darrow agreed, stating that he did, indeed, expect to raise the question of insanity regarding "the one who shot the pistol."

Kelley then argued that, if Darrow was going to raise that defense, he had to reveal "who shot the pistol." Darrow had been holding the insanity card close to his vest, and nobody knew if he would play it or who the defense would say had done it.

There were inklings, of course.

Russell Owen had reported in *The New York Times*, at the end of jury selection:

> *Two alienists who figured in notorious murder trials of Southern California and Arizona, arrived here tonight to confer with Clarence Darrow, the Chicago lawyer who heads the defense counsel for Mrs. Granville Fortescue and three naval men on trial for second degree murder.*

This exchange in the courtroom between Kelley, Darrow, and Judge Davis marked the first time Darrow revealed to the prosecution that he would actually be relying on an insanity defense, which was quite rare for the time:

MR. KELLEY: *We object to any further testimony of Lieutenant Massie on this subject, unless we are informed that the plea of insanity is to be presented in his behalf.*

MR. DARROW: *I don't think that makes the slightest difference. Of course counsel has stated many times to the jury that each one is responsible for what all did, if they were connected in an enterprise of this sort,* [103] *which, perhaps, would be true if they had reason to foresee what might follow from their act. I don't think we need to go further at this time. The Court is familiar with it, and so is counsel. That statement was made openly and it is just exactly as we stated it.*

MR. KELLEY: *We have the right, if the Court pleases, at least we feel we have the right, in the event the plea of insanity is relied upon with reference to any of these defendants, relying upon further information that certain well-known psychiatrists have come here, ostensibly to testify in this case, we have the right to know which defendant this plea is going to be presented for, and the right to examine by alienists, doctors, psychiatrists or other persons, the party who it is claimed was insane at the time the murder was committed.*

THE COURT: *Under our law, Mr. Kelley, the plea of insanity puts in issue the sanity of all. There is no special plea of insanity required.*

MR. DARROW: *Counsel has been very accommodating to us, and if he says he wants some doctors to come in here and hear the testimony, why I would be perfectly willing to accommodate him by even calling another witness, although I would rather finish with him [Massie] as I*

---

[103] This reflected the law of conspiracy, which Darrow hated.

> started. Nobody whom we claim is insane, we not may see fit to submit them to his physician. That will come up later. But certainly they have the right to be here in court, and if he makes any such request we will try to meet him fairly in the matter.

Darrow would later concede:

> The evidence will show in this case that the defendant Massie, now on the stand held the gun in his hand from which the fatal shot was fired in this case.

And so, Kelley learned, when it was too late to have his own alienists examine Massie since the trial had already started, that Darrow was going to rely upon an insanity defense and in whose hands he would place the murder weapon. Although Kelley hired his own alienists, their opinions would be limited to their observations of Massie at trial.

He learned the hard way that Clarence Darrow was not above playing dirty.

Massie had not testified during the Ala Moana Case, instead spending, according to his testimony in the Massie Case, only one day in the courtroom during that prior trial while the rest of the time he was at sea on maneuvers. But he had to testify here, even though it could be risky for a defense lawyer to put his client on the stand to face cross examination. I say "had to" because Darrow was relying on not only an insanity defense, but also on the unwritten law—the supposed right of a husband to avenge his violated wife.

To succeed, he needed the jury to hear and see Massie as Darrow wanted to portray him: a poor, deranged husband in the grip of emotion and uncontrollable impulse when he pulled the trigger and dispatched the man who defiled his wife to the great beyond.[104]

---

[104] Not that Darrow believed in the "great beyond;" he didn't believe

In addition to the obvious problem that it wasn't Joe Kahahawai who defiled Thalia Massie—in fact, the Pinkerton Detective Agency would later question whether anybody did—there was another more serious factual problem with the theory, which we'll discuss later.

Darrow led Massie through a description of Thalia's appearance when he arrived home that night—blood pouring from her nose and mouth, her lips crushed and bruised.

He testified that Thalia repeatedly said, "I want to die! I hope to die." And when the police brought in her assailants for identification, Massie said, "I was there and later she told me, 'They are the ones.' I said, 'Don't let there be any doubt, darling.' She said, 'Don't you know if there were any doubt I'd never draw another free breath?'"

Massie described the kidnapping of Joe, bringing him into the Fortescue house, and efforts to coax a confession. "And suddenly he [Kahahawai] said, 'Yes, we done it.' The last thing I remember was that picture that came into my mind, of my wife when he assaulted her and she prayed for mercy and he answered with a blow that broke her jaw."

DARROW: *Did you have a gun in your hand when you were talking to him?*

MASSIE: *Yes, sir.*

DARROW: *Do you remember what you did?*

MASSIE: *No, sir.*

DARROW: *Do you know what became of the gun?*

MASSIE: *No, I do not, Mr. Darrow.*

---

in heaven or hell.

And there it was: deep emotional pain, anger, irresistible impulse, and then blackout. Both defenses—insanity and unwritten law—wrapped up nicely. There was, of course, a reason why Massie had no recollection of shooting Joe: because he didn't do it, something Darrow well knew.

Now it was time for cross-examination by Kelley, but Massie stuck to his fugue state story. He described the moment of his arrest when the defendants were stopped with Joe's body in their car. "Here is the way it was, Mr. Kelley. It was all vague. I could see figures and I think I knew they were people, and I could tell something about the distinction in dress, but it was all very vague."

In fact, he couldn't even remember when he finally snapped out of it. "That is something that has baffled me. I can't recall the first thing. I have thought a great deal about it. Everything was vague and blurred at times and then I would clear up and blur again."

Massie also confirmed that Eugene Beebe had, in effect, put the kidnapping plot into his head in the first place, though he was vague about specifics of his conversation with Beebe.

> KELLEY: *You had been advised by Mr. Beebe that a confession obtained from any of these defendants by force could not be used, is that correct?*
>
> MASSIE: *He made particular reference to not beating him.*
>
> KELLEY: *Did he say anything about threatening him with a gun?*
>
> MASSIE: *I don't remember.*

Later, Massie repeated his encounter with Beebe about the issue, and that Beebe "told me that the case was in such a condition now that a confession would be necessary." However, Beebe had also told him that no force could be used nor marks visible on the confessor.

For his part, Beebe testified simply that he discussed the beating of Horace Ida with Massie, and:

> *I told him I had read the newspaper accounts and seen the pictures in the newspaper which showed bruises across the boy's back, and I told him a confession obtained under the circumstances of that case was not admissible in Court.*

He denied any further conversation about confessions obtained under duress or coercion.

Interestingly, Kelley also pressed Massie on cross-examination as to whether he had asked Beebe "if the unwritten law could be invoked in the Territory of Hawaii." The question seemed to suggest some foresight and planning to use it if the attempted coercion of a confession led to violence. In other words, it suggested that Massie, *et al*, anticipated at least the possibility of killing a confessor.

That sounds an awful lot like premeditation.

Massie denied remembering whether he had, in fact, asked that question of Beebe, though he left open the possibility.

> KELLEY: *You might have asked him [Beebe] if the unwritten law could be invoked in the Territory of Hawaii, but you don't recall it now, is that correct?*
>
> MASSIE: *Yes, I suppose so. I don't recall it; I know that it is true.*

To further the notion that there was premeditation, setting up an unwritten law defense before actually killing Kahahawai, consider this line of questioning:

> KELLEY: *Do you know an artist here, by the name of Luquines?*

MASSIE: *It doesn't register. I don't know anyone by that name.*

KELLEY: *You don't recall knowing any person who is an artist or an etcher?*

MASSIE: *Is it a lady?*

KELLEY: *No, it's a man. First name Huck?*

MASSIE: *It doesn't register with me. I am not saying that I do not, but at the present time I can't recall him.*

KELLEY: *Did you tell anyone two or three days before Kahahawai was killed that you ought to take him out and shoot him?*

MASSIE: *Not that I can recall.*

KELLEY: *Do you deny that you did?*

MASSIE: *I give you the same answer I have before, Mr. Kelley.*

KELLEY: *You don't remember?*

MASSIE: *I do not.*

KELLEY: *There was nothing wrong with your mental set-up then, was there?*

MASSIE: *I never was as miserable and upset and nervous and sick at heart in my life.*

KELLEY: *Was that mental or physical?*

MASSIE: *I don't know.*

KELLEY: *Did you ever tell Mr. Beebe that you felt like taking Kahahawai out and killing him?*

MASSIE: *Not that I recall.*

KELLEY: *You might have?*

MASSIE: *My same answer, Mr. Kelley. I want to be accurate.*

The nature of the question implied that Kelley may have had information about a conversation with Beebe. Or maybe he was just shooting in the dark. We'll likely never know if any such conversation occurred between Massie and either the mysterious Luquines or attorney Beebe, because Kelley didn't follow up on it with either of them.

But ain't it curious?

Although Kelley wasn't able to make any headway into debunking Massie's story due to the witness's strategic memory loss, he did get a few sarcastic shots in. When Massie testified that he couldn't remember getting into the Buick with the body in the backseat, and said, "For all I know I might have gone to China and back," Kelley responded, "Too bad you didn't."

And then there was this somewhat moving exchange:

KELLEY: *Did Kahahawai appear frightened?*

MASSIE: *Yes.*

KELLEY: *He was trembling?*

MASSIE: *Yes.*

After Massie left the stand, Darrow put on a succession of minor witnesses before calling his key experts: Dr. Thomas Orbison and Dr. Edward H. Williams—the "alienists."

He counted on Orbison and Williams to convince the jury that, at the time he pulled the trigger, Tommie Massie was suffering from *Dementia Americana*.

What they actually accomplished, though, was to bore the jurors into glassy-eyed comas as Orbison testified that Tommie was suffering from "delirium with ambulatory automatism" originating in the "internal glandular apparatus."

At one point Judge Davis even felt compelled to admonish Darrow that, "The questions are becoming interminably long. I wish you would shorten them."

Thalia Returns to the Stand

The most dramatic moment in the trial came during the last witness called by Darrow: Thalia Massie, star of the Ala Moana Case.

When Darrow attempted to take her through the events that she claimed happened on Ala Moana Road, Kelley objected: "We are not retrying the Ala Moana case." He argued that the issue was Tommie's mental condition on the morning that Kahahawai was shot, and that all that was relevant from Mrs. Massie were the things she said to Tommie that might have affected his state of mind.

Judge Davis overruled the objection, and Darrow took Thalia through that terrible night, starting with the phone call from Tommie that brought him running home to her and how she had undergone "an operation to stop pregnancy."

Then Kelley started his cross-examination, which lasted only eight minutes. To set it up, we've got to first step back a few months. In the spring of 1931, Thalia learned that she was pregnant, but she lost the baby in mid-summer. She sought counseling with Dr. Lowell Kelly, a 25-year-old assistant professor at the University of Hawaii, who was in the process of designing what would ultimately be a twenty-year longitudinal analysis of marital compatibility among 300 married couples. It became known as the Kelly Longitudinal Study, and was based on a battery of psychological tests, plus a questionnaire he had designed, and which Thalia answered.

As an aside, it's interesting to note that Dr. Kelly later wrote that Thalia's "personal and emotional problems were beyond his competency" and that "I became convinced that she was in need of psychiatric treatment and so advised her husband by telephone."

After Professor Kelly told this to Tommie, Thalia canceled her next appointment, and Kelly never spoke to her again.

Flash back to the trial as John Kelley began his cross-examination of Thalia. After a few random questions, Kelley approached the witness stand, withdrawing a folded piece of paper from his breast pocket. It was the questionnaire Thalia had answered.

"Did you have a psychopathic examination at the university last summer?" the prosecutor asked.

"Yes. I went to see Professor Kelly."

John Kelley handed her the paper, which he had unfolded. "Is this your handwriting?" he asked.

According to *The New York Times* report the next day, "There came a transformation from the pathetic looking figure into a woman who, with low voice but blazing face, turned on the prosecutor."

"Where did you get this?" she asked.

"I'm asking the questions, not answering them. Has your husband always been kind to you?"

In a rage, Thalia began tearing up the page into pieces. "Don't you know this is a confidential communication between doctor and patient? I refuse to say whether that is my handwriting or not."

One person started clapping in the courtroom then the clapping spread to others, including the defendants. Judge Davis banged his gavel, restoring order to the room.

"Thank you, Mrs. Massie," Kelley said, "at last you have shown yourself in your true colors."

When he announced that he was through with the witness, Thalia lurched from the witness stand, bent at the waist as if in pain, and stumbled toward Tommie, who was rushing to catch her.

"What right does he have to say that I don't love you?" she asked. "Everybody knows I love you."

And now everyone in the courtroom knew what the paper said.

The defense rested on April 20, 1932. After Kelley put on his own alienists in rebuttal, who testified that Tommie was sane but merely angry, Dr. Faus, who had performed the autopsy on Joe, was recalled as the trial's final witness. He testified for only three minutes, concluding that Joe would likely have remained conscious for up to five minutes after being shot, and that it took about twenty minutes for him to die.

Darrow later claimed that "Kahahawai lived but a few moments," [cclxxxi] which is not only inconsistent with this testimony from Dr. Faus, but it is consistent with Darrow's pattern of diminishing the suffering of crime victims. Recall that he argued in Leopold and Loeb that the family of Bobby Franks didn't really suffer, nor for that matter did Bobby, himself, because his death was accomplished in such a short time.

There were four closing arguments at the close of evidence. On Tuesday, April 26, Barry Ulrich, the assistant prosecutor opened, and was followed by George Leisure for the defense. The two heavyweights were to come the next day, with the order reversed: Darrow would go first for the defense, followed by Kelley for the prosecution.

With the whole country listening in by live radio that second day, Darrow spoke for 4 hours and 20 minutes. He started in the morning, took a nap during the lunch break, then returned in the afternoon to finish. According to the official records, he completed his argument at 2:23 PM, Honolulu time. Kelley started his closing at 2:38 and the jury began its deliberations at 4:30.

Blowhard

Chapter Twenty-Three: Darrow's Final Courtroom Bloviation

This case illustrates the working of human destiny more than any other case I have handled. It illustrates the effect of sorrow and mishap on human minds and lives, and shows us how weak and powerless human beings are in the hands of relentless powers.
—Clarence Darrow

JUST EXACTLY WHAT did Clarence Darrow have to say to that Hawaiian jury? It almost paralleled Leopold and Loeb, where he pled his clients guilty to killing Bobby Franks.

Similarly, here, no one disputed that his clients had kidnapped and killed Joe Kahahawai. In the prior case, his goal was simply to minimize the punishment without explicitly condoning the act. Therein lay the big difference, because in Massie he attempted to justify or excuse the conduct.

The testimony he extracted from his clients, particularly Tommie Massie, had followed the notions of temporary insanity and applying the unwritten law—defined by Bouvier's Law Dictionary and Concise Encyclopedia, the 1914 edition, as "A supposed rule of law that a man who takes the life of his wife's paramour or daughter's seducer is not guilty of a criminal offence [sic]."

The defense theory was that Tommie, in an insane blackout, squeezed the trigger of the gun in his hand at the moment that Joe confessed to raping his wife, even though he would have been privileged to do so, anyway, as the husband of the maltreated spouse, regardless of sanity.

It was a belt-and-suspenders approach, striving for excuse and justification all at once.[105]

Insanity would provide a legal excuse, that he couldn't be held responsible for an act over which he had no control (shades of Leopold and Loeb), while the unwritten law would say that whether he was insane or not was irrelevant; he was justified in killing Joe.

The Unwritten Law

Let's take a moment, though, to remember that the unwritten law presupposes that Joe Kahahawai was, in fact, guilty of raping Thalia Massie.

You can't be justified, even under the unwritten law, for killing someone who *did not* rape your wife. Or, for that matter, if your wife had never been raped in the first place.

Both of those issues were in serious doubt, neither of which Darrow bothered to investigate thoroughly, or even cursorily, beyond simply reading mainland newspapers and accepting his clients' version of events. He didn't even pay heed to the legal nicety that there had been a hung jury in the rape trial, such that the Ala Moana Boys had not been convicted and were, thus, entitled to a continuing presumption of innocence. Darrow presumed, and argued to the jury, guilt.

Later, Darrow's biggest complaint about Judge Davis was that he wouldn't give the jury an instruction validating the unwritten law defense. Instead, Davis told the jury:

I instruct you, Gentlemen of the jury, that no man may

---

[105] Or maybe it was the old dog-bite sequence of defenses: I don't have a dog; that's not my dog; my dog doesn't bite.

> *take the law into his own hands, and that no amount of mere mental suffering or worry, no amount of mental harm, injury, or shame caused to one man by another, not causing insanity, can or will furnish legal justification for the taking of the life of that other, and that the alleged fact, **if it be a fact** that the deceased in this case had assaulted or ravished the wife of one of the defendants in this case, cannot and does not furnish any legal justification to any of the defendants to kill said deceased and furnishes no defense to any of them.*[106] [emphasis added]

But let's assume for the sake of argument that Joe committed the actual crime of rape, that the "alleged fact...be a fact."

Darrow obviously accepted that as fact. He also accepted as fact that his clients killed Joe Kahahawai.

Now, try to reconcile his argument that Tommie Massie was justified in doing so with his arguments in the Leopold and Loeb case that his clients were victims of their own endocrine systems and heredity and, accordingly, were not responsible for their bad acts—and there could be no justification for the State sending them to the gallows.

In that case, he said, "I do not know what it was that made these boys do this mad act...because someone in the past sinned against them."

In his 1924 debate on capital punishment with Judge Alfred J. Talley of the Court of General Sessions in New York City, Darrow argued:

> *All people are products of two things, and two things only—their heredity and their environment. And they act*

---

[106] Darrow later groused about the verdict: "We finally agreed that the judge was to blame. This is always a first-rate alibi; the judge should not have instructed them so much on the side of the State." *The Story of My Life* at p. 477.

> *in exact accord with the heredity which they took from all the past, and for which they are in no wise responsible....*[cclxxxii]

Notice he said "all people." By logical definition of the words, that would include the Ala Moana Boys, assuming they were guilty, and so "they are in no wise responsible" for any alleged assault of Thalia Massie.

He also stated in the Leopold and Loeb case that if the State executed his clients for killing young Bobby Franks, "that act will be infinitely more cold-blooded, whether justified or not, than any act that these boys [Leopold and Loeb] have committed or can commit."

Assuming, then, that Joe Kahahawai raped Thalia Massie, doesn't it stand to reason under Darrow's philosophy that he was driven to that act by forces over which he had no control?

And that executing Joe for the rape, as Tommie Massie and his cohorts effectively did, "will be infinitely more cold-blooded, *whether justified or not*...." [emphasis added]

So how, then, could he walk into a Honolulu courtroom and argue that Tommie Massie, Grace Fortescue, Albert Jones, and Edward Lord were justified in killing Joe and, therefore, should be excused?

That becomes a particularly damning question when you realize that Joe and his buddies were almost certainly innocent of the assault on Thalia.

More Windbaggery

Let's look more closely at Darrow's argument, yet another exercise in windbaggery.

It lasted four hours and twenty minutes, just a breezy chat by Darrow standards, not even in the ballpark of his twelve hours in Leopold and Loeb.

Maybe, now in his mid-70s, he really was wearing down.

But he still made the most of those few hours to live up to his reputation for bloviation. He vented to a nationwide audience listening in by radio about his poor, poor clients and the dirty deed done to them by the Ala Moana Boys, a deed that drove those poor folks—God bless 'em—to commit an act that would, if they were convicted for it, "sanctify" the penitentiary in which they would be incarcerated.

Darrow started with one of his old standbys, that forces beyond our control dictate our actions. He had perfected it in Leopold and Loeb with a measure of success, so why not dust it off and try it again?

> *This case illustrates the working of human destiny more than any other case I have handled. It illustrates the effect of sorrow and mishap on human minds and lives, and shows us how weak and powerless human beings are in the hands of relentless powers.*

But then he launched into another recurrent theme that now, in most states, is no longer permissible.

The Golden Rule

It's called the "Golden Rule" argument, and it asks jurors to decide a case, not on the facts and the law, but instead on their own biases and prejudices—exactly what *voir dire*, or jury selection, is designed to weed out.

After setting the table with a description of devastating mental effects on Massie caused by the assault on his wife—"Massie's mind had been affected by all that was borne upon him: grief, sorrow, trouble, day after day, week after week, month after month"—Darrow asked the all-male jury this rhetorical question:

> *What do you think would have happened to any one of you under the same condition? We measure other people by ourselves. We place ourselves in their place and say, 'How would we have acted?'*

That is the essence of the Golden Rule as embodied in the Bible: "Do unto others as you would have them do unto you." *Luke* 6:31 (KJV).

Darrow returned to the Golden Rule multiple times in his argument, to borrow a Biblical metaphor from *Proverbs* 26:11 (KJV), "like a dog returning to his vomit."

It was almost brilliant in its simplicity.

Put yourself in the shoes of these defendants, he pleaded. Would you have done the same thing had it been you? If so, how can you possibly convict them of a crime for an act that you, yourself, would have committed under the same circumstances? Ignore the law. Judge them based upon what you would have done and how you would want a jury to judge you for it.

At one point, Darrow referenced people in the community supposedly spreading false rumors about Thalia's behavior— "terrible stories" that "I don't believe true."[107] He asked the jurors, "May I ask what effect they would have had on you and how would you have stood them?" Then again, later, another rhetorical question: "Gentlemen, you are asked to send these people to the penitentiary. Do you suppose that if you had been caught in the hands of fate—would you have done differently?"

Maybe a more accurate rhetorical question might have been, "If the guilt of your wife's attacker had not been proven in a court of law, and in fact that guilt was questionable at best,[108]

---

[107] See discussion above of Thalia's reputation. Although in this instance, some of the specific rumors may have been false, they were largely based in fact. Thalia was known for her extracurricular activities, to borrow a euphemism, particularly when her husband was away on maneuvers. A more recent rumor was that, rather than a tryst gone wrong, Thalia's physical injuries were inflicted upon her by her drug dealer, who provided her with opium. That has never been proven, but it does provide food for thought.

[108] Let's not overlook the possibility that Thalia's injuries had been, to some extent, administered by her own husband. There was some evidence that the injuries that the Clarks and the Bellingers reported seeing when they picked up Thalia on Ala Moana Road were not as

instead of waiting for a new trial, would you have kidnapped him, taken him to your home, and shot him?" But why mess up a good Golden Rule argument with the facts?

Darrow returned again toward the end of his argument with one of the most blatant requests that the jurors apply the Golden Rule. And it was not really a request. Rather, it was a statement that, unless they put themselves in the place of the defendants, then they had no right to judge them.

It was a heavy burden, a guilt trip, he placed on their shoulders.

> *No man can judge another unless he places himself in the position of the other before he pronounces the verdict. If you can put yourself in his place, if you can think of his raped wife, of his months of suffering and mental anguish, if you can confront the unjust, cruel fate that unrolled before him, then you can judge—but you cannot judge any man otherwise.*
>
> *If you put yourself in Tommie Massie's place, what would you have done? I don't know about you or you or you or you*[109]*—but at least 10 out of 12 men would've done just what poor Tommy* [sic] *Massie did. The thing for which you are asked to send him to prison for the rest of his life.*

And finally, just before taking his seat, he asked the jurors to take the case "as a case of your own," or as if they were the defendants.

Only then, he said, "I'll be content with your verdict."

---

severe as those found by medical personnel when she was finally examined at the hospital. Some speculate that her added injuries were incurred at the hands of her husband between his arrival home and the advent of police.

[109] Reportedly, "you, or you, or you, or you" was accompanied by finger-pointing by Darrow from juror to juror.

Darrow's Clients were the Real Victims

In keeping with his argument in Leopold and Loeb, where he referred to his clients as these "unfortunate boys," Darrow pretended that somehow his clients in the Massie Case were the victims, not the perpetrators.

He contended that the only reason they were on trial for their freedom was because something happened to them—Thalia was raped and "in the twinkling of an eye…the life of the family was changed and they are now here in this court for you to say whether they will go to prison—for life!"

But he forgot one crucial fact: interposed between the alleged rape and the trial, during that metaphorical twinkling of an eye, they kidnapped and killed a man who was almost certainly innocent of the initial crime. They weren't mere passive victims of fate; they were active perpetrators of a crime. *That* was why they were facing prison.

Similarly, in Leopold and Loeb he had argued that his clients were on trial because of things that had happened to them—the "terrible misfortunes of Dickie Loeb and Nathan Leopold"—while overlooking what they had done.

Then, in a fit of rhetorical handwringing, he bloviated, "Is there a more terrible story anywhere in literature? I don't know whether there is—or who it was—or where I can find that sad tale but right here." He later referred to it as a "story as terrible, as cruel, as any story I ever heard."

Several sadder, crueler, more terrible tales immediately leap to mind. A fourteen-year-old boy snatched off the street, bludgeoned with a chisel and choked to death by a rag stuffed down his throat, stripped, doused with acid, and then shoved into a culvert.

Or perhaps an innocent young man snatched off the street in front of the justice building, driven to a home and shot, dragged into a bathroom to drown in his own blood, then his lifeless body driven off to be dumped in the ocean.

And they almost got away with it. But, as John Kelley

would argue in his closing, "Another five minutes, a shade up in the window of the car, and the body of Joseph Kahahawai would have been consigned to the deep forever. But an omnipotent God said, 'Thou shalt not kill,' and the hand of fate saved Kahahawai's body from the sea so that it might rest in a Christian grave." [110]

Mothers

Other similarities here to Darrow's Leopold and Loeb argument also jump out, although I suppose this was the *Reader's Digest* condensed version.

Darrow obviously had his themes to which he returned over and over, like a dog returns to...well, you understand. Not the least of those themes was his attempt to tug at heartstrings about mothers. Recall that in Leopold and Loeb, he claimed the whole affair was harder on the mothers of the two killers than on the mother of the victim because, after all, Bobby Franks simply "left his home and went to his school and...never came back."

The mothers of Nathan Leopold and Richard Loeb, however, would forever be tortured, wondering if somehow the homicidal maniac gene was passed down to their offspring from them.

They would have to ask themselves the questions:

> *How came my children to be what they are? From what ancestry did they get this strain? How far removed was the poison that destroyed their lives? Was I the bearer of the seed that brings them to death?*

---

[110] This argument from Kelley bears some similarity to that of Robert Crowe in the Leopold and Loeb case, who said, in reference to Leopold's eyeglasses being dropped at the scene, "And nothing in my judgment but an act of God, an act of Providence, was responsible for the unraveling of this terrible crime."

He then cited the poem by A.E. Housman, "The Culprit," bemoaning the fate of a mother whose child was to be executed for committing murder.

In the Massie case, he went to similar lengths to extoll the virtues of motherhood and wring every last bit of sympathy he could from the jurors for Grace Fortescue. He might even have topped his Leopold and Loeb hyperbole. For starters, he reminded the jurors that "[p]oems and rhymes have been written about mothers," though he graciously demurred from reciting any to them. The Leopold and Loeb jury should have been so lucky.

Instead, he went off on this tangent about Grace Fortescue:

> *Here is the mother. What about her? They wired to her and she came.... I don't want to bring forth further eulogies which are more or less worth while [sic], but I want to call your attention to something more primitive than that. Nature. It is not a case of the greatness of a mother. It is the case of what nature has done. I don't care whether it is a human mother, a mother of beasts or birds of the air, they are all alike.*
>
> *To them there is one all-important thing and that is a child that they carried in their womb. Without that feeling which is so strong in all life, there would be no life preserved upon this earth. She acted as every mother acts. She felt as your mothers have felt, because the family is the preservation of life. What did she do? Immediately she started on a long trip to her daughter. The daughter was married and a long way off, but she was still her daughter. I don't care if a mother is seventy-five and her daughter fifty, it is still the mother and the child.*
>
> *Everything else is forgotten in the emotion that carries her back to the time when this was a little baby in her arms which she bore and loved. Your mother was that way and my mother, and there can be no other way, because life can be preserved in no other way. The mother started*

> *on a trip of 5,000 miles, over land and sea, to her child. And here she is now in this courtroom waiting to go to the penitentiary.*
>
> *Gentlemen, let me say this: If this husband and this mother and these faithful boys go to the penitentiary, it won't be the first time that a penitentiary has been sanctified by its inmates.*[111]
>
> *When people come to your beautiful Islands, one of the first places that they will wish to see is the prison where the mother and the husband are confined because they moved under emotion. If that does happen that prison will be the most conspicuous building on this Island, and men will wonder how it happened and will marvel at the injustice and cruelty of men and will pity the inmates and blame Fate for the cruelty, persecution and sorrow that has followed this family.*

Not a single word uttered about Esther Anito, Joe's mother. Didn't she carry Joe in her womb, wasn't Joe once a little baby in her arms, wasn't Joe's mother "that way," as was "your mother" and "my mother"?

It's not surprising that he ignored Esther, just as he downplayed the grief of Flora Franks, whose son fell prey to predators who killed just to prove they were smarter than everyone else. In fact, Darrow had even asked at one point that Esther Anito be removed from the courtroom because, as prosecutor John Kelley held up Joe's clothing, including a blood-spattered shirt with a distinctive bullet hole in it, she began to weep audibly.

No pity from Darrow for her.

But John Kelley wasn't buying it, referring to Grace and her co-defendants as "three able men and a cold calculating woman." He also had not forgotten Joe's mother for one

---

[111] "Sanctified," defined by *Merriam-Webster* as "set aside to a sacred purpose or to religious use." Interesting term to be used by an atheist.

moment. In his rebuttal to Darrow, he said:

> Mr. Darrow has spoken of mother-love. He points to Mrs. Fortescue as 'the mother' in this courtroom. Well, there is another mother in this courtroom. Has Mrs. Fortescue lost her daughter? Has Massie lost his wife? No, she sits there between them. But where is Joe Kahahawai?

There was No Intent (Just Gross Indifference)

As Darrow bounced back and forth between justification and excuse, he emphasized the notion that there was no intent to kill Joe Kahahawai, reprising his excuses for the McNamara brothers in Los Angeles.

He denied, though, that Tommie's purpose was to obtain a confession in order to convict his wife's alleged rapists.

> He wanted to get a confession. For what? To get somebody imprisoned? No—that did not concern him—he was concerned with the girl, whom he had taken in marriage when she was sixteen—sweet sixteen.

Maybe, though, that was Grace's purpose.

> Mrs. Fortescue was worrying about the delay of what she thought was justice, and what other people thought was justice. I fairly well know what the law is, but I don't often know what justice is—it is a pattern according to our own conceptions.

But kill? No, they never intended that—though they were certainly prepared to kill, handguns at the ready, loaded and pointed at Joe—as if lack of intent excused what happened. In fact, even though "they formed a plan to take Kahahawai to their house and get a confession," they, remarkably, "never conceived it to be illegal—it was the ends they thought of—not the means."

Sounds remarkably like his justification of the McNamaras, doesn't it?

Darrow told the jury:

> *They did not want to kill—they made no plan to kill—they didn't know what to do when it happened."*

He continued:

> *There is nothing in this evidence to indicate that they ever meant to kill—there was never any talk about killing as far as this evidence is concerned.*

I believe that to be an accurate statement of the facts. I don't believe they intended to kill Joe Kahahawai, because they needed his confession and they needed him alive for the retrial. The problem was that they didn't care if they killed him or not. They recklessly disregarded Joe's rights and his life, with fatal consequences, just as Darrow's clients did when bombing the *Los Angeles Times* building.

"I didn't mean to" doesn't excuse or justify the crime, although lack of intent may lessen, but not eliminate, accountability.

Ends Justify the Means

Darrow further devolved into his end-justifies-the-means philosophy that had been on display in Idaho and Los Angeles.

He claimed that the defendants didn't conceive their plan to be illegal—you know, dummying up a subpoena and forcing Joe into a car at gunpoint, taking him to a house and holding him against his will, staring in the face of four people and two guns, scared to death, in order to force a confession out of him.

But how could they not have thought their means were illegal? Darrow, himself, knew better. His own clients back in Chicago, Nathan Leopold and Richard Loeb, had been sentenced to life imprisonment for killing Bobby Franks, *plus* 99 years for the kidnapping. I guess it depends upon whether you adhere to Darrow's notion that justice depends upon one's personal conceptions.

While it was most likely that this was an unintended killing, there is such a thing as a felony murder rule.

This provides that if someone is killed during the commission of a dangerous or specifically enumerated crime, regardless of intent, it can still constitute murder, typically first degree or premeditated murder.

Here, the accompanying felony would have been the kidnapping at gunpoint. This principle would have held all four defendants liable for the killing regardless of who fired the shot. Darrow knew that, which he proved when he said, as quoted above when arguing that it did not matter who pulled the trigger on the fatal shot, "each one is responsible for what all did, if they were connected in an enterprise of this sort...."

Loyalty

Switching briefly to the two sailors, Edward Lord and Albert Jones, Darrow praised them for their loyalty to Tommie Massie, as if loyalty justified killing an innocent man.

He asked, rhetorically, "Are Jones and Lord, two common seamen, bad? There are some human virtues that are not common—loyalty, devotion. There isn't a single thing that either of these two boys did that should bring censure."

Other than, of course, willingly participate in the kidnapping and murder of Joe Kahahawai. And there is some reason to believe, by virtue of a confession he made to Grace Fortescue, that Albert Jones was previously involved in the kidnapping and beating of Horace Ida.[cclxxxiii]

It Doesn't Matter who Fired the Shot

One of Darrow's more interesting arguments, as quoted above, had to do with his failure to divulge to the prosecution, ahead of time, who the defense contended actually fired the shot.

It's of no consequence who fired that shot. I am arguing

the facts and the only facts as you get them. Is there any reason in the world why Massie, on top of all these other troubles, should assume the added burden of assuming the responsibility of his killing?

He went on to question why the prosecution even cared. "Again, I say, I cannot understand why the prosecution raises a doubt as to who fired the shot and how."

But then, in the next breath, he conceded that it was Tommy Massie who fired the shot, although Massie's testimony was essentially to the effect of "I had the gun in my hand and it went off. I don't really know what actually happened."

In closing, Darrow said that Massie "saw the picture of his wife pleading, injured, raped, and he shot. There could have been nobody else."

Darrow had to put the gun in Tommy's hand because otherwise, notwithstanding the felony murder rule, neither the insanity defense nor the unwritten law made sense. It was Tommie's wife who supposedly had been raped. It was Tommie, the aggrieved husband, who was suffering mental anguish. It was Tommie, the aggrieved husband, who had the right to avenge what had befallen his wife.

If anybody else had pulled the trigger, these defenses simply wouldn't make sense.

The prosecution had logical questions because the testimony was that Tommie's gun was a .45 while the .32 belonged to Jones.

The fatal shots were fired by the .32.

When Jones was later captured, he had the .32 with an empty clip on his person. So it was legitimate for the prosecution to assume that Jones was the one who pulled the trigger, but that wouldn't fit with Darrow's defense.

He had to put the gun in Tommie's hand at the key moment.

Victims, Again

In the same way Darrow tried to portray Leopold and Loeb as mere victims of their heredity, he continued to portray his clients in the Massie Case as victims.

As quoted before, he said they were in court because they were "bound up in a criminal act committed by someone else in which they had no part."

In other words, the only reason they were there was because of what somebody else had done to Thalia, not because of their own actions in response to that.

As Darrow droned on, he reiterated that they were there because of what had happened to them. He pleaded with the jurors to "take these poor, pursued suffering people, take them into your care as you would have them take you if you were in their place."

But whatever you do, he said, do not think of "heaping more sorrows on their devoted heads, to increase their burden and add to their wrongs." After all, "Can anyone say that they are of the type on whom prison gates should close to increase their sufferings? Have they ever stolen, assaulted, forged?"

Well, no, but they kidnapped and killed.

Don't forget that.

Crazy, Again

Although Darrow had played his insanity cards close to the vest before trial, tricking Kelley, he was not at all hesitant to play that card with the jury.

He contended that all the woes that had happened to Thalia had weighed heavily upon Massie's mind, along with horrible rumors that had been spread about his wife:

> [W]hat effect did they have on Massie? May I ask what effect they would have had on you and how you would have stood them? Massie attended to his day's duties as best he could. He went back and forth, nursing his wife,

> working all day and attending her at night for weeks. It was all that any husband could do or any man could do. He lost sleep. He lost courage. He lost hope. He was distraught! And all this load was on his shoulders.
>
> Any cause for it? Our insane institutions are filled with men and women who had less cause for insanity than he had. Everyone knows it. The mind isn't too easy to understand at the best. But what happens to the human mind? It does one thing with one person and another thing with another. You know what it did to Massie's. Do you think he is responsible or has been from that terrible night?

And later, "Tommie for months had been subject to delusions and fears that bring insanity."

Darrow Assumed the Ala Moana Boys were Guilty of Rape

Not merely content with justification under the unwritten law, he had to rely upon excuse, which is what the insanity defense was. I noted earlier that both of these defenses depended upon Joe Kahahawai and the other Ala Moana Boys having actually been the ones who were guilty of the attack on Thalia Massie.

However, the evidence in the rape trial clearly showed that was not the case. Darrow apparently did not care to look into the facts any deeper than getting his client's version of events. He just assumed the guilt of the Ala Moana Boys.

Likewise, Irving Stone, a Darrow apologist, did the same in his biography of Darrow. In describing the facts of the case, Stone wrote as fact:

> Mrs. Massie had gone only a short way up the road when a car containing two Hawaiians, one Chinaman, and two Japanese pulled up at the curb; they were apparently intent upon hijacking one of the native women on her way to the service bungalows, a practice that had been going

> on for a number of months. One of the Hawaiians and one of the Japanese jumped out and grabbed Mrs. Massie. When she struggled with them Kahahawai, a famous Island athlete, slugged her with his fist and broke her jaw. Then they threw her into the backseat of the car and drove down the Ala Moana Drive to an abandoned spot where the five men ravaged her. Mrs. Massie stumbled back to the road, was found by white motorists and taken to her home. She was immediately transferred to the hospital where the following morning she identified four of her assailants.[cclxxxiv]

Stone got most of his information—the "main sources of this biography," he called it—from the papers of Clarence Darrow, "sold to me by Mrs [sic] Darrow," and other Darrow-centric materials, as well "personal contributions" from Darrow friends and family.

It's not unreasonable to assume a bias in favor of Darrow rather than critical commentary, which probably explains the Darrow-friendly version of the biography. Stone obviously placed no reliance on, and maybe didn't even read, the trial transcript from the Ala Moana Case, nor on the Pinkerton Report, which would have told a completely different story of the alleged assault of Thalia Massie.

Darrow bought his clients' story, lock, stock, and barrel. He claimed that "no one raised even a doubt about this story," which ignored the fact of a full-length trial that had taken place, not only raising doubts about the story but also blowing huge holes in it.

He said that Thalia Massie identified her assailants and provided information to the police, but he never acknowledged her inconsistencies in identifying the assailants, nor that her story changed from telling to telling to telling.

If he had dug into the facts even a little bit, or into the prior trial, he would not have been able to say to the jury that, in the Ala Moana Case, it was "a strange circumstance, indeed, that the jury disagreed in that case. I don't know. I don't see why."

Willful blindness, I suppose. Or, maybe it was possible that he really did know of serious questions about his clients' story but disregarded them because it didn't fit his preferred narrative. Neither outcome reflects well on him. He was either derelict or deceitful.

Hearkening back to his tactics in the Leopold and Loeb case, Darrow referred to his client as "Tommie," then felt compelled to explain why he did so. "I say Tommie because he will never be anything else to me. I have not known him long, but I have learned to love him and respect him."

In the Leopold and Loeb case, he had been chastised by the judge, following objection from the prosecutor, for referring to his clients by their nicknames of Babe and Dickie. Yet he insisted upon doing so, probably in order to personalize and soften them to the jury. He likely had that same purpose in Massie, believing it would be harder for a jury to convict "Tommie" than to convict the "Defendant" or "Lieutenant Massie."

In a final spout of bloviation, Darrow put the fate of his clients in the hands of the jury—the guilt trip ploy—with these words:

> *All right, gentlemen, you have the power. But let me say to you that if on top of all else that has been heaped upon the devoted heads of this family, if they should be sent to prison, it would place a blot upon the fair name of these islands that all the Pacific seas would never wash away.*

In true Darrow fashion, he ended by patting himself on the back for being such a great human being and trying to ease the racial tension and strife in Hawaii, which his clients had actually exacerbated.[112]

---

[112] This is similar to the way he patted himself on the back in Leopold and Loeb for having "stood here for three months as one might stand at the ocean trying to sweep back the tide.... I know the future is with

I'd like to think I had done my small part to bring peace and justice to an island racked and worn by strife. You have not only the fate, but the life of these four people. What is there for them if you pronounce a sentence of doom on them? What have they done?

You are a people to heal, not to destroy. I place this in your hands, asking you to be kind and considerate both to the living and the dead.

Apparently that entreaty did not extend to Joe Kahahawai.

Blowhard

Chapter Twenty-Four: Paradise Lost

I felt, as we went away, that we were leaving behind the island more peaceful and happy than I had found it, for which I was very glad.
—Clarence Darrow

PROSECUTOR JOHN KELLEY spoke for less than half of Darrow's time—one tends to be more focused when addressing relevant issues instead of esoteric matters appealing solely to emotion although, as noted in the prior chapter, he had felt compelled to directly respond to some of Darrow's flights of fantasy—and the case was submitted to the jury at 4:30 PM.

The jurors took a preliminary ballot before adjourning for the night, 7-5 for acquittal. They picked up where they left off the next morning and hammered at each other to try to reach a consensus.

Bystanders reported hearing loud and angry voices coming from the jury room.

The *Chicago Tribune*'s Philip Kinsley wrote:

> The first manifestation that the jurors were deadlocked came late [Thursday] afternoon, when the seven Caucasian members came out of the jury room and stood on the balcony in the light rain. Their five colleagues of

Oriental and native strain stayed inside.

At 4:00 PM on Friday, April 29, Judge Davis called the jurors back to the courtroom.

First he asked if a verdict had been reached, to which foreman John Stone said "no." Then Judge Davis asked: "Is there any prospect of your reaching a verdict?...Yes or no?"

Stone answered, "Yes, I think so."

The answer stunned the courtroom, as well as the participants.

This had started to feel like a reprise of the 97-hour hung jury in the Ala Moana case, and everyone was already gearing up for a similar result and the necessity of another trial.

Maybe Darrow would have to earn his fee, after all.

Leniency Recommended

True to its word, at about 5:30 PM, the jury handed down its verdict: guilty of manslaughter, with leniency recommended.

Nobody really knew what "leniency recommended" meant, though it was clear the jury had at least some sympathies toward the defendants. As some jurors later explained to inquisitive reporters, the *haole*, or white, jurors didn't believe the shooting of Kahahawai was premeditated but was more or less a sudden, impulsive act.

That actually tracked with the testimony. But they also didn't believe the story of Tommie's temporary blackout when he supposedly fired the fatal shot. In fact, they didn't even believe that it was Tommie who had shot Kahahawai, nor did they believe that Joe had confessed, triggering (literally) that fatal shot.[113]

They did believe that something tragic had happened to Thalia, though they couldn't know then that the Pinkerton Detective Agency would later debunk her claims. Still, overall, they sympathized with the ordeal of Thalia's family and reached

---

[113] Smart jury.

the manslaughter verdict as a compromise. They added the request for leniency in sentencing to take into account those sympathies.

But the lawyers knew something that the jurors didn't: Under Hawaiian territorial law, Judge Davis had no room for discretion in imposing a sentence, notwithstanding the recommendation of leniency. The law of manslaughter required him to sentence each of the defendants to the maximum of ten years at hard labor.

Judge Davis announced that they would reassemble for sentencing a week later, then he adjourned court. Speaking to reporters outside the courtroom in his typical bombastic style, Darrow called the verdict "a travesty of justice and on human nature, and on every emotion that has made us what we are from the day the human race was born." He added, "I couldn't believe it. I couldn't think or understand how anybody could be that cruel."

Darrow would later fiercely criticize Judge Davis for his charge to the jury that insisted that they follow the law instead of their emotions. It was those instructions that "did the mischief," he said.

> ...Judge Davis had told the jury in a dozen different ways that they must not be human; the law allowed them to think, but did not permit them to feel, in spite of the fact that they were born to feel. No one expects the law to be human, but it must be logical though the heavens fall, and all the earth with it.[cclxxxv]

It was almost as if Darrow never understood his role as *law*yer.

Then Darrow amended his complaint to inject a bit of racism. "A jury of white men would have acquitted," he wrote. So, Darrow claimed that he lost because of the judge and the jury. But isn't that the way it's supposed to work?

Grace spoke more directly in the trial's aftermath.

> *I expected it. I felt all along that we would be unable to get a fair and just trial in Honolulu. American womanhood means nothing even to white people in Hawaii.*

Later, while back on the *USS Alton*, she was reported to have said that they had killed the wrong person—they should have shot the two Williams, Heen and Pittman, the attorneys for the Ala Moana Boys at the rape trial.

A Miscarriage of Justice

On Wednesday, May 4, the defendants and their lawyers gathered in Judge Davis's courtroom where, at 10:30 AM, he pronounced sentence on all four of the defendants: ten years at hard labor in Oahu Prison.

Strangely, no one seemed upset. Under enormous pressure from the military leadership and private businesses in Hawaii, as well as political pressure from the mainland and the federal government, including threats to declare martial law in Hawaii unless the defendants were pardoned, territorial governor Lawrence Judd had reached a fateful decision that he had coordinated with Darrow in advance of the sentencing hearing.

The lawyers and their clients left the courtroom and walked across the street to Iolani Palace, where Governor Judd officed. There, Judd signed a formal order for commutation, the language of which had been jointly prepared by Darrow and Judd. Judd then went outside his office to where the press had gathered for a scheduled conference.

At approximately 11:10, Judd announced:

> *The four defendants in the so-called Fortescue case were sentenced this morning in accordance with Territorial law to ten years in prison. Acting on a petition of the four defendants, joined by counsel for the defendants and in view of the recommendation of the jury, I am commuting the sentence to one hour in custody of the High Sheriff.*

Since the sentences had been handed down at 10:30 AM, along with a warrant for their incarceration, they had about 20 minutes left to serve. After serving out their hour, Jones and Lord returned to their naval posts and, on May 7, Grace, Tommie, and Thalia, now celebrities back on the mainland, boarded the ocean liner *Malolo* for San Francisco, along with Clarence and Ruby Darrow.

The miscarriage of justice was complete.

But even after the verdict and the commutation in the Massie case, Darrow—who apparently just couldn't help himself—continued to rewrite history just as he had during the trial.

He added an addendum chapter to his memoir *The Story of My Life* in which he misstated, presumably intentionally, facts surrounding the aftermath. For example, he claimed that he was "informed but cannot state it as a fact, that every one of the jurors asked Governor Lawrence Judd to commute the sentence." [cclxxxvi]

While it's true that the jury recommended "leniency" as part of its verdict, there is no corroboration for Darrow's assertion that every juror, or even that *any* juror, made such a request to the governor. He didn't identify his source for this alleged information. But given his penchant for embellishment, it is at least plausible that there was no such source other than his active imagination and his desire to paint history more favorably to himself and his views than existed in reality.

Darrow asserted that the "attorney general came to see me; the prosecution did not like the verdict; he said the governor could help us out if he wanted to, which we admitted would be fine." [cclxxxvii]

We might be able to forgive Darrow's confusion of the position of attorney general with the City and County Prosecutor for Honolulu,[114] but there is no evidence that the

---

[114] Michael Lilly, former Attorney General for the State of Hawaii, advises that, beginning in 1932, the Honolulu prosecutor's office was

Territory's attorney general, Harry Hewitt, made any intercession for a pardon.

Prosecutor John Kelley decidedly did not.

And if the prosecution truly didn't like the verdict, it was the failure of the jury to convict for second degree murder that caused the indigestion, not a guilty finding in general.

While Judd acknowledged that "pardons for the four were demanded," nowhere does he state that he was contacted by any juror in the case making those demands.

Rather, in his memoir, he said that those demands came from such sources as the mainland press and the United States Congress, as well as from some in the business establishment in Hawaii, though even that is not overly clear. Frank Atherton, head of Castle and Cooke (one of Hawaii's "Big Five" of industry) recommended pardons, but pardons were opposed by Clarence H. Cooke, president of the Bank of Hawaii, and John Waterhouse, president of Alexander and Baldwin, another of the Big Five.[cclxxxviii]

Darrow claimed that, after several conferences with Judd, "it was arranged that the governor should pardon our clients," but that was later amended to be a commutation, not a pardon. Still, Darrow wrote, "...we were pretty well satisfied, either way."[cclxxxix]

For his part, Judd denied any consideration of, or arrangement for, pardons. He described his meetings with Darrow this way:

> *"What are you going to do?"* he [Darrow] asked. *"Full pardons are indicated in the circumstances."*
>
> *"I'll commute the sentences to one hour,"* I informed

---

placed under the control and supervision of the Attorney General, so it's at least possible that Darrow was simply confused. However, John Kelley was not the AG; Harry Hewitt was, and there is no corroboration that I am able to find that Hewitt made any such request of Darrow.

> him. "I can do nothing more."
> Darrow bowed his head a moment, in seeming assent, and took his leave. "So be it," were his parting words.

Darrow came to Judd's office again the next day and "'turned on' his courtroom presence...demanding, not asking" for full pardons. When Darrow accused Judd of "breaking a pledge" if he didn't pardon the defendants, Judd replied, "Whose pledge?... Not mine certainly. I have never given even an intimation, anywhere at any time, that I would grant pardons in these cases." [ccxc]

Judd explained his rationale for a commutation, instead of a pardon, to an aide.

> They'll remain felons. Commutation does not condone the crime, but merely expiates the servitude imposed by law. Then we'll retry the assault case and clear the air. [ccxci]

Even though Judd denied promising pardons, that didn't stop Darrow from lying about it. Judd lamented that, for a while after the trial, he became "preoccupied" with Darrow's antics, as the lawyer "was spreading the report among newspapermen that I had promised to pardon Massie and his codefendants." [ccxcii]

Judd would later write that he regretted even commuting the sentence. "I acted under the heaviest congressional pressure and against my better judgment. Had I possessed facts which I later learned, I doubt if I would have commuted the sentence." [ccxciii]

And Darrow's final word on this particular issue?

It seems he couldn't resist one last lie, writing in his memoir that at least Tommie Massie was pardoned. "We knew that if we ever wanted a pardon, we would get it, as we have, in the case of Lieutenant Massie." Simply not true. None of the defendants was pardoned.

The bigger stretch of the post-trial truth, though, is

Darrow's claim that the attorney general[115] of Hawaii asked him to help prosecute a retrial of the Ala Moana case, a request he said he declined because prosecution just wasn't his cup of tea, and prosecutor John Kelley's lack of enthusiasm for re-trying that case in the first place.

> *I had been asked by the attorney general if I would come into the case with him and his associates to help prosecute the assailants of Mrs. Massie, for which I was offered a fee; but I explained that I had never prosecuted any one, and it was too late for me to begin now.*[ccxciv]

Besides, he felt sure the prosecution "wanted no further trouble and would be glad to get rid of the case" if Thalia were to leave the islands, thus removing their star witness from being able to testify.

We have only Darrow's highly dubious word for his uncorroborated assertion that he was asked to assist in prosecuting a retrial. As for his belief that the prosecution would be "glad to get rid of the case" if Thalia was no longer available to testify, that flies in the face of Governor Judd's stated intention that the case be retried. Prosecutor Kelley even took steps to subpoena Thalia *to prevent her departure* and compel her attendance at the retrial.

The effort to serve a subpoena led to a brouhaha of its own. As Professor Stannard wrote:

> *Honolulu authorities insisted that Thalia remain for the rape trial, and they announced their intention to use legal means to keep her in the islands. The result was a minor comedy of subterfuge and frustration. Thalia and the others were brought alongside the ship [the Malolo] in a*

---

[115] Again, let's not quibble with Darrow's inability to properly identify the office of the prosecutor, even though he had just spent several weeks dealing with him in the trial.

navy minesweeper and sneaked aboard through a cargo bay while Captain Wortman wrestled with a police officer, successfully preventing him from serving Thalia with a subpoena.^{ccxcv}

Governor Judd described the attempt at service as a "melodrama" that included "a chase through passageways and even a physical tussle between [Navy] Captain Wortman and process-server Dewey Mookini...." ^{ccxcvi}

No Retrial for the Ala Moana Boys

And so the *Malolo* sailed for the mainland with Darrow and his clients on board. In his delusion about what he had accomplished for his fee in the Massie case, Darrow wrote, "I felt, as we went away, that we were leaving behind the island more peaceful and happy than I had found it, for which I was very glad." ^{ccxcvii}

He was either still lying or he was delusional.

After Darrow's and his clients' departures, John Kelley immersed himself in the trial record of the Ala Moana Case. The unavailability of Thalia Massie was the least of his concerns. Instead, he was deeply troubled by gaping holes in the evidence. He was so concerned that he prevailed upon political leaders to engage The Pinkerton National Detective Agency to conduct an exhaustive investigation into the case and its background facts. The investigation kicked off in June of 1932, the month following sentencing in the Massie case, and the Pinkertons issued a detailed report in October.

The report concluded not only that it was "impossible to escape the conviction that the kidnaping and assault was not caused by those accused," (i.e., the Ala Moana Boys didn't do it!) but also that it was highly unlikely that Thalia Massie had even been raped at all.

> *We have found nothing in the record of this case nor have we thru [sic] our own efforts been able to find what in our estimation would be sufficient corroboration of the*

> statements of Mrs. Massie to establish the occurrence of rape upon her. There is a preponderance of evidence that Mrs. Massie did in some manner suffer numerous bruises about the head and body but definite proof of actual rape has not in our opinion been found.

It also said the failure of the prosecution to secure a conviction of the Ala Moana Boys was "inevitable," given that their alibis were firm and Thalia's story was highly suspect. The report was publicized by the mainland press. Darrow was quoted as rejecting the report, even though he had not read it, and reasserting his belief in the guilt of the Ala Moana Boys.

Doth he protest too much?

For reasons stated in the report, with neither Thalia's nor Darrow's unavailability for a retrial identified as a factor or even a consideration, Kelley dismissed the Ala Moana case. He wrote in his Motion for *Nolle Prosequi*:[116]

> The evidence adduced at the trial of said defendants was such that it is not surprising that a verdict of conviction was not obtained, and in view of the fact that the above mentioned investigation uncovered no new or additional evidence, there certainly is no more likelihood that a conviction could be obtained on a retrial of the case.

This is remarkably consistent with even Darrow's own recollection of the retrial prospects, at least according to Governor Judd. He said that Darrow told him, "It's foolish to talk about retrying the case.... There is no chance for conviction."[ccxcviii]

Perhaps this was an inadvertent slip of honesty by Darrow, though he made no mention of it in his memoir and, if he did say it, it begs the question: Was he cognizant all along of the holes in the prosecution's evidence in the Ala Moana Case? Did he know

---

[116] Latin for "we shall no longer prosecute."

that Joe Kahahawai was innocent?

I guess we'll never know, and Darrow certainly didn't tell us.

You're Goddamn Right I Shot Him

So what really happened in that house in Manoa? About thirty years later, Albert "Deacon" Jones gave an interview to Peter Van Slingerland of *Look Magazine* in which he revealed the actual events. In that interview he said:

> *Massie asked him a question and Kahahawai lunged at him. I say 'lunged.' Somebody else might say he just leaned forward.... I shot him.... You're goddamn right I did. I shot him right underneath the left nipple and to the side. When that slug hit him he just went over backwards on the chaise longue. The bullet didn't go through him. It stayed in his body. That was the climax, right there.*[ccxcix]

Did Darrow know that the key fact upon which he based his defense was a lie, and that it was Jones, not Tommie Massie, who fired the fatal shot?

He, of the jury bribes in the Haywood and McNamara cases. He, of the suppressed experts' report and theft of the trial transcript in Leopold and Loeb. He, of the countless other iniquities across the years of his legal career.

Could it be that, in the last case of his career, Clarence Darrow engaged in the unethical and illegal act of suborning perjury? Of knowingly putting a witness on the stand to lie? Given his history, it wouldn't be surprising.

And the evidence says that he did. When Van Slingerland asked Jones if Darrow knew who had shot Joe, Jones said:

> *I told [Darrow].... at the very end of the trial, about the last day or two.... That seemed to me to be Mr. Darrow's idea to let Tommie take the rap, because, if it had been either Lord or I that was up there, they'd say,*

'What in hell was he doing in it, anyway?' But Tommie had a motive and the reason. After all, it was his wife.[ccc]

Despite knowing that Jones fired the shot, Darrow argued to the jury that "Massie...shot... There could have been nobody else." He reiterated it in his memoir: "Even though Thomas Massie shot accidentally, or while his mind was a blank...."[ccci]

And, despite knowing that Tommie Massie's testimony was false, Darrow praised it in his memoir. "I cannot recall any whose testimony was more impressive than that of Lieutenant Thomas H. Massie and his wife, Thalia."[cccii]

Darrow was long since dead by the time Van Slingerland interviewed Deacon Jones, but Jones had no apparent motive to lie. His statement was consistent with evidence at trial that Kahahawai was killed with Jones's gun, not the one Tommie possessed.

We also know that, when arrested, Jones had, in his pants, the clip from the .32 with a missing bullet. It also supports the jury's belief that it was not Tommie who fired the fatal shot.

Still, as noted, it would be consistent with Darrow's ethics—or lack thereof—to suborn perjury. That's not too far removed, after all, from bribing jurors and paying off witnesses.

But before we leave the Massie Case, here is one last highly dubious statement by Darrow in his autobiography as he reflected on Hawaii and his time there:

> *...I would like to believe that this favored land might prove to be the place where the only claim to aristocracy would be the devotion to justice and truth and a real fellowship on earth.*[ccciii]

Said the man who really didn't even believe in justice other than something based upon one's personal conceptions and who put a witness on the stand to lie, resulting in a great miscarriage of justice of his own making and thereby nearly setting off a race war in that favored land.

PART SIX
Stop the Presses

History has its truth, and so has legend. Legendary truth is of another nature than historical truth. Legendary truth is invention whose result is reality. Furthermore, history and legend have the same goal: to depict eternal man beneath momentary man.
—Victor Hugo

Mike Farris

Chapter Twenty-Five: The Hard Death of a Legend

Legends die hard. They survive as truth rarely does.
—Helen Hayes

TO SET UP one's self as the ultimate arbiter of the correct, proper, and just outcome of any situation does more than merely smack of arrogance.

What it smacks of is a God complex, which is ironic for one who questioned the very existence of God. On the other hand, perhaps it is easier to exalt yourself and your own opinion and judgment if you don't have to worry about offending or supplanting God.

The beauty for Clarence Darrow, philosophically, was that his approach freed him from restrictive rules and chains of honesty and veracity that shackled mere mortals. How liberating that must have felt. No ethical or legal restraints, at least as far as he saw it, to interfere with achieving his desired ends. As long as he didn't get caught. But in Los Angeles, he did.

As Shakespeare's Hamlet said in his "To be or not to be" soliloquy, "Ay, there's the rub."

Darrow's sin lay not so much in his legal acumen, nor in his philosophies or causes, but rather in his usurpation of the justice system, often in a mean-spirited manner, for his own ends, even at the expense of justice. From his *Übermensch* viewpoint, he got to call the shots. In some respects, he was the poster child for why ethical rules and codes of professional conduct were promulgated, so that lawyers weren't able (at least theoretically) to elevate their beliefs and positions over the greater good of the justice system.

This book has been harsh to Darrow, but in the view of the author, deservedly so. Then again, maybe John T. Scopes's view of William Jennings Bryan should apply here. Recall that Scopes wrote in his memoir (with my substitution of Darrow for Bryan):

> [Darrow] *was, like most of us, an individual who had contributed both good and bad, and a fair man would pity him for the bad he brought to the world, and love him for the good.*

On the South Side of Chicago,[117] a bridge crosses a lagoon in Jackson Park, near the Museum of Science and Industry.

It was dedicated by Mayor Richard Daley, in 1957, as the Clarence Darrow Memorial Bridge because it was a favorite of Darrow's, and it was there that his ashes were spread after his cremation.

Interviewed shortly before his death on March 13, 1938, Darrow reportedly said that if there was such a thing as an afterlife, he would return to the bridge on the anniversary of his death.

In the years since it was dedicated in his name, people have gathered annually on the bridge on March 13 to watch for him.

He has yet to appear.

---

[117] In the Jim Croce song, that was the home of *Bad, Bad Leroy Brown*.

Blowhard Bibliography
Published Materials

Baatz, Simon, *For the Thrill of It: Leopold, Loeb, and the Murder That Shocked Chicago,* New York: Harper, 2008.

Baillie, Hugh, *High Tension: The Recollections of Hugh Baillie*, Harper & Brothers Publishers 1959.

Barrett, Nina, *The Leopold and Loeb Files,* Midway, 2018.

Barrymore, Ethel, *Memories*, Harper & Brothers, 1955.

Black, Coby, *Hawaii Scandal*, Honolulu: Island Heritage, 2002.

Blum, Howard, *American Lightning: Terror, Mystery, The Birth of Hollywood, and the Crime of the Century*, Crown Publishers, 2008.

Boyd, Tyler L., *Nellie Kenyon: Trailblazing Tennessee Journalist,* Waldenhouse Publishers, Inc., 2021.

Burns, William J., *The Masked War: The Story of a Peril That Threatened the United States by the Man Who Uncovered the Dynamite Conspirators and Sent Them to Jail*, Forgotten Books, 2015.

Checkoway, Julie, *The Three-Year Swim Club: The Untold Story of Maui's Sugar Ditch Kids and Their Quest for Olympic Glory*, Grand Central Publishing, 2015.

Cohn, Alfred and Chisholm, Joe, *Take the Witness*, Frederick A. Stokes Company, 1934.

Cowan, Geoffrey, *The People v. Clarence Darrow: The Bribery Trial of America's Greatest Lawyer*, Times Books, 1993.

Darrow, Clarence, *Absurdities of the Bible*, Haldeman-Julius Publications, 1925.

Darrow, Clarence, *Crime: Its Cause and Treatment*, Kaplan Publishing, 2009, reprinted from Thomas Y. Crowell, 1922.

Darrow, Clarence, *Plea of Clarence Darrow in His Own Defense to the Jury that Exonerated Him of the Charge of Bribery at Los Angeles, August 1912*, Golden Press, 1912.

Darrow, Clarence, *Resist Not Evil*, Breakout Publications, reprinted from the original in 1902.

Darrow, Clarence, *The Story of My Life*, Charles Scribner's Sons, 1932, reprinted in Da Capo Press, 1996.

Darwin, Charles, *The Origin of Species: By Means of Natural Selection or the Preservation of Favored Races in the Struggle for Life*, Merrill and Baker, 1859.

Day, A. Grove and Kirtley, Bacil F., ed. *Horror in Paradise: Grim and Uncanny Tales from Hawaii and the South Seas*, Mutual Publishing Co., 1986.

Farrell, John T., *Clarence Darrow: Attorney for the Damned,* Vintage Books, 2012.

Garner, Bryan A., *Black's Law Dictionary, 11th Edition,* Thomson Reuters 2019.

Ginger, Ray, *Altgeld's America: The Lincoln Ideal Versus Changing Realities*, Markus Weiner Publishing, 1958.

Gompers, Samuel, *Seventy Years of Life and Labor: An Autobiography of Samuel Gompers*, E.P. Dutton, Inc., 1925.

Grover, David H., *Debaters and Dynamiters: The Story of the Haywood Trial*, Oregon State University Press, 1964.

Higdon, Hal, *Leopold & Loeb: The Crime of the Century,* University of Illinois Press, 1975.

Hunter, George William, *A Civic Biology: Presented in Problems.* American Book Co., 1914.

Jensen, Richard J., *Clarence Darrow: The Creation of an American Myth*, Greenwood Press, 1992.

Johnson, Nelson, *Darrow's Nightmare: The Forgotten Story of American's Most Famous Trial Lawyer*, Rosetta Books, 2021.

Judd, Lawrence M. (as told to Hugh M. Lytle), *Lawrence M. Judd & Hawaii: An Autobiography,* Charles E. Tuttle Co., 1971.

Kersten, Andrew E., *Clarence Darrow: American Iconoclast,* Hill and Wang, 2011.

King, Greg and Wilson, Penny, *Nothing But the Night: Leopold & Loeb and the Truth Behind the Murder that Rocked 1920s America*, St. Martin's Press, 2022.

Larson, Edward J., *Summer for the Gods: The Scopes Trial and America's Continuing Debate Over Science and Religion*, Basic Books,1997.

Lawrence, Jerome and Lee, Robert E., *Inherit the Wind*, Ballantine Books, 1955.

Levin, Meyer, *Compulsion,* Simon and Schuster, 1956.

Leopold, Nathan, *Life Plus 99 Years*, Doubleday & Company, Inc., 1958.

Lukas, J. Anthony, *Big Trouble: A Murder in a Small Western Town Sets Off a Struggle for the Soul of America*, Touchstone, 1997.

McManigal, Ortie E., *The National Dynamite Plot,* Leopold Classic Library, reprinted from The Neale Company, 1913.

Mencken, H.L., *A Religious Orgy in Tennessee: A Reporter's Account of the Scopes Monkey Trial*, Melville House Publishing, articles originally published in *Baltimore Sun* in 1925.

Olasky, Marvin and Perry, John, *Monkey Business: The True Story of the Scopes Trial,* Broadman & Holman Publishers, 2005.

Owen, Russell, "Hot Lands and Cold," in *We Saw It Happen: The News Behind the News That's Fit to Print*, eds. Hanson W. Baldwin and Shepherd Stone, World Publishing, 1938.

Packer, Peter and Bob Thomas, *The Massie Case*, Bantam Books, 1966.

Papke, David Ray, *The Pullman Case: The Clash of Labor and Capital in Industrial America*, University Press of Kansas, 1999.

Robinson, W.W., *Bombs and Bribery,* Dawson's Book Shop, 1969.

Robinson, W.W., *Lawyers of Los Angeles: A History of the Los Angeles Bar Association and of the Bar of Los Angeles County*, Los Angeles Bar Association, 1959.

Rosa, John P., *Local Story: The Massie-Kahahawai Case and the Culture of History*, Honolulu: University of Hawaii Press, 2014.

Ross, Christian, *The Father's Story of Charley Ross The Kidnapped Child*, John E. Potter, 1876.

Scopes, John T. and Presley, James, *Center of the Storm: Memoirs of John T. Scopes,* Holt, Rinehart and Winston, 1967.

St. Johns, Adela Rogers, *Final Verdict,* Doubleday & Company, Inc., 1962.

Stannard, David E., *Honor Killing: How the Infamous "Massie Affair" Transformed Hawaii*, Viking, 2005.

Steffens, Lincoln, *The Autobiography of Lincoln Steffens,* The Chautauqua Press, 1931.

Stirling, Yates and Buell, Mabel A., *Sea Duty: The Memoirs of a Fighting Admiral,* G.P. Putnam's Sons, 1939.

Stone, Irving, *Clarence Darrow for the Defense,* Doubleday, Doran & Company, Inc., 1941.

Tietjen, Randall (ed.), *In the Clutches of the Law: Clarence Darrow's Letters*, University of California Press, 2013.

Van Slingerland, Peter, *Something Terrible Has Happened*, Harper & Row, 1966.

Vine, Phyllis, *One Man's Castle: Clarence Darrow in Defense of the American Dream*, Amistad, 2004.

Weinberg, Arthur (ed.), *Attorney for the Damned: Clarence Darrow in the Courtroom*, University of Chicago Press, 1989.

Weinberg, Arthur and Weinberg, Lila (ed.), *Clarence Darrow: Verdicts Out of Court*, Elephant Paperbacks, 1963.

Weinberg, Arthur and Weinberg, Lila, *Clarence Darrow: A Sentimental Rebel*, Athenum, 1987.

Wright, Theon, *Rape in Paradise*, Mutual Publishing, 1966.

Yale, Charles Harrison, *Clarence Darrow*, Jonathan Cape, 1931.

Court Cases

Aguillard v. Treen, 634 F. Supp. 426 (E.D. La. 1985)
Brady v. Maryland, 373 U.S. 83 (1963)
Edwards v. Aguillard, 482 U.S. 578 (1987)
Epperson v. Arkansas, 393 U.S. 97 (1968)
Escobedo v. Illinois, 378 U.S. 478 (1964)
John Thomas Scopes v. The State of Tennessee, 278 S.W. 57 (Tenn. 1927)
Lemon v. Kurtzman, 403 U.S. 602 (1971)
Miranda v. Arizona, 384 U.S. 436 (1966)
Pettibone v. Nichols, 203 U.S. 192 (1906)
Powell v. Alabama, 287 U.S. 45 (1932)
Walters v. Radiation Survivors, 473 U.S. 305 (1985)

Court Records

Trial transcript for The State of Idaho v. William D. Haywood

Final Report of the Los Angeles Grand Jury (regarding *Los Angeles Times* bombing)

Pleadings and documents for People of the State of California v. J.J. McNamara and J.B. McNamara

Trial transcript for The People of the State of California v. Clarence Darrow (Lockwood bribery trial)

Trial transcript (partial) for The People of the State of California v. Clarence Darrow (Bain bribery trial)

Trial transcript for People of the State of Illinois v. Nathan F. Leopold, Jr. and Richard Loeb

Trial transcript for State of Tennessee v. John Thomas Scopes

Trial transcript for Territory of Hawaii v. Ben Ahakuelo, et al.

Trial transcript (partial) for Territory of Hawaii v. Grace Fortescue, et al.

Newspapers, Magazines, and Periodicals

Appeal to Reason
Baltimore Sun
Chattanooga Times
Chicago Daily News
Chicago Inter-Ocean
Chicago Times
Chicago Tribune
Collier's
Coronet

Denver Post
Forbes
Honolulu Advertiser
Honolulu Star-Bulletin
Honolulu Times
Life
Los Angeles Times
Memphis Commercial Appeal
New York Sun
New York Times
New York Tribune
Rutgers Law Review
San Francisco Examiner
Smithsonian Magazine
St. Louis Dispatch
The Forum
The New Yorker
True Detective
Wayland's Monthly
Why Dayton?

Internet and Video

Merriam-webster: www.merriam-webster.ccm

University of Minnesota, The Clarence Darrow Digital Collection: https://librarycollections.law.umn.edu/darrow/index.php

Bryan College: https://www.bryan.edu

Geoscience Research Institute: https://grisda.org

Fiorini, John Carl, *Deviants of Great Potential: Images of the Leopold Loeb Case*. Master's thesis, College of William & Mary, 2013. https://scholarworks.wm.edu/cgi/viewcontent.cgi?article=3402&context=etd

Mike Farris

Studs Terkel Radio Archive: John T. Scopes discusses the "Scopes Monkey Trial" of 1925. https://studsterkel.wfmt.com/programs/john-t-scopes-discusses-scopes-monkey-trial-1925.

Zwonitzer, Mark (writer/director), *The Massie Affair* (documentary), Arlington, VA: PBS *American Experience*, 2005.

Clarence Darrow, one-man show by Henry Fonda (1974)

Compulsion, starring Orson Welles, Dean Stockwell, and Bradford Dillman (1959)

Inherit the Wind, starring Spencer Tracy and Fredric March (1960)

Endnotes

Chapter 1: Dazzlement or Bafflement
[i] Adela Rogers St. Johns, *Final Verdict* (Doubleday & Co., Inc. 1962), at p. 480.
[ii] Id. at p. 435.
[iii] Alfred Cohn and Joe Chisholm, *Take the Witness* (Garden City Publishing Co., Inc. 1934) at p. 222.
[iv] Geoffrey Cowan, *The People v. Clarence Darrow: The Bribery Trial of America's Greatest Lawyer* (Times Books 1993).
[v] *The Story of My Life* at p. 1.
[vi] *The Story of My Life* at p. 7.

Chapter 2: The Legend of Clarence Darrow
[vii] Id. at pp. 32-33.
[viii] John A. Farrell, Clarence Darrow: Jury Tamperer? *Smithsonian Magazine*, December 2011.
[ix] Gerald F. Uelmen, *Fighting Fire With Fire: A Reflection on the Ethics of Clarence Darrow*, 71 Fordham Law Review 1543 (2003).
[x] *Final Verdict* at p. 403.
[xi] W.W. Robinson, *Bombs and Bribery* (Dawson's Book Shop 1969) at p. 45.
[xii] Hugh Baillie, *High Tension: The Recollections of Hugh Baillie* (Harper & Brothers 1959) at p. 27.
[xiii] *Final Verdict* at p. 507.

Chapter 3: Bombs
[xiv] J. Anthony Lukas, *Big Trouble: A Murder in a Small Western Town Sets off a Struggle for the Soul of America* (Touchstone 1997) at pp. 724-725.
[xv] Id. at pp. 331-332.
[xvi] Id at p. 504.
[xvii] John F. MacLane, *A Sagebrush Lawyer* (Pandick Press 1953) at p. 158.
[xviii] David H. Grover, *Debaters and Dynamiters: The Story of the Haywood Trial* (Oregon State University Press 1964) at p. 207.
[xix] Id. at p. 211.
[xx] Howard Blum, *American Lightning: Terror, Mystery, the Birth of Hollywood, and the Crime of the Century* (Crown Publishers 2008) at p. 24.
[xxi] Nelson Johnson, *Darrow's Nightmare: The Forgotten Story of America's Most Famous Trial Lawyer* (Rosetta Books 2021) at p. 36.
[xxii] Id. at p. 44.
[xxiii] *The Story of My Life* at p. 171.

[xxiv] Irving Stone, *Clarence Darrow for the Defense* (Doubleday, Doran & Co., Inc. 1941) at p. 247.
[xxv] *The Story of My Life* at p. 173.
[xxvi] *The People v. Clarence Darrow* at p. 118.
[xxvii] Id. at pp. 121-122.
[xxviii] *The Story of My Life* at p. 175.
[xxix] *The People v. Clarence Darrow* at p. 122.
[xxx] Randall Tietjen, ed. *In the Clutches of the Law: Clarence Darrow's Letters* (University of California Press 2013) at p. 163.
[xxxi] Id. at p. 164.
[xxxii] *The People v. Clarence Darrow* at p. 166.
[xxxiii] *American Lightning* at p. 73.
[xxxiv] *The People v. Clarence Darrow* at p. 174.
[xxxv] Id.
[xxxvi] Id. at p. 175.
[xxxvii] *Darrow's Nightmare* at p. 23.

Chapter 4: Necessity Knows No Law

[xxxviii] *The People v. Clarence Darrow* at p. 136.
[xxxix] Id. quoting from Wood letter to Ehrgott.
[xl] William J. Burns, *The Masked War: The Story of a Peril that Threatened the United States by the Man Who Uncovered the Dynamite Conspirators and Sent Them to Jail* (George H. Doran Co. 1913) at p. 25.
[xli] *The Masked War* at p. 271.
[xlii] Id. pp. 272-273.
[xliii] *In the Clutches of the Law* at p. 163.
[xliv] *The Masked War* at p. 285.
[xlv] Id. at p. 284.
[xlvi] *The People v. Clarence Darrow* at p. 300.
[xlvii] *The Masked War* at p. 266.
[xlviii] Id. at 266.
[xlix] Id. at 270.
[l] *The People v. Clarence Darrow* at p. 161.
[li] *Final Verdict* at p. 424.
[lii] Lincoln Steffens, *The Autobiography of Lincoln Steffens* (Harcourt, Brace and Co. 1931) at pp. 671-672.
[liii] Id. at p. 672.
[liv] Id. at p. 681.
[lv] All quotes in this paragraph were cited in *The People v. Clarence Darrow* at pp. 264-265.

Chapter 5: The Trials and Tribulations of Clarence Darrow

[lvi] Letters quoted in this section can be found in *In the Clutches of the Law*.
[lvii] *Final Verdict* at pp. 435, 482.
[lviii] Id. at 432.
[lix] Id. at 480.
[lx] *The People v. Clarence Darrow* at pp. 288-289.
[lxi] Id. at 289.
[lxii] *Final Verdict* at 461.
[lxiii] Id. at p. 458.
[lxiv] *High Tension* at p. 20.
[lxv] *Final Verdict* at p. 458.
[lxvi] Id. at 460.
[lxvii] Id.
[lxviii] Id. at 463.
[lxix] Id.
[lxx] *Clarence Darrow for the Defense* at p. 325.
[lxxi] Id.
[lxxii] Id. at p. 324.
[lxxiii] Martin Maloney, "Clarence Darrow" in Marie Hochmuth, editor, *A History and Criticism of American Public Address, Vol III* (Longmans, Green and Co. 1955), at pp. 262, 300, and 307.
[lxxiv] *High Tension* at p. 12.
[lxxv] Nathan Leopold, *Life Plus 99 Years* (Doubleday & Co., Inc. 1958) at p. 54.
[lxxvi] Ethel Barrymore, *Memories: An Autobiography of Ethel Barrymore* (Harper and Brothers 1955), at p. 158.
[lxxvii] *High Tension* at p. 12.
[lxxviii] Id. at p. 15.
[lxxix] *Debaters and Dynamite* at p. 223.
[lxxx] Arthur Weinberg, ed., *Attorney for the Damned: Clarence Darrow in the Courtroom* (University of Chicago Press 1957) at p. 487.
[lxxxi] *High Tension* at p. 12.
[lxxxii] *Final Verdict* at p. 452.
[lxxxiii] Id. at p. 499.
[lxxxiv] Id. at p. 500.
[lxxxv] Id. at p. 501.

Chapter 6: That's Not My Dog

[lxxxvi] *The Story of My Life* at p. 187.
[lxxxvii] Id. at p. 42.
[lxxxviii] *In the Clutches of the Law*, at pp. 204-205.

[lxxxix] *Final Verdict* at p. 448.
[xc] Id.
[xci] Id.
[xcii] Id. at p. 502.
[xciii] *The Story of My Life* at p. 182.
[xciv] Id. at p. 181.
[xcv] Editorial, *Collier's,* August 24, 1907 at pp. 5-6.
[xcvi] Letter to Editor of *Collier's,* September 21, 1907, at p. 11.
[xcvii] Comment on Darrow letter to editor of *Collier's*, September 21, 1907, at p. 12.
[xcviii] Letter to Editor, *Collier's*, October 26, 1907, at p. 9.
[xcix] Editorial, *Collier's*, November 30, 1907, at p. 7.

Chapter 7: Did He or Didn't He?
[c] Farrell, "Clarence Darrow: Jury Tamperer?"
[ci] Letter dated January 12, 1904, from Wright to Wood in the Charles Erskine Scott Wood Papers held at the Bancroft Library at the University of California, Berkeley, cited in *The People v. Clarence Darrow*.
[cii] Ray Ginger, *Altgeld's America: The Lincoln Ideal Versus Changing Realities* (Funk & Wagnells 1958), p. 269.
[ciii] Id.
[civ] *The People v. Clarence Darrow* at p. 52.
[cv] Id. at p.434.
[cvi] John Farrell, *Clarence Darrow: Attorney for the Damned* (Vintage Books 2012) p. 278.
[cvii] *High Tension* at p. 27.
[cviii] *Bombs and Bribery* at p. 46.
[cix] *Final Verdict* at p. 447.
[cx] Id. at p. 421.
[cxi] Id. at 442.
[cxii] Id. at p. 507.
[cxiii] Id. at 44.
[cxiv] *Clarence Darrow for the Defense* at p. 324.
[cxv] *Final Verdict* at 454.
[cxvi] Id. at p. 403.
[cxvii] Id. at 506.
[cxviii] Id. at 507
[cxix] *The People v. Clarence Darrow* at p. 436.
[cxx] Arthur & Lila Weinberg, *Clarence Darrow: A Sentimental Rebel* (Putnam 1980) at p. 262.
[cxxi] Id.
[cxxii] *Clarence Darrow for the Defense* at p. 322.

[cxxiii] Id. at p. 323.
[cxxiv] Id at p. 344.
[cxxv] *The Story of My Life* at p. 190.
[cxxvi] Id. at pp. 203-204.
[cxxvii] *The People v. Clarence Darrow*, p. 371.
[cxxviii] *Attorney for the Damned* at p. 247.
[cxxix] *Darrow's Nightmare* at p. 300.
[cxxx] Farrell, "Clarence Darrow: Jury Tamperer?"
[cxxxi] *High Tension* at p. 23.
[cxxxii] Farrell, "Clarence Darrow: Jury Tamperer."
[cxxxiii] *The People v. Clarence Darrow* at p. 438.
[cxxxiv] Id. at p. 439.
[cxxxv] Id. at p. 159.

Chapter 8: Smartest Guys in the Room
[cxxxvi] *The Story of My Life* at p. 459.
[cxxxvii] *In the Clutches of the Law* at p. 292.
[cxxxviii] *The Story of My Life* at p. 232.
[cxxxix] *Life Plus 99 Years* at p. 57.

Chapter 9: My Kingdom for a Lawyer
[cxl] Id. at pp.54-55.
[cxli] *The Story of My Life* at p. 232.
[cxlii] *Clarence Darrow for the Defense* at pp. 380-81.
[cxliii] Id.
[cxliv] *The Story of My Life* at p. 232.
[cxlv] *Clarence Darrow in the Courtroom* at p. 17.
[cxlvi] *The Story of My Life* at p. 83.
[cxlvii] Id. at pp. 361, 368.

Chapter 10: A Plea in Mitigation
[cxlviii] Greg King and Penny Wilson, *Nothing But the Night: Leopold & Loeb and the Truth Behind the Murder that Rocked 1920's America* (St. Martin's Press 2022), p. 194.
[cxlix] Id. at pp. 58-59.
[cl] *The Story of My Life* at p. 413.
[cli] Id. at 422.
[clii] Republished in *Verdicts Out of Court* at pp. 429-436.
[cliii] *The Story of My Life* at p. 234.

Chapter 11: Someone Else's Fault

[cliv] *The Story of My Life* at p. 81.
[clv] Id. at p. 83.
[clvi] This portion of the record was reported in Nina Barrett's *The Leopold and Loeb Files: An Intimate Look at One of America's Most Infamous Crimes* (Midway 2018), p. 242.
[clvii] *In the Clutches of the Law* at p. 199.
[clviii] *Nothing But the Night* at pp. 74-75.
[clix] Id. at p. 77.
[clx] Id. at p. 78.
[clxi] *Life Plus 99 Years* at p.72.
[clxii] Id. at p. 78.

Chapter 12: What Goes Around

[clxiii] *Nothing But the Night* at p. 215.
[clxiv] *Life Plus 99 Years* at p. 305.
[clxv] *Nothing But the Night* at p. 267.
[clxvi] Id. at p. 268.
[clxvii] Id. at p. 269.
[clxviii] *Life Plus 99 Years* at p. 26.
[clxix] Id. at p. 50.
[clxx] Id. at p. 49.
[clxxi] *In the Clutches of the Law* at p. 296.
[clxxii] Edward J. Larson, "Murder Will Out: Rethinking the Right of Publicity Through One Classic Case," 62:1 *Rutgers Law Review* 131, at pp. 136-137.
[clxxiii] Meyer Levin, *Compulsion* (Simon and Schuster 1956).
[clxxiv] *Life Plus 99 Years* at pp. 370-371.
[clxxv] Id. at p. 376.
[clxxvi] *Compulsion* at p. 237.
[clxxvii] Id. at p. 252.
[clxxviii] Id. at p. 261.
[clxxix] Fiorini, John Carl. Deviants of Great Potential: Images of the Leopold Loeb Case. Master's thesis, College of William & Mary, 2013. https://scholarworks.wm.edu/cgi/viewcontent.cgi?article=3402&context=etd
[clxxx] *In the Clutches of the Law* at p. 294.
[clxxxi] https://librarycollections.law.umn.edu/darrow/trials_details.php?id=1
[clxxxii] Baatz, Simon, *For the Thrill of It: Leopold, Loeb, and the Murder That Shocked Jazz Age Chicago* (Harper Perennial 2008), p. 458.
[clxxxiii] *Nothing But the Night* at p. 229.
[clxxxiv] Id. at p. 229.

Chapter 13: An Act Prohibiting
[clxxxv] Marvin Olasky and John Perry, *Monkey Business: The True Story of the Scopes Trial* (Broadman & Holman Publishers 2005), p. 25.
[clxxxvi] *The Story of My Life* at p. 249.
[clxxxvii] *In the Clutches of the Law* at p. 306.
[clxxxviii] Edward J. Larson, *Summer for the Gods: The Scopes Trial and America's Continuing Debate Over Science and Religion* (Basic Books 1997), p. 15.
[clxxxix] Id. at p. 54.
[cxc] Id.
[cxci] Marquis Jones, "Around Town at the Scopes Trial," *The New Yorker* (July 4, 1925).
[cxcii] John T. Scopes and James Presley, *Center of the Storm: Memoirs of John T. Scopes* (Holt Rinehart and Winston 1967), p. 53.
[cxciii] Id. at pp. 55-56.
[cxciv] Id. at p. 60.
[cxcv] Id.
[cxcvi] Id. at p. 4.
[cxcvii] Id. at p. 62.
[cxcviii] *Monkey Business* at p. 12.

Chapter 14: Under the Big Top
[cxcix] F.E. Robinson, *Why Dayton – of all places?* (Andrews Printery, Chattanooga 1925)
[cc] Id. at p. 3;
[cci] Id. at p. 15.
[ccii] Id. at p. 17.
[cciii] Id.
[cciv] *Summer for the Gods* at pp. 96-97, 100.
[ccv] Id. at p. 100.
[ccvi] Id..
[ccvii] *Center of the Storm* at p. 67.
[ccviii] Id. at p. 72.
[ccix] Id.
[ccx] *Summer for the Gods* at p. 102.
[ccxi] Id. at p. 100.
[ccxii] H.L. Mencken, *A Religious Orgy in Tennessee: A Reporter's Account of the Scopes Monkey Trial* (Melville House Publishing 2006).
[ccxiii] Tyler L. Boyd, *Nellie Kenyon: Trailblazing Tennessee Journalist* (Waldenhouse Publishers Inc. 2021) p. 62.

Chapter 15: Send in the Clowns

[ccxiv] *A Religious Orgy in Tennessee* at p. 66.
[ccxv] George William Hunter, *A Civic Biology: Presented in Problems* (American Book Company 1914), p. 195.
[ccxvi] https://studsterkel.wfmt.com/programs/john-t-scopes-discusses-scopes-monkey-trial-1925
[ccxvii] *The Story of My Life* at p. 258.
[ccxviii] Id. at p. 256.
[ccxix] Id. at p. 257.
[ccxx] Id.
[ccxxi] Id. at p. 259.
[ccxxii] Id.
[ccxxiii] Id.
[ccxxiv] Id.
[ccxxv] Id. at 265.
[ccxxvi] Id. at 257.
[ccxxvii] *In the Clutches of the Law* at pp. 307-308.
[ccxxviii] *The Story of My Life* at p. 270.

Chapter 16: The Sun Stood Still

[ccxxix] Id. at p. 267.
[ccxxx] Id at p. 249.
[ccxxxi] Id. at pp. 259-260.

Chapter 17: Folding the Tent

[ccxxxii] *The Story of My Life* at p. 268.
[ccxxxiii] Id. at p. 276.
[ccxxxiv] *Nellie Kenyon* at p. 75.
[ccxxxv] Id. at 64.
[ccxxxvi] Id.
[ccxxxvii] *Clarence Darrow for the Defense*, at p. 464.
[ccxxxviii] *The Story of My Life* at 271.
[ccxxxix] Id. at p. 277.
[ccxl] Id. at 272.
[ccxli] Id.
[ccxlii] Id. at pp. 272-273.
[ccxliii] https://www.bryan.edu/about/
[ccxliv] https://www.bryan.edu/about/core-values/
[ccxlv] https://forbes.com/advisor/education/best-online-masters-in-human-services/
[ccxlvi] *Summer for the Gods* at p. 200.

ccxlvii *A Religious Orgy in Tennessee*, at p. 117.
ccxlviii *Center of the Storm* at pp. 216-17.
ccxlix *The Story of My Life* at p. 276.
ccl *Center of the Storm* at pp. 233-34, 240.
ccli Id. at 243.
cclii Id. at 273.
ccliii Katherine Ching, The Teaching of Creation and Evolution in the State of Tennessee, Geoscience Research Institute (1974); https://grisda.org/origins-01086.

Chapter 18: I Better Go to Hawaii

ccliv Mike Farris, *A Death in the Islands: The Unwritten Law and the Last Trial of Clarence Darrow* (Skyhorse Publishing 2016) at p. xiii.
cclv (Grand Central Publishing 2015), p. 225.
cclvi *In the Clutches of the Law* at p. 431.
cclvii Id. at p. 432.
cclviii *The Story of My Life* at p. 460.
cclix Id. at p. 459.

Chapter 19: The Ala Moana Case

cclx Stannard, David E., *Honor Killing: How the Infamous "Massie Affair" Transformed Hawaii*, (Viking 2005), p. 36.
cclxi Thirteen Correspondents of *The New York Times*, *We Saw It Happen: The News Behind the News That's Fit to Print* (Simon and Schuster 1938) at p. 220.
cclxii *Honor Killing* at p. 36.
cclxiii Id. at p. 38.
cclxiv *The Story of My Life* at p. 463.
cclxv *Honor Killing* at p. 40.

Chapter 20: Hung Jury

cclxvi Stirling, Yates, *Sea Duty: The Memoirs of a Fighting Admiral* (G.P. Putnam's Sons 1939), p. 250.

Chapter 21: The Murder of Joe Kahahawai

cclxvii *The Story of My Life* at p. 459.
cclxviii *We Saw It Happen* at p. 221-222.
cclxix *In the Clutches of the Law* at pp. 431.
cclxx *The Story of My Life* at p. 459.
cclxxi *Clarence Darrow for the Defense* at p. 503.
cclxxii *A Sentimental Rebel* at p. 372

cclxxiii Andrew E. Kersten, *Clarence Darrow: American Iconoclast* (Hill and Wang 2011), p. 228.
cclxxiv Theon Wright, *Rape in Paradise* (Mutual Publishing 1966), p. 212.
cclxxv Id.
cclxxvi *The Story of My Life* at pp. 458-459.

Chapter 22: Darrow's Final Trial
cclxxvii *Honor Killing* at p. 311.
cclxxviii *The Story of My Life* at p. 469.
cclxxix Id. at pp. 469-70.
cclxxx Id. at pp. 470-71.
cclxxxi Id. at p. 467.

Chapter 23: Darrow's Final Courtroom Bloviation
cclxxxii *Clarence Darrow in the Courtroom* at p. 98.
cclxxxiii *Honor Killing* at p. 233.
cclxxxiv *Clarence Darrow for the Defense* at pp. 500-501.

Chapter 24: Paradise Lost
cclxxxv *The Story of My Life* at 476.
cclxxxvi Id. at 480.
cclxxxvii Id. at 480.
cclxxxviii Judd, Lawrence M., *Lawrence M. Judd & Hawaii* (Charles E. Tuttle Co. 1971), pp. 199-200.
cclxxxix *The Story of My Life* at p. 478.
ccxc *Judd & Hawaii* at p. 203.
ccxci Id.
ccxcii Id. at 204.
ccxciii Id. at 168.
ccxciv *The Story of My Life* at p. 481.
ccxcv *Honor Killing* at p. 391.
ccxcvi *Judd & Hawaii* at p. 212.
ccxcvii *The Story of My Life* at p. 481.
ccxcviii *Judd & Hawaii* at p. 211.
ccxcix Peter Van Slingerland, *Something Terrible Has Happened*, (Harper & Row, 1966), at p. 318.
ccc Id. at 322.
ccci *The Story of My Life* at p. 467.
cccii Id. at 475.
ccciii Id. at 482.

www.ingramcontent.com/pod-product-compliance
Lightning Source LLC
Chambersburg PA
CBHW020047170426
43199CB00009B/195